BOOKS BY VINCENT BROME

Jung   1978

The Ambassador and the Spy   1973

Freud and His Early Circle   1968

Operating Theater   1968

Four Realist Novelists   1966

International Brigades: Spain 1936-1939   1966

Frank Harris   1959

Six Studies in Quarreling   1958

Way Back   1958

Aneurin Bevan   1953

H. G. Wells   1951

JUNG

JUNG

by Vincent Brome

Atheneum

NEW YORK

1978

TO ANGELA
Who made it possible

Contents

Acknowledgments

I wish to acknowledge, with thanks, permission to quote from the following books: C. G. Jung's *Memories, Dreams, Reflections*, recorded and edited by Aniela Jaffé, published by Collins and Pantheon Books, a Division of Random House Inc.; *The Freud–Jung Letters*, edited by William McGuire, published by Routledge & Kegan Paul, Hogarth Press and the Princeton University Press; *Letters of C. G. Jung*, 2 vols, edited and selected by Dr Gerhard Adler and Aniela Jaffé, published by Routledge & Kegan Paul and Princeton University Press; *The Collected Works of C. G. Jung*, published by Routledge & Kegan Paul.

Preface

THE LONG PILGRIMAGE into Carl Gustav Jung's life began as far back as 1957 when I first encountered John Layard in Cornwall. He spoke of his meetings with Jung so vividly and reconstructed his model of the psyche with such enthusiasm that I determined one day to write about the man who had come to represent the only serious rival to Freud. Confronted by the range and erudition of Jung's work, resolution quailed, but I continued to accumulate material, only to be side-tracked into writing a biography of Havelock Ellis. Still, occasionally, recording Jungian interviews and material, Freud seemed more closely related to Ellis than Jung and I next completed a study – *Freud and His Early Circle*.

By 1971 it was difficult any longer to ignore the steadily enlarging Jungian dossiers. The appearance of Jung's *Memories, Dreams, Reflections* in 1963 provided a frame for the early and last days in his life and several memoirs began to appear. However, it was 1972 before I settled down to a task of intimidating proportions. First came the inevitable rereading of his works which led into a labyrinth easily open to misinterpretation since the paths sometimes twisted into definitions beset by misty ambiguities. The ancillary literature included studies by E. A. Bennet, Aniela Jaffé, Laurens van der Post, Paul J. Stern and Barbara Hannah. For those who are interested a complete bibliography appears at the end of this book.

Inevitably Jung's home in Küsnacht, the C. G. Jung Institute and the Burghölzli Mental Hospital in Zürich had to be visited and a long pilgrimage to the 'holy places' in Switzerland undertaken. Over the years I have conducted a series of interviews with some thirty people who have known him, including: Dr Gerhard Adler, A. I. Allenby, Ruth Bailey, Dr E. A. Bennet, Hugo Charteris, Dr Michael Fordham, Liliane Frey-Rohn, Barbara Hannah, Dr James Hillman, Aniela Jaffé, Dr Ernest Jones, Franz Jung, the son of C. G. Jung, John Layard, E. Naef-Wolff, M. Odermatt, Bertrand Russell, Dr Anthony Storr, Alix Strachey, H. G. Wells, Lancelot Whyte.

I have also consulted: Adler's daughter Alexandra Adler, Dr M. Balint, Ean Begg, Professor Martin Bleuler, Professor Henri Ellenberger, John Freeman, Dr Maurice Green, Dr Joseph Henderson, Kenneth Lambert, Dr A. Maberley, Dr J. Moore, J. B. Priestley, Dr Marian C. Putnam, Professor Paul Roazen, Marthe Robert, Dr Charles Rycroft and Judith de Taves, daughter of Izette de Forest. There are a number of other personal sources which for reasons of protecting the people involved I must keep confidential. Considerable hazards beset the path of anyone who tries to set down the truth of what he finds in the early history of psychoanalysis and analytical psychology.

Both the collected letters of Jung edited by Gerhard Adler in collaboration with Aniela Jaffé and the Freud–Jung letters edited by William McGuire were obviously important sources. I also have the advantage of testimony from Ernest Jones at considerable length, and I have read the Parelhoff correspondence and a number of other unpublished letters. These were in the six boxes of Ernest Jones's papers for his *Life and Work of Freud* to which Mrs Jones kindly gave me access. An unpublished document provided by Dr Gerhard Adler afforded a very interesting account of the life of Toni Wolff. The typescript of Hugo Charteris's interview with Jung included a number of revealing unpublished details. Dr Michael Fordham provided a collection of Jung letters, some of which do not appear in the Collected Letters. Ean Begg allowed me to see some unpublished letters from Emma Jung. A correspondence with Franz Jung, son of C. J. Jung, was useful. Jones's papers included the following unpublished letters which provided a very good background to the early psychoanalytic history:

Letters to Dr Jones from James Putnam, 1910–17
Letters from Marie Bonaparte to Freud, 1949–57
Jones's correspondence with James Strachey, 1950–6
Correspondence with A. A. Brill, 1926–36
Correspondence with Sandor Ferenczi, 1911–13. A selection of a large number of unpublished letters
Correspondence with Max Eitington, 1928–43
Letters to Otto Rank, 1920–3
Letters from Hanns Sachs, 2 September 1911, 19 July 1912, 17 August 1912, 7 July 1913

Many periodicals, technical and popular, had to be consulted, and the references are given in the Notes or listed in the Bibliography.

It should be made clear that this is primarily a biographical study interweaving outlines of the different phases of his work as they interlock with his life, until the complete model is reconstructed and analysed in Appendix I.

For the rest, I have spent many years studying the history of psychoanalysis and analytical psychology; was a friend of the late Ernest Jones, Freud's biographer; have met several of the survivors of the immediate Freud–Jung circle and personally encountered the subject of this biography on two occasions. However, this does not set out to be a definitive work. That will have to wait another thirty years before it can be written.

I should like to thank Dr Peter Johnson, who accompanied me on my Swiss travels and gave invaluable advice and aid. Máire NicSuibhne cleared up many knotty points. James Wright's impeccable editing was indispensable.

VINCENT BROME

JUNG

Prologue

THERE WERE OCCASIONS in his eighties when, meeting Carl Gustav Jung on a cold winter day, one encountered a tall, slightly bent man wrapped in a full-length, fur-lined dressing-gown with a dark skull-cap fitting tightly on the white hair, and it was as if the timeless figure of his own mythological creation – the Old Wise Man – had materialised in the flesh. There were other occasions when those who visited him at his beautiful house beside the upper lake of Zürich found him – at first sight – disarmingly casual, but frequently came away with the image of a man whose complex personality and powerful intellect had come to terms with 'natural' life and whatever mysterious forces lay hidden in the unconscious.

Calling upon Jung at Bollingen, the visitor knocked on a heavy wooden door set in a thick stone wall which seemed literally to grow out of the earth. The wall, the door and the oddly shaped towers rising beyond it all held hints of the medieval. As you waited it was not uncommon to hear the ringing sound of an axe falling upon wood, because there was no coal, gas or electricity in this strange house. According to the time of day, and depending on his mood, you might see Jung wearing a workman's green apron, busily chopping wood, or a scholarly person deeply immersed in reading a book. Still a tall, well-built man, it was customary for him to come to his feet with a brilliant, slightly mischievous smile and fall into easy conversation. 'So you've come all this way just to listen to me,' he said to one American professor from Indiana University. 'It's extraordinary what illusions people have about me.' The broad forehead and powerful chin remained from earlier years, but now he had mellowed, and there was a softness in the face, the white hair and the informality of manner. To the surprise of one patient who came to the house at Bollingen he rose to greet her with the words, 'So you are in the soup, too?' Disconcerted at first, the patient – a young woman – quickly discovered the depth of awareness hidden behind what seemed a frivolous initiation.

At eighty-three Jung was the modern high priest of a psychotherapeutic tradition reaching far back into ancient mythology which diverged widely from Freud's materialism and the measurable world of science. A sage – almost an oracle – living out his last years in distinguished isolation, many famous men and women came from all over the world to pay homage as they might to a holy man, or to pose questions which he alone, they believed, was equipped to answer.

A new climate had become apparent in wide areas of intellectual and public life. A renaissance of the irrational had turned thousands of young people toward psychedelic experience, Indian gurus, and experiments with semi-mystical rituals. Reason as a means of solving some of our biggest problems had proved inadequate, and social institutions become dubious shrines of fossilised values. Science was suspect, and the ancient cult of astrology in the ascendant once again among more people than would care, openly, to admit it. In this mental and spiritual climate Jung's deep roots in myth, symbol, magic, the occult and the religious attitude to life were magnetically attractive. Many people like J. B. Priestley, H. G. Wells, Sir Montagu Norman and Sir Herbert Read turned to his works, searching for that rejuvenation from wellsprings which, in their view, were deeper than anything reason, politics, Freud, Marx or Marcuse could offer, and his appeal overran many apparently exclusive boundaries.

It was at the 1938 congress of the International General Medical Society for Psychotherapy at Oxford that I first encountered Jung. He was chairman of the conference, but he also outlined fourteen points upon which he thought there was agreement in all schools of psychological thought. In his sixty-third year, still tall and command-ing, he bore down upon me that hot summer day. 'I understand', he said, 'you are writing a biography of H. G. Wells.' His manner of speech was staccato, almost explosive. He spoke with a decided accent and placed tremendous emphasis on certain words.

I admitted what somehow seemed a crime, since the outlooks of Carl Gustav Jung and Herbert George Wells were vastly different.

'Tell me,' he said, 'why does he *so hate* religion?'

His eyes brimming with intelligence through his gold-rimmed spectacles, his manner charming, I was nonetheless aware of the masked scrutiny of the trained analyst, but the first impact of his personality was not as overwhelming as it had once been to the early Freudian circle. The voice was still deep but warm, the eyes penetrating but alight, every other moment, with puckish humour. Within a few minutes I felt at ease in the company of what appeared to be one of the most civilised of men.

Analysing the extraordinary contradictions in H. G. Wells's work, Jung admitted that he found his particular brand of 'rational scientism' temperamentally alien. I have a memory of his referring to the works of Karl Popper with words something like: 'It's a pity Wells doesn't read German, because he might have found enlightenment in Karl Popper's *The Logic of Scientific Discovery*.[1] There we saw some of the shortcomings of science properly exposed.'

'But medical science has played a big part in your own career,' I said.

'As a boy I was powerfully attracted to two fields – comparative religion and science. I became the *luckiest of men*. I managed to marry two *very disparate* subjects. Later I wanted to *divorce science* because it appeared to me to be getting ideas *above its station*. But it did not work out like that.'

We talked on for some time, and I was aware of a curious anomaly.

Instead of the great man talking about his ideas, his books, work or experience, he seemed more interested in finding some 'frame' through which he could suitably view and examine my own psyche. Continually the exchange came back to my immature ideas and ambitions, and the whole conversation was laced with quips and jokes.

It was at the same congress that Jung received the first D.Sc. offered by Oxford University to a psychotherapist. Dr Michael Fordham records: 'his reply of thanks was flowery and unusual to English tastes and I found it embarrassing. But worse was to follow. As he came down with the University dignitaries Jung gave his close assistant C. A. Meier an enormous wink which convulsed Meier and several others besides. . . . It seemed like a calculated insult to the University. I don't think so, however; it was just Jung unable to resist being a *gamin* and showing his humorous disrespect for ceremony . . .'.[2]

Ernest Jones had a very different impression of Jung. He told me that Jung could 'easily become a cantankerous and stubborn man incapable of making concessions in argument'.[3] Freud, of course, on one classic occasion, referred to him as 'brutal and sanctimonious', but that phrase occurred as the two men were tearing apart in the late-Freudian battles. Any such rich and complex character as Jung, of course, would be subject to widely varying moods and involve what can only be described as multiple personalities. Certainly one of those personalities had ceaseless intellectual curiosity, great humanity, depth of imaginative insight and concern for his patient, but there were many others.

Elizabeth Osterman encountered another incarnation when she visited him for the first time at Bollingen in 1930 while returning from Greece via Switzerland to the United States.

> As I stood waiting before the door I was somewhat nervous but was reassured by the sounds of wood chopping coming from behind the wall. I was trying to accustom myself to the fact that I was actually going to meet the man who indirectly had influenced my adult life so profoundly, who, in fact, had changed its entire course.[4]

Ten years before, a kind of dream-vision had deflected her career from straight medicine into psychological medicine, and the dream had occurred 'when working through a deep analysis with one of [Jung's] students in San Francisco'.

Jung greeted her warmly, and she had an immediate sense of *rapport*. 'At the water's edge we settled into comfortable chairs and through that afternoon the conversation wandered back into the prehistory of the earth, into the depths of the psyche, into the wonders of nature around us.'

After two hours Elizabeth Osterman looked at her watch for fear that she was keeping Jung too long. 'Never mind your watch,' he said, and went on talking. There was about the statements he made an immediacy and simplicity in total contradiction to his great erudition.

What she described as 'a remarkable force' emanated from him. 'He seemed at once powerful and simple; real the way the sky and rocks and trees and water around him were real. . . .'

Miss A. I. Allenby first encountered Jung at the end of the Second World War, and the idea of meeting the great man filled her with apprehension, but 'the moment I entered his intimate little study I felt completely at ease. All the people I know who have met Jung have told me the same.'[5]

In the following years she spent many hours discussing 'matters of great personal importance with him in his study, and always he gave the same lively attention to whatever I had come to consult him about. The man who has left us the fruits of an incredible amount of work . . . never seemed to be hurried when one was with him.'

Recounting, on one occasion, a dream which she found obscure, Jung suddenly broke off to search his bookshelves for correlative documents, resumed his seat, read out the relevant passages and related the available evidence to corresponding experiences of his own. There was no sense in which the Master displayed special insights to enlighten his patient, but instead he worked with the patient in a co-operative search 'for the meaning of it all'. 'It seemed to me as if his capacity to listen and to absorb every detail did not diminish in old age, but on the contrary increased.'[6]

If that conjures up a very solemn, silver-haired sage, Miss Allenby corrected the image with an account of his great gusts of laughter as he laced his exposition with illustrative anecdote. One story in particular recurred from a number of witnesses. Intended to demonstrate the proposition that one should not feel guilty about events which occur 'on their own account' and over which one had 'no control', it concerned the reaction of a shrewd old Swiss peasant to a stroke of lightning which damaged the village church. When the pastor moved round the village collecting contributions for repairs, the peasant exclaimed, 'Are you asking me to pay Him for destroying His own house!' And Jung with a Homeric laugh commented, 'That man got it right!'[7]

Miss Allenby finally remarked:

> At bottom Jung was . . . a passionate moralist. His morality is different from that in which most of us have been brought up: it is at the same time more permissive and more exacting. It is above all a morality deeply rooted in faith – faith in the value of the individual and faith in the creative potentiality of the unconscious.

Another view of Jung's personality was given by the analyst Anneliese Aumüller. As a young student spending a few weeks in Zürich, a friend invited her to a party, and there, marked out among the assembled company, was Jung. Some twenty people were in the room.

He talked about his experiences in Africa, his encounters with natives of practically every part of the world. . . . His voice seemed to belong to an ancient Chinese story-teller. I found myself walking through the jungle with many new eyes open. . . . I could suddenly perceive the world with senses of whose existence I had never known before.

It was her first encounter with Jung, and it opened doors which 'never closed again'.[8] Many years passed before she saw Jung again, and in those years catastrophe overtook Europe. The Nazis rose to dominate Germany, the Second World War broke out, refugees multiplied, the horror of the concentration camps was revealed and chaos overtook European civilisation.

Once more she returned to Zürich to consult Jung, brimful of problems, dreams, complexities, but to her dismay Jung did not seem to appreciate 'how desperately I wanted to talk to him. He just glanced at me, and then looked out of the window into his garden and started to tell me quiet little stories: about the long preparation the bushmen took the evening before a hunt; how many years of learning it took a disciple of Zen Buddhism before he dared to try to hit the target.'

His soliloquy became preoccupied with exploring 'the pitch black darkness of a tower where there was no chance of any light', and Anneliese Aumüller's impatience approached despair.

The following morning Jung greeted her with a smile which conveyed elements of the sarcastic. 'You were quite unhappy last night and thought me a nasty, un-understanding man, didn't you?' She admitted as much, and at once Jung began a swift exposition of one flaw in Western civilisation, which would never, as he put it, 'let things happen'. He analysed the Chinese concept of Wu-Wei, which meant achieving a balance between activity and passivity. One of his most appreciated authors translated Wu-Wei as 'Doing nothing, but also not doing nothing.'

Anneliese Aumüller commented:

When I went back to war-terror and fear I had learnt not to jump immediately *in medias res*. I no longer wanted to solve the problem or complex but was able to smell out the climate a little more and to let things happen . . . even to let the patient leave in despair in order to give the unconscious a chance to say what it thought to be good.

In other words, some problems were not immediately soluble, and it was better to let them develop their own inner resolution in collaboration with the unconscious.

Joseph L. Henderson was successively a patient, a student, a colleague and a friend over many years. He first saw in Jung the image of the philosopher or man of wisdom.[9] 'It was hard to realise how at an earlier time he had been so much more exclusively the psychologist and psychiatrist in the scientific sense.' These two images, the scientist and the philosopher, clashed on first acquaintance, and then, meeting him a second time, they suddenly fused into a 'humanist in the old Renaissance style, in whom an authentic scientist and artist met in a man of philosophic temperament and training'. Unlike most philosophers, Jung was also a man who put his theories into practice on such a scale and with such wide-ranging influence that Dr Henderson was deeply impressed.

On perhaps his tenth meeting, yet another embodiment of his chameleon personality emerged – that of the European Christian Protestant – to modify his reverence. 'This I did not envy and it . . . provoked the same rebellious anti-father feelings from which I had expected Jung to cure me . . . in him I thought I detected a far more deeply moral critic than my own father had been.'

Yet another image then arose to challenge the austerity of the father-figure – that of a Swiss peasant in faded blue denims and sandals, 'drinking wine and throwing meat to his dogs with gargantuan generosity. There was nothing gross or self-conscious about this; it was all an expression of true Homeric piety.'[10]

As if to flaunt the complexity of Jung's personality, yet another of the multiple selves within his overtly integrated persona would come riding up from a tradition apparently different from all the others which made Jung, at times, into the modern equivalent of the old shaman, a person of uncanny perception and frightening unpredictability of behaviour. 'This was the side of him which could never endure boredom and managed to keep him in hot water with someone all his life.' It could cause an abrupt breaking away from a person – where communication between them had run dry – in a manner which was rude. Indeed, one witness testifies to a Swiss-German bluntness approaching and sometimes realising rudeness. Jung himself enlarged on this, but before quoting irrefutable evidence from the Shaman himself let Dr Henderson describe a lighter aspect of Jung's nature.

> I remember a party at his house in which we were held to a relentless game, with everyone sitting in a circle throwing a ball from one to the other to frustrate the unfortunate victim who had to stand in the centre and try to intercept the ball. This seemed to go on for hours, with Jung as the evil genius who kept it going. Various mishaps occurred during the evening. I fell down and broke my glasses, a very proper Bostonian lady lost her pearls, and just as the party seemed destined to fall to pieces by this shattering of personas, the unbounded pleasure of our host asserted itself, baptising us all to harmony again.[11]

At a much deeper level Dr Henderson remarks that 'when I have gone all over my memories of Jung's personality and character, sifted and simplified the images they evoke, there is left a sense that he was not just a mixture of them all but something separate and whole. . . . He was the most deeply rooted man I ever met, whether in his actual life or in his philosophic and religious commitment. . . .'

On my own second and last meeting with Jung, I encountered a man who emanated a kind of certainty. Given his high cheek-bones and fresh complexion, he could easily be mistaken for a countryman, and the 'excellent brain was so unexpected in the peasant's frame'.[12] Certainly, for all his erudition, Jung had a gift for communicating with people in many walks of life when he put himself out to do so. H. F. Ellenberger claims that in the gatherings which followed the meetings of the Medical Association for Psychotherapy he would strip off his jacket and dance and yodel far into the night, but Jung's son Franz denies this.[13]

Jung believed that a good psychiatrist must sometimes get away from the consulting-room to explore the taverns, prisons, stock exchanges and churches. A contradiction arose between the man firmly anchored in reality who enjoyed good food, sailing, pipe-smoking and moun-taineering, and the metaphysician who was fascinated by the occult. He could move with disconcerting speed from the loftiest speculation to an analysis of good coffee-making, cook an excellent meal, swear elo-quently and face a threatening mob of Africans with immense courage. Modern art, modern music and women in trousers he abhorred. Conversationally brilliant, wit was not something he prized, but he sometimes practised it with skill. On one occasion, asked if simple ignorance were not the root of most of the troubles in the world, he replied: 'No, it's not ignorance – it is that so many people know things which are simply not so.'

Yet another side of his character came through at a meeting of the Eranos Society.[14] In full flood of delivering a paper, Herbert Read became aware of a growling voice which erupted from the body of the hall like occasional rolls of thunder. The voice repeated – at intervals – two phrases explosively: 'That's mine!' and 'That's yours!' As Herbert Read plunged deeper into his subject the interruptions became louder. Suddenly, the powerful figure of Jung stood up, made his way ruthlessly along the row of disciples and stormed out of the hall. Within minutes there came from the floor above the hall the sound of a man clumping about, his footsteps expressing his fury more violently than his words. Dr Michael Fordham arrived late for the lecture and encountered the same figure storming down the stairs again, swearing with an unexpected range of four-letter invective.[15] Jung told Fordham that his wife had stolen (!) the key to his flat above the lecture-hall and that he could not get in.

Certainly, Jung was a man capable of great rages, sometimes the result of a long accumulation of repressed aggression, but he rarely held a grudge.[16] He could, as we have seen, be rude to those who bored him. He could literally eject a visitor who had become intolerable, and his invective against his enemies included phrases like 'slimy bastard',

'empty gasbag', 'a pisspot of unconscious devils', and might even mount
to the point of physical threats – 'I would have softened up his
guttersnipe complex with a sound Swiss thrashing.'[17]

In total contradiction, he was the sensitive scholar who carried
intelligence into the high places of intellect, and his erudition in many
languages was redeemed from pedantry. Capable of creating a new
model of the human psyche, half his life was spent speculating about the
nature of Man. Suffering himself at one stage to the point of near-
madness, he understood the suffering of others and sometimes converted
pain into an Elizabethan zest for living. That, at least, was how his
disciples saw him.

One fundamental key to his rich and complex psyche only became
apparent very late in life. 'There was a daimon in me and in the end its
presence proved decisive. It overpowered me and if I was at times
ruthless it was because I was in the grip of the daimon.'[18]

He offended some people because the daimon insisted that if they did
not understand him, then that was the end of the matter. He had no
toleration of alien people unless they happened to be patients in
treatment. 'I had to obey an inner law which was imposed on me and
left me no choice.' Although he was able to become intensely interested
in people for a time, 'once I had seen through them the magic was gone'.
He made a number of enemies because of the daimon. 'A creative
person has little power over his own life. He is not free. He is
captive. . . .'

This lack of freedom in his inner life was a great sorrow to him, and he
found himself forced to say on occasion, 'I am fond of you, indeed I love
you, but I cannot stay. . . .'[19] In the end he regarded himself as literally
the victim of these forces.

As we shall see, the flattery of his disciples was subject to severe
qualification and the picture drawn in this prologue had less pleasant
aspects which will be examined in detail. We have so far touched in an
outline of the myth. Behind it we shall eventually confront the actual
man.

When all this is said, what were the influences which combined to
produce a person so rich in contradictions, what beginnings gave birth
to such a multiplicity of personas, and how did he achieve the smiling
serenity of the Old Wise Man so often presented in his last days?

Chapter 1
Forebears

CARL GUSTAV JUNG tended to identify during many periods of his life with his grandfather, also named Carl Gustav, a legendary figure in Basel.[1] From his childhood grandfather Jung (1774–1864) revealed a combative temperament, and remained a forceful personality throughout his life. At school one day he is alleged to have challenged a bully of enormous proportions with words equivalent to 'Hit someone smaller than yourself.' The bully subsided, confronted by the concentrated fury of a boy who had not yet experienced many of the harsh realities of the outer world.[2]

The son of a German doctor, Jung's grandfather grew up in the austere atmosphere of Basel and eventually went to Heidelberg University to study medicine, but his mind was full of the music of the Romantic poets. He wrote poetry, and was sometimes to be found on a summer evening walking through the woods singing student-songs of his own composition.[3] At twenty-three an incident occurred which dramatically changed the course of his life. As Gustav Steiner later wrote:

> Driven by idealistic notions and following his God-inspired duty, Carl Ludwig Sands [a friend of Jung] had assassinated a Russian Councillor said to be a symbol of the reactionary movement. As a result the police had a good pretext to move in and Jung's grandfather was arrested and spent a year in prison in Berlin. It is questionable whether he himself felt as innocent as posterity claimed him to be. The police found a hammer and an axe belonging to the assassin in his room.[4]

Carl Gustav Jung was locked away without trial, and emerged to find his public character stained and his medical career apparently in ruins.[5]

Embittered, he abandoned the country of his birth, set out for France and found there the illusion of a freer, more stimulating intellectual climate where the rhetoric of the barricades was common parlance. In Paris the café life absorbed him, and the combination of an occasional absinthe with bursts of revolutionary talk gave a fresh stimulus to his life. It was there that he met Alexander von Humboldt, who suddenly recognised in him a possible candidate for a new post which the Medical School at the University in Basel had just created. The Director was searching for a person with sufficient drive and initiative to reorganise the school, and Humboldt immediately recommended the voluntary exile Jung.

Steiner gives a different version of this episode, in which von
Humboldt stumbled on Carl one day sitting on a bench in the open, and
found the young man to be almost starving. It was, Steiner states, as
much for humanitarian reasons as for any belief in his talents that von
Humboldt agreed to recommend him.

Whether Jung's 'criminal record' interfered or the bureaucratic
wheels ground slowly, the appointment was mysteriously delayed, and
Jung found himself forced to apply for authorisation to give private
lectures in Basel. When at last they offered him the medical post, he
became a Swiss citizen and quickly made his mark.[6]

Accounts of his behaviour as a family man vary.[7] One source
described him as a tyrannous father, another as boisterous and prank-
playing, and a third as 'the most considerate of men'; but on one
characteristic most accounts agree. When dealing with colleagues or
recalcitrant students at the University, his 'irresistible' charm reconciled many feuding parties and won the hearts of young and old alike.

Three children were born to his first wife before she suddenly and
unexpectedly died. Audaciously, within a very short time Carl Jung
was wooing the daughter of the Mayor of Basel, Sophie Frey, and
bearding the Mayor in his office to ask for her hand in marriage. No
reliable details of the encounter remain, but what began as a quiet
discussion was said to have become explosive when the Mayor made it
clear that he had no intention of granting Jung's request.

In keeping with the irrational side of his nature, which marked Carl
Jung out from most of his conforming colleagues, he retired to a local
tavern, drank a few beers and suddenly, in roistering mood, proposed
marriage to one of the waitresses. At first, this was taken to be the result
of a fit of pique or simply a bad joke, but when it became clear that he
intended to carry through his morganatic madness the story set the
University by the ears and produced widespread consternation. It was
almost as if he wished to punish the Mayor by discrediting himself and
holding the Mayor responsible.

The subsequent marriage added notoriety to his already considerable fame, and his career suffered a temporary setback. He rode out the
storm with a personality which by now reinforced charm with great
strength of character.

Once again death intervened to change the direction of his life. When
his wife Aniela had borne him two more children, the ex-waitress in her
turn died, and now came an unexpected climax to his emotional life.
Once more he bearded the Mayor at his home and again asked for the
hand of the Mayor's daughter. Little is known about the reactions of
Sophie Frey herself, but it has been suggested that she deliberately
remained single in the hope that one day a wife who was 'nothing more
than a waitress' must pall on a man as distinguished as Carl Gustav
Jung. This time the Mayor consented to the marriage.

From now on the career of Jung the elder went from strength to strength. One of the most distinguished doctors in Switzerland, he became Grand Master of the Swiss Freemasons, Rector of the University, wrote plays and scientific treatises under different pseudonyms, and sired in all thirteen children.

One factor which may have influenced his career reverberated down the centuries and even created echoes in his grandson's lifetime a hundred years later. Rumour had it that Jung the elder was in fact an illegitimate son of the great Goethe.

Early photographs show him sitting splendidly in a big armchair, with noble brow, silver locks and visionary eyes, and resonances do arise of a less poetic, less subtle Johann Wolfgang von Goethe, but the evidence for the family connection is ill-defined, and illegitimacy probably a romantic legend.

Toward the end of his life his grandson told Aniela Jaffé:

> The wife of my great-grandfather [Franz Ignaz Jung, d.1831] Sophie Ziegler and her sister were associated with the Mannheim theatre and were friends of many writers. The story goes that Sophie Ziegler had an illegitimate child by Goethe and that this child was my grandfather, Carl Gustav Jung. This was considered virtually an established fact. . . . Sophie Ziegler-Jung was later friendly with Lotte Kestner, a niece of Goethe's 'Lottchen'. This Lotte Kestner settled in Basel, no doubt because of these close ties with the Jung family.[8]

The legend persisted stubbornly down the years, and Jung would sometimes relate it with a certain 'gratified amusement', but his attitude remained ambivalent. One moment he felt that any proliferation of the story was in bad taste because there were 'too many fools who [told] such tales of the unknown father'. At another he solemnly investigated his origins like a genealogist. Unfortunately, the existing family-tree breaks off with Sigmund Jung at the beginning of the eighteenth century, since the municipal archives of Mainz were burned down in the course of a siege during the War of the Spanish Succession.

One other vital link with the adult Jung became apparent in Sophie Ziegler's character. Writing to Ewald Jung in January 1960, Jung said: 'Sophie Ziegler-Jung's mental illness has absorbed me again. The only documents relating to this are some letters of hers in my possession. The handwriting shows no schizophrenic traits but rather, for all its character, an emotional ravagement such as can be observed in psychogenic melancholias.'[9] Jung was to have, in middle-age, a major mental breakdown. Could it be traced to hereditary sources?

Two other aspects of Carl Jung's life and work were reflected in his maternal grandparents – the religious and the occult. His maternal grandfather Samuel Preiswerk (1799–1871) was a man of strong personality whose carefully prepared sermons were said to include occasional heresies, despite the fact that he would have his daughter sit for hours behind him to prevent the evil spirits intervening. There is some evidence to show that the daughter was herself only too anxious to introduce heresies which would put fresh fire into his pompous outpourings. Erudition frequently inhibits spontaneity, but despite the premeditation which distinguished most of the more important decisions in his life it did not save Samuel Preiswerk from making bad mistakes. Some of these troubles were represented in his poems, of which he wrote an inordinate number, but they appear to have been no more distinguished than his sermons. As a theologian he could pursue a narrow thread of argument with Jesuitical subtlety, but there was nothing of the Jesuit in his straightforward Christian beliefs, and the hymns he wrote reflected the simplicity of his creed. Perhaps the best literary work he left was a Hebrew grammar, which reflected his bias in favour of the Jews, and there is some evidence to show that the passion which failed to vitalise his sermons was poured into a number of Palestinian writings. Professor Ellenberger says in his book *The Discovery of the Unconscious* that Preiswerk was considered a precursor of Zionism and 'actively defended that idea'. For the rest, he married twice, had one child from his first wife and no fewer than thirteen from the second.

The subject of this biography came from a long line of pastors, and the religious influence was strong, repeating itself in his maternal grandparent Samuel Preiswerk, but a second preoccupation played an important part in Samuel Preiswerk's life.[10] As Professor Ellenberger puts it, 'According to family tradition he had visions and conversed with the world of spirits. . . .' Indeed, an extraordinary ritual repeated itself every week with unfailing regularity.[11] A special chair was set aside in Samuel Preiswerk's study for the spirit of his first wife, whose death had deeply disturbed him, and every week she came to occupy the chair and communicate – by what means is not clear – with her husband. His second wife, who believed that spiritual infidelity was close to physical infidelity, would have tolerated, it seems, the threat of a living mistress better than this intangible rival whose powers no material laws could challenge.[12] However, it would be a mistake to imagine that a remarkable battle of psychic wits did not take place at a level far removed from the commonplace. Preiswerk's second wife – Jung's grandmother – was said to possess the gift of second sight, and several members of her family claimed parapsychological abilities.[13]

Serious biography is not a place for psychic speculation, but it is hard to believe that on those disturbing Wednesdays, when the first wife reinvaded the household of the second wife Augusta Faber, she did not invoke her psychic gifts to challenge and perhaps overwhelm her resuscitated rival. The eternal triangle raised to the psychic level becomes an intriguing possibility which would have appealed to Jung. Indeed, here – as, once again, we shall see – echoes recurred sixty years later in the life of Carl Gustav himself.

Turning to Jung's parents, the face of the father Paul Jung which looks out from so many photographs has the same fine forehead as the paternal grandfather, but the features are more intellectual and less poetic. Tapering away to a bearded chin, the triangular features have an intensity and austerity different from those of the grandfather. Authoritarianism and a degree of passion are evident, but photographs rarely capture more than a particular mood, and frequently mislead.

That Jung had a 'strong resentment towards his father' is clear from the reminiscences he compiled with Aniela Jaffé, but he did not describe his father as tyrannical. Professor Ellenberger once met an old lady who had known Jung's father well in her youth, and she said he was 'a quiet, unassuming, kind-hearted man who knew how to preach to peasants and was uniformly loved and respected by his parishioners'.[14] Public and private personalities frequently differ, and it may not be surprising to find Jung himself saying that his father often quarrelled with his mother. On Jung's evidence outbursts of rage and irritability were commonplace.

The father's career was not distinguished. He studied Oriental languages in Gottingen and completed a thesis on the Arabic version of the Song of Songs.[15] According to Jung, 'his days of glory ended with his final examination' and 'thereafter he forgot his linguistic talent'.[16] Assigned to the small parish of Kesswil on the shores of Lake Constance, in 1875, when his son was six months old, he moved to Laufen, the castle and vicarage above the Falls of the Rhine. Already serious rifts in his marriage to Emilie Preiswerk were becoming apparent. In 1879 he moved again, to Klein-Hüningen, a small village which was regarded as part of Basel city, to become the Protestant chaplain of the Friedmatt Mental Hospital, bringing his son into indirect contact with a world in which he was, many years later, to specialise. Jung made no mention of the coincidence in his reminiscences, and it may have no real significance. It is reasonable to assume that Jung the elder would talk about the patients to his wife, but no one knows how far any of these references penetrated the consciousness of a very young child.

Thereafter, Jung later wrote, his father 'lapsed into a sort of sentimental idealism and into reminiscences of his golden student days, continuing to smoke a long student's pipe. . .'.[17]

Paul Jung fell in love with and married Jung's mother Emilie Preiswerk under the most conventionally correct circumstances. Very little evidence remains of their early relationship, but Jung had two memories of his mother. One recalls a slender young woman wearing a dress 'made of black printed all over with green crescents' who could be happy and laughing but was subject to fits of depression. The second impression came from a later period:

My mother was a very good mother. She had a hearty animal warmth, cooked wonderfully and was most companionable and pleasant. She was very stout and a ready listener. She also liked to

talk and her chatter was like the gay plashing of a fountain. She
had a decided literary gift as well as taste and depth. But this
quality never properly emerged; it remained hidden beneath the
semblance of a kindly fat . . . woman, extremely hospitable, and
possessor of a great sense of humour.[18]

Publicly, Mrs Jung conformed to all the understood conventions of
the day and accepted ready-made values based on Christian principles,
but privately there sometimes appeared a person so strikingly different
that Jung spoke of her later in life as being two people. An unconscious
aspect of her personality would suddenly break through the crust of the
conforming mother and reveal a power and resolution at variance with
the plump compliance of her public self. It was a 'sombre, imposing
figure possessed of unassailable authority – and no bones about it', Jung
wrote. One personality was innocuous and human, the other uncanny.
The second personality emerged rarely, but each time the experience
was unexpected and frightening. 'She would then speak as if talking to
herself but what she said was aimed at me and usually struck to the core
of my being so that I was stunned to silence.'

In his mother the duality of a warm-hearted, deeply religious person
and a woman whose psychic powers expressed themselves in a second
personality emerged to impress the growing boy.

Chapter 2

The First Years

CARL GUSTAV JUNG was born on 26 July 1875, in the village of Kesswil, in the canton of Thurgovia on the shores of Lake Constance. Switzerland in 1875 was a country where women wore skirts which almost swept the ground, the family was sacred and unquestioned, the relations between the sexes required chaperons for innumerable innocent occasions, religion penetrated all areas of life, a prolonged engagement preceded marriage, and sex was regarded by some as an unfortunate prerequisite of reproduction. The conspiracy of silence about sexual matters remained profound and premarital intercourse was heavily frowned upon.

It has been said that Switzerland is sexually one of the most puritan countries in the world. Certainly, in 1875 any blunt mention of sexual activity in polite circles was not merely taboo but a sure invitation to social ostracism. Searching for explanations of hysteria, crippling complexes and compulsive anxiety, Swiss doctors recoiled from the possibility that these had anything to do with sex. Homosexuality was a criminal condition, impotence an unfortunate derangement of the sexual organs, cunnilingus and fellatio regarded by large numbers as unpleasant perversions, and many men married women in total ignorance of the nature of their anatomy.

In the wider perspective, the Protestant ethic held sway everywhere. Personal integrity, honesty and cleanliness were reinforced by hard work, ambition and the imperative of social as well as personal progress. In the eyes of many poverty was synonymous with idleness, the unemployed were victims of their own vices, criminals incapable of treatment, and the role of women essentially that of wife and mother of children. Large families were common, and contraception only practised in its crudest forms by those who had a pact with the devil of sensuality.

In contradiction to the popular view today of Switzerland filling her coffers on the proceeds of prolonged, if not prostituted, peace, Jung's grandparents had known a period when Switzerland became enmeshed in the French Revolution and Napoleonic Wars. Civil strife broke out between 1815 and 1830, when the farmers tried by force to abolish the privileges of the city patriciate in several cantons and armed fighting arose on a widespread scale. Jung's parents would have been very much aware of the days when Switzerland mobilised against – of all giants to challenge – Russia, and they were certainly involved in the religious struggles which continued far into their son's lifetime.

Professor Ellenberger claims that Jung 'reflected to a high degree not only the characteristics of the Swiss mentality but also the spirit of his home town, Basel, his ancestors and his family'.[1] A self-contained political unit with its own government, ministerial departments and administration, Basel in the year of Jung's birth had only 50,000 inhabitants and was sufficiently localised for large groups of people to know one another personally.

> Since the Renaissance Basel had remained one of the hearths of European culture. In his childhood Jung, when walking in the streets, could see the eminent historian philosopher Jacob Burck-hardt or old Bachofen: he heard talk about Nietzsche everywhere, whom so many people had known: and he was infallibly identified as 'the grandson of the famous Carl Gustav Jung'.[2]

The Reverend and Mrs Paul Jung had a surprisingly small family – only three children. It seems that either sexual relations broke down – Jung's later evidence supports this view – or they practised some form of contraception. Carl Gustav was the second son, his elder brother Paul – born in August 1873 – having died a few days after his birth. The third child was a girl, Johanna Gertrud, born on 17 July 1884, nine years later – an interval, once more, with interesting implications. A much simpler, less intellectual person than Jung, she greatly admired her distinguished brother and lived in his shadow all her life.

Very little is known of the first few months of Jung's life, but within six months the family moved from Kesswil to Laufen. The Pfarrhaus or presbytery has been called 'one of the germinal cells of German culture',[3] and it was in this spacious house that Jung's first attempts to cope with reality began. The presbytery stood in isolation near the Laufen castle with a big meadow reaching back to the sexton's farm, and from no great distance came the constant murmur of the Rhine Falls, a background music to Jung's childhood memories.

At the age of eighty-three Jung wrote: 'My memories begin with my second or third year. I recall the vicarage, the garden, the laundry house, the church, the castle, the Falls, the small castle of Worth . . . .'[4]

One especially vivid memory remained from these very first days, and this first indelible impression predisposed the child to respond to the pleasure of being alive. 'I am lying in a pram, in the shadow of a tree. It is a fine warm summer day, the sky blue, a golden sunlight darting through green leaves. The hood of the pram has been left up.' He had just awakened, he said, 'to the glorious beauty of the day and . . . a sense of indescribable well being'. The sun was playing through the leaves, beautiful blossoms adorned the bushes, and everything was 'wholly wonderful, colourful and splendid'.[5] It is difficult to imagine a better response to the beginnings of life for any child. Eighty-three years later his reactions may have lacked the spontaneous joy of this two-year-old response, but he sometimes recaptured a glowing serenity in the presence of nature. Between these two idyllic episodes stretched an eternity of experience, harsh, disturbing, exciting, satisfying and profound, driven by a cannon pulse of physical and intellectual energy and an underlying zest for living which even the worst moments could never quite overwhelm.

Clearly, his mother in the first few years of his life surrounded him with that warmth and affection which most psychiatrists regard as a prerequisite of a well-adjusted person. The very earliest memories were frequently happy ones. 'I am sitting in our dining room on the west side of the house, perched on a high chair and spooning up warm milk with bits of broken bread in it. The milk has a pleasant taste and a characteristic smell.'[6]

Childhood amnesia easily obliterates memories too unpleasant to recollect, and Jung admitted that there may have been early episodes he successfully suppressed all his life. 'But generally speaking my very early years were happy ones. The troubles came after that. People seem to polarise their earliest memories and create one of two myths, one being an idyll, too consistent to be true, the other early years of sheer misery.'[7]

I once discussed a nightmare I had as a child with Jung, and he remarked, 'I had some pretty good ones too.' My nightmare concerned a plague of bees swarming over my bed, each one of which was dressed in black with white stiff reversed collar, resembling clergymen. A spasm of religious revulsion had overtaken me as a result of learning for the first time what terrible retribution awaited me if I failed to conform to the precepts of the Christian faith. Jung remarked, 'I suffered occasionally from a similar visitation. It was all about a man in a long, black garment and broad hat coming out of a wood. It certainly struck fear into my heart. But he wasn't a clergyman – as you call it – he was a Jesuit.'

In his very earliest years he recalled that it was his aunt, not his mother, who took him out in front of the house one day and said, 'Now I am going to show you something.' Stretching away into the distance was the road to Dachsen, and there on the far horizon the interlocking chain of the Alps. Magnificent in the crimson glory of the sunset, they should have inspired awe but, as he later said, 'At that age I was no respecter of persons or places.'

In *Memories, Dreams, Reflections* he develops the episode. 'I was told . . . the next day . . . [that] the village children would be going on a school outing to the Uetliberg, near Zürich. I wanted so much to go too. To my sorrow I was informed that children as small as I could not go along, there was nothing to be done about it.' But the incident took on symbolic significance. 'From then on the Uetliberg and Zürich became an unattainable land of dreams, near to the glowing snow-covered mountains.' Again in old age he remarked, 'I became one of the lucky ones – I reached my unattainable land.'

The invocation of his aunt in his earliest memories was revealing. From the first years the hyper-sensitive child became dimly aware of reactions between his parents which troubled him. At three years of age 'general eczema' attacked him and, assuming it was nervous eczema, the cause of the strain seems self-evident. Reading between the lines of his reminiscences, it is clear that he suffered from powerful tensions created by his parents, and at one point he becomes quite explicit: 'My illness in 1878 must have been connected with a temporary separation of my parents.' His mother spent several months in a Basel hospital. Attempts to check which hospital she went to have failed because the records have been destroyed, but two facts point strongly in an interesting direction. The date of the boy's illness is in dispute. If it happened to be 1879 instead of 1878, that was the year when the family moved again, to Klein-Hüningen where his father became chaplain of the Friedmatt Mental Hospital. Jung implied that his mother's illness was brought on by mental stress as a result of the difficulties of the marriage, but the evidence is insufficient and confusing. Certainly, her absence deeply disturbed her son. One of the images which constantly recurred later in life was of himself, 'restive, feverish, unable to sleep', being carried by his father, who paced up and down, singing his old student-songs. 'I particularly remember one I was especially fond of and which always used to soothe me – "Alles schweige, jeder neige . . .". To this day I can remember my father's voice singing over me in the stillness of the night.'[8]

It is possible to piece together a dangerously influential period at the crucial age of three when an aunt, twenty years older than his mother, took care of Jung, his father did his best to compensate for the missing mother, but a bad outbreak of eczema troubled the boy. Collectively these events left a lasting impression. 'From then on, I always felt mistrustful when the word "love" was spoken. The feeling I associated with "woman" was for a long time that of innate unreliability. "Father", on the other hand, meant reliability and – powerlessness.'[9]

Powerless to replace the missing mother, powerless to control the events which had removed his mother, or powerless to control the boy's distress and illness? Retrospective insights into childhood motives are frequently unreliable, and words like 'powerless' would certainly not have occurred to a boy of three or four years old. Whatever it was, the removal of his mother had thrown his world into confusion, and he turned to his father, his aunt and his mother's maid for assurance.

The maid left a deep impression. She was slim with black hair and an olive complexion. She would pick him up to lay his head against her shoulder, and far into life he could remember 'her hairline, her throat, with its darkly pigmented skin and her ear'.

Beyond the physical reassurance of her body there was something 'very strange' about her, as if she 'belonged not to my family but only to me', and was 'connected in some way with other mysterious things I could not understand'. In short, the girl became a component of his anima – a term elaborated later, but for the moment very roughly stated as the female component in the male personality.

It was the maid who came rushing in one day and shouted: 'The fishermen have found a corpse. It came down the Falls – they want to put it in the washhouse.' Jung's father agreed to accept the corpse, and the four-year-old boy, his curiosity fully aroused, tried to get a glimpse. Pushed back into the house again, his determination to see the corpse grew, and he waited patiently until all the fuss had subsided and stole out once more. The washhouse door was locked, but – his curiosity unabated – he wandered round the house until he came to an open drain running down a slope, and there he saw 'blood and water trickling out'. He commented in *Memories, Dreams, Reflections*, 'I found this extraordinarily interesting.' Ernest Jones told me that he had once discussed this episode with Jung much later in life and Jung had said, 'That was the beginning of a preoccupation I seemed to develop with corpses. Of course, it was not so much the corpse in those days – it was trying to accommodate the idea of death.'[10]

The water from which the corpse had been taken also became a preoccupation and when Jung went one day to visit some friends of the family who owned a castle on Lake Constance, he 'couldn't be dragged away from the water. . . . The lake stretched away and away into the distance. This expanse of water was an inconceivable pleasure to me, an incomparable splendour.'

Symbolically the experience became fused in his mind with the two great traumas of birth and death, and even as a boy he determined that whatever else happened in life he must live near a lake. 'Without water', he thought, 'nobody could live at all.'[11] As everyone knows, his last beautiful home was by a lake.

Another experience associated with the Falls persisted clearly in his memory until the age of eighty, linking earlier and later years. One day, while his father and mother were still 'separated', he remembered a pretty young girl with blue eyes and fair hair leading him 'on a beautiful autumn day' through rows of golden chestnut trees along the Rhine below the Falls. This girl later became his mother-in-law. 'I did not see her again until I was fully adult.'[12]

That his parents' marriage underwent strains, quarrelling and at least one prolonged break is clear; but Jung had a great reluctance to talk about their difficulties, and what evidence is available comes from second-hand sources. One source suggests sexual problems to explain the nine-year gap between the two children at a time when most clergymen would have recoiled from contraceptive devices even if they had been available, and this could have led to mental stress in his mother. Externally the mother's plump, warm, loving personality made this analysis dubious, but it was Jung himself who familiarised the world with the principle of a persona, projected to conceal the 'true' personality.

Albert Oeri wrote of this period: 'I first set eyes on Jung during the time his father was pastor at Dachsen am Rheinfall and we were quite small.' The fathers of both boys were old school-friends and they wanted their children to play together, but 'nothing could be done about Carl who sat in the middle of the room and occupied himself with a little bowling game and wouldn't pay the slightest attention to anyone else'. Why did he remember the first meeting so clearly? 'Probably because I had never come across such an a-social monster before. I was born into a well populated nursery where we played together or fought but in any case always had contact with people, he into an empty one, his sister had not yet been born.'[13]

Nonetheless, there were some lighter moments and an occasional childish prank. 'He wanted me to join him in teasing a cousin whom he regarded as a sissy. He asked the boy to sit on a bench. . . . When the boy complied he burst into whoops of wild Indian laughter, an art he retained all his life. The sole reason was an old souse sitting on the bench. He hoped his sissy cousin would smell of schnapps.'

Sometimes louder, sometimes softer, the roar of the Rhine Falls became the inexhaustible muttering of an unseen presence connected with death, drowning and the inexplicable disappearance of people. The boy himself nearly became one of the victims. Crossing the bridge over the Falls to Neuhausen one day, he had one leg under the protective railing and was 'about to slip through' when the maid caught him just in time. Either a playful child had unconsciously flirted with death or a very distressed child had tried to plunge to his own extinction. Jung himself believed that such accidents pointed to 'an unconscious suicidal urge'.

It looked very much as if the relative happiness of the first two years had gone, and in his third and fourth years he began to experience night fears and many disturbances. Whether these were more pronounced than those of any average childhood is open to question, but they preceded more severe disturbances. There remained a contradiction between the majestic beauty of the Rhine Falls and the hidden ogre who swept people to their death over the rocks and brought processions of 'solemn men in long frock coats' carrying black boxes. 'My father would be there in his clerical gown speaking in a resounding voice: women wept: I was told that someone was being buried in this hole in the ground . . . then I would hear . . . that Lord Jesus had taken them to himself.'

It was this Lord Jesus who now created disturbing confusions in the growing perceptions of a very sharp mind. The boy's mother had taught him to pray to Lord Jesus every night, but he was very painfully aware that the same Lord Jesus 'took people to himself', which meant locking

them up in black boxes and burying them deep in damp holes in the
ground.

The prayer she chose was:

Spread out thy wings, Lord Jesus mild,
And take to thee thy chick, thy child.
If Satan would devour it
No Harm shall overpower it,
So let the people sing!

From being a benevolent old gentleman like the owner of the castle
on the hill, Lord Jesus became a sinister figure closely associated with
'the gloomy black men in frock coats, top hats and shiny black boots'.

Growing conflict in Carl's mind crystallised one hot summer day
when he was sitting outside the house, playing in the sand. He does not
seem to have had many playmates as a child, and his mother presently
left him alone in the roadside sand. Suddenly there emerged from the
wood on the brow of the hill a figure like an apparition so engulfed in
black clothing from head to foot that he could not immediately
determine its sex. Granted almost spectral grace, the figure descended
the road, and as it drew closer he could see that 'it really was a man
wearing a kind of black robe that reached to his feet'.

In the rush of his reaction he remembered his father talking about the
evil activities of certain Jesuits, and immediately a confused association
between the words 'Jesus' and 'Jesuits' arose in his mind and he recalled
the sense of danger conveyed by his father's voice and manner.
Simultaneously it occurred to him that this was a man disguised as a
woman, because he planned to bring evil influences into the house of his
father.

'Terrified, I ran helter skelter into the house, rushed up the stairs and
hid under a beam in the darkest corner of the attic.' He remained
cowering there for perhaps fifteen minutes, and when he dared to poke
his head out of the window again there was no trace of the menacing
figure.[14]

All these were external events. Internally, dreams, conflicts and
anxieties created the usual ferment in the mind of a boy scarcely four
years old trying to accommodate the hundred new impressions which
now made up his everyday life. The conventional struggles between
mother and son when the boy refused to go to bed were replaced, while
she was away, by battles with his father, and on one occasion he was
gathered up, struggling and kicking, to be carried forcibly to his
bedroom. The austerity revealed by photographs of Jung senior was
seldom translated into tyrannical behaviour, but he was more than
capable of imposing his will on a rebellious boy.

Shortly afterwards Carl Gustav experienced a very powerful dream
which preoccupied him for the rest of his life. He dreamt that he was
wandering in the meadow which stretched away to the sexton's farm

when he stumbled on a stone-lined hole deep in the ground. Peering into it, he saw a stairway leading into the black earth and, full of apprehension, decided to discover where it led. Suddenly his passage was blocked by a thick brocaded curtain, and with great hesitation he pulled the curtain aside to discover, opening before him, a long rectangular chamber with an arched ceiling cut out of solid rock. Immense flagstones stretched in perspective down the chamber with a rich red carpet leading from the entrance to a raised platform on which stood an ornate golden throne. There was no questioning the magnificence of the throne, but instead of a splendid monarch in all his regalia there reared out of the throne, with organic certainty, what the child at first thought to be a tree, so high and thick and powerful was its presence. His eye travelled upward in alarm, along its immense height to the ceiling and, retreating down again, suddenly realised that this was no ordinary tree. Instead of bark, human skin covered the tower and, beneath the skin, flesh and blood replaced wood; but, most alarming of all, the top of the tower created the illusion of a rounded head with no face or hair but with – still more sinister – 'a single eye gazing mysteriously upwards'.

The dim light, which failed to illumine the far corners of the room, intensified around the head and eye, creating a kind of aura, and suddenly the boy had a terrible fear that the whole apparition would come to life and crawl towards him like a gigantic worm. 'I was paralysed with terror. At that moment I heard from outside and above me my mother's voice. She called out, "Yes – just look at him. That is the man-eater." '[15]

Fear gave way to sheer panic in the boy's mind, and he came awake sweating and trembling. The following evening when his father tried to get him to bed he fought to prevent it, and for many evenings afterwards fear of sleep reproducing the dream kept him awake far into the night.

Later in life he admitted that the dream haunted him for years, and gave the following interpretation which for the present writer has unconvincing elements: '. . . what I had seen was a phallus and it was decades before I understood that it was a ritual phallus. I could never make out whether my mother meant " *That* is the man-eater" or "That is the *man-eater*." ' The first interpretation meant for Jung that the devourer of little children was not Lord Jesus but the phallus. 'In the second case . . . the man-eater in general was symbolised by the phallus so that the dark Lord Jesus, the Jesuit and the phallus were identical.'

There followed an erudite elaboration of the elements of the dream which seemed to confuse rather than enlighten. The phallus had an *abstract* significance because it was enthroned by itself or – 'ithyphallicly' in the Greek – upright. He interpreted the hole by which he had entered the underground chamber as a grave, and the grave itself 'an underground temple whose green curtain symbolised the meadow, in other words the mystery of Earth with her covering of green vegetation'. He developed the description of the carpet as not merely red but blood red, and concluded: 'the interpretation of the *orificium urethrae* as an eye with the source of light apparently above it points to the etymology of the word phallus . . . in the Greek, shining bright'.

Events in real life which surrounded the occurrence of the dream – the conflicts between his father and mother, their temporary separation, and the boy's inability to assimilate growing tensions of the Oedipal situation – re-echoed the fear it generated. Assume for the moment that, like most boys, he had seen his father's penis at some time and found it huge if not menacing. If the tree becomes a phallic symbol – ritualised or not – a grave leading down to a blood-red carpet suggests, just as sharply, a womb, and together the components of intercourse. Whether Jung ever glimpsed some detail of sexual intercourse between his parents we do not know, but the phallic symbol can easily be read as the threatening father in the context of the quarrels with his wife, and the mother's exclamation – 'That is the man-eater' – a good description of what she had come to regard as her dangerous and destructive husband. Brilliantly combining so many elements in Jung's four-year-old world, it spelt out the struggle between father and mother, his own growing awareness of sexuality, the threats of the father's introjected imago and the many anxieties besetting him.

Jung himself saw it quite differently. 'Through this childhood dream I was initiated into the secrets of the earth. What happened then was a kind of burial in the earth and many years were to pass before I came out again. Today I know that it happened in order to bring the greatest possible amount of light into the darkness.' His intellectual life, he concluded, first began to stir in his unconscious at that time.[16]

Whichever interpretation the reader accepts, one other conflict in these very early years set the seed for self-exploration and intellectual struggle. The experience of the threatening Jesuit coming over the brow of the hill and the 'frightful revelation' of the 'underground' Jesus made the actual Lord Jesus 'never quite acceptable . . . lovable . . . or real'. As for Christian doctrine, 'it seemed to me a solemn masquerade, a kind of funeral at which the mourners put on serious mournful faces but the next moment were secretly laughing and not really sad at all'. The Lord Jesus became a god of death, crucified as a bloody corpse, and serried ranks of gentlemen clad in black frock coats and shiny black boots – eight uncles were parsons – reminded him constantly of burials. Religious gentlemen aroused fear more than respect, and as he grew up his attempts 'to take the required positive attitude to Christ' never quite overcame his distrust. Meanwhile in 1879 another move came, to yet another home with fresh experiences to be assimilated.

Chapter 3

Village School to Gymnasium

WHEN CARL WAS FOUR his father accepted a new parish at Klein-Hüningen, a small village on the shores of the Rhine largely inhabited by fishermen and peasants. It was a patriarchal village with limited educational resources, and Carl had no alternative but to go to the local school. Once again his new home was an old, rambling house which required resources far beyond those of a country parson. It had been the seat of a rich patrician family whose coat of arms with three roses can still be seen over one of the doors, and here, in his fourth and fifth years, his growing awareness invaded the world of art. The house, built in the eighteenth century, had one big dark panelled room full of period furniture with many 'old paintings' on the walls. Among them he discovered a minor copy from Guido Reni's workshop of David and Goliath which so held his fascinated attention that he would steal into the room and 'sit for hours gazing at all the beauty'. In the account he gave later, a very revealing phrase followed: 'It was the only beautiful thing I knew.'[1]

Loneliness, a lack of beauty, and quarrelling parents continued to characterise these childhood years, driving him deeper and deeper into his private self. Games played in total isolation became steadily more important to him. Presented with a set of bricks, he created a series of dizzy towers only to destroy them with deliberately engineered earthquakes brought about by shaking the table, or he dashed down in an exercise-book drawings intended to represent every kind of naval battle, or set his toy soldiers regularly at each other in scenes of frightful carnage.

At six years old came the first experience of school. Forced to mix with the sons of peasants and farmers, the experience reinforced distinctions between the classes and produced alienation not only from his fellow-pupils but also from himself. The Carl Jung who studied Latin, tried to read the books in his father's library and behaved with the restraint required by a middle-class Swiss family became at school a prank-playing local boy of much coarser calibre.[2] The change disturbed him. It seemed to him that the external world beyond his parents' home was 'dubious if not altogether suspect', and at a deeper level still vaguely hostile. Rigorous in his devotions, he said his prayers every night, and this preserved a ritual protection against evil forces, but every day the threatening shadows renewed themselves. As the burgeoning beauty of the world revealed fresh wonders to the growing boy which delighted all his senses, the shadows continued to mount in

fear of fathers homosexuality

the background and qualified his spontaneous response.

The hostile world crystallised one day in the form of a bullying schoolmate – a farmer's son – who taunted him with his 'fancy' manners. Physically strong, there were sensitivities in Carl which, at this stage, inhibited any exploitation of his strength. When fisticuffs threatened, he did not retaliate. The school bully became a growing nightmare, until suddenly and unexpectedly the boy left school to work on his father's farm. From his recorded reminiscences it is clear that, if conflicts arose at school, tensions continued to multiply at home. 'All sorts of things were happening at night, things incomprehensible and alarming. My parents were sleeping apart. I slept in my father's room.'[3]

Curious nocturnal happenings at the door of his mother's bedroom included the materialisation of a 'faintly luminous indefinite figure whose head detached itself from the neck and floated along in front'. Whether someone entered or left her room in reality or whether the boy underwent anxiety dreams in which decapitated people drifted about the house remains uncertain. Certainly, a number of fresh nightmares assailed him, one of which – a set of telegraph wires, crowded with birds which grew thicker and thicker until they threatened to fill the room – brought him awake in terror. Far more significant, he now developed what he described as a pseudo-croup which brought on very distressing choking fits. During one attack he stood at the foot of the bed, his head bent back over the bed-rail, while his father tried to take the strain of his shaking body with his arms. Suddenly he had a vision. 'I saw a glowing blue circle about the size of a full moon and inside it moved golden figures which I thought were angels. The vision was repeated and each time it allayed my fear of suffocation.' The salvation offered by the Christian creed became embodied in the vision, but physically to all intents and purposes he appeared to be suffering from an anxiety state which returned again and again to disturb his sleep. Psychologically the message spelt out became easily translatable at the simplest level – the tensions in the house made the atmosphere choking.[4]

Religious teaching at school brought him regularly to church, but nothing could overcome his dislike of the 'church atmosphere' or his particular revulsion from Catholic priests. One day his mother took him to Arlesheim, where she showed him a Catholic church, and he slipped away from her, in mingled fear and curiosity, to peer through the open door. Hardly had he glimpsed the richly arrayed altar before he fell forward and struck his head on a piece of projecting iron. When his mother picked him up he was bleeding, in pain and screaming at the top of his voice. A mixture of guilt and shame revived his memory of the Jesuitical dream to explain the accident. It was their fault that he stumbled and screamed.[5]

The accident remained imprinted so indelibly on his memory that for thirty years afterwards, whenever he entered a Catholic church, fear of falling leapt to his mind, and the sight of a Catholic priest revived

cut off from body by father

anxieties which adult understanding should have dissolved long before.

At school he absorbed the elements of reading, writing and arithmetic, but nobody made any attempts to stimulate his imagination. His father had already given him Latin lessons and taught him to read, with the result that his performance dazzled his fellow-pupils, but a double alienation from school and home drove him into an attempt to propitiate the gods and withdraw inside himself.[6] A failure to adjust to his own identity or the external world was represented one day when he sat on a stone embedded in the slope which led to the garden wall. The question arose in his mind: 'Am I the one who is sitting on the stone, or am I the stone on which he is sitting?' As he stood up from the stone another puzzle arose: Which was human and which was stone now? A powerful conviction that the stone 'stood in some secret relationship' to him drove him to sit on it for long periods, superficially fascinated by the relationship between the animate and the inanimate but fundamentally troubled by the problem of his own relationship to the outside world. The problem intensified over the next two years to the point where, one day, he took out the wooden ruler which was an obligatory part of his school equipment and carved one end into the shape of a mannikin wearing a top hat, frock coat and black boots. From pieces of wool he made a bed in his pencil-box for the mannikin, sawed him off and reverently put him to sleep alongside a specially coloured stone which he had recovered from the Rhine. The stone was an old treasure 'painted with water colours to look as though it were divided into an upper and lower half'.

Carried out in secrecy, as if he were fulfilling some private ritual not to be exposed to the common gaze, he took his pencil-case, mannikin and stone up to an attic, long forbidden because of rotten floorboards. Swiftly, he hid the box under a loose floorboard and immediately felt a flood of relief. No one could ever find it there. It was safe, and he was safe. 'The tormenting sense of being at odds with myself was gone.'[7]

The whole elaborate episode could be seen as concentrating multiple aspects of his life at that time. The stone, carefully divided into halves, represented the two sides of his own developing nature, the black, frock-coated mannikin figure combining the father who caused disruption at home with the Jesuitical threat of external reality. Brought together, in the same bed, they were reconciled in enforced harmony and the 'sense of being at odds with myself was gone'.

Over the next few weeks, he retreated to the attic, took out his pencil-case and communed with the mannikin figure whenever threatened with punishment by his parents or by situations which endangered his sense of security. The ritual containment of reality was further developed by leaving in the box on each occasion what he described as 'a scroll', on which he had written in his own 'secret language' messages whose precise significance he never recollected. Thus he created a miniature world at one remove from reality in which he deposited his secret thoughts and conducted a dialogue with substitutes for internal and external figures, brought by this means under his control.

'The episode with the carved mannikin formed the climax and the conclusion of my childhood,' he said. It also reverberated far into life, and thirty years later, working on the preliminary studies for *Wandlungen und Symbole der Libido*, he found some evidence of a cache of stones near Arlesheim which vividly recalled the coloured stone he had recovered from the Rhine. Further research revealed the equivalent of his mannikin figure in the Telesphoros or 'little cloaked god' of the ancient world which stood on the monuments of Asklepios reading from a scroll.[8]

It was much later in life that Jung seized on the coincidence to formulate, for the first time, the theory that archaic psychic components enter the unconscious mind without any conscious cultural teaching. Rigorous search in his father's library failed to yield any printed source which could have inspired his childhood ritual, and he concluded that some inherited response had been stirred from a level deeper than the personal unconscious, or any source of acquired knowledge. Here were the beginnings of a first demonstration of the workings of the collective unconscious.

If, to the detached observer, there seem to be weak links in the chain of reasoning, it is possible to understand how a man so obsessed with the idea of the collective unconscious should fasten on every scrap of evidence which supported it.

The birth of his sister (1884) made an even deeper impact than normal on the growing boy, partly because it came as such a surprise. He had explained away his mother's habit of lying in bed as sheer idleness, and when his father suddenly announced, 'Tonight you've been given a little sister,' it took him unawares. There followed an experience which reinforced his growing belief that too many people were practising forms of deception for reasons which he could not understand. His father took him to his mother's bedside, and she 'held out a little creature that looked dreadfully disappointing'. It had 'a red shrunken face like an old man's, the eyes closed and probably as blind as a young puppy's'. Was this what a baby should look like, or had his mother given birth to a monkey instead? His parents concocted the same dismal story about the stork bringing the baby, and immediately a problem arose in Carl's mind. If the stork were the immortal harbinger bringing animals as well as human beings into the world, it would mean a whole series of rapid and complicated journeys to explain the arrival of kittens, calves and a litter of puppies, and a remarkable inflation of the stork's powers to carry a cow or even a calf. 'Besides the farmers said the cow calved, not that the stork brought the calf.' They were trying to conceal from him something that had happened to his mother, and his uneasiness developed into plain distrust as all his questions failed to elicit any clear answer. The displacement of a degree of his mother's affection on to her baby daughter was inevitable, but Jung never recollected any strong sense of deprivation or jealousy. Certainly, as his sister demanded more attention, he would retreat to the attic, to his box and the mannikin, recording more messages in his secret language, but he could not recall any other compensatory strategies.

His mother developed a new habit; she constantly reprimanded him for his appearance. Their neighbours were a prosperous couple with three children, accustomed to city ways, who appeared on Sundays in frilly frocks, white gloves and patent leather shoes, a combination which excited total scorn in the young Carl. They deliberately avoided mixing with badly dressed, poorer and rougher types. His mother, infuriated by his indifference, would sometimes explode angrily: 'Why do you get so dirty – why do you behave like a little lout – look at those children. They are an example to you.'

Her anger was counter-productive. One day it drove Carl to seek out the son of the family next door and give him a 'good hiding'. His mother was appalled. In tears she poured out her protest; she had loved him, looked after him, brought him up properly, and now he had done a thing like this. It was terrible. As for Carl, 'I had not been conscious of my fault: on the contrary I was feeling pretty pleased with myself for it seemed to me that I had somehow made amends for the incongruous presence of this stranger in our village.'[9]

Asked, in later life, 'Did you often have violent thoughts about people when you were young?' Jung replied, 'Only when I got mad . . . then I beat them up.'[10]

Shattered by his mother's comments, Jung retired to play behind an old spinet while his mother continued to fume from her window-seat; but suddenly she muttered something which made him prick up his ears. 'Fancy keeping a litter like that – dressed-up little monkeys.' Relief swept over him. His mother understood how he felt, but even at that age he knew he must 'keep perfectly still and not come out triumphantly'.

Sometime in his boyhood years there occurred an episode which he did not mention in *Memories, Dreams, Reflections* and left in doubt all his life. He became the victim of a sexual assault by a man whose identity was never disclosed. In the austere patterns of behaviour which conditioned all those families he came to know, it would be difficult to credit that such an episode ever occurred but for a letter he wrote to Freud twenty-two years later: 'Actually – and I confess this to you with a struggle – I have a boundless admiration for you both as a man and researcher, and I bear you no conscious grudge. So the self preservation complex does not come from there: it is rather that my veneration for you has something of the nature of a "religious" crush because of its undeniable erotic undertone. This abominable feeling comes from the fact that as a boy I was the victim of a sexual assault by a man I once worshipped.'[11]

father?   child sex abuse victim

The precise date of the sexual assault is impossible to ascertain from the evidence available, but its effect on the boy must have been profound. Whether any convincing links between the assault and the 'undeniable erotic undertone' of his later relation with Freud can be established is uncertain, but Jung himself certainly admitted the connection twenty-two years later, which meant that the experience left an indelible impression over all those years.

It also tended to reinforce a new identification with his mother. Earlier experience had thrown doubt on the reliability of women in his childhood world, and now the doubt repeated itself with men, but in a much more deeply disturbing way. No woman had ever violated him sexually. This was the final outrage. The tie with the mother deepened. However, many years later Jung claimed: 'When it comes to personal feeling I had a better relation to my father who was predictable than with my mother who was to me a very problematical something.'[12] In the same interview, answering the question 'Did your father try to beat you?' he said, 'Oh, no, not at all. He was very liberal and he was most tolerant and most understanding.'[13]

However, the mother's imago was certainly introjected to the point where, in the middle of a near-breakdown when he was thirty-nine, a woman's voice spoke to him out of the depths of his collective unconscious.

The experience also clarified the two sides of his mother's personality, which again reflected itself in the interpretation he gave to his own dual self. By day his mother was a straightforward, loving, relatively simple woman without any special powers, 'but at night she seemed uncanny'. Then, she became 'one of those seers who is at the same time a strange animal like a priestess in a bear's cage'. In this incarnation she was archaic and ruthless, a person given to direct expression of 'natural' truths without the intervention of politeness or respectability.

Identification with the mother intensified when he said, 'I, too, have this archaic nature and in me it is linked with the gift – not always pleasant – of seeing people and things as they are.'[14] Many years later his psychological model converted these experiences into the theory that every child had two mothers.

In his eleventh year his life once more changed dramatically, and he was suddenly thrown into a world splendid out of all proportion to the impoverished limits of a local preacher's son. He entered the Gymnasium in Basel and there encountered expensively dressed boys who spoke a refined French and German, behaved with gracious ease and had more pocket-money than he had ever dreamt possible. Suddenly, it was borne in on him that his father's life-style did not represent the peak of prosperity and that a number of fortunate beings lived in a world dominated by big houses, rich dinners, and beautiful carriages drawn by fine horses. His shoes with holes in them and worn trousers suddenly became embarrassing. He heard casual talk of expeditions into the snowy mountains near Zürich, and some boys told him – with the patronage of cosmopolitan world-travellers – that they had frequently been to the seaside and actually stayed there for four weeks at a time. Two profound impressions emerged from those first few weeks in the company of these grand beings; he had been born to comparative poverty, and his father's anxieties had a much firmer basis than he had ever imagined. Since his mother always seemed the stronger of his two parents, Carl tended to sympathise more with the sufferings of his father, but he swung to and fro in the storms which developed between them and desperately tried to find some equilibrium by assuming what he described as the role of 'superior-arbitrator'.

The insecurities bred by parental tensions, relative poverty and his mother's persistent evasion of embarrassing questions were further reinforced by the realisation of a world of new wonders, but now his attempts to cope with his parents' quarrels inflated his sense of self-importance and further complicated the conflicts within his own personality. 'My unstable self assurance was one moment strengthened and another weakened.'[15]

His mother re-activated an old habit which contributed further stresses. Whenever he received an invitation to one of the grand houses of his new schoolfellows, she would deliver a series of admonitions which were fresh ground for embarrassment. Proudly dressed in his modest finery – best suit, spotless collar, polished shoes, darned socks – he would set out from the house, only to hear his mother calling after him, 'You're sure you washed your hands? Do you have a handkerchief? Don't forget to wipe your nose. And remember to give the regards of your mamma and papa.'[16]

It was bad enough to find that his best Sunday suit looked so much less stylish than those of his new friends, but to be harangued about his personal habits in the presence of every passing stranger was an affront to his dignity. Whenever self-confidence struggled to renew itself, confronted by one or other of the splendid new homes he now visited, 'a sense of the grandeur and power of these people came over me. I was afraid of them, and in my smallness wished that I might sink fathoms deep into the ground.'

The first of his two developing personalities reacted with fear, but the second became openly rebellious, refused to convey his parents' regards, defiantly proclaimed that his neck was dirty and recalled the little man in the frock coat and top hat locked away in the attic who could give him reassurance in another dimension.

At the Gymnasium he attended classes in mathematics, divinity, languages and art. Bored by divinity, puzzled by algebra, utterly incapable of drawing in the art class, his reactions combined to produce a new sense of failure. 'A kind of silent despair' developed, 'which completely ruined school for me'. It was further reinforced by a fierce hatred of gymnastics. 'I was going to school to learn something, not to imitate the apes.'[17] A new streak of timidity, partly the result of a number of minor physical accidents, partly the company he now kept, also made him ripe for bullying, but according to his son Franz Jung: 'No one bullied him. He was much too big and strong.'[18]

One successfully survived brawl he described in some detail. Singled out by teachers who thought him crafty, whenever a row developed he immediately came under suspicion, but on this occasion seven boys lay in ambush and suddenly attacked him. Jung suddenly fell into one of his violent rages, seized a boy by both arms and swung him round like a scythe, mowing several of his attackers to the ground. The others hastily retreated, and the affair might have been forgotten, but one of the vanquished reported the brawl to the headmaster, who promptly blamed Carl. His belief in an irreductible quantity of injustice in the world was reaffirmed by the punishment duly meted out. However, 'no one dared to attack me again'.

When it came to mathematics, what appeared to be easily accepted truths to other boys were brought under the scrutiny of a mind working in another dimension. The boy with an unusual approach to any form of diagrammatic abstraction simply found that he did not know the true nature of numbers. 'They were not flowers, not animals, not fossils . . . they were . . . mere quantities.' No one could give him a satisfactory definition of numbers, and it disturbed him that his teacher saw no reason even to ask the question. Why not, he wondered, reverse the process if the logic held true – a becoming apple-tree, b becoming box and x becoming a question-mark? Far more confounding: 'If $a = b$ and $b = c$, then $a = c$ even though by definition a meant something other than b and, being different, could therefore not be equated with b let alone c.' In short, algebra seemed to Carl nothing better than a clever box of numbered tricks devised to confound the peasantry.

While his mathematics master ploughed boldly through his lessons, scribbling formulae on the blackboard, the young Carl posed question after question in silent incomprehension. Intimidated by what seemed to him his own shortcomings, he should have failed hopelessly in mathematics, but one remarkable faculty now came to his aid on all occasions. He had a very unusual gift for fixing words and signs photographically in his mind. As his son Franz says, 'He had a wonderful memory. He worked in rather short bursts but with great intensity.'[19]

Most of the masters continued to regard him as stupid, and the Latin teacher alone gave him any encouragement. As we know, his father had taught him Latin since he was six, and his proficiency so pleased the teacher that he allowed him to escape the more boring lessons and sent him on errands to the library to collect books into which Carl dipped as he walked, deliberately delaying his return to the hated classroom. Carl freely admitted in maturity that most of his schoolfellows did not like him, but his recollections of those days were ambiguous. Certainly, he did achieve a number of friendships, 'mostly with shy boys of simple origins'.

Oeri recalled that Carl staged a duel on one occasion between two fellow-students from the Gymnasium in the parsonage garden. When one boy hurt his hand Carl was distressed, but the incident disturbed his father far more because he remembered a boy, seriously injured in a duel, being carried into his house one day.[20]

Oeri claimed that Carl's mathematical inadequacies were in fact hereditary, reaching back three generations. Carl's grandfather admitted – after hearing a lecture about a photometrical instrument – that mathematics baffled him too. He never blamed his children for their inadequacies. They were in their inheritance.[21]

Oeri added: 'He would not have received his diploma if the need for a definite report of proficiency in all subjects had been rigorously enforced. He was frankly an idiot in mathematics.'[22]

Despite this, his performance in school slowly improved, but as he observed the struggles of those below to keep pace with him sympathy for them took the pleasure out of his success. He came to hate all competition and deliberately restrained his powers in order not to reach the top of the class. In one supreme month, against all intention, his abilities broke through and drove him to the top, and he regretted the occasion.

The incident now occurred which reinforced his belief that his teachers as well as his classmates shunned him. Bored by German grammar and syntax, his performance in the German class remained mediocre and whenever, as frequently happened, the subjects set for composition seemed to him either silly or shallow he took no trouble. Thus he slipped through with average marks and reinforced the anonymity he sought. He tended to sympathise with boys from poor families not only because they sprang from origins similar to his own but also because 'in their simplicity' they noticed nothing unusual about him. He wanted to remain the unnoticed norm which gave him protection from abuse, and the ruse worked successfully until one day the incident burst on him 'like a thunderclap'.[23]

A subject had been given that day which excited his imagination, and he set to work with a will to produce what he thought to be a proficient but certainly not brilliant essay. Assessing the work of a score of pupils, the master began with the essay written by the boy at the top of the class and progressed what Carl imagined to be downwards. As essay after essay was examined and classified without his own name being mentioned his heart sank. To be top of the class gave a dangerous brilliance to his name, but to be bottom produced an abysmal distinction open to the worst kind of abuse. He wanted neither, but least of all to be forced into the lowest grade.

At last, every essay except Carl's had been assessed, and then the teacher paused before he said with premeditated malice, 'Now I have one more composition – Jung's. It is by far the best and I ought to give it first place. But unfortunately it is a fraud.' Turning on Carl he added, 'Confess now – where did you copy it?'[24]

Jung leapt up to proclaim his innocence. He had not copied it. He had taken great trouble to write a good essay.

'You're lying,' the master snapped back.

There followed charge and countercharge – 'You are lying' – 'I am not' – which steadily mounted in intensity, until at last the teacher said ominously, 'I would have you thrown out of school if I knew where you had copied it.'[25]

His schoolmates were smiling, some maliciously, some with approval that he had duped the Old Ogre. All his attempts to clear himself failed, and now the aggressive side of his temperament burst out and he swore vengeance on the teacher in jungle terms. The man who later in life could erupt into fierce anger was very clear in the boy clamouring to bring savage retribution down on his enemy's head.

Day after day he sought for some means of redress but came to the conclusion that he was powerless. The fact that one of the teachers had told his father, 'He works well – but he's just about average,' did not distress him. That this idiot teacher should now regard him as not only stupid but also morally degenerate totally dismayed him.

Grief, rage, gloom mingled to produce one of the most distressing experiences of his schooldays, but then, suddenly and unexpectedly, 'there was a . . . silence as though a soundproof door had been closed on a noisy room'. Some second personality stepped out of the seething emotional pit to climb to a high place and look down with reflective calm, analysing all the contradictory elements. In maturity he regarded these two selves as his No. 1 and No. 2 personalities, an over-simplification which might have occurred to a schoolboy but not to the fully developed, sophisticated and infinitely complex Jung.

Remembering the mental illness which troubled him for four years between 1913 and 1917, it is interesting to see the beginnings of what some clinicians regarded as a schizophrenic breakdown, although he strongly denied any such diagnosis. Referring to personalities One and Two, at one point Jung thought of No. 2 as a self-contained person involving 'something other than myself'. He put it poetically: 'It was as though a breath of the great world of stars and endless space had touched me, or as if a spirit had invisibly entered the room – the spirit of one who had long been dead and yet was perpetually present in timelessness until far into the future.'

It was No. 2 which now came to his rescue, dissipated his anger and tried to see the whole episode from the teacher's point of view. Others might have said that he invoked his capacity for objectivity and sufficiently distanced events to see them impersonally, but Jung insisted on personification. This stupid master didn't understand his true nature any more than he did himself, and both distrusted one another. That was the message conveyed by Personality No. 2.

The incident crystallised an impression which had been growing for some years. He was simultaneously a schoolboy in the late nineteenth century who struggled to grasp the elements of algebra and a man who lived in the eighteenth century, a person 'not to be trifled with', powerful, influential and very distinguished. This second personality wore a white wig, satin trousers and buckled shoes, and 'went driving in a fly with high concave rear wheels between which the box was suspended on springs and leather straps'.

Identification with such a person first occurred when a very antique green carriage drove in reality past the house one day with every appearance of hurtling out of the eighteenth into the nineteenth century. Carl became very excited, and suddenly felt overwhelmed by the idea that it came from 'my time'. The conviction was further reinforced when he stumbled on a terracotta statuette of two figures at the home of an aunt, one representing a doctor famous in Basel in the late eighteenth century – Dr Stuckelberger – and the other one of the doctor's patients.

Old Stuckelberger, according to legend, was crossing the Rhine Bridge one day when this patient accosted him and poured out a long series of complaints which Stuckelberger cut short with the words: 'Of course there must be something wrong. Stick out your tongue and shut your eyes.' The patient obeyed at once, whereupon Stuckelberger silently hurried away and many passers-by fell to laughing at the funny old lady standing alone with her eyes shut in such an idiotic pose. The statuette represented the woman with shut eyes and tongue sticking out, but the detail which riveted Carl's attention in the representation of the doctor was a pair of shoes, and particularly the buckles on the shoes. Suddenly the conviction seized him that these were the shoes he had worn in his earlier incarnation as a distinguished gentleman of the eighteenth century. So powerfully did his identification become that he underwent a kind of metamorphosis in which he literally felt those shoes on his feet and his body tingled with the spirit of another person.

He first concluded that it must be his grandfather frequently recollected in conversations with his father, who provided the driving force of what threatened to become a hallucination; but his grandfather reached maturity in the nineteenth not the eighteenth century. In old age he dismissed the possibility that the figure could have been that of Goethe, allegedly a relative of his, 'because I first heard this tale from strangers'. In a number of instances it can be shown that his memory in *Memory, Dreams, Reflections* was faulty, and it seems odd that such a persistent legend, of which most Swiss German families would be proud, should not have been mentioned by his father. The dates, too, point to the splendid figure of Goethe. What more natural impulse than to compensate for the stumbling schoolboy's inferiorities by identifying with the Olympian figure of his alleged eighteenth-century forebear?

Whatever the explanation, the sense of a dual personality not only persisted far into life until he heard the voice of a second personality speaking inside his head; it also provided an empirical basis for his theory of opposites and, since the second personality became a woman in his self-analysis, set the first seed for the concept of anima and animus.

Jung was quick to deny any pathological explanation of these early experiences: 'the play and counter-play between Personalities No. 1 and No. 2 which has run through my whole life has nothing to do with a "split" or dissociation in the ordinary medical sense. On the contrary, it is played out in every individual.'[26]

Two qualifications occur. Roughly coincidental with his double-identity experience came a series of fainting fits which led to something resembling a breakdown in the growing boy, and just such a breakdown, with far more powerful evocation of unconscious material, overtook the adult man. Strictly, for the boy the precipitating event was nothing to do with this division of personality, and in the man the nature of the illness, as we shall see, was not a straightforward breakdown.

Chapter 4

Early Religious Struggles

IN HIS TWELFTH YEAR Carl was standing in Basel Cathedral square after morning classes, waiting for a friend, when one of several boys 'larking about' around him suddenly gave him a push which knocked him to the ground. His head hit the kerbstone as he fell, and everything went black. He claimed in maturity that even as he felt the blow the thought flashed through his mind: 'Now I won't have to worry about school anymore.'[1] Half-unconscious, he lay there 'longer than was strictly necessary' until some people helped him to his feet, discovered his identity and took him to the home of two spinster aunts.

There followed a prolonged period of disturbances when it was difficult to distinguish between a boy deliberately exploiting the accident and a genuine series of minor collapses which finally drove him to leave school for six months. His worried parents consulted one doctor after another, and each one solemnly averred that the trouble had quite different roots. A recommendation that the boy should take a holiday carried him away to new surroundings at Winterth, where more of his innumerable relatives lived. There the railway station, representing the conflicting lines of his developing life, came to fascinate him and he spent hours watching the trains converge if not clash. It is not clear whether the fainting fits diminished during the Winterth visit, but by implication they seemed to cease altogether, which underlined the combined stress of school and family life as the cause of what was really a psychic illness. Returning home, the doctor now diagnosed the trouble as epilepsy, at which the growing boy simply laughed, but it confirmed his parents' determination to keep him away from school.

Freed from all the doubts, intrigues, quarrels and injustices of school during the next few weeks, life seemed like paradise. He could roam freely through the countryside, indulge to the limit a kaleidoscope of daydreams, draw page upon page of doodles and conjure scenes of battle carnage which satisfied his burning desire for conquering life at one remove. Sheer loafing occupied a good deal of his time, interspersed with reading, collecting and occasional visits to his father's library, but everything combined to produce a wonderful sense of holiday.

It was in his father's modest library that he sought out books which might resolve his growing dilemma about religion and God. Volume after volume simply repeated the conventional interpretation of both until he stumbled on Biedermann's *Christliche Dogmatik*, a book which described religion as 'a spiritual act consisting in man's establishing his own relationship with God'. Biedermann struck an original note, but it was a note unacceptable to the growing scepticism of a teenaged boy. 'My religion recognised no human relationship to God for how could anyone relate to something so little known as God?'

While his reading developed, the fainting fits were banished suddenly one day by the sheer accident of overhearing a visitor say to his father, 'Is your son any better?' His father replied, 'It's a sad business. The doctors no longer know what is wrong with him. They think it may be epilepsy. It would be dreadful if it were incurable. I have lost what little I had, and what will become of the boy if he cannot earn his own living?'

The words rang dramatically in Carl's ears. Recalling those days to an unexpected person he said, 'I had seen how poor we were compared to other families who sent their children to the Gymnasium, and had a sudden fear of further poverty. I was frightened of what adults later referred to as destitution. I must work to relieve my father's worries and save myself from becoming even poorer. Poverty suddenly seemed like a haunting ogre to me – and indeed on the death of my father did very seriously threaten me. . . .' Jung commented to Ernest Jones: 'I reacted at once to my father's words.'[2]

He hurried away to his father's study and renewed his Latin lessons in earnest, but within a few minutes fell forward in one of the most spectacular fainting fits he had yet experienced. Recovering rapidly, he did not abandon his studies but concentrated grimly and pushed on with his reading – only to sense another collapse approaching. It came fifteen minutes later, but again he did not succumb and summoned all his dwindling reserves of willpower to outface the attack. A third followed, and he rallied his weakening powers to cope with it, suddenly afraid that this time he must be vanquished. Ten minutes later he was still working. Fifteen minutes later he knew that he had triumphed, and a sense of exhilaration ran through him. 'Suddenly I felt better than I had in all the months before.'

The attacks ceased from that day, and what he later came to see as a psychological device to avoid the school he so much hated, surrendered to a tremendous effort of will carrying with it a message for the treatment of patients which he disinterred effectively years later. 'That was when I learned what a neurosis is . . . the whole affair was a diabolical plot on my part.'

Still troubled by religious conflicts, he now began probing deeper into his father's small library. He must know more about God. He turned back to Biedermann once more and in the chapter 'The Nature of God' found a description of His personality 'to be conceived after the analogy of the human ego: the unique, utterly supramundane ego who embraces the entire cosmos'.

Contradictions at once arose. Anthropomorphic concepts introduced personality, and personality introduced character. If God were everything, how could he possess a distinguishable character? Analogies with human personality involved limiting factors which were dismaying. His own ego had two contradictory elements and was subject to those familiar shortcomings which haunted most human beings – self-deception, vanity, laziness, irresponsibility. What could they have to do with a divine being? Further research revealed a plethora of negative and positive definitions which remained very unsatisfactory, and he looked in vain for any explanation of the dark side of God's character – his wrath, his apparent vindictiveness, his intolerance of the in-adequacies of the creatures he had by definition brought to life.

When Carl read that God, although sufficient unto Himself and needing nothing outside, had created the world to His satisfaction, he was further bewildered. If He looked upon His creation as good, it did not correspond with the reality as seen by one young boy not yet aware of the hubris of his questioning. The world which unfolded week by week to Carl Jung was as horrible as it was beautiful. Not yet sixteen, the life of a small village concentrated the realities of disease, suffering, old age and death perhaps more clearly since they were not lost in a city crowd, but nakedly evident in each isolated human being. Had God also derived satisfaction from the Devil, whose operations were so evident in the daily life of the village? What were described by Biedermann as the 'wonderful harmonies of natural law' became more and more to resemble for Carl 'a chaos tamed by fearful effort' and the glory of the star-lit firmament 'an accumulation of random bodies without order or meaning'. In short, Carl had come gravely to doubt whether God had filled the natural world with His goodness and, if He had, why was it a goodness beyond his comprehension? Worse still, it now seemed to him that Biedermann's enormous tome on Christian dogmatics was not only 'fancy drivel', but also – even more dis-reputable – ' a specimen of uncommon stupidity whose sole aim was to obscure truth'.[3]

At the core of his growing disillusion Carl felt a new pity for his father, who had 'fallen a victim to this mumbo-jumbo' and still preached a mistaken message. Already, everything his father said, all his theorising about life, his beliefs and evaluations had come under such suspicion that when Carl heard him preaching about grace it all sounded 'stale and hollow' like a legend memorised and repeated by someone who had totally lost his convictions. Since Carl's first personality was too shy to challenge his father directly and he could not quite surrender to the authority placed in his hands by his second personality, stalemate supervened and produced a terrible sense of frustration.

Somewhere there existed an all-permeating quality called grace, but none of the six parsons on his mother's side or the two uncle-parsons on his father's managed to convey the experience in their interminable theological discussions. Depressed, worried and sometimes sleepless, Carl rummaged through his father's library and underwent contorted attempts at intellectual analysis in search of this most prized, beautiful and elusive state of mind-spirit called grace.

The deeper he penetrated into the thickets of theological thinking, the more he came to understand the tragedy of his father's life. The more he read, the less sympathetic he found his father's outlook. Carl's response to that final mystery of the church, Holy Communion, reaffirmed his father's failure to commit his son to the one true faith as he and most clergymen of the day saw it.

In accordance with custom a wheelwright, whose skills with the lathe he had often admired, became Carl's godfather, and it was this taciturn old man, transformed by a top hat and frock coat, who accompanied him to the church for his first communion. Small pieces of bread baked, as Carl knew, by the inferior local bakery, and wine in a pewter jug from a local tavern of not very high repute were waiting beside the altar at which stood, in the full solemnity of his robes and office, Carl's father. Correctly sonorous, Pastor Jung rolled out the prayers from the Liturgy and then began the ceremony which the boy watched with detached wonderment, if not distaste. One gloomily pious person after another swallowed his piece of bread, supped the wine and returned the cup to the pastor, and Carl failed to detect any change whatever in the recipients. The same depressing atmosphere which accompanied most of the religious ceremonials he had experienced filled the church all over again, and Carl could not help comparing it with the life and vitality of what he regarded as its secular equivalent.

'Suddenly my turn came. I ate the bread: it tasted flat as I had expected. Then the wine of which I took the smallest sip was thin and rather sour.' There followed the interminable repetition of bread and wine carried out in steadily mounting gloom. At last the congregation broke up, and Carl emerged into the sunshine freshly aware of his new black suit and felt hat. Externally, strolling proudly around, he felt a new young grandee, but internally there was only a disturbing sense of emptiness.

It took several days before the full import of his disillusion came home to him. Deeply embroiled in spiritual struggles with Christian dogma, he had graduated to the highest 'pinnacle of religious initiation' and waited for the sudden upsurge of – what was it? – divine grace, a new communion between himself and the universe or something full of fire accompanied by unearthly lights, a revelation on the road to Damascus. Instead it was all words, dull flat words with much talk of Him but absolutely no realisation of the divine presence which by now Carl not only expected but in one sense craved. His boyish imagination romantically infused religious experience with vast despairs and overpowering elation. He had expected an overwhelming sense of union with – he paused and thought – Jesus; but Jesus was only a man who had died 1860 years ago. Called the Son of God, he must be like the Greek heroes and as such quite inviolable to human interpenetration. So what on earth was the real significance of this 'wretched memorial service with the flat bread and the sour wine'? Suddenly the conclusion was inescapable. Communion had turned him fatally against the Church, and he would never again risk the terrible disillusion of repeating the ceremony. Church for him no longer represented a shrine of spiritual life, but had become a place of death.[4]

Even worse, it sharpened his understanding of the tragedy of his father's professional life. As he later wrote, 'he was struggling with a death whose existence he could not admit. An abyss had opened between him and me, and I saw no possibility of ever bridging it.'

Retrospective analysis of the thoughts of the schoolboy by an old man in his eighties must be subjected to sceptical scrutiny. Suspicion arises that Jung the elder injected a degree of sophistication into the boy's thinking which would have been unusual even in such an unusual person. 'I could not plunge my dear and generous father . . . who had never tyrannised over me, into that despair and sacrilege which were necessary for an experience of divine grace.'

Disentangling present distortion from past fact, one experience does come through clearly. Carl felt that he had suffered 'the greatest defeat of his life' and his expectation of a meaningful relationship with the universe through religious experience had been shattered.[5]

This decisive watershed in spiritual thinking was reinforced by another experience, the precise date of which is difficult to determine. A long and tormenting struggle with religious questions had broken his sleep and left his mind in a ferment of uncertainty, but one area of conflict resolved itself in a most unsuspected way. Examining the long line of his ancestors, known and unknown, he pushed his genealogical roots right back to the beginning of life and those first real or mythological people Adam and Eve. If God had created them with all their imperfections, were they responsible for their own actions? Creatures created in God's own likeness, they yet 'committed the first sin by doing what God did not want them to do, but how was that possible? They could not have done it if God had not placed in them the possibility of doing it.' Only one conclusion seemed possible: 'it was God's intention that they should sin'.

Temporarily released from one tormenting conflict, he was promptly thrown by another. What exactly did this very confusing God want with him, and what in all the enormous complexities of all the options open to him could possibly be defined as the right one? His final formulation of a new principle did not seem very clear. 'Is it not possible that God wishes to see whether I am capable of obeying His will, even though my faith and my reason raise before me the spectres of death and hell?'

Re-examined over the next few days, he found this reasoning satisfactory, but when he finally screwed his courage to the sticking-point and leapt forthwith into hellfire it took the most extraordinary form. He had a vision one day of the arching empyrean, and high in the fine air above the world God sat on his golden throne; but as he watched 'from under the throne an enormous turd' fell upon the 'sparkling new roof', shattering it and breaking 'the walls of the cathedral asunder'.[6]

No worse desecration could have been conceived, no more vivid symbolism of lost religious faith. Instead of deepening his despair, the daydream gave a tremendous sense of exhilaration and release, and he literally wept in his new-found 'happiness and gratitude'. Expecting damnation for such an act of blasphemous desecration, 'grace had come upon me and with it unutterable bliss'.

Desperately shifting his strategy to meet each new doubt, the young boy twisted and turned, exploring alleys long familiar to theologians as if they were freshly pioneered country. From time to time religious discussions broke out with his father, and Carl still believed that if only he could convince his father of what he referred to as 'the miracle of grace' it would resolve his spiritual problems. Unfortunately, his father countered all arguments with the words 'One ought not to think but believe', and the boy would say, 'Give me this belief' – whereupon his father, despairing of enlightening this stubborn son of his, would shrug his shoulders and 'turn resignedly away'.

Extraordinarily, at the age of eighty-three, after a lifetime spent redefining what religious experience meant, Jung turned full circle and answered John Freeman's television question 'Do you now believe in God?' with 'I don't need to believe. I know.'[7]

More and more time was spent in his father's study, deepening and widening his reading, sometimes in secret for fear that his father should suspect the distillation of further heresy. German translations of English classic novels, German literature, poetry, drama, history – he moved recklessly from one field to another, slowly graduating toward natural science. Personality No. 2 had broken through so many religious confusions only to be confronted by yet another closed door, and it was a relief to give full play to Personality No. 1 where one book yielded to another with an inconsequential ease that required little effort. Until suddenly one day his mother's No. 2 personality intruded on this feast of reading and said to him, 'You must read Goethe's *Faust*.'

Now he plunged into *Faust* with growing excitement. Here was a man who took the Devil seriously and even 'concluded a blood pact with him'. Here was a book which confronted the adversary 'who had the power to frustrate God's plan to make a perfect world'. In Carl's eyes Faust turned out to be an unsatisfactory character who far too easily gambled away his soul and made too much display of its destruction; but clearly 'the weight of the drama and its significance lay chiefly on the side of Mephistopheles'. As for the somewhat frivolous angels who finally tricked Mephistopheles, they were really not made of the sterner stuff required to cope with such an intelligent devil. Whether a sceptically minded, very perceptive boy with all his antennae freshly attuned to new experience really analysed Faust in these terms, or whether the eighty-three-year-old Jung once more retrospectively injected his own mature questioning into his early reading is difficult to determine. Certainly his approach to *Faust* matched his independent and highly sceptical approach to religion, but what final impression did the book leave? 'At last I found confirmation that there were or had been people who saw evil and its universal power and – more important – the mysterious role it played in delivering man from darkness and suffering.'

Faust led him into another field of reading – philosophy, and now he turned to his father's library once more, only to find a desert. Philosophers were questioning thinkers and the elder Jung far too uncertain of his own faith to risk exposing it to such scrutiny. One book alone, Krug's *General Dictionary of Philosophical Sciences*, dared to deal with the subject in any detail, and even there Carl found himself baffled by the complicated expositions which verged on an unqualified assertion that God existed, only to retreat into doubt. 'God derived from good, and his existence could not be proved', but 'the innateness of the idea of God' existed '*a priori* in man, if not in actuality at any rate potentially'. Why, Carl said to himself, does not this man abandon all these elaborate qualifications and roundly proclaim what he himself clearly at this stage believed – that God existed?

Chapter 5
Intellectual Beginnings

IN HIS EARLY TEENS Carl's parents constantly confronted him with the question 'What do you want to do in life?' From his fifteenth year onward, the question frequently recurred, and his two personalities clashed in an attempt to find an answer. Science, with its discoveries based on empirically verified facts, fascinated him, but the metaphysical implications of comparative religion drew him with equal power. 'Science met to a very large extent the needs of Number One personality whereas the humane or historical studies provide[d] beneficial instruction for Number Two.'[1]

An interview conducted in 1959 extracted this reply about his early ambitions: 'Originally I wanted to be an archaeologist. . . . I hadn't the money: the study was too expensive. So my second love then belonged to nature, particularly zoology . . . that meant natural sciences.'[2]

From his sixteenth year onward Carl's depressions diminished as No. 1 personality began to emerge to dominate No. 2. The struggle between his two selves became a struggle between a powerfully emerging ego – or, in his terms, self – and an imperfectly realised collective unconscious. His reading widened and deepened as part of the reconciliation process. Plato, Pythagoras, Empedocles and Heraclitus presented attractive systems of thought, although he found Plato unnecessarily long-winded and Pythagoras and Empedocles 'like pictures in a gallery . . . somewhat remote'. The only writer who conveyed 'the breath of life' – Schopenhauer – he found very difficult to understand, which was hardly surprising in a boy of sixteen. Within the embalmed convention of Swiss education, he brought to bear an irreverent scepticism for great writers which shocked some of his teachers and led to complete incomprehension when he calmly implied that the Schoolmen 'left him cold'. As for Aristotelian intellectuals, they, he said, employed logical trickery to prove something about which they really knew nothing – an attitude even more outrageous to his mentors.

And then, suddenly, he came upon Schopenhauer, and here at last was a writer who struck a profoundly responsive chord.[3] Instead of attempting to bring the suffering, cruelty and injustice of the real world into a divine harmony, Schopenhauer had the courage to see it for what it was and stated bluntly that 'a fundamental plan underlay the sorrowful course of human history and . . . the blindness of the world-creating Will'.

Schopenhauer's suggestion that man should pit his own puny intellect against the All-Powerful Will and redirect the purpose of the cosmos seemed hopelessly unsatisfactory to Carl, since a blind will would be impervious to such a minuscule rebellion. In a vivid image Jung said, at the age of eighty-three, that it was like a child holding a mirror up to the sun 'expecting the sun to be dazzled by the mirror'.

Schopenhauer led him through a labyrinth of reading into the works of Kant, and here, in the *Critique of Pure Reason*, he thought he had discovered a new flaw in Schopenhauer's system. Schopenhauer hypostatised metaphysical assertions, giving mental concepts factual reality or, in Jungian terms, endowing 'a mere noumenon – a *Ding an sich* – with special qualities'. At this stage of Carl's development the discovery of this intellectual confidence trick from Kant's examination of philosophic theory afforded him even more satisfaction than the salutary recognition that a great philosopher like Schopenhauer shared his own pessimistic view of the world.

The realisation that he had a mind of his own capable of challenging, with adolescent hubris, writers given exaggerated respect by his teachers brought about a slowly accelerating change in his personality. Out of the thin, pale, shy and distrustful boy there emerged a far more communicative person whose intellectual appetites drove him in all directions with a voracity which surprised his father, who said to a friend one day, 'The boy is interested in *everything* – but heaven knows where he will end up.' As Carl began to make friends more easily, he came to the conclusion that poor boys were not necessarily at a serious disadvantage with rich ones, and risked expressing his heretical views about life and literature ever more freely. Temporarily that caused a setback. He was accused of vanity and conceit, of being a humbug and a braggart. Destructively, a teacher once again revived the charge of cheating in a different form. Struggling to convey some of his ideas to paper, he had written an essay on 'The Meaning of *Faust*' which cost him many hours of effort, polishing the style and reorganising the content. This essay, the teacher said, 'is downright brilliant but [it] is tossed off so carelessly that it is easy to see how little serious effort went into it'.[4] There followed a forceful homily on the impossibility of getting through life with such a slapdash approach to matters of such profundity.

When Carl protested that he had spent hours working in great detail on the essay, the teacher simply replied, 'You cannot make me believe that. It was tossed off frivolously. . . .'

This attack reinforced his schoolmates' jeering at what they regarded as his pseudo-knowledge when he spoke of Kant and Schopenhauer – philosophers not in the school curriculum – and once more he retreated into himself, concealing his 'budding erudition' even from his parents. One small family group alone amongst his adult acquaintances would have regarded his talk as anything but pretentious boasting. This was his uncle on his mother's side, then pastor of St Aban's in Basel, at whose house he 'had permission' to lunch every Thursday. Despite the uncle's subtle attempts to press theology on Carl as his most suitable subject for further study, the conversation at lunch was intellectually daring.

'It was marvellous experience for me to discover that anything of this sort existed at all, for in my home surroundings I had never heard anyone discussing learned topics.' Several years passed before Carl realised that his father's refusal to explore ideas was a defence against the profound doubts which already disturbed his Christian faith. 'He was taking refuge from himself and therefore insisted on blind faith.'[5] Thus the luncheons at his uncle's became oases of intellectual excitement, and his aunt noticed the avidity with which the boy followed every exchange. Nonetheless, Jacob Burckhardt was regarded by all present as too much of a freethinker, and Nietzsche's name too outrageous even to achieve mention. Comfortably ensconced in a world which excluded fundamental doubts, they had little idea of the duplicities practised by this sharply aware boy who carefully concealed the scientific realism toward which his studies now drove him.

Once again the oasis of intellectuality failed him. When he discovered that Kant could be invoked at his uncle's lunch-table to destroy their opponents' ideas but never to question their own convictions, the boy lost faith once more. Stimulation still occurred, but with diminishing intensity, and he was forced to develop his duplicity. Too young and inexperienced to challenge openly the comfortable world of closed conviction, he concealed his heresies which condemned him to what he regarded as cheating. That they had a vested interest in maintaining their beliefs intact, since it was their paid profession, did not quite reconcile him to his cowardice, and his two opposed personalities constantly challenged each other in renewed conflict. Slowly, Thursdays turned into black days for Carl, days when the stimulation surrendered to a sense of intellectual dishonesty.

Swinging from one personality to the other, he knew that his No. 1 personality must sooner or later make up his mind what he wanted to do in the world – a recurring anxiety reinforced by long and serious talks with his father. 'Be anything you like except a theologian,' his father said to Carl's great relief. By tacit agreement he did not go to Communion, avoided church as much as possible and recoiled from the thickets of theological exegesis.

Four remaining episodes stood out in his memory of the days which preceded his entry into university. Still subject to bouts of ill health, when his fitful appetite worried his parents they packed him off on one occasion to Entlebuch, where for the first time he encountered someone in touch with the world of scientific wonders which steadily exerted a stronger allure. In reality the scientist was a friend of his father, with no more than a Ph.D. in chemistry, but to Carl he became the man 'who understood the secret of the stones'.

The second experience, a visit to a distillery, fulfilled a couplet later familiar to him from Wilhelm Busch:

But now there comes a kicker:
This stuff you see is liquor.

In fact, though still a schoolboy, he emerged 'shamefully, gloriously, triumphantly drunk' and opened a path which led, on the death of his father, to some serious drinking which receives no mention in his reminiscences. Bursting into one of those eloquent passages which lift the reminiscences – confused though their organisation is – out of the commonplace, he later wrote: 'No. 1 and No. 2 were no more; caution and timidity were gone and the earth and the sky, the universe and everything in it that creeps and flies, revolves, rises or falls, had all become one.'[6] The third memory took him back with vivid awareness to the day his father pressed a ticket into his hand and he entered a strange locomotive which appeared to kneel in reverence to Mount Rigi, while the cog-wheel mechanism drove it up through the incredible sweep of ravine and valley to the uttermost pinnacle where the world suddenly leapt into the empyrean and a vast abyss fell away at his feet, cloud-filled, vertiginous, empty beyond endurance. The moment was sublimal. He felt 'this is it, my world, the real world . . . no schools, no unanswerable questions, where one can *be* without having to ask anything'.[7]

Later, sitting beside Lake Lucerne on the same trip, he suddenly saw himself as an independent adult, elegantly at ease on the terrace of a very expensive hotel, wearing a beautiful new suit and a stiff black hat, toying with an expensive cane and waiting to be escorted aboard a luxury liner which would carry him back toward the mountains and the sublime vision they alone could offer. 'For many decades this image rose up whenever I was wearied from overwork. . . .' But the daydream, constantly reactivated in times of stress, never really achieved fulfilment until he approached old age.

The fourth memory carried him back to Sachseln where, on one occasion, his father was on holiday and visited the hermitage at Flueli to consider the beatified relics of Brother Klaus. Klaus appeared to divide his time, with less than saintly devotion, between his cell and his house, and it occurred to Carl that this was the ideal way of life: 'the family in one house, while I would live some distance away in a hut with a pile of books and a writing table and an open fire where I could roast chestnuts and cook my soup on a tripod'.

It closely resembled the life he finally led between Küsnacht and Bollingen.

Chapter 6

University and a Career

CARL GUSTAV JUNG passed his final examinations – luckily, according to Oeri[1] – in the spring of 1895 and, wasting no time, by 18 April of the same year had registered as a medical student at the Medical School of Basel University.[2] Now a much more confident young man who had at last resolved the problem of a career, he remained surrounded by serious family problems.[3] His father's health had deteriorated, the family had little money, and his mother remained unqualified for anything other than domestic work.

His desire to become an archaeologist had been frustrated by the lack of courses in that subject at Basel University. Zoology offered the dubious rewards of school-teaching but at least fell within the province of the natural sciences which still attracted him. The sirens of philosophy continuously whispered in his ear, but how to combine metaphysical speculation with scientific fact remained a problem. Suddenly, out of the blue, the idea had come to him – why not be a doctor? By now he was trying with youthful bravado to live by a motto of his own devising: 'Never imitate'; and it was this principle which had, until now, prevented him from following in the footsteps of his paternal grandfather, once a distinguished doctor. Perhaps it was the obvious fact that medicine satisfied his need for natural science which crystallised his resolve, but the first stumbling steps on the threshold of maturity were beset by fresh difficulties.

The evidence of three witnesses differs widely on his character at this stage, but they all agree on sudden financial complications.[4] Albert Oeri had known Jung from boyhood onward, and with the exception of one year's illness which forced them apart he could have left a continuous detailed record. Both men were born in the same year, both knew each other's family and they drank, made merry and confided in each other.[5]

Within a relatively short period, between his seventeenth and nineteenth years, a person so new emerges from the old Carl Jung that something approaching a metamorphosis transforms him. Instead of being an anonymous figure eternally buried in the dimmest corner of the University library, as everyone expected, he boldly joined the Zofingia – the Swiss student society – and asserted himself in a manner which quickly marked him out from his fellows.[6] Now a big, strong young man six feet one inch tall, with a deep resonant voice and considerable command of language, he plunged into every debate organised by the society and approached each subject heretically.

Between the years 1892 and 1894 his vehement discussions with his father sometimes broke into open quarrelling, which multiplied the tensions already a daily occurrence in family life. His father's health continued to deteriorate, and he complained constantly of mysterious abdominal pains for which the doctors could find no explanation. When he confided to his son that he felt as if there were 'stones in his abdomen', Carl shrewdly wondered, with a first flash of psychiatric insight, whether his father were not inducing the symptom psychically. It seemed to Carl that his father's days of glory had really ended with his dissertation on the Arabic version of the Song of Songs, and a long process of decline had led to such serious religious doubts that his whole choice of profession had become a strain. He sat in his study deliberately smoking the long pipe from his student days, sinking deeper into sentimental reminiscences of a long-dead past. His God had failed him, his marriage had revealed appalling shortcomings, his son vehemently disputed what remaining beliefs he still cherished, and the world could only be faced by a regression to the golden days of his student years. A martyr to Christian charity, 'he did a great deal of good – far too much' – and as a result a tired, irritable, over-exploited man frequently fell into angry scenes despite his strenuous attempts to live a devout and devoted life.

Paradoxically, it was the son who had been allowed a glimpse of the true nature of God, and the father who failed to realise the revelation which should have been his by professional persuasion. Once Carl heard his father praying desperately for some gleam of light from the silent Godhead, and cursed the theological dogma of the Church which made true communion impossible for a man who so much desired it. Compounding the paradox, the son who claimed direct experience of divinity discussed such experiences intellectually with his father, and this, to a person of his temperament, was 'like a red rag to a bull'.

By the winter of 1895 it became clear that his father was approaching a death which still seemed to have no clear-cut medical basis, and his decline became rapid.[7] Presently 'Carl had to carry him round like a heap of bones for an anatomy class';[8] and at last, in the autumn of 1895, he became a complete invalid. It was the final humiliation. The once so strong, striding and always erect Paul Jung had collapsed into an emaciated shadow of his former self and become a burden to everyone.

As the father declined, the son blossomed. It was almost as if, phoenix-fashion, a new person were released from his entanglements with the dying man, and he plunged enthusiastically into the life of the University. And then, on 28 January 1896, he returned home from an anatomical lecture, asked how his father was, and his mother said, 'He's very weak – but still the same.'

When they went into the bedroom Carl saw that his father had become delirious, but he managed to whisper something to Frau Jung, who translated the incoherent message to her son, warning him with her eyes that it was necessary to lie. 'He wants to know whether you have passed the state examination.' Typically, in the moment of death, the confused mind of Carl's father had thrown up an altruistic question; and Carl duly lied, 'Yes, it went very well.'[9]

Great relief appeared on his father's face, and he sank back in a coma once more. Shortly afterwards Carl entered the bedroom alone to find his father breathing deeply and regularly. Then came 'a rattling in his throat', and he could see that death was approaching. Instead of calling his mother, he stood there – fascinated – because he had 'never seen anyone die before'. No sense of urgency drove him to bring his mother into communion with her husband in his last moments, and what might have been a loving son had almost become a cool observer. It speaks volumes for his relationship with his father that he could remain so classically detached until at last – suddenly – the old man stopped breathing. Hurrying out to his mother, he found her sitting by the window in the next room, busy with that eternal anodyne for living and dying – knitting. 'He's dying,' he said – lying, one supposes, because of guilt. When she came to the bed and saw that he was dead, she said in wonderment, 'How quickly it has all passed.'[10]

If there were elements of relief in the death of his father, it nevertheless led Carl into days of gloom. The complexities of their relationship were sharply focused by his mother's comment some days later, which may have been a soliloquy not intended for his ears: 'He died in time for you. . . . You did not understand each other, and he might have become a hindrance to you.' Carl felt it was his mother's No. 2 personality speaking to the 'surrounding air', but the message came through clearly: 'You are free of the inhibitions which your relationship with your father imposed on you.' At first disturbed by the sense that part of his life had irrevocably disappeared and left him standing alone on the edge of an abyss, the new and more confident Carl quickly adjusted as some part 'of freedom and manliness awoke in me'.

A second shock came when he discovered, according to Ruth Bailey, that his father had left only £200 with which the whole family had to face the future.[11] For a time he was under pressure from his mother's relations to look for a clerk's job in a business-house to earn money immediately, and it is salutary to think that this could easily have happened, so severe were the economic pressures. Three relatives now came to the family's aid. An aged aunt gave him the right to sell her collection of antiques on a commission basis, and he quite enjoyed doing this, displaying considerable bargaining skill. His mother's youngest brother made her a small allowance and an uncle on his father's side gave Carl a long-term, interest-free loan to keep him at University. Collectively, with the addition of small sums he later earned as a junior assistant, the money carried him over a difficult period. With that capacity for romanticising the past characteristic of most great men, he wrote in *Memories, Dreams, Reflections*: 'I would not have missed this time of poverty. One learns to value simple things.'

Carl now took over the management of the family finances, and became responsible for giving the 'housekeeping money to my mother every week because she was unable to economise and could not manage money'. Step by step he assumed several of the roles lately fulfilled by his father, and finally, at the great age of twenty, became head of the family, underpinning his authority by taking over his father's room.

When they could not meet the bills for the big rambling vicarage, Oeri records that 'Carl's mother moved into a house near Bottminger Mill in the Basel suburban community of Zinningen together with both children'. She was, he adds, 'a wise and courageous woman'.[12]

That the whole Jung family now had to pinch and scrape to make ends meet is clear, and it must have prematurely burdened Carl with great responsibilities to have to play the father surrogate so early in life.

Whether in reaction to intense study and family worries, or whether it occurred as a natural part of developing manhood faced with its first serious challenge, another change now took over Carl's personality – a change unrecorded in the reminiscences: a third and unsuspected self presently materialised.

It was a roistering, extrovert self, capable of getting drunk and likely to assert itself with an abrasive force which even some of his fellow-students found difficult to take. Liberation from the shadow of his father's presence produced a person who sometimes sat in the Zofingia pub right through the night, steadily drinking, usually beer, until at first light he remembered his mother and sister waiting for him at home. Then he would wander back, with all the appearance of a hangover, and on the way, flower by flower, painfully put together a placatory bouquet which he presented to his mother, sometimes in person, sometimes leaving it at her bedside as she slept.

There is no available record of how she reacted to her son's developing character. Many students delighted in this new person. Carl became known as 'The Barrel', and 'was a very merry member of the Zofingia student club, always prepared to revolt against the League of Virtue as he called the organised fraternity brothers. He was rarely drunk but when so . . . noisy. He did not think much of school dances, romancing the housemaids and similar gallantries. He told me once that it was absolutely senseless to hop round a ballroom with some female until one was covered with sweat.'[13]

According to Oeri there followed an episode which crystallised the entirely unexpected buccaneering element in Jung's new self. Dancing one night in the grand Heiten Platz at the Jofingen Festival, he concentrated his attention on a beautiful young student from French Switzerland, and suddenly became aware that all his protestations about time-wasting sweat were false; he had fallen in love. That was normal enough. The original element appeared two weeks later. He strode into a jeweller's shop, confidently examined a number of rings, selected not one but two, put twenty centimes on the counter and hurried off toward the door again. The proprietor promptly called after him, pointing out that twenty centimes were useless, even as a down payment, and demanded the return of the rings. Jung threw the rings on the counter, cursed the proprietor for interfering with his engagement and stormed out of the shop.[14]

How he explained his dilemma or disengaged himself from the girl remains unknown. Oeri simply states: 'The Barrel stayed unaffianced.' Preoccupations with the occult came through clearly in these early student days. Carl led a group of students who read widely in occult literature, conducted parapsychological experiments and converted spiritualists like Zollner and Crookes into heroic martyrs of science. Already a dog-lover, he would earnestly lecture a young dachsund he had acquired, claiming that the animal not only understood every word but also had parapsychological potential which caused it to whimper whenever occult presences were active.

It was this sense of unknown forces at work in a non-material dimension which produced another surprising reaction. He spent many hours in the student pub known as the Brio, and late at night with a group of close friends, when the roistering was over, never seemed anxious to set out for home. Slowly it became apparent to Oeri that he disliked walking alone through the sinister Nightingale Woods which lay between the pub and his home in Bottminger Mill. At the door of the pub he would plunge into animated discussion and the company would find themselves following him into the woods, drawn by the magnet of his conversational powers. Pausing at certain spots, he would dramatically describe historic incidents, never failing to say at a special tree, 'On this spot Doctor Götz was murdered.'

Another surprise now supervened. Called up at nineteen, Carl hated his first brief period of military conscription, but as a result he owned and carried a revolver. He would offer this for his friends' protection on their return journey from the pub. Oeri took advantage of his offer on one occasion, and recorded: 'I was not afraid of Dr Götz's ghost nor of living evil spirits, but I was afraid of Jung's revolver in my pocket. I had no mechanical knowledge and did not know whether the safety catch was on or off.'[15]

On 28 November 1896 a student meeting called to honour Professor Ehren von Immermann gave Carl a chance to address the students on a subject already dear to his heart – 'The Limits of Exact Science'. Opening with some ironical pleasantries about the nature of current thinking, he turned sharply into his subject with a description of 'our intellectually impoverished time'.[16] It is difficult to achieve a good English translation of the key passages of his lecture, but the gist can be summarised.

In the concert of the great world orchestra the constantly recurring theme centred around the beloved self or ego. People were interested in money, honour, power – nothing of any consequence – and all the great issues which for epochs had occupied the civilised world were largely non-existent for the cultivated. Who was looking for truth without also searching for money? Wasn't most of our scientific work done to satisfy conceited egos, or to further the rusty system of materialism which dominated our thought? Even those who did think about the important issues lacked the necessary intellectual vigour, which explained the shallowness of most cultivated conversation. It did not require any great percipience to recognise the inadequacy of present scientific dogma, and any critique of empirical theory led inevitably into metaphysical thinking which reached out into the grand assumption of transcendental life.[17] Carl then gave several illustrations of phenomena in objective reality which were difficult to examine scientifically because 'their appearance depended on the special nature of certain qualities' – such as hypnotism.[18]

Sustained applause broke out at the end of his paper, and even the Praesidium of the Student Association congratulated him, but in the discussion which followed he was strongly attacked by the medical students, who argued that scientific research could only be conducted in the natural sciences, which certainly excluded phenomena like hypnotism. Jung attempted to justify exact research in metaphysical matters, and some members of the natural sciences and mathematics school supported him. Provoked as they were, the theological students remained silent.[19]

Much of the evidence for these student debates comes from Jung's student friend Gustav Steiner. A few years younger than Jung, his recollections of those days were vivid. At their first meeting when he told Jung he was studying German history, Jung remarked, 'I am the great-great grandson of a natural son of Goethe's. He said it, apparently, without assuming "any great airs".'

Carl returned to the theme of his first paper in a second, delivered in the summer of 1897 – 'Thoughts about Psychology'. Once again he violently attacked the totally unjustified lack of interest in metaphysics because it could not be substantiated by experience. Steiner says in his reminiscences: 'Despite superfluous and not at all popular outbursts by Jung, he succeeded in holding the attention of his audience.' The President did not hesitate to criticise 'the too abrasive tone of his polemic', even if it could be justified by the narrow-minded thinking of his critics.[20]

By the winter of 1897–8 he had asserted his dominance over the students to the point where, against considerable opposition, he was elected president. The medical and law students fought a vigorous campaign against him because they resisted any further proliferation of scientific discussion. As Ellenberger noted, 'throughout . . . Jung . . . maintained the ambiguous relationship with the theological students that he was to have later with many religious ministers'.[21]

The seeds of so many later attitudes were apparent in these debates: his capacity for explosive argument, his preoccupation with the problem of evil, his peculiar form of theological agnosticism, and his 'absolute conviction when speaking of the *soul* . . . as immaterial, transcendent, outside of time and space – *and yet to be approached scientifically*'.[22] (My italics.) One of the main channels of enquiry for this scientific approach was an area of investigation regarded by many as insusceptible to scientific analysis. 'Among the means of obtaining cognisance of the soul were the study of somnambulism, hypnosis and spiristic manifestations. Thus to Jung spiritism was not a matter of occultism but of unknown psychic phenomena that needed to be investigated with proper scientific methods.'[23]

Jung wrote of this period: 'My student days were a good time for me. Everything was intellectually alive and it was also a time of friendships. . . . We argued over Schopenhauer and Kant, we knew all about the stylistic niceties of Cicero and were interested in theology and philosophy.'

Puzzled by the absence of any serious analysis of the psyche in his omnivorous reading, he came to the conclusion that without it the insights of science – subject as they were to severe limitation – would never have arisen. C. G. Carus mentioned the psyche in passing, but none of the authors Jung read paused to examine the inner psychology of man. At first sight a casual observation, it was to have profound repercussions on his intellectual development.

Reinforcing his new preoccupation with psychology came the discovery, in the library of a classmate's father, of a book on spiritualistic phenomena dating from the seventies. The scepticism he brought to bear in theology evaporated with spiritualism. He sought out and read every possible book on the subject, ploughing heroically through masses of literature, from Eschenmayer to Passavant, from Kerner to Görres, concluding with an excited skimming of seven volumes of Swedenborg. The observations of the spiritualists may at first reading have struck him as 'weird and questionable' but they were also the first accounts he had read of 'objective psychic phenomena'.

A certain lack of intellectual rigour was apparent in Jung's approach to a subject destined to become all-important, when he concluded that the repeated proliferation of stories of ghosts and psychic phenomena throughout the world was evidence for their validity. We have seen today a similar rash of evidence spread across the world about flying saucers, without adding any reliable evidence of their existence. Straining to achieve immortal life, many people cling to any shred of evidence in favour of a spiritual dimension – and spiritualism, poltergeists, ghosts, all reaffirm the craved potential. No such scepticism troubled Jung. 'They added another dimension to my life . . . the world gained depth and background . . . Kant's Dreams of a Spirit

Seer came just at the right moment and soon I also discovered Karl Duprel who had evaluated these ideas philosophically and psychologically.'

Dismayed to find that his new enthusiasms met with scorn among many of his fellow-students, his mother's No. 2 personality came to his aid and fully approved his expanding researches. He did not yet know that psychological investigation of spiritualistic phenomena was to become part of the subject of the thesis he submitted in 1902 for his doctorate, but he simply felt that he had been 'pushed to the brink of the world'.

Another incident occurred in the summer of 1898 which reinforced his growing absorption in spirit phenomena. His mother sat knitting in the dining-room one day while he studied in the adjoining room with the door ajar; his fourteen-year-old sister was away at school and the maid busy in the kitchen. At the centre of the dining-room stood the big round walnut table which had passed down the family from his paternal grandmother and was probably seventy years old. Suddenly Carl heard a 'report' so loud that he abandoned his books and hurried into the dining-room to find his mother 'sitting flabbergasted' in her armchair, the knitting fallen from her hands. She stammered out 'W-w-what's happened . . .?', staring at the table-top. Miraculously, a split had appeared, running from the edge of the table not along any joint but across the wood to the centre. The eighty-three-year-old Jung, recalling the episode, wrote: 'I was thunderstruck – how could such a thing happen? A table of solid walnut that had dried out for seventy years – how could it split on a summer day in the relatively high degree of humidity characteristic of our climate?' His mother darkly commented, as perhaps would most people of her generation and upbringing, 'That means something.'

A certain temperamental predisposition is required to share Jung's excitement at this incident. An expert in timber behaviour has assured me that the vagaries of wood-shrinkage over such a very long period could easily reconcile the split in rational terms.[24] No one can predict at precisely what point shrinkage will cease or a dramatic collapse of supporting structures reproduce a pistol-shot; but something else now happened, of an even more remarkable nature.

Two weeks later Carl returned from the University to find the three women of the household 'in a great state of agitation'. Another report, this time said to be deafening, had echoed through the house from the direction of a heavy, old-fashioned sideboard, but no equivalent split had appeared. Jung's scientific curiosity was fully aroused, and he rigorously scrutinised every surface of the sideboard for further evidence, without success. Opening the sideboard, he found a bread-basket containing bread and a bread-knife – and now the mystery, for him, was even more astonishingly explained. The blade of the knife had broken in several pieces. Scrupulously checking the immediate history of the knife, Jung cross-examined the maid, who claimed that it had been used at four o'clock in the afternoon and was then intact. To be more precise, whether the maid, his mother or his sister bore witness to this fact is unclear, but Jung completed the imaginative leap from the deafening report to the broken knife with growing excitement.

The next day he hurried off to a well-known cutler, who examined the blade technically, pronounced it sound and reported that 'someone must have deliberately broken it piece by piece'.

Once again the scepticism he brought to religious thought was modified by 'psychic phenomena'. Without question something very remarkable appeared to have happened, but it was no less remarkable that Jung failed to press home his enquiries. A predisposition to believe in psychic phenomena, derived perhaps from his mother's second personality, might have inhibited scientific scrutiny. As in other incidents later in life, it never struck him as odd that whatever forces were at work should dissipate their powers on frivolous table- or knife-splitting. Subliminal influences from another dimension are surely demeaned by such parlour tricks, even when sheer virtuosity split the knife three ways at a single stroke.

Searching for fresh data, Jung now became interested in the séances held by some relatives with a girl, not yet sixteen years old, as medium. Perhaps the secrets of the psychic powers which split the knife could be unravelled through the psychology of people said to possess them. Jung's account does not disclose the girl's name, but she was the granddaughter of Samuel Preiswerk – Hélène Preiswerk – and he began to attend her séances with a mind so open that the oddest coincidences did not appear to arouse his suspicion.[25] For two years he religiously attended and recorded these séances, which finally formed an important part of his doctoral thesis, but if we consider the number of points where coincidence came close to fraudulence it is surprising that her reputation lasted so long.

Not that Jung by any means swallowed the evidence whole. 'We had results in the form of communications and tapping noises from the walls and the table. Movements of the table independently of the medium were questionable and I soon found out that limiting conditions imposed on the experiment generally had an obstructive effect.'

Nonetheless he accepted the autonomy of the 'tapping noises' and concentrated his attention on the 'content of the communications'. When absorbed in her semi-somnambulistic states, Hélène Preiswerk remained aware of her surroundings, but frequently took on a second personality named Ivènes, a person diametrically different from Hélène. Ivènes was restrained and dignified, Hélène unstable and frivolous. Ivènes took her inspiration from her grandfather, the Reverend Samuel Preiswerk, and frequently spoke in his low, dignified manner, but she claimed to have travelled to the planet Mars and described its canals and flying machines. Two types of spirit possessed the girl, one solid and dour, the other extrovert and exuberant, and Jung carefully noted that these characteristics corresponded with the conflicting aspects of her everyday personality between which she oscillated sometimes with alarming rapidity. She could also reincarnate several of her dead relatives with consummate skill, reproducing their precise tone of voice.

Presently these early performances gave place to fantastic elaborations which were psychologically fascinating and would have enriched the records of any modern psychoanalyst. Indeed, Jung did not fail to bring a double vision to Hélène Preiswerk's extraordinary fantasies, but he continued to keep an open mind about their origin. Passing through many incarnations scattered with considerable profligacy down three centuries, Fräulein Preiswerk played out in various trance-like states a number of roles, sometimes abandoning her customary Basel dialect to speak perfect High German with considerable ease. She insisted throughout that it was the spirits of the dead who spoke through her with such ventriloquial effect, and fiercely discounted any latent acting virtuosity. Yet the sheer repetition of her roles made the whole performance suspect as she passed from being the Seeress of Prevorst in the nineteenth century to the Countess of Thierfelsenburg in the fifteenth century, from Madame de Valours in the thirteenth, when she was burnt as a witch, to a christian matyrdom under Nero in Rome. Many characters accumulated from her many roles until she became the centre of an immense fantasy network. Not only was every new person she met immediately assimilated into her family systems, but also shortly after meeting Jung she claimed to have been the young woman seduced by Goethe, which literally made her Jung's great-grandmother!

Of these early séances one other fact which Jung once more took in his stride needs to be emphasised. Introduced to Justinus Kerner's book *The Seeress of Prevorst*, in which Friedericke Hauffe, the daughter of a village gamekeeper, frequently spoke in an unknown language, Hélène Preiswerk immediately 'magnetised herself . . . and talked in an unknown language which vaguely resembled a mixture of Italian and French'.[26]

Of course, Jung did attempt to trace the sources of her mediumistic performances, discovered Kerner's *Seeress of Prevorst* and linked one remarkable session with talks she had heard about Kant's cosmogony; but he failed to mention that the history of old Basel families was common knowledge to many Basel citizens.

For two years Jung sat through these sessions, recording, checking, analysing, and it was six months after he withdrew from the circle that Fräulein Preiswerk was finally caught red-handed in outright deception. He described the occasion in his thesis: 'She wanted to revive the wavering belief in her supernatural powers by genuinely spiritualistic experiments like apports, etc., and for this purpose concealed in her dress small objects which she threw into the air during the dark séances. After that her role was played out.'[27]

As Ellenberger remarked, 'It seems that only much later did Jung realise that his young cousin had been in love with him and had multiplied her mediumistic revelations in order to please him.'[28]

The final details of the story were revealed by Jung in a seminar given in Zürich in 1925.[29] Some years after these sessions, the girl travelled to Paris to become a dressmaker, and, passing through that city, Jung went to visit her. Once again an element of naïveté appeared in his reaction to the discovery that she had forgotten all about her days as a medium – one of many defence mechanisms someone psychologically disturbed might assume against recollection of a too painful past.

From the scientific spirit which characterised his research into this and many other cases finally emerged a deeply thought-out academic thesis which gave a profound analysis of the interlocking relationship between psychic and spiritualistic phenomena and was enthusiastically reviewed by Théodore Flournoy.[30] Any scepticism about the phenomena Jung investigated has to take into account his emphasis on its psychological roots. He was not simply another recruit to the gullible ranks of spiritualism; his purpose was much more genuinely scientific.

Straightforward medical training seemed far removed from such matters. Following the first introductory course, Carl became a junior assistant in anatomy, quickly made his mark and was selected by the demonstrator to take charge of the course in histology. 'I interested myself primarily in evolutionary theory and comparative anatomy,' he wrote, adding, 'I also became acquainted with neo-vitalistic doctrines.'

His unconscious identification with the life of animals made the vivisection classes in physiology repellent. He could never quite free himself from the feeling that warm-blooded creatures were too closely allied to human beings to be regarded as just 'cerebral automata', and he did not see the necessity of vivisection classes. 'I had imagination enough to picture the demonstrated procedures from a mere description of them.' Inevitably, his examination results in physiology were poor, and he just 'scraped through'.

The precise direction his career was to take now became the focus of fresh analysis. Until his parapsychological experiences with Hélène Preiswerk, his ambitions had remained confined to straight medicine, in which he hoped to specialise either in surgery or internal medicine. Later in life he believed that but for economic factors his preference for pathology and his special training in anatomy would have made surgery his final choice. He had run into debt with his uncle, with the tradespeople and an occasional friend, an extremely painful experience to a young man of his fierce integrity. His immediate expectation of becoming an assistant in a cantonal hospital was unrealistic. Jobs in clinics were dependent on the backing of their chiefs, and with his capacity for making enemies he did not expect to be a popular candidate.

Professor Immermann, who had been present at his first address to the student society, did not like Jung very much, but by now a much more sympathetic person, Frederick von Muller, had taken his place as Director of the Medical Clinic. A man who shared Jung's freshly formulated view that asking the right questions was halfway toward solving problems, he became so interested in Jung's work that he suggested taking him as his assistant to Munich where yet another new post already awaited him. Persuaded, at this point, that internal medicine was the correct field for him to work in, Jung easily accepted the invitation, only to have the whole orientation of his choice dramatically changed by reading a single book.

Since the instructor in psychiatry had failed to excite Jung's imagination, and visits to psychiatric clinics had left him unimpressed, he had no predisposition to enter the field with any enthusiasm. That, at least, is the impression given by his reminiscences. In fact other sources reveal that he spent one winter semester between 1898 and 1899, and another in the summer of 1900, attending *two* courses given by Professor Wille at Basel in psychiatry.[31] It was obligatory to attend one psychiatric semester, but not two. It is possible to fault his memory at a number of points in the medical material of his reminiscences, but, whatever the truth, he certainly left his study of psychiatric *literature* to the last days before the state examination. When he opened Krafft-Ebing's *Lehrbuch der Psychiatrie*, his mood was deeply influenced by the current attitude of the medical world to the whole subject – one of contempt.

Mental patients in those days were frequently isolated in clinics, almost like lepers, the director was 'locked up in the same institution with his patients', many forms of mental illness were accepted as incurable, and the few practising psychiatrists regarded as eccentrics if not quacks.

Nonetheless it is difficult to see why the opening passage of Krafft-Ebing's preface and one subsequent remark in the following pages had such a powerful effect on Jung. The preface began: 'It is probably due to the peculiarity of the subject and its incomplete state of development that psychiatric textbooks are stamped with a more or less subjective character.' Then came a description of psychoses as 'diseases of the personality'.

'My heart', Jung wrote, 'suddenly began to pound. I had to stand up and draw a deep breath. My excitement was intense for it had become clear . . . in a flash of illumination, that for me the only possible goal was psychiatry.'[32] Spelling out this sudden impact, he said: 'Here was the empirical field common to biological and spiritual facts, which I had everywhere sought and nowhere found. Here at last was the place where the collision of nature and spirit became reality.' The result was that he decided to apply for a post in the famous Burghölzli Psychiatric Hospital in Zürich.

When Professor Muller heard the news he was astonished, and at first hostile. Jung's friends shared this reaction. He must be mad to throw up the chance of becoming Muller's assistant in Munich in favour of the witchcraft of psychiatry, with all its uncertainties as a career. Once again his old sense of alienation returned. He was an outsider, a person antipathetic to others, and the scar from the past gave him renewed pain. He referred to it in fact as a reopened wound, but nothing could deflect him from his purpose. As he said somewhat grandiloquently: 'It was as though two rivers had united and in one grand torrent were bearing me inexorably towards distant goals.'

At the moment of resolution he encountered a minor setback in the subject in which he should have excelled – pathological anatomy. In most examinations he successfully anticipated what questions would be asked, and perhaps it was sheer overconfidence in pathological anatomy that made him overlook some moulds in the corner of a slide already encumbered with 'all sorts of debris'. As a result he fell just short of the highest marks.

Coincidentally a good bargain struck from one of his aunt's antiques left him with surplus money for the first time since his father's death, and he indulged the impossible extravagance of going to the opera. The following day, compounding extravagance, he took a holiday trip to Munich, and the rhythm of the train-wheels matched the intoxicating arias from Bizet's *Carmen* in his mind. Art, music, literature combined in Munich with a tremendous sense of relief that the plodding pilgrimage through the requisite fields of medicine was at last, in its boring sense, over. He felt liberated. It was the first week in December, and spring nowhere near, but the sap seemed renewed in him.

Chapter 7

The Young Psychiatrist

JUNG ARRIVED at the Burghölzli Psychiatric Hospital in Zürich one bitter winter day early in December 1900 and was escorted by the receptionist to the waiting-room. Within a few minutes Professor Eugen Bleuler, Director of the Burghölzli, strode into the room, gave a few brief words of welcome and, despite Jung's protests, insisted on carrying his case and showing him to his room. Jung became aware from this very first encounter that he was dealing with a man dedicated to work, duty and austerity. Rumours of these characteristics had long circulated in the outside world, but now, inside the Burghölzli, they revealed themselves in all their formidable reality. In effect, as Ellenberger says, 'From this moment on the young man was to live in a kind of psychiatric monastery.' A staff meeting took place every morning at 8.30 a.m., but long before that every resident psychiatrist was expected to have made the first rounds of the wards for which he was responsible. It meant rising between 6.30 and 7 a.m. and carrying out detailed duties before the staff meeting. There were no secretaries and the residents had to type their own case-histories. Food was reasonably plentiful but plain, and the slightest deviation from the regulations regarded as dereliction of duty. Complicating the normal process of examination, diagnosis and prescription, the patients were such as required a high degree of tolerance and persistence. Three times a week a special meeting – the Gemainsame – was held during which the staff discussed the case-histories of new patients, under the direction of Bleuler. Evening rounds were made between 5 and 6.30 p.m., and the day's note-taking frequently not completed until ten o'clock. The main doors of the hospital were firmly closed and locked at 10 p.m., only the senior residents were granted keys and, when the younger members asked to borrow one, reasonable justifications had to be forthcoming.

In a personal communication to Professor Ellenberger, Dr Alphonse Maeder, a colleague of Jung at the Burghölzli, said: 'The patient was the focus of interest. The student learned how to talk with him. Burghölzli was in that time a kind of factory where you worked very much and were poorly paid. Everyone from the professor to the young resident was totally absorbed by his work. Abstinence from alcoholic drinks was imposed on everyone.'

It must have been hard for Jung the Barrel, accustomed to normal bouts of drinking, to find all such indulgences cut off, but Maeder adds, 'Bleuler was kind to all and never played the role of chief.'

It is difficult to believe, from what followed some years later, but

Professor Jakob Wyrsch also confirmed this: 'Bleuler never blamed a resident. If something had not been done he would just enquire about the reasons for the omission. There was nothing dictatorial in him. He often came to the residents' room after lunch and took coffee with them. Then he would ask about new developments in medicine or surgery, not to test the knowledge of the residents but just to keep himself informed.'[1]

In recollection Jung did not share this idealised view of Bleuler. Astonishingly, only a single line is given to Bleuler in his reminiscences, and he depreciates the kind of work undertaken by the staff. 'From the clinical point of view which then prevailed the human personality of the patient, his individuality did not matter.' His colleagues were not interested, he said, in answering the profoundly complicated question: What actually takes place inside the mentally ill? 'Patients were labelled, rubber-stamped with a diagnosis and for the most part that settled the matter.'[2] As Ellenberger points out, many of those who worked with Bleuler in the Burghölzli contradicted this view, praised Bleuler and regarded him as reasonably open-minded.

Jung's old friend Albert Oeri called on him in these early days and was shown round the Burghölzli. Oeri found it frightening. Most of the patients looked strange and were restless, either turning in their beds, pacing round the wards or simply standing staring into space. One sat up and spoke eagerly to Jung, and suddenly 'a heavy fist whizzed through the air right next to me'.[3] An irritated patient behind Jung's back had suddenly tried to punch him, but a very nimble Jung was accustomed to evasive action. Jung laughed outright at Oeri's frightened reaction and said 'that man can hit with great force – you'd better keep your distance – but you are a bit of a sissy'. He did not seem at all intimidated by the thought of physical violence. Indeed, asked later whether he had ever been physically assaulted he said: 'No.' Asked why, he replied, 'Because they know I'd hit back.'[4]

Oeri had lunch in the hospital, and Jung talked avidly about the old days, but it was amazing, he said, to see 'this old sinner following his master into abstinence and looking so sourly at a glass of wine it was liable to turn to vinegar'.[5]

As at school, Jung did not easily adjust to the new community of the Burghölzli. Within a week he withdrew once more into his own private world and, in what spare time remained from the exhausting routine, read volume by volume through the entire fifty-volume course of the *Allgemeine Zeitschrift für Psychiatrie*. Observing his colleagues became as much part of his work as observing his patients, and he secretly compiled statistics on their heredity from which he gained 'much instruction'. Clearly he was unimpressed by some of their personalities and techniques.

'I need scarcely mention', he later wrote, 'that my concentration and self-imposed confinement alienated me from my colleagues.' There was even a day when he is said to have publicly mocked his chief, Bleuler; but that came much later.[6]

For the moment, he had entered a psychiatric monastery, but refused to submit to vows which required him to believe 'only in what was probable, average, commonplace and barren of meaning'. Much more exciting prospects quickly opened to his probing mind, and one big question constantly recurred: 'How did the human mind react to the sight of its own destruction?' Already it seemed to him that psychiatry was 'an articulate expression of that biological reaction which seizes upon the so-called healthy mind in the presence of mental illness'.

Professionally the way was stubborn, difficult and in the beginning unsympathetic. Personally a similar adjustment had to be made. Leaving Basel for Zürich meant a break with his mother, sister and family roots going back centuries, but Basel had become 'stuffy' for Carl, and the belief of Basel's citizens that theirs was the only civilised town, provincial. Closely classified in Basel as a respectable intellectual, the son of a parson and the grandson of the great Dr Carl Gustav Jung, he belonged to a 'specific' category which did not appeal to him. Paradoxically Zürich, a centre of commerce, attracted him more than Basel, which was proud of its cosmopolitan intellectualism. Tradition weighed heavily on the city of Basel, but in Zürich the 'air was free'.

In recollection he emphasised the emotional upset his mother underwent when he broke away from her and went to Zürich, and implied that he himself remained undisturbed, but his ties with his mother were still very close.[7] His mother bore the pain of the break bravely, helped by her daughter – a home-loving, conventional person completely at variance with her brother. Physically delicate, his sister had none of her brother's drive and initiative, but now the very fact that 'she was born to live the life of a spinster' made her role as her mother's companion acceptable if not satisfying.

His mother could not quite see why he had abandoned a sensible career in down-to-earth medicine for the intangibilities of psychiatry. She would stare uncomprehendingly at the psychiatric charts he pinned to the walls of his room and wonder what they had to do with the health of human beings.[8]

One other experience reached a minor resolution in Jung's first year at Burghölzli. Several periods of military training, each lasting no more than a few weeks, reached their climax in 1900 when he 'received the grade of lieutenant' in the Swiss Army. As he said in a confidential burst to a colleague some years later: 'The military arts have their satisfactions – I let loose a lot of aggression in them. But the only satisfactory role is that of general.'[9]

Now approaching twenty-six years of age, an upstanding person of magnificent physique, Jung's sheer physical presence was already beginning to make felt those dynamic qualities which later contributed to the charisma of a great man. On occasions he might be withdrawn, but nobody could ignore him. He certainly became intolerant of orthodox psychiatry, but simultaneously reacted with enthusiasm to the work of Breuer, Freud and Janet. As early as 1900 he read the first edition of Freud's *The Interpretation of Dreams*, but lacking the experience required for its proper assimilation, put the book aside, quite unaware that a second reading would provide another watershed in his life. He did, in fact, prepare a summary for Bleuler which was discussed at a 'report evening' in the Burghölzli, but his interest remained luke-warm.[10]

Jung's relations with Eugen Bleuler fluctuated. Before he became director of the Burghölzli, Bleuler had lived in the Rheinau Mental Hospital, cheek by jowl with his patients, and developed the qualities of a saint living among lepers. Simultaneously Professor of Psychiatry at the University of Zürich and Director of the Burghölzli, he was one of the great pioneers of psychiatry who revised the entire concept of dementia praecox, renaming it schizophrenia.

On the basis of his clinical research Bleuler had developed a new approach to schizophrenia. In contradistinction with the purely *organicist* theories that were prevalent at the time, Bleuler developed a theory that would be called organo-dynamic today. He assumed that schizophrenia derived from an unknown cause (perhaps from the action of toxic substances on the brain) in which heredity played an important part. In the chaos of the manifold symptoms of schizophrenia he distinguished primary or physiogenic symptoms, caused directly by the unknown organic processes, and secondary or psychogenic symptoms deriving from the primary symptoms.[11]

According to some who worked with him at the Burghölzli, Bleuler experimented with what were regarded as revolutionary techniques, such as suddenly transferring a patient to a ward with quite different patients, discharging severely ill patients to confront normal family life again, or giving an apparently irresponsible patient considerable responsibilities.[12] Jung observed these techniques with concentrated attention, but felt that they dealt with the symptoms rather than the cause of the illnesses. One such technique – work therapy – then startlingly new, he did find full of possibilities. Moreover, several witnesses from those days confirm that Bleuler had 'miraculous success' with a number of patients, although no long-term follow-up evidence was ever recorded.[13]

Bleuler believed that the basic symptom of schizophrenia consisted of 'loosening the tension of association', a phrase capable of several interpretations, one of which included dissociation – as when the word 'right' did not any longer imply the word 'wrong'. Bleuler asked Jung to experiment with word-association tests, and Jung launched himself into widescale research with colleagues and patients. The results were exciting.[14] The test paradigm involved reading a list of words to the patient, asking for the first associated word and recording the varying time-intervals and logical predictability of the respondent's choice.

One woman, a dressmaker born in 1845, had been admitted to the Burghölzli in 1887 and remained there for twenty-five years. 'Before admission she had for several years heard voices that slandered her. For a time she contemplated suicide by drowning. She explained the voices as invisible telephones. They called out to her that she was a woman of doubtful character.'[15]

She wrote a letter to the Superintendent:

> With these lines I suggest you most urgently to discharge me forthwith. My head is *clearer* than ever as I have already remarked in my last letter. What I have to suffer secretly on account of novelties of all descriptions is unfortunately known to me alone and is too shattering for my health as well as for my mind. Unfortunately they have gone so far as to torture poor victims to death with secret brutalities for I suffer more than you can imagine.

The patient developed vivid delusions of inheriting millions, of having her spinal marrow torn out by night, and her bed stuck full of needles. She was given the following word-association test:[16]

Stimulus word	Reaction	Reaction time (seconds)
Pupil	Now you can write Socrates	12.4
Father	Yes mother	7.6
Table	Sofa	3.8
Head	Yes irreplaceable	14.8
Ink	Nut-water	9.0
Needle	Thread	11.4
Bread	Butter	3.4
Lamp	Electricity, kerosene	6.4
Tree	Fruit	6.0
Mountain	Valleys	9.4
Hair	Hat	6.2

It is possible to read several of these replies as having, if not normal logic, a logic of their own, but Jung commented: 'Among these reactions there are some that sound quite incomprehensible. The first reaction – pupil/Socrates – is really a startling reaction for a dressmaker; it looks very affected and immediately suggests a complex constellation. . . .' Later Jung found that ink/nut-water in her responses was the result of associating dark-brown water with black ink, and commented: 'But how does the patient get nut-water? It is again a complex constellation like Socrates. . . .' At this stage Jung defined the term 'complex' in Janet's terms – an 'idée fixe subconsciente' – but he attempted to analyse the complexes in the original meaning of the term given by Ziehen. In word-association tests Ziehen, like Jung, found that the reaction time was longer when the stimulus word related to something unpleasant in the mind of the patient. 'Sometimes by picking out several delayed responses one could relate them to a common underlying representation that Ziehen called *gefühlsbetonter Vorstellungskomplex*.'[17] In others words an emotionally charged complex.

Repeated applications of word-association tests did produce a number of weird replies in the case of the dressmaker, and there was no doubt that certain words were highly charged with emotional blocks. As Ellenberger said: 'In this way [Jung] found himself able to identify a great number of complexes into three groups: dreams of happiness, complaints of suffering injustices and sexual complexes. The seemingly incoherent utterances of the [dressmaker] thus expressed a systematic wish fulfilment to compensate for a life of toil and deprivation.'

As his research developed, one question persisted in Jung's mind: Why were the complexes so resistant to treatment in dementia praecox? Some time elapsed before he put forward the hypothesis derived from Bleuler that dementia praecox produced a toxin which had a 'noxious action on the brain thus rendering the disease irreversible'.

A second potential use for the word-association tests became clear to Jung when another patient told him of his missing wallet which he suspected had been misappropriated by his eighteen-year-old ward. Jung subjected the ward to an association test, and after the first trial run became convinced that he had merely to begin a second test with the words 'You have stolen' and a confession would be forthcoming. This is exactly what happened. A similar case brought to him concerning money stolen by one of the nurses he solved with equal facility. The word-association tests shifted suspicion from the nurse supposed to have committed the crime and revealed the actual culprit.

For a time these results opened up exciting prospects. Had he discovered an infallible means for exposing concealed or unconscious thoughts and, if so, would they be admissible evidence in court? Unfortunately, a major flaw quickly revealed itself. Subjective feelings of guilt were dependent on so many personal experiences that they bore no correspondence to the *objective* guilt required by a court of law. In other words, guilt not connected with the crime might bring a guilty response in a person innocent of the particular crime at issue.

However, one of the earliest cases encountered by Jung in the Burghölzli proved dramatically criminal indeed. Every routine exploration had been carried out on this young woman patient before she entered Jung's care. Originally diagnosed as a melancholic, following the tests she was reclassified as schizophrenic – or, in those days, suffering from dementia praecox. This was Bleuler's diagnosis. Too young and inexperienced openly to challenge his chief's conclusions, Jung felt Bleuler was wrong, and his first interview with the woman led him to believe that here was a case not of schizophrenia but of deep depression. Already influenced to a minimal extent by his reading of Freud's *Interpretation of Dreams*, his word-association tests were now reinforced by attempts to interpret the patient's dreams. The results were spectacular. Combining two relatively new techniques he uncovered material – directly, he later said, from her unconscious – which all previous tests had failed to produce. Many a novelist would have welcomed the material as it emerged and completed a dramatic pattern.

Still a young girl, the patient had fallen in love with the son of a wealthy industrialist, but fierce competition from other girls made her doubt her chances of winning the man despite her prettiness. A rumour eventually reached her that the industrialist's son did not, in fact, care for her, and partly out of pique she decided to marry another, less attractive man.

Five years went by. The marriage was reasonably successful, and she had two children. Then, one day, an old friend arrived at the house, and they began reminiscing about the past. 'Your marriage came as a shock to that young man,' she said, naming the son of the wealthy industrialist. She then revealed what turned out to be traumatic for the patient. The wealthy man's son *had* cared for her, and she need never have married her second choice.

No one else in the Burghölzli had uncovered any of these remarkable details, and Jung now found, with growing excitement, that her depressions began from the day of her friend's visit. Far more tragic events slowly and reluctantly came to the surface as Jung pressed home his new techniques.

Several weeks after the shattering revelation the woman was bathing her four-year-old daughter when she noticed the child sucking the sponge, an act full of hazard in an area where the water was very impure. As if in a trance, she continued staring at the child without interfering, and then compounded her crime by deliberately, if somnambulistically, giving her son a glass of impure water to drink. In the event the boy survived, but the girl died. Simultaneously the woman's depression deepened, and she began to behave so irrationally that she was taken into a mental hospital, finally passing into Jung's hands at the Burghölzli. Still a relatively raw recruit to psychiatry, Jung found himself responsible for a woman who was clearly a murderess and had already attempted suicide. Moreover, he strongly disagreed with his colleagues' diagnosis and their proposed course of treatment. In his view this was a case of 'psychogenic disturbance and not . . . of schizophrenia'.

But how to treat her? Should he speak frankly to her and confront her with the real cause of her illness? 'I was faced with a conflict of duties altogether without precedent in my experience.' Collectively his colleagues were against confronting her with the truth which might simply, in their view, drive her 'even more crazy'. In his autobiographical study Jung commented: 'To my mind the effect might well be the reverse'; but gives no convincing reason why he arrived at this conclusion. Steeped as he already was in the beginnings of psychological mysteries, it seems unlikely that he would have proceeded blindly into the unknown, but the conclusion of his own account of the case reads somewhat romantically: 'to accuse a person point blank of murder is no small matter. . . . But the result was that in two weeks it proved possible to discharge her and *she was never again institutionalised*.'[18] (My italics.)

One takes Jung's word for it, but a glimmering of doubt arises about the sustained efficacy of merely unravelling the story at the surface level to the patient. Abreaction was not a word in his vocabulary, at this stage, and whether his treatment re-created the experience remains unclear. The condensed account in his reminiscences could be misleading, and conceivably the 'two weeks' did successfully generate a cathartic reaction.

Certainly, Jung decided to mask the truth he had discovered about Frau X from his colleagues, for fear they might invoke the law to deal with a person who was clearly a murderess. 'Fate had punished her enough: it seemed to me more meaningful that she should return to life in order to atone . . . for her crime.'

The library of books he now read developed a parallel growth and rhythm with his creative research. A wide range of psychological, psychiatric and medical books available at the turn of the century were reinforced by such philosophers as Schopenhauer, Kant, Nietzsche and Hartmann. They opposed the 'natural sciences' to the 'philosophy which engaged him as a medical student', but before the end of his student period he was to find the two approaches reconciled in Krafft-Ebing's *Handbook of Psychiatry*, a dramatic moment in his intellectual development.

Meanwhile his medical dissertation was published in 1902. Delivered before the Faculty of Medicine in the University of Zürich, the 1902 title-page stated that the author was at that time First Assistant Physician in the Burghölzli Clinic. As we have seen, it dealt with *The Psychology and Pathology of So-Called Occult Phenomena* and opened with Hélène Preiswerk's story under the title 'A Case of Somnambulism in a Girl with Poor Inheritance (Spiritualistic Medium)'.

Summing up the case, Jung admitted that there was something 'extremely immoderate, unsteady, almost protean' in Hélène Preiswerk's character which was only partly explained by the fluctuating psychological states of puberty. There remained a pathological residue which expressed itself in bizarre reactions. 'It gets its specific cast from certain features that must be regarded as hysterical.' Her semi-somnambulistic states in which table movements, automatic writing and hallucinations occurred he described as 'the appearance of various automatisms which point to the activity of a subconscious independent of the conscious self'.[19] Dealing with the first category – table movements – he countered any suspicion that Hélène Preiswerk was , consciously manipulating the table herself, by claiming that 'unconscious motor phenomena are not only a frequent occurrence among hysterical persons', but could also be induced fairly easily in normal persons. 'With most subjects', given enough patience, 'motor automatisms will be obtained'.[20] Thus, tables could be made to react by normal as well as abnormal people through unconscious motor impulses.

Elaborating the exposition, he said that 'through the gradual increase of auto-suggestion the motor areas of the arm are isolated from consciousness' or, in other words, 'the perception of slight motor impulses is veiled from the mind'. As the analysis developed it became less clear: 'The intention to formulate necessarily affects the motor component of the verbal representation most of all, thus explaining the unconscious overflow of speech impulses to the motor area.'

Jung's attempts to explain the psychic mechanisms underlying automatic writing, the second category, did not develop in any great detail because 'the automatic writing of our patient never came to very much'. He then admitted that most of the experiments were carried out in the dark and in most cases the automatic writing 'passed over into semi-somnambulism or ecstasy'.

The third category, hallucination, led into a most complex exposition of contributory forces. Any attempt to summarise the densely reasoned details of his very impressive thesis is impossible without rewriting it, and the serious reader must turn to the original for accurate re-capitulation; but certain key sentences do reveal the trend of Jung's thought: '. . . the patient was in a state of partial hypnosis and furthermore a subconscious personality having the closest ties with the speech area had already constituted itself'.[21]

Postulating a split-off part of Hélène Preiswerk's personality, Jung argued that it seized upon the nearest available material in association with Jung's family and spoke with the voice of his grandfather. He also suggested that hypnagogic images such as distinguished Hélène's performances when she reincarnated historical figures were associated with the dream images of normal sleep. Moreover, mentally disturbed people frequently believed themselves to be Napoleon, the King of Spain or Hamlet, and there were connections between the origins of these delusions and the hallucinatory personalities speaking through Hélène Preiswerk. As for the swarm of open and secret love affairs, sexual adventures and illegitimate births which characterised some of Hélène's outpourings, these could be traced, Jung said, to her budding sexuality. 'From this point of view the whole essence of . . . her enormous family is nothing but a dream of sexual wish-fulfilment.'

Throughout the thesis Jung's attitude is subtly ambivalent. On the one hand he appears anxious to give scientific respectability to para-normal phenomena by elaborate observation, research and technical analysis. On the other his temperamental predisposition to believe in the psychic is qualified by the psychological explanations he elaborates. The balance is so beautifully maintained in many sections of the thesis that it almost becomes a work of art. In others he blatantly accepts occurrences without sufficient evidence to convince the strictly scientific mind.

Grossly oversimplifying the theme of the thesis, it tried to answer the infinitely complex question: Are psychic powers rationally explicable as special psychological states or are they powers of a different order?

Either Jung wrote the thesis at a time when his relationship with Professor Bleuler was very good, or else he mouthed the usual acknowledgements which accompany academic works of this kind: 'I would like to express my warmest thanks to my reverend teacher Professor Bleuler for his friendly encouragement and the loan of books. . . .' Later their relations became very ambivalent.

Chapter 8

Family Life Begins

DURING THE WINTER OF 1902–3 Jung took leave of absence from the Burghölzli and went to study under Janet in Paris, where his relative poverty sometimes drove him to eat nothing more than a bag of roast chestnuts for dinner.[1] By now he had already met his future wife, Emma Rauschenbach, daughter of a wealthy Schaffhausen industrialist. According to his son Franz, Carl Jung met his wife-to-be when she was little more than a small girl.[2]

According to Stephen Black, by a remarkable premonition he selected Emma at the age of sixteen, when he first saw her at the top of a staircase of a famous Zürich hotel. ' "She was about fifteen or sixteen . . . and I said to a friend of mine – I was twenty-one then – I said, 'That girl is my wife.' " '

' "Before you had spoken to her?" '

' "Yes – 'That's my wife.' I knew it." '[3]

The stories can be combined without conflict. At first glance it is astonishing that in his reminiscences Jung should have made only two brief references to her, but in the light of subsequent events the omission becomes explicable. For the moment a long acquaintance with this attractive girl blossomed into full-scale romantic love, and Gerhard Adler, who has read the love-letters which passed between them, testifies to their colour and beauty.[4]

The relationship followed a completely conventional pattern except for one important fact. When Jung first proposed to Emma she turned him down, and it must have come as a considerable shock. However, there were romantic evenings beside the lake, boating picnics on hot summer afternoons, trips to the mountains, and a number of quarrels and reconciliations. On his second proposal she accepted him, but one other fact remains in dispute – whether they slept together before they were married. All the evidence is against such an 'unnatural occurrence' as one survivor from those days, Alphonse Maeder, put it. It remains one of the supreme ironies of psychoanalytic history that Jung, who modified the sexual etiology of human behaviour in his theoretical models, was tormented by the threat – and in at least one case the reality – of his own unfaithfulness, while Freud, a stalwart defender of the sexual faith, remained unremittingly within the fortress of monogamy.

Whether as a last fling before marriage, or because his career demanded it, the Parisian visit preceded his marriage by a few months and produced some unexpected reactions. Certainly he attended the lectures and demonstrations which Janet was then giving, but he also surrendered himself to the pleasures of a city which so exhilarated him that it induced 'a mild state of intoxication'. He visited Notre-Dame, the Louvre, the Bastille, Versailles and the Boul Mich; he spent hours wandering along the Seine, but came to the conclusion that most of the books offered by the *bouquinistes* were rubbish. There is little evidence available of his companions, or even which cafés he frequented, but at least two well-informed sources agree that 'he was not a particularly assiduous student'.[5]

Janet had become the Professor of Experimental Psychology at the Collège de France in 1902 and, as was the rule for such remote beings, he lectured only once a week, which would have exposed Jung to the dangers of enforced leisure. Janet's lectures explored the normal and morbid emotions, consciousness, hysteria and psychotherapy, all subjects which already fascinated Jung. Freud, of course, had already published his *Studies in Hysteria* (1894), giving his reasons for rejecting Janet's theory that hysteria resulted from congenital mental weakness which facilitated the 'splitting of consciousness'.[6] Freud believed that the active process of repressing an incompatible idea resulted in the substitution of a somatic innervation or conversion; that is, a powerful sexual impulse, when repressed, was converted into hysteria. Jung must have been familiar with their conflicting views, and he continued to read, sporadically, while in Paris. He met a number of assistants in the Experimental Psychology Department, and, before he left, one encouraged him to visit them again as soon as possible – 'since Paris is far ahead of anywhere else'.

He returned to the Burghölzli early in 1903, full of talk about Janet and his theories, but professional matters were, temporarily, overwhelmed by his marriage to Emma Rauschenbach on 14 February 1903. She was twenty-one, and Jung twenty-eight; she was the product of a fine old Swiss German family and the special education which accompanied her class, he came from quite different roots. A very rare photograph taken in 1902 shows a stout young man with white waistcoat, watch-chain, drainpipe collar, bow tie and immaculate cufflinks, looking with all the pride of a brilliant young doctor at the camera, while Emma, in long skirts and a blouse reaching high up around her neck, stands shyly close to him with a touch of apprehension in her face. A good-looking young woman, she could not be said to be beautiful, but she had great charm and a social grace not revealed by the photograph. No one could deny her attractions or her wealth. They spent their honeymoon at Lake Como, and much later Jung said to a psychiatric colleague, 'Honeymoons are tricky things. I was lucky. My wife was apprehensive – but all went well. We got into an argument about the rights and wrongs of distributing money between husbands and wives.' Laughing, he added, 'Trust a Swiss bank account to break into a honeymoon in Italy!'[7]

All Jung's financial troubles were now definitely at an end, and his life-style underwent a number of changes. Unexpectedly, he did not leave the Burghölzli and set up home outside. He occupied a three-roomed flat below the top floor on the right of the entrance to the main building, immediately above Eugen Bleuler's flat. A long, low-lying construction, symmetrically arranged with projecting blocks at either end and a grouping of three entry-blocks at the centre, the Burghölzli was built on the heights overlooking the lake of Zürich. The building had a certain austere elegance, but there were trees and gardens at the front and a line of hills at the back. Jung from his front windows overlooked the trees and gardens, which pleased him.

Meals were no longer institutional meals, but specially cooked to his taste, clothes were no longer a random accumulation of convenient garments, but selected and bought in his wife's company, entertaining no longer a near-impossibility, but easily available. None of this was allowed to interfere with the iron routine of his work.

The first years of his married life were successful and suffered no more than the 'misunderstandings' which he thought common to most married couples.[8] Within a year Emma Jung was pregnant, and a daughter, Agatha, was born on 26 December 1904. There followed Anna, born 8 February 1906; Franz, born 28 November 1908; Marianne, born 20 September 1910; Emma, born 18 March 1914. Whether Jung practised contraception is not established, but in a letter to Freud he wrote that all was well with the family except for another 'false alarm' about a possible pregnancy. 'One tries every conceivable trick to stem the tide of these little blessings but without much confidence. One scrapes along one might say from one menstruation to the next. The life of civilised man certainly does have its quaint side.'[9] Ellenberger recorded, 'His wife was an exceptional woman, an extremely capable mother and housewife with lively interests who became his collaborator and [eventually] applied his psychotherapeutic methods.'

They spent the remaining months of 1903 adjusting to married life and finding deep satisfaction at many levels. In the monastic atmosphere of the Burghölzli hints of a surrender to the fleshpots surrounded the newly married couple. Nonetheless, Emma charmed Jung's colleagues, and even Bleuler agreed that Jung had made 'a very good choice'. It was not easy being married to a dedicated man, and at the outset Emma knew that her husband was just such a person. The story is told that when in the winter of 1904 he developed a severe cold and Emma tried to keep him in bed he said, 'The Burghölzli is much more important than a brood of second-rate bugs,' and promptly went off to work.[10]

If the years 1903–4 dramatically changed his personal life, they also brought profound changes in his professional development. As early as

1900, as we have seen, Jung had read Freud's *The Interpretation of Dreams* and laid the book aside without fully grasping what a pioneering work it represented. He was then just twenty-five years old, an earnest, truth-seeking person still groping in the mists of so many possibilities for the precise direction which his career should follow. 'I lacked the experience to appreciate Freud's theories,' he wrote of that time. 'Such experience did not come until later.' Three years' work in the Burghölzli had now given him fresh professional confidence, and in 1903 he once more took up *The Interpretation of Dreams*. Suddenly he detected a coincidence between his own and Freud's work which was at first exciting and then disturbing.

The repressive mechanism Freud found at work in dreams he had discovered in his word-association tests. 'In response to certain stimulus words the patient either had no associative answer or was unduly slow in his reaction time . . . such a disturbance occurred each time the stimulus word had touched upon a psychic lesion or conflict.' Differences arose in the 'content' of repression. Where Freud found a hidden sexual impulse or experience, Jung was 'familiar with numerous cases of neurosis in which the questions of sexuality played a subordinate part'. There remained enough parallels between their work to excite Jung when he realised that hundreds of miles away in Vienna another pioneer was probing into related problems and getting closely similar answers, but anxieties followed close on the heels of the excitement. Was this man about to trump every card he played, pioneering one step ahead in matters which Jung thought purely the result of his own original research? It had been the fate of many a scientist working in his laboratory, and the human psyche had in some respects become his laboratory. Moreover, the years 1903–5 concentrated a number of achievements which seemed to predict not an original scientific but a brilliant university career for Jung as an academic psychiatrist. Appointed First Oberarzt at the Burghölzli – roughly equivalent to Clinical Director – he became in effect Deputy Director under Bleuler of the whole hospital. Within a few months he also took over direction of the outpatients department and was granted the much coveted title of Privat Docent or, in English terms, Lecturer in Psychiatry at Zürich University. In the same year he also became senior physician at the Psychiatric Clinic.

At this time hypnosis was commonly used in treating patients, and whenever he lectured Jung frequently investigated patients by this means. One early case remained in his memory all his life. It concerned a fifty-eight-year-old lady who entered the lecture theatre on crutches, led by her maid, and quickly plunged into an account of her illness which centred around the painful paralysis of her left leg. It had been Jung's intention to use the patient to demonstrate hypnosis to the students, but when he interrupted the flood of her narrative to say 'I am now going to hypnotise you', suddenly and without any effort on his part she fell into a trance. An uninterrupted flow of words then poured from her, vividly evoking the most remarkable dreams, and Jung, unaware at this stage of the real nature of the unconscious, thought she must have passed into a 'kind of delirium'. As he later wrote, 'the situation was gradually growing rather uncomfortable for me. Here were twenty students present to whom I was going to demonstrate hypnosis', and here the patient had promptly hypnotised herself. He now tried to bring the patient awake, without success, and suddenly felt alarmed. Could it possibly be that he had, inadvertently, probed into a latent psychosis which had taken possession of the patient and might firmly maintain its grip for an indefinite period? Reverting to the crudest form of stimulus, he shook the patient by the arm, and still she did not respond. Between concealing his alarm from the students, working on the patient and thinking ahead to a final course of action he felt himself sweating; and then at last the woman suddenly came awake. Immediately Jung said, 'I am the doctor, and everything is all right.' Almost simultaneously she cried out, 'But I am cured!' – and thereupon threw away her crutches and walked out of the lecture room. Jung tried to cover his embarrassment by saying at once to the students, 'Now you've seen what can be done with hypnosis!' Convinced that she would relapse within twenty-four hours and her leg become paralysed again, Jung contacted her a few days later, but she was still walking freely, and insisted later that she was completely cured.

In the middle of the summer semester the following year she suddenly entered the lecture room once more, and now she complained of acute pains in her back of very recent origin. Pressed to explain the precise date of the new symptom, she finally traced it to the day she read the newspaper account of Jung's new lecture course, and Jung immediately wondered what special significance he, as a person, had for her. Once more he began his lecture, again she fell into a trance, and precisely as before the pain in her back vanished after she recovered consciousness. Fascinated by the exact repetition, Jung asked her to wait until the lecture was over, and then began to explore her history more rigorously. Detail by detail the mosaic of her life fitted into a pattern which revealed its hidden meaning. She had been married twice, and a feeble-minded son, the result of the first marriage, not only played a major part in her life but was also at that moment holding a very minor job in the Psychiatric Department of the Burghölzli. Unaware of his identity for the obvious reason that he went under the name of his mother's first husband, Jung had failed to see any connection between the two. Carried away on the tide of recollection, the mother now revealed that she had desperately wanted a brilliant son who would become a distinguished man, and suddenly the pieces of the psychiatric puzzle fell into place. She had projected her idealised son on to Jung, and not only saw in him a man who could work miracles but also actually made sure that a miracle was, under her very eyes, performed – by curing herself.

She had realised her dream vicariously through Jung, adopted him as her son 'and proclaimed her own miraculous cure far and wide'. As Jung finally commented: 'In actual fact she was responsible for my local fame as a wizard and since the story got around I was indebted to her for my first private patients.' In effect his psychotherapeutic practice was launched by a mother 'putting [him] in place of her mentally ill son!'[11]

With refreshing simplicity Jung finally remarked about the case: 'Naturally I explained the whole matter to her in all its ramifications. She took it very well and did not again suffer a relapse.'[12] This was the language of the untrained layman, implying that exposition was sufficient to bring about a cure, but it fitted, in one sense, those unsophisticated days and the fact that this was his 'first real therapeutic experience'.

For a time Jung continued to use hypnosis as an instrument of investigation for university demonstrations, but gradually he found it more and more unsatisfactory. During 1904–5 he organised a special laboratory for experimental psychopathology, assisted by Franz Riklin and Ludwig Binswanger. Among his other associates were two Americans, Charles Ricksher and Carl Petersen, who wrote papers for American journals which pioneered Jung's reputation abroad. Jung directed research into psychic reactions, as in the word-association tests, and wrote his paper 'On the Psychological Determination of Facts'.[13] Ludwig Binswanger reinforced the impact of his work by writing a doctoral thesis around what was then known as the psychogalvanic effect.[14]

Another case-history still available in the archives of the Burghölzli concerned a woman regarded as incurably mad by some of the staff. Jung persuaded her to tell him three of her dreams, and the process of dream recollection accelerated day by day. Within a short time he was under pressure to release her into the outside world again, and at last decided to take the risk. In his final interview he made a determined effort to retest her sanity, and when he asked her whether she had dreamt the night before she replied: 'Yes – but I am not going to tell you what I dreamt.' This he took to be a reaffirmation of a great improvement in her rationality. Written across her case-history in Jung's handwriting is the word *Erlassen* – 'discharged'.[15]

By now Jung was becoming steadily more embroiled in the work and thinking of Freud. His rereading of *The Interpretation of Dreams* had left a lasting impression, but he did not carry out his intention of addressing a letter to Freud. Academic life still strongly attracted Jung, and he was about to complete yet another paper intended to advance his university career, but Freud was definitely *persona non grata* in the academic world, and any connection with him might have been damaging. Important people mentioned him surreptitiously, but at congresses he was discussed only in the corridors and never on the floor. 'Therefore the discovery that my association experiments were in agreement with Freud's theories was far from pleasant to me.'[16]

Uncertain whether to mention Freud when he first published his findings in 1906,[17] Jung suddenly heard what he described as the devil whispering to him that such an acknowledgement was quite unnecessary: 'After all, I had worked out my experiments long before I understood his work.' His No. 2 personality then intervened to protest, 'If you do a thing like that as if you had no knowledge of Freud it would be a piece of trickery. You cannot build your life upon a lie.'

Whereupon the devil stopped whispering in his ear, the prowling person who wanted to exploit the very repression with which Jung's discoveries were so much concerned capitulated, and Jung decided openly to sympathise with Freud and his findings. Nonetheless, from the very beginning a sense of rivalry existed on Jung's part, and this conflict over the ethics of priorities was first to enliven, then dismay and finally split apart many members of what became the Wednesday Viennese circle.

In March or early April of 1906 Jung at last brought himself to write a letter to Freud, sending him a copy of his Diagnostic Association Studies, and Freud replied on 11 April 1906:

Dear Colleague,
Many thanks for sending me your Diagnostic Association Studies which in my impatience I had already acquired. Of course your latest paper Psychoanalysis and Association Experiments pleased me most because in it you argue on the strength of your own experience that everything I have said about the hitherto unexplored fields of our discipline is true. I am confident that you will often be in a position to back me up but I shall also gladly accept correction.

Yours sincerely,
DR FREUD[18]

How right Freud was. Within a few weeks Jung found himself in a position to take up the cudgels on Freud's behalf in private and public. In public the occasion was the congress in Baden-Baden in May 1906 when Gustav Aschaffenburg, Professor of Psychiatry and Neurology at Heidelberg, vigorously denounced Freud's method as wrong in most cases, objectionable in many, superfluous in all, and completely immoral anyway. According to Ernest Jones, Freud's biographer, Hoche reaffirmed Aschaffenburg, describing psychoanalysis as an evil method proceeding from mystical tendencies and full of dangers to the medical profession. Jung replied to this outburst – but not according to Ernest Jones – very effectively.[19] Jung did not share Jones's view that Aschaffenburg's criticism of Freud's theory was an outright attack from every corner of the scientific and moral compass. 'If I try to answer Aschaffenburg's – on the whole – very moderate and cautious criticism

I do so in order to prevent the baby from being thrown out with the bath water.'[20]

Jung pointed out that Aschaffenburg confined his criticism exclusively to Freud's interpretation of the role of sexuality and that his wider psychology of 'dreams, jokes and disturbances of ordinary thinking' remained intact. Jung by no means committed himself to Freud's point of view, and wrote: 'Freud has not examined all the hysterias there are. His proposition is therefore subject to the general limitation which applies to empirical axioms.' It was even possible, he continued, that there were several forms of hysteria distinct from those with which Freud dealt, and implied that they might, if discerned, be open to quite other than sexual interpretation. Ellenberger states that Jung's paper was a sharp rejoinder to Aschaffenburg, but it is full of compromise and clearly foreshadows the differences which were later to develop between Freud and himself.

It remains true that, in the climate of opinion then prevailing, Jung's paper was a bold and very brave one, risking association with someone regarded by many as disreputable.

Chapter 9

Friendship with Freud –
First Phase

JUNG'S CORRESPONDENCE with Freud was to run on for ten years, finally erupting in a quarrel which bore witness to the complex interplay of two uniquely rich personalities. For the moment all was sweetness and light. On 5 October 1906 Jung wrote thanking Freud for sending him a collection of various short papers,[1] and once again revealed severe reservations: '. . . your therapy seems to me to depend not merely on the affects released by abreaction, but also on certain personal rapports and it seems to me that though the genesis of hysteria is predominantly, it is not exclusively, sexual'.[2]

The letter revealed that Jung had treated a case which first drew Bleuler's attention to Freud's theories and, whereas at that time Bleuler had fiercely resisted Freud's whole approach, he was now 'completely converted'.[3]

Freud's reply on 7 October quickly stressed Jung's ambivalent position: 'Your letter gave me great pleasure. I am especially gratified to learn that you have converted Bleuler. Your writings have long led me to suspect that your appreciation of my psychology does not extend to all my views on hysteria and the problem of sexuality.'

For reasons of principle Freud said he did not propose to answer Aschaffenburg's attack. However, if he did so, his reply would be much more severe than Jung's. He eagerly awaited Jung's forthcoming book on dementia praecox, because 'whenever a work such as yours or Bleuler's appears it gives me the great and to me indispensable satisfaction of knowing that the hard work of a lifetime has not been entirely in vain'.

Still addressing Jung as 'dear colleague', by 6 December 1906, Freud had become much more personal and wrote: 'As you know I suffer all the torments that can afflict an "innovator", not the least of these is the unavoidable necessity of passing among my own supporters as the incorrigible self-righteous crank or fanatic that in reality I am not. . . .' Devoting, as he was, ten hours a day to psychotherapy, it gave him a resistance 'to being urged to accept opinions that differ from my own'. Speaking of the transference process, later to become a theoretical split between them, Freud said that it provided the 'impulse necessary for understanding and translating the language of the ucs [unconscious]'. In fact, he concluded, 'One might say the cure is effected by love. And actually transference provides the most cogent, indeed, the only unassailable proof that neuroses are determined by the individual's love life.' In the many refinements which Freud's theories underwent during the course of his life, already sexuality was giving place to Eros with its constituent emotional elements.

It is possible to unravel from the letters which followed these opening shots between the two great pioneers of psychoanalysis some of the inner workings of Jung's three-year-old marriage. Now a handsome, dashing young man of thirty-one at the height of his powers, with quite new and dazzling professional prizes within his grasp, Jung's horizons were widening in all directions.

A dream occurred one night which revealed what can only be described as a 'restlessness' in his marriage. Under the pseudonym of Mr X in *The Psychology of Dementia Praecox*[4] he recorded the dream in considerable detail, and launched into a labyrinthine interpretation which seemed to overlook a simpler, more obvious exegesis. Concealing the dreamer's true identity, he wrote that a friend once told him: 'I [dreamt] I saw horses being hoisted by thick cables to a great height. One of them, a powerful brown horse which was tied up with straps and was hoisted aloft like a package, struck me particularly.' As he watched, the cable suddenly snapped, and the horse came crashing down. 'I thought it must be dead. But it immediately leapt up again and galloped away. . . .'

In the dream the horse seemed to be dragging a heavy log, but despite this it proceeded at a tremendous pace. Full of galloping impetuosity, the horse was on the verge of causing a second accident, when suddenly another, smaller horse ridden by a second person came up alongside and headed off the runaway. When the first horse threatened to break away again a cab joined in the chase, drove in front of the two horses and brought the first horse to a 'still slower gait'. The account finished with the words: 'I then thought now all is well, the danger is over.'

In a letter, unfortunately missing, Freud, who had read of this dream in *Dementia Praecox*, put his unerring finger on one key to its interpretation. Freud used the phrase 'the failure of a rich marriage', and Jung admitted in his next letter that it referred to 'something essential that is undoubtedly contained in the dream though not in the way you think'.[5]

Jung's wife, of course, was rich, and, although Jung hastened to affirm, 'I am happy with my wife in every way,' the very next phrase qualified that statement: 'So there has been no sexual failure, *more likely a social one*.'[6] (My italics.) It is difficult to know precisely what that meant. Jung now admitted to Freud that his wife had turned him down when he first proposed to her. Currently it was also clear that his new and distinguished colleagues, clamouring for his exclusive attention, frequently overlooked his wife, and Emma Jung – a very intelligent and active woman – did not like this.[7]

An interpretation of the dream different from Jung's readily occurs.

Stresses had arisen in his marriage for very complex reasons, and the 'powerful brown horse' hoisted aloft in straps could easily be seen as Jung, trapped in a net of family responsibility and professional ambition, forced to concentrate on getting to the top. When the cable breaks, instead of killing the horse, it releases him to dash away, but encumbered by a heavy log which still does not prevent his proceeding at 'a tremendous pace'. Freud in a later letter asked why Jung did not interpret 'log' as 'penis', and Jung, without rejecting the analogy, said the chief reason was his inability to present his dream impersonally. 'My wife therefore wrote the whole description (!!).'[8]

If we accept the log-penis interpretation, it so easily reads as a restless desire to break out of the sexuality of his marriage and indulge in an outside affair, which within a very few years was what he did. Jung explicitly denied in his letter of 29 December 1906 that there was any sexual failure between Emma and himself, but then came a very revealing phrase: 'The rationalistic explanation "sexual restraint" [in the dream] is, as I have said, merely a convenient screen pushed into the foreground and *hiding* an *illegitimate sexual wish that had better not see the light of day.*' (My italics.) This can be read to reaffirm a desire for infidelity, but later in the correspondence between the two men Jung openly admits a homosexual element in his relationship with Freud. Was he already aware of this element in his nature, which so much better fits his phrase 'an illegitimate sexual wish that had better not see the light of day'? It would also correspond with the image of dragging the log-penis into the light of day or admitting the homosexual impulse only under powerful duress.

In his book *The Psychology of Dementia Praecox* Jung elaborated a quite different and richly complex interpretation of the dream by means of word-association, and came to a number of very different conclusions. The mountain, or great height, to which the horse was being hoisted, associated with the picture he had recently seen of a skyscraper under construction, clearly linking with his ambition to develop his career in America. The straps carrying the horse, willing or unwilling, associated with the tourists Jung despised, who were hoisted to the highest peaks like 'sacks of flour'. Of course it was possible, he said, to be hoisted up to the top of a profession as well as to labour one's way up, but he himself had 'never needed anybody's help', and the horses in the dream were other people who reached the top 'not by their own efforts'. Attempting to clarify the identity of the dreamer, Jung asked himself for associations with the word 'log' and suddenly recalled that he 'used to be nicknamed the "log" on account of his powerful stocky figure'. Decoding the rider who heads off the first horse in the dream, he saw him as checking his 'sexual impetuosity'. The words 'a rider came up on a little horse' associated with a pregnant woman he had seen in his boyhood and the question he had put to his mother – 'Does she have a little horse under her clothing?' His wife was in fact pregnant at this time.

Thus the dream finally meant to Jung: 'The wife's pregnancy and the problem of too many children impose restraints on the husband. This dream fulfils a wish since it represents the restraint as already accomplished.' Compressing many of the contradictory hopes and disappointments of 'an upward-striving career', it also camouflaged 'an extremely personal matter which may well have been accompanied by painful feelings'.[9]

Several brief letters now followed arranging Jung's first meeting with Freud in Vienna which took place on a cold blustery Sunday (3 March)[10] at ten o'clock in the morning, with Emma present. According to Ernest Jones, Jung 'had much to tell Freud and to ask him, and with intense animation he poured forth in a spate for three whole hours. Then the patient, absorbed listener interrupted him with the suggestion that they conduct their discussion more systematically. . . .'

Ernest Jones told me that Freud regarded the first meeting with Jung as very important because he had seldom encountered a man with such wide-ranging knowledge and so much lively sympathy for the mechanism of neuroses. There was also an intellectual dynamism which injected tremendous verve into their talk, and, above all, Jung's unrestrained imaginative flow captivated Freud. According to Jung, Freud was 'the first man of importance I had encountered; in my experience up to that time no one else could compare with him'. As a result their talk became a marathon exchange which ran on, with brief breaks, for thirteen hours and but for sheer exhaustion might still have continued twenty-four hours later. The two giants of psychoanalysis had met and grappled for the first time in that academic atmosphere which permitted fierce discussion without rancour.

At the outset Jung tried to introduce qualifications into sexual motivation, but Freud said that, as his experience widened, he would find himself in agreement with the Viennese school. In retrospect Jung recalled that a peculiar passion informed every sentence which Freud uttered concerning sex. 'There was no mistaking the fact', he wrote, 'that Freud was emotionally involved in his sexual theory to an extraordinary degree. When he spoke of it, his tone became urgent, almost anxious, and all signs of his normally critical and sceptical manner vanished. . . .'[11]

Jung made no allowance for the double impact of Freud's passionate temperament and the magnitude of his 'discovery', heightened in turn by the twin forces of anti-Semitism and the scorn – if not open abuse – of Viennese medical circles.

Martin Freud, one of Freud's sons, has given his impressions of Jung on his first visit to Bergasse 19: 'Jung had a commanding presence. He was very tall and broad-shouldered, holding himself more like a soldier than a man of science and medicine. His beard was purely teutonic with a strong chin, a small moustache, blue eyes and closely cropped hair.'[12]

Jung never communicated with Frau Freud as Freud later communicated with Frau Jung. Indeed, 'he never made the slightest attempt to make polite conversation with mother or us children but pursued the debate which had been interrupted by the call to dinner. Jung on these occasions did all the talking and father, with unconcealed delight, did all the listening.'[13]

Martin Freud's sister Mathilde went shopping with Jung while he was in Vienna, and as they came into the main street they found it lined with soldiers because the Emperor was about to pass. 'Excuse me!' Jung said abruptly, and simply ran off to join the crowd like an enthusiastic boy.

According to Binswanger, then on the staff of the Burghölzli, he accompanied the Jungs and was received by the Freud family. With Jung he attended the Wednesday meeting of 6 March, and both entered the discussion.[14] Binswanger remained in Vienna while Carl and Emma went to Budapest, Fiume and, at last, Abbazia.[15] There occurred an incident to which Jung later referred in a letter to Freud. It was a remarkable episode in which he developed a sudden infatuation for another woman, and its power matched a similar episode several years later where the details are fully authenticated.

Immediately after the visit Freud wrote to Jung: meeting you 'was most delightful and gratifying; I should like to repeat in writing various things that I confided to you by word of mouth, in particular that you have inspired me with confidence for the future, that I now realise that I am as replaceable as everyone else, and that I could hope for no-one better than yourself . . . to continue and complete my work.'[16]

Jung replied four days later: 'I only fear that you over-estimate me and my powers. With your help I have come to see pretty deeply into things but I am still far from seeing them *clearly*. . . .'[17]

It was in April 1907 at the First International Congress of Psychiatry and Neurology in Amsterdam that the differences between Aschaffenburg and Freud again brought Jung hurrying to the latter's defence. Freud had himself been invited to attend, but he wrote to Jung: 'They were evidently looking forward to my having a duel with Janet. . . . I hate gladiator fights in front of the noble rabble and cannot easily bring myself to put my findings to the vote of an indifferent crowd.'[18] Freud was, in fact, away on holiday when the Congress took place and, suddenly overcome by a qualm of conscience that someone should be fighting his cause in his place, he sat down and wrote another letter to Jung. 'I don't know whether you will be lucky or unlucky but I should like to be with you just now, enjoying the feeling that I am no longer alone.' If Jung needed any encouragement, he 'could tell [him] about [his] long years of honourable but painful loneliness'. These years began, Freud said, as soon as he glimpsed the new world of sexual pathology, when even his closest friends failed to understand what he was trying to do and he reached a point where he himself wondered whether he was 'in error'. In later storms and difficulties he clung to *The*

Interpretation of Dreams 'as to a rock in the breakers', until he reached the calm certainty that this was his chosen path and waited for a voice from the outside world which would respond. When it came, he wrote to Jung, 'It was yours!'

By now Jung's paper replying to Aschaffenburg had brought letters from two German professors warning him that his academic career would be in jeopardy if he continued to defend Freud. Jung replied, 'If what Freud says is the truth I am with him. I don't give a damn for a career if it has to be based on the premises of restricting research and concealing truth.'[19]

The correspondence between the two men was continuous through-out the next few months, technically analysing case-histories, express-ing views about colleagues, exchanging mutual regard and moving – magisterially in some letters – toward the day when their joint theories would be heard and accepted throughout the world. A proliferation of new technical terms occurred in the correspondence which would confuse any layman trying to understand the many case-histories.

Jung clearly outlined in *The Psychology of Dementia Praecox* (1907) his approach to what we now call schizophrenia. Combining prolonged clinical experience with theoretical models, he came to the conclusion that his evidence 'pointed above all to a quite central disturbance'. Janet called it 'dissociation, abaissement du niveau mental', Gross disintegration of consciousness, Neisser disintegration of personality, but Jung gave it quite new meaning: 'Whereas in the healthy person the ego is the subject of his experience, in the schizophrenic the ego is only *one* of the experiencing subjects. In other words, in schizophrenia the normal subject has split into a plurality of subjects or into a plurality of *autonomous complexes*.'[20]

In its most elementary form, splitting took the form of paranoia, and the classic persecution-mania burst through all rational restraints, producing a self-contained second personality. Talking to what appeared to be a perfectly normal patient, Jung would let drop the word 'Freemason', and 'suddenly the genial face . . . changes, a piercing look of abysmal distrust and inhuman fanaticism meets us from his eyes'. The rational, smiling human being has suddenly been converted into 'a hunted, dangerous animal surrounded by invisible enemies'. His second, split personality had risen to the surface. In other words, a highly charged emotional complex had cohered into a personality of its own.

Jung now set out to isolate and describe the many different kinds of complex, from the 'accidental' and the 'normal' to differences in complexes between men and women. In men, the social pressures to succeed produced a preoccupation with money and ambition and their correlative complexes. These preceded the erotic complexes. In women, the priorities occurred with erotic complexes based upon pregnancy, children, marriage and household matters. Permanent complexes tended to occur in patients suffering from hysteria and dementia praecox.

Hysterical complexes could usually be traced to 'one great tenacious complex related to an old secret wound', and the patient could, by careful treatment, become capable of assimilating the wound into a newly healed psyche. In dementia praecox the complexes were deeply rooted, if not permanently fixed, and were very difficult or almost impossible to eradicate. Jung's outpatient clinic at this time was 'studded with [schizophrenic] thorns' which were sharpest among the uneducated whose transferences were so atrociously crude that it made analysis a very tough job indeed.

Jung published his findings in his important book *The Psychology of Dementia Praecox* (1907), where the influence of Flournoy and Janet is still strong, but, if Bleuler receives due acknowledgement, there is no disguising strong reservations about Freud's approach to the subject. Refined definitions enrich the book with complexes related to a single event, others to a continuous situation, some conscious, partly conscious or fully conscious, assessing the kind of emotional charge which distinguishes one from another.

A detailed account of a sixty-year-old woman demonstrates Jung's clinical approach to dementia praecox as we have already seen.[21] As usual Jung surrounded his findings with many cross-references, one of which came from Flournoy, who concluded that a patient named Hélène Smith indulged the romances of her sublimal imagination as a compensation for the mediocrity of her life. Comparing his findings in the case of the sixty-year-old woman with his exploration of sixteen-year-old Hélène Preiswerk, Jung found that sublimal romances in one imprisoned the patient in her delusions but in the other were an attempt to break out of the barriers to her future development. One was suffering from dementia praecox, the other a very powerful recurrent hysteria.

But why was it possible to treat successfully the most complicated complexes in hysteria and not those in dementia praecox? Searching for the cause in *The Psychology of Dementia Praecox*, he repeated the conclusions of his earlier researches: a specific concomitant of the affect – a toxin or poison – 'caused the final fixation of the complex and injured the psychic function as a whole'. Freud took a different view. Selecting a case of dementia praecox, he demonstrated the principle of conversion by which intolerable experiences were repressed and indirectly reappeared in complexes, splitting off parts of the personality.

Their letters continued to weave a network of point and counter-point, converging in some aspects, diverging in others. There is about many of the letters a pioneering excitement, as they hew out paths in unknown forests of the psyche which yield the most stimulating insights only with the greatest difficulty.

No special dispensation inoculates psychoanalysts against vilification of their colleagues, and when Jung went to Paris once more in June 1907 to talk to Janet he came back not only a disappointed but also a vituperative man. Janet, he said, had only the most simplistic understanding of dementia praecox and refused to assimilate the new idea, which left him 'stuck in a groove'. He is, Jung added, 'merely an intellect but not a personality, a hollow causeur and a typical mediocre bourgeois'.[22]

Freud replied on 1 July, and two key sentences are worth quoting. He was very glad that Jung 'gained the impression that the days of the great Charcot [were] past, and that the new life of psychiatry is with us, between Zürich and Vienna. So we have emerged safe and sound from a first danger.'

In July 1907, Jung went off once more for his regular three weeks' military service which involved a working day from five in the morning till eight in the evening and left him 'always dog tired'. When he returned to the Burghölzli he found an enormous backlog of work waiting, and Professor Bleuler and Karl Abraham the first assistant immediately went on holiday. The Secretariat of the Amsterdam Congress was demanding the manuscript of his lecture, and Jung worked far into the night trying to make it more palatable. 'Just now I am working on the latest development of your views – the detailed introduction of sexuality into the psychology of hysteria,' he wrote to Freud on 12 August 1907. Frequently near despair in his struggle with words, he consoled himself that ninety-nine per cent of the public would never understand what he was trying to say. He was becoming more and more convinced, he said, that Freud had got to the heart of the matter when he attributed widespread resistance to their theories as 'based on ill will'.

Karl Abraham, a person destined to become a powerful member of the Freud circle, recurs in a number of letters about this time. Abraham studied psychiatry in Berlin, joined the staff of the Burghölzli at the end of 1904 and became first assistant to Bleuler. Two years younger than Jung, Jones said of him: 'He was alive and hopeful, however irksome or sinister the prospect, and his buoyancy together with the confidence that went with it often contributed materially to bringing about a more successful issue than at first seemed possible.'[23] Jung had a very different view of him while he worked at the Burghölzli. Abraham refused on one occasion to collaborate with Jung in preparing a paper which, Jung said, was just as well because Abraham was definitely not his type. Jung drew a picture of a lone wolf who waited in the background to pick up talk between Bleuler and Jung and then would 'suddenly step into the limelight with a publication'.[24] Developing his criticism, Jung said Abraham was unpopular with patients and intelligent but not original. He admitted a touch of personal venom because he was jealous of Abraham, who also corresponded – independently – with Freud.

On 19 August, Jung admitted to Freud that his powerful ambitions were sometimes responsible for his fits of despair, and Freud replied: 'If a healthy man like you regards himself as an hysterical type I can only claim for myself the "obsessional" type, each specimen of which vegetates in a sealed-off world of his own.' In total contradiction to Jung's view that something strange about his own personality made him repellent to many people, Freud roundly declared: 'all hearts are open to you'.[25]

Between 2 and 7 September, Jung hurried off to Amsterdam for the First International Congress for Psychiatry, Psychology and the Assistance of the Insane. He reported back to Freud on 11 September. The first speaker was an Italian, Bezzola, who inveighed against Freud and Jung, their books, work and even – their income! 'It's enough to make one die of laughter or burst a blood vessel.' Konrad Alt, director of a sanatorium at Achtspringe in Saxony, proclaimed a reign of terror against the new psychoanalytic school, and Professor Zichen of Berlin congratulated him. General applause greeted one attack after another, and when Jung tried to justify their theories all his attempts were said to be faked.

By 25 September, Jung was himself attacking a member of the Viennese circle: 'I consider Eitington a totally impotent gasbag. Scarcely has this uncharitable judgement left my lips than it occurs to me that I envy him his uninhibited abreaction of the polygamous instinct. I therefore retract impotent as too compromising. He will certainly never amount to anything. . . .'

It would distort Jung's letters to select his attacks upon early members of the Freudian circle as representative. They were not. These letters are alive with rigorous thinking and humanity, but his very special relationship with Freud lies at the root of his severe criticism of men like Bleuler, Abraham and Eitington.

Weygand received similar treatment. 'He is a super-hysteric, stuffed with complexes from top to bottom so that he can't get a sensible word out of his gullet: he is even dumber than Aschaffenburg.'

By now, Freud had become for Jung the surrogate father, a person he could warmly relate to and admire, unlike his own real father. Their correspondence was alive with mutual psychoanalytic insights in which Freud played the role of the father analyst, and, at this stage, the positive transference from Jung was strong enough to induce jealousy for those rivals who clamoured for Freud's attention if not love. Jung's attacks were explicable in these terms, but there was another much more important factor, which we have already seen, breaking through in a letter dated 28 October 1907. 'Actually – and I confess this to you with a struggle . . . my veneration for you has something of the character of a "religious" crush.' Claiming that it did not trouble him, he still found it slightly ridiculous if not disgusting, because it had undeniable erotic undertones. 'This abominable feeling comes from the fact that as a boy I was the victim of a sexual assault by a man I once worshipped.'[26]

Extraordinarily, within a few years Freud himself was to admit similar complications, not with Jung but Fliess, in a letter to Ernest Jones: 'There is some piece of unruly homosexual feeling at the root of the matter.'[27] And in another letter to Ferenczi: 'Since Fliess' case. . . . A part of homosexual cathexis has been withdrawn and made use of to enlarge my ego.'[28]

It was interesting to find in the current climate of sexual repression that both the masters of psychoanalysis were prepared to admit bisexual elements in their natures, but it seemed to trouble Jung rather more than Freud.

Recollections of the sexual assault still 'hampered' Jung 'considerably' and made strong transference from any of his colleagues 'downright disgusting'.[29] Worse still, when Freud or Bleuler entrusted him with personal confidences, he feared them from Freud and simply found them offensive from Bleuler. He concluded a letter which had already cost him a great deal to write with the words: 'I would rather not have said it.'

Once more the identity of the person he worshipped as a boy, who assaulted him, needs to be clarified, but, so far, we have no reliable evidence on which to speculate.

What remains clear is that Jung already found himself in a considerable turmoil about the conflicting and what must have been to him deeply disturbing elements in his psyche. Another five years were to pass before he deliberately plunged into that psyche with a form of self-analysis which laid bare a number of new and remarkable truths.

Now Ernest Jones appeared for the first time in Jung's life. He was a young Welsh doctor who was already in touch with Freud and very sympathetic to his theories. Toward the end of November 1907 he travelled to Zürich to spend a week with Jung.[30] The latter had written a very friendly letter looking forward to his visit and inviting him to lunch at what Jones regarded as the ungodly hour of eleven o'clock – an indication of the early rising which distinguished Jung's routine. Jones did indeed receive a warm welcome and was surprised at the charm which this big, powerful man with his strong face and direct manner could generate. In Zürich, at the time, were the Americans Brill and Petersen, both from New York, working with Jung on Veraguth's psychogalvanic phenomenon, and, when Brill began to explain the elements of their work to Jones, Jung interrupted with the words: 'We didn't invite Dr Jones here to teach him but to consult him.'

A group called the Freudian Society of Physicians had been formed in Zürich by this time, and with few exceptions the members were drawn from the Burghölzli and two or three other clinics in Zürich. Twelve members attended the first meeting on 27 September 1907 at which H. W. Maier discussed the sexual symbolism of a catatonia. The second meeting, a fortnight later, brought twenty members together, with Karl Abraham reporting on 'purposivity in sexual dreams', and, according to Jung, everything 'went very well' with the liveliest discussion.[31] By 30 November, Jung records twenty-five members as present, and 'Professor Bleuler opened the proceedings with some priceless doggerel aimed at [Freud's] critics'.

By the time Jones arrived in Zürich, Abraham had decided to leave the Burghölzli and move to Berlin, with the result that he was not, to Jones's regret, present at the session of the Freudian Society which Jones attended. The level of discussion impressed Jones, but if Abraham was absent, the great neurologist von Monakow more than compensated. Bewildered by the new terminology for what he regarded as old-fashioned techniques, von Monakow said, 'I have been practising psychoanalysis for twenty-five years.'

'Jung clashed forcibly with Monakow once or twice,' Jones told me.[32]

But he could change his mood like a chameleon. One moment the big, vibrant, charming chairman of the group and the next a vociferous intervener who, when confronted by opposition, put his case with a vigour which some thought – well – pretty rough. I liked him at the time. He did not mince his words. He was forthright and – at that stage – neo-Freudian to the point where you wouldn't have known the difference. However, there certainly was a difference all right. I could see he seemed very uncomfortable with the idea of monosexuality, not that that was a good description of Freud's position at the time. Freud acknowledged the instinct to eat as at least as strong as sexuality, but one was freely indulged, the other repressed, taboo'd, smothered – hence his concentration on sexuality. I think Jung was partly the ventriloquist victim of Swiss puritanism. He could not go along – entirely – with Freud – even if he wished to – and he didn't. Why he didn't is very complicated. I had the impression at the time that he was suffering from a good deal of stress – some internal conflicts I could only guess at – which he did not bring into the open. He seemed to get along very well with his wife in public. I've no idea what it was like in private. He could be a witty man. When I asked him what he thought of the new Dadaism then sweeping Zürich, he said: 'It is too idiotic for any decent insanity.'[33]

It was during this visit that Jones suggested the idea of 'a general gathering of those interested in Freud's work', and Jung set about organising the first historic Congress of Psychoanalysis which took place five months later in Salzburg.

Jung wrote to Freud immediately after Jones's visit saying that, although Jones was 'convinced of the Theoretical necessity of [Freud's] views', he had not understood them in any depth because of his splendid isolation in London. However, 'he will be a staunch supporter of our cause for beside his intellectual gifts he is full of enthusiasm'.[34]

Chapter 10

Freud – the Second Phase

BY 15 FEBRUARY 1908, Jung was in a depressed state, partly as a result of a prolonged bout of influenza but also because of family troubles. His scientific work came to a stop, he felt gloomy and apathetic, and readily admitted to Freud that 'a complex connected with my family played the very devil with me'. Still organising what was in effect the first congress, he insisted – against the advice of Ernest Jones – on calling it the Zusammenunft fur Freud'sche Psychologie. Jones wanted to use the title International Psychoanalytical Congress, but Jung persisted in sending out the invitations under the title he had selected. From Jones's point of view it converted a scientific into a personal congress and gave Bleuler good reason for criticism.

In the midst of clinical work, lecturing, writing and researching, Jung was simultaneously trying to launch a new psychoanalytical journal, but was considerably disheartened by the complexities of its birth. The American sympathiser and colleague Dr Brill had just translated Jung's *The Psychology of Dementia Praecox* into English, and Jung wrote to Freud saying that Brill would like to attempt a similar translation of *Studies in Hysteria*, which Freud had written in collaboration with Breuer, but Brill wanted to exclude Breuer's theory.

Freud replied on 17 February 1908: 'Since I have not yet had the honour of being translated what you write is a great temptation. But I shall resist it. I should have to ask Breuer for his consent to this disjunction and I don't want to. Besides, I know he would be hurt.' Moreover, he added, his case-histories were no less antiquated than Breuer's theories and did not seem to him worth translating. On 20 February, Jung wrote repeating that the undeserved gift of Freud's friendship was a great moment in his life, but that he desired to develop it, not as equals, but as 'that of father and son'.

By now arrangements for the first organised conference of Freudians was well under way, and Freud wrote on 5 March 1908: 'From your quarter eighteen persons are expected, from Vienna there will be ten or twelve, perhaps as many as fifteen.' The harmony between the two men, vying for surrender to each other's precedence, is clearly shown in Freud's remark: 'If you must give me the honour of the first lecture then I think you ought to deliver the last one.'

A small cloud appeared just before the conference in Freud's letter of 14 April 1908. 'Three of your papers are lying on my desk. The first one you did in collaboration with Bleuler displeases me with its hesitations and concern over the good opinion of E. Meyer.'[1]

Jung had not been well for the previous few weeks. 'All sorts of things' had 'played the devil' with him and another prolonged bout of influenza driven him to go to Baden to take the thermal baths. Obviously the strain of simultaneously lecturing, writing, treating patients, family tensions and organising the first international congress of a rebellious pioneer band were beginning to show. He reacted strongly to Freud's letter. 'Your last letter', he replied on 18 April 1908, 'upset me. I have read a lot between the lines.' Something far more interesting appeared when he replied to the criticism of a joint paper with Bleuler. Lacking as Bleuler does, Jung wrote, sufficient clinical experience, he tends to stress the organic side of dementia praecox. 'I think *very many* cases of dementia praecox are due exclusively to purely psychological conflicts.' However, he added, there were others where 'a physical weakness of some kind precipitates the psychosis'. This seriously modified his previous position, where the stress fell on somatic etiology. Jung apologised for the 'dryness' of his letter and said that there was a smile behind it even if it did not come through.

Freud, all magnanimity, opened his reply: 'Happy Easter! Hard feelings must not be nursed. If I was cranky and seemed so, there is much more room – in this case – for a somatic than for a psychogenic aetiology.' Like Jung, he said, he was completely exhausted by work and a lack of recreation which he feared might interfere with his contribution to the Salzburg congress. Then he added: 'What I mean is I am not angry with you.' Freud proceeded to praise 'not only your insight but also your fine artistic feeling and the seeds of greatness'.

The historic first conference of what was to become the International Psychoanalytical Congress took place at the Hotel Bristol on 26 April 1908. At fifty-two Freud was still a handsome man with greying hair, a fine moustache and a full pointed beard. The power of his presence gave the illusion of height to his personality, but he was barely 5 feet 8 inches tall. When roused to passionate argument, his flashing eyes added a panache which was by no means missing from Jung. Not quite thirty-three, Jung, equally handsome in a quite different way, overtopped Freud with his 6 feet 1 inch, and could, in turn, bring passion into his utterance. Freud had filled out with middle-age, but Jung remained without superfluous flesh. His gold-rimmed spectacles gave his face the austere look of the scholar, but, once carried away in response to a challenge, every feature became animated. Both men could be explosive, and both had to control a considerable capacity for anger. At the Salzburg conference they succeeded.

One of the first social tasks carried out by Jung in Salzburg was to introduce Ernest Jones to Freud. Jones left a description of Jung at variance with the person who emerged in his letters. The letters were serious, sometimes gloomy, referring to overwork, and even sometimes despair. Jones wrote: 'I could best describe Jung as a breezy personality. He had a restlessly active and quick brain, was forceful or even domineering in temperament and exuded vitality and laughter: he was certainly a very attractive person.'[2]

The members of the conference sat around a long table, with Freud at its head, and Jung persuaded Freud to deliver the opening paper on 'The Man with Rats', which he did in a low conversational voice. Beginning at the Continental hour of eight in the morning, he spoke without ceasing for three hours and then broke off to suggest that 'perhaps you have had enough'.[3] Unanimously the conference, still hanging on his every word, agreed that he must continue, 'which he did until nearly one o'clock'.

Curious contradictions arise about Jung's paper. First, it was not published and has not survived in its original form, although Jung contributed an abstract to Rank's report on the conference. Second, Jones's account of the lecture does not correspond to the qualifications of Jung's own ideas which he had introduced in earlier letters to Freud. Talking to Jung and Abraham during the conference, Freud had suggested that dementia praecox differed from any neurosis merely in having a much earlier point of fixation. Abraham and Jung both read papers on dementia praecox at the congress, and Jones commented: 'but whereas Abraham took full advantage of Freud's hints and even came to the conclusion that what was called "dementia" in this disease was due, not to any destruction of intellectual capacities but to a massive blocking of the feeling process, Jung on the other hand merely repeated his opinion that the disease was an organic condition of the brain produced by a hypothetical toxin'.[4]

Drinking coffee with Jones during a break in the conference, Jung confided to him that he thought it a pity Freud had no followers in Vienna worthy of his name. 'They are either Bohemian, degenerate or highly eccentric,' he said, 'and some of them do not even clearly understand the techniques they profess.'[5] Jones flatly contradicted this description of the Viennese delegates to me: 'Certainly their clothing might seem a little flamboyant in keeping with Viennese custom, but they were all serious-minded doctors who faithfully tended their patients, and only an occasional drunken bout brought out what appeared to be an occasional violent prejudice.' They were also, he said, very cultured people, quite at home in 'both German and Classical literature'. However, from the bitterness, backbiting and feuds which slowly overran the Viennese circle, it is clear that there was some truth in Jung's remarks.

A side committee at the Salzburg Congress, led by Jung, decided to launch a periodical exclusively concerned with psychoanalysis, and over the years the *Jahrbuch fur Psychoanalytische und Psychopathologische Forschungen* developed no less than eight satellite periodicals. Originally Jones had suggested that it should be international, accepting papers in three languages, but negotiations with the American psychiatrist Morton Prince to amalgamate his *American Journal of Abnormal*

Psychology came to nothing.[6] Directed by Bleuler and Freud, the appointment of Jung as editor further exacerbated the Viennese section who felt that not only were the positions of power passing to their Zürich rivals, but also even the courtesies of consultation had been ignored.

Fully aware of the jealous undercurrents at work between those from Zürich and those from Vienna, Freud wrote a letter to Abraham after the conference saying that the first gathering was a 'promising test'. The letter commented on the conflict which had arisen between Abraham and Jung, but much deeper doubts and suspicions underlay what could nevertheless be regarded as a historic event. In the eyes of Freud's Viennese circle – Adler, Federn, Rank, Stekel, Wittels and others – they had supported him from the outset, and the enthusiasm with which Freud greeted the newcomer Carl Jung seemed out of all proportion to his contribution. When Freud stood alone, the Viennese had rallied round him, and now here was this upstart Jung receiving over-enthusiastic attention. Jones commented: 'Their attitude was accentuated by their Jewish suspicion of Gentiles in general with its rarely failing expectation of anti-Semitism. Freud himself shared this to some extent.' It was to take two years of smouldering resentment before these early troubles grew to explosive proportions, but after the conference Jung wrote to Freud claiming that 'on balance the results were very good and this bodes well for the success of our *Jahrbuch*'.

As for Freud: 'So you too are pleased with our meeting in Salzburg. It refreshed me a great deal and left me with a pleasant after-taste. I was glad to find you so flourishing and every suspicion of resentment melted away when I saw you again and understood you.' By now Freud was addressing Jung as 'Dear Friend', but Jung still kept his distance with 'Dear Professor Freud'.

The first documented acknowledgement of a side-rift in the Zürich–Vienna circle became evident in Freud's letter. He wanted, he said, to ask Jung a great favour. It had not escaped his attention that trouble arose at the congress between Abraham and Jung which seemed to him most unfortunate. 'I regard [Abraham] as a man of great worth,' Freud wrote, 'and I should not like to be obliged to give him up though there can be no question of his replacing you in my eyes.'

Writing to Abraham almost simultaneously, Freud said: 'I recollect that your paper led to some conflict between you and Jung. . . . Now I consider some competition between you unavoidable and within certain limits quite harmless.'[7] Freud unhesitatingly believed that Jung was in the wrong, but he would not like, he said, any really bad feeling to come between them, and he hoped that Jung might find his way back to views (Freud's views) which Abraham still expressed.

Already signs of the quarrel which was to explode volcanically were clear, but so were Freud's attempts to reconcile the preliminary antagonists. Since Abraham had revealed himself as a faithful disciple, it would have seemed reasonable that Freud should write to Jung and ask him to keep the peace. Instead, he now pleaded with Abraham: 'Thus you will be doing me a great personal favour if you inform him [Jung] in advance of what you are going to write and ask him to discuss with you' any objections.

As if to suspend further comment on an explosive situation, the letters between Freud and Jung turned away to concentrate on the case of Otto Gross. Once an assistant in Kraeplin's clinic in Munich and a member of the first psychoanalytical congress, he was now tragically sick. Freud had sent Gross to Jung for treatment, because his 'self defence mechanism rebelled against' treating him himself. Jung spent long, exhausting weeks analysing Gross, whose symptoms were extravagant, but Jung never seemed to tire, because 'in spite of everything he is my friend' and 'at bottom . . . a very good fine man'.

Chapter 11

The Quarrel Develops

How THE PRESSURE of their multiple activities allowed these two men to conduct their prolonged, detailed and sometimes beautifully written correspondence remains a mystery, but the letters are full of references to 'at long last I have a quiet moment' – 'I write under some strain' – 'I still have an unspeakable amount of work to do'.

Gross in particular occupied Jung for tremendously sustained analytical sessions. He sacrificed days and nights to him, and it is interesting that in 1908 he put more emphasis on early infantile material than he did later in life, spending three weeks exclusively analysing Gross's childhood experiences. Slowly he came to the conclusion that, although Gross had occasional insights into profoundly repressed experiences, 'they were nevertheless overwhelmingly powerful . . . drawing their affects from inexhaustible depths'. Momentarily, as Jung then put it, he 'stopped the leak', but 'the next moment it opened up again'. There followed a marvellously vivid description of the way in which Gross lived in a constantly renewed childhood where, despite every analytic attempt, he still reacted 'like a six year old boy'.

Jung constantly resisted what he knew to be a disastrous diagnosis, but in the end told Freud that it all pointed with terrifying clarity to only one possible conclusion – dementia praecox. Much more significant, in his letter to Freud dated 19 June 1908 he said that for him the experience 'was one of the harshest' in his life because in Gross he uncovered several aspects of his own nature 'so that he often seemed like my twin brother – but for the dementia praecox'. It was almost as if he had a premonition of the breakdown, similar in some respects but different in others, which was to overtake him and might indeed already be fermenting in the immensely complex pressures which surrounded him. He said of Gross, 'he will never be able to live with anyone in the long run and it causes him much sorrow', but he would not have 'missed this experience for anything' because it gave him 'a unique insight into the nethermost depths of dementia praecox'.

By July the quarrel with Abraham was troubling Freud again, and he wrote to Abraham: 'I greatly deplore your quarrel. . . . I am afraid that, with the exception of what you did recently for my sake, there is a lack of desire for a satisfactory harmony on both sides.' Abraham must, he added, for the sake of the cause, find some means of reconciliation.

This was loading the evidence in favour of Jung. Abraham had made conciliatory overtures to Jung, and he had ignored them, yet here was Freud complaining of Abraham's 'lack of desire for . . . harmony'.

When Abraham again made a brief reference to the Zürich situation, it disturbed Freud afresh. Abraham was at some pains to explain his 'tactlessness' in a letter dated 16 July, which steadily mounted, as if carried away by its own momentum, until it read like a wholesale condemnation of the Zürich group.

Freud replied on 20 July saying that he was thinking of going to Zürich where he intended to try to clear up the feud himself. 'I think a great deal more favourably about Jung, but not about Bleuler. On the whole it is easier for us Jews as we lack the mystical element.'

By 23 July he reinforced that message in a long letter which acknowledged Abraham's paper on dementia praecox, and said that it was marred for him because it brought his quarrel with Jung into the open again. Freud found himself in a difficult position. He now revealed clearly, for the first time, that he had originally thrown out the dementia praecox idea to both men 'and had no intention other than that each should take it up and work on it independently'. Now he complained, with somewhat tortured logic, that Abraham, by adopting it, was forcing Jung into opposition. Again Freud made no reference to the real kernel of the trouble: Jung had rejected the formulation of the idea as presented to him by Freud and insisted on his own interpretation.

'When I go to Zürich . . . at the end of September', Freud continued to Abraham, 'I shall try to make good what can be made good. Please do not misunderstand me. I have nothing to reproach you with.'

In September, Freud duly travelled to Zürich and spent several days talking far into the night with Jung – exploring, in the first place, his relationship with Abraham. He explained to Jung, Jones thought very unwisely, Abraham's difficulties and suspicions, and Jung expressed regret at what had happened.

Freud stayed for three days between 18 and 21 September, in Jung's Burghölzli flat and established a warm relationship with Emma Jung, who found Freud 'a delightful man – on the gloomy side perhaps – I talked to him once about my own troubles'.[1]

Jung took Freud round the wards and brought his special attention to the case of Babette S. A phenomenally ugly old woman, Freud listened to Jung's analysis of her case with what Emma later referred to as 'an odd puzzled look'. Brought up in the dirty, narrow streets of Zürich old town, with a drunken father and a prostitute sister, Babette succumbed to a paranoid form of dementia praecox at thirty-nine, and when Jung first met her had been institutionalised for twenty years. He explained to Freud what it cost him in long, tormented hours of observation, talk and analysis to try to decode the completely irrational utterances of this bewildered, unkempt old lady whose case seemed, instantly to Freud, incurable. When she cried, 'I am Socrates' deputy,' what she really meant was 'I am falsely accused like Socrates.' Or 'I am the double polytechnic irreplaceable' meant 'You may think I am a very inferior person but in fact I am very important.'[2] Anticipating Ronald Laing, Jung saw that there was a method in her madness, a special logic, the key to which enabled a good analyst to decode many of her outpourings. Freud listened 'with that shrewd half sceptical look'[3] which characterised his reaction to what he called 'surface analysis' but accepted Jung's proposition that hidden behind the demented split-off person there remained a background personality which could still be called normal. As Jung pointed out, it needed only a burst of actual physical illness for that normal personality to reassert its ascendancy. Freud's final comment was revealing: 'You know, Jung, what you have found out about this patient is certainly interesting, but how in the world were you able to bear spending hours and days with this phenomenally ugly female?' Such a reaction had never occurred to Jung. He looked upon her as a pleasant old lady who 'had such lovely delusions and said such interesting things'.[4] Acknowledging to Freud his failure with Babette – because she had been sick far too long – Jung still believed that sympathetic identification with the patient's personality and suffering did have a therapeutic effect.

According to Jones, during the September visit Jung revealed to Freud that he had resigned his job as assistant to Bleuler at the Burghölzli, but a later letter from Freud to Jung stated that Bleuler had in fact deprived Jung of 'a teaching post'.[5]

By October, Jung was once more 'undergoing another exhausting bout of military duty' which, combined with family troubles, the Bleuler battles and guerrilla warfare with Abraham made him lose his zest for work – a rare experience. However, by the time his military service finished on 30 October, he was almost his old self again.

On 12 November, Freud was writing to Jung: 'I agree with you completely. It is an honour to have plenty of enemies!' – and the phrase had repercussions all over again with Abraham. In the same month Abraham sent Jung his paper 'Intermarriage between Relatives and Neurosis' for publication in the *Jahrbuch*, and now fresh troubles developed between them.

Jung rounded off this phase of their still unfinished feud with the melancholy comment that it was all too depressing and meant that he 'dare not ask [Abraham] for further abstracts'. He bore him no grudge, he concluded. He 'wanted to live at peace with Abraham but Abraham had to make a show of goodwill as well'.

For the moment, as another preliminary skirmish with Jung subsided and peace among his followers was temporarily restored, Freud gave his attention to a major rearrangement of his domestic life. His sister, Frau Rosa Graf, had a flat opposite his, and when she decided to leave it he moved in with his family, destroying in the process a mass of documents and letters, including some from Jung, Abraham and Ferenczi.

Chapter 12

First Visit to America

FOR NEARLY SIX YEARS Jung's marriage had pursued a reasonably equable course, with no more than the usual number of quarrels and misunderstandings. As we have seen, three children were born – Agatha (26 December 1904), Anna (8 February 1906) and Franz (28 November 1908). Whenever his wife was about to be confined Jung dropped all his professional duties and gave his full attention to her.[1] Freud sent him a congratulatory telegram on the birth of Franz in 1908, and Jung replied by letter: 'You can imagine our joy.' The birth was easy, and Jung commented: 'Too bad we aren't peasants any more otherwise I could say – Now that I have a son I can depart in peace.'

On the evening before the birth, when Emma's labour-pains were beginning, Jung was talking to his four-year-old daughter Agatha. He pulled her on to his knee, kissed her gently and said, 'What would you say if you got a little brother tonight?' Instantly and without a moment's reflection Agatha retorted, 'I should kill him.' Freud had pointed out, and Jung confirmed, that in childish jargon the phrase 'I will kill him' has a very different connotation from its adult equivalent. The expression 'to kill' looked very alarming but in child language only meant 'get rid of'.

The baby was born in the very early morning and, when 'all traces . . . had been removed together with the bloodstains',[2] Jung went into his daughter's bedroom to tell her the news. Agatha looked at first surprised and then very tense, whereupon Jung gathered her up, carried her into his wife's bedroom and showed her the new arrival. Her reaction disappointed the whole family. Emma still looked very wan, the new baby resembled a pink blancmange, and Agatha simply stared with a combination of suspicion and apprehension. Released from her father's arms, she ran out of the room and carefully kept her distance from her mother for the whole morning – unusual behaviour in a child who normally would not leave her mother alone. Suddenly, in the afternoon, she rushed back into the room, flung her arms round her mother's neck and asked anxiously, 'But, Mamma, you don't have to die, do you?'

Agatha had been troubled by the problem: Why is Granny so old, and what will happen to her anyway? Evasive about the facts of birth, Jung had not avoided the realities of death, and Agatha knew that Granny would die, go to Heaven and eventually become a child again. Since, in her logic, somebody had to die in order to make a child, she now worried about the certain death of her mother.

To relieve the pressures on Emma, Agatha was sent to stay with her grandmother for a few weeks, where the old myth about the stork was reiterated in answer to her questions. When she returned home, Jung hired a nurse to cope with the new young baby and the chores involved with a family now numbering five. Still suspicious about her baby brother, Agatha developed a fierce hostility to the nurse, refused to be undressed by her and, when the nurse embraced Franz, shouted at her, 'That's not your little brother – he's mine.'

Clearly Jung did not believe in giving blunt expositions on sexual intercourse to a girl of four, but the bewildering puzzles in her new situation drove Agatha to every kind of disobedience. One blackmailing phrase she reiterated passionately: 'I shall go back to Granny.' To which Emma would reply, 'But I shall be sad if you leave me. . . .' 'Ah,' Agatha would retort, 'but you've got baby brother.'

Inevitably the crucial question arose a number of times: 'Do you still love me too – not just Franzli?' And Emma tried to give her complete assurance, but some indestructible centre of suspicion spread into many areas. One was a fear that her mother had taken to lying. When she said one day, 'Let's go into the garden,' Agatha frowned and said, 'I don't believe it. You're not lying, are you?' Emma was forced to accompany her at once to the garden and demonstrate truthfulness.

Agatha's sense of impending doom expressed itself when she fastened on the story of the Messina earthquake and had to be told over and over again how every bit of wood, every stone in the road and all the people had been destroyed. Then came the question 'Are there any earthquakes in Zürich?' Despite immediate reassurance she came back again and again to the question. Her possible displacement by her brother and the danger of losing her mother's love were obviously symbolised in the Messina catastrophe.[3]

'What enchantment such a child is,' Jung commented to Freud. 'My wife', he added, 'is of course nursing [Franz] herself, a pleasure for both of them.'

Freud, in reply, struggled to relate Agatha's behaviour to th. t of the boy in his famous case, Little Hans, where Freud uncovered a co.nplex based on the boy's belief that all children had peni at birth and were in danger of castration. Jung quite rightly resisted this, clinching his argument with the words 'Agatha has never heard of little Hans.'

By March 1909 the building of a new house at Küsnacht involved long discussions with builders, architects and his wife. Nerves became frayed. Jung's life was already strenuous without these complications. His son, when asked for an account of an average day in his father's life, said that he had a daily schedule which he followed with some regularity. Sometimes he worked with his patients in his consulting-room, sometimes in the garden. His correspondence became a burden which interfered with more important matters. He did quite an amount of his writing on Saturdays, Sundays and during holidays.[4]

The daily routine would include lunch at 12.30 and supper at seven, Jung frequently eating with the family. In leisure hours they shared many things – swimming, building, painting, sailing, camping.[5] Often he took a walk beside the lake with his dog. Occasionally some part of the evening was given over to writing papers, books or letters, especially at this stage letters.

Now that his fame was spreading abroad and invitations to lecture in America, England and Germany multiplied, a colleague said to him one day, 'Why don't you give up your patients?' And he replied, 'Oh, no, I need their stimulus.' In the steadily mounting complications of his professional and social life Emma Jung found herself beginning to be pushed, slowly, into the background. A woman of considerable intelligence and many interests, she tried to keep pace with the mounting demands of her husband's life, but in these relatively early days she had little time to spare to collaborate with him professionally.

Certainly she shared his troubles, and the psychiatric politics of Zürich became the centre of discussions between them. By January 1909, Jung reported to Freud that the 'little [psychoanalytic] circle' in Zürich was thriving with at least twenty-six participants but 'a revolution is going on among our pedagogues'. Oscar Pfister, a Protestant pastor of Zürich, appeared for the first time in his correspondence with Freud as 'a clever man' beginning a campaign to spread Freud's ideas. Jung found his mixture of medicine and theology highly sympathetic, regarded him as altogether a 'splendid fellow', and made him, within a year, a founder member of the Swiss Psychoanalytic Society (1910).

By 19 January, Jung told Freud that Bleuler had 'quietly handed the teaching post for mental hygiene over to Riklin'[6] and had not even consulted Jung about the appointment. Jung commented, 'This is the second time a teaching post has slipped through my fingers not without Bleuler's passive connivance.' It meant a severe setback to his chances of academic promotion, but a much wider and more important horizon had already opened up. In December 1908, Freud's international fame became clearly evident when Stanley Hall, then President of Clark University, Worcester, Mass., invited him to visit America to give a course of lectures. Shortly afterwards, to Freud's delight, a similar invitation was issued to Jung. Freud wrote to Oscar Pfister, 'You too must have been impressed by the great news that Jung is coming with me to Worcestor. It changes my whole feeling about the trip and makes it important.'

In February of 1909, Freud was welcoming Jung's proposed visit to Vienna and saying, 'Splendid that you are bringing your wife.' When Freud telegraphed Jung asking for the date of his arrival in Vienna, no less than two weeks elapsed before Jung replied. 'I have been under terrific strain day and night,' he said, one of the worst stresses being a woman patient who spread scandalous rumours about his conduct. He had treated her some time before and 'pulled her out of a sticky neurosis', but a situation very familiar to any analyst, in which a positive transference became uncontrolled love, expressed itself in her case by an overwhelming desire to have Jung's child. Jung discussed every step in the developing situation with his wife, and two phrases in his letters to Freud indicate that it must have caused considerable disturbance. The woman, he said, 'kicked up a vile scandal solely because I denied myself *the pleasure of giving her a child*' (my italics).

Tempted or not, he protested that he had always behaved like a gentleman to her. 'Before the bar of my rather too sensitive conscience,' he wrote, 'I nevertheless don't feel clean.'⁷

The same letter revealed elements in his nature of which until then he had been either unaware or the power of which he underestimated. 'Until now I had a totally inadequate idea of my polygamous components despite all self-analysis.' He had evidently been through the fire of severe temptation and emerged not only unscathed but also with his whole morality reinforced. The full details of what took place between himself and his wife are not available, but if the episode 'churned [him] up hellishly inside' it also gave him very revealing insights into his own hidden self.

Nor was the story of the patient who preyed on him by any means done. Some time later it came as a shock to Jung to learn that she had begun, all over again, to circulate fresh rumours about Jung's impending divorce and remarriage to a girl student. The identity of the patient can now be revealed. Sabina Spielrein, of Russian origin, practised in Geneva as Dr Spielrein, and her case-history was in fact published in abbreviated form in Jung's Amsterdam lecture, to which he referred as of 'blessed memory'. He now admitted to Freud that he had prolonged his relationship with her over the years because he feared that she would suffer a hopeless regression if he withdrew his support.

Whether Hell knows no fury like a woman scorned may be uncertain, but psychiatry knows no virago like a patient refused the analyst's child, and it seemed as if Sabina Spielrein sought her revenge by trying to wreck his reputation. 'I need hardly say', Jung commented, 'that I have made a complete break.'

Unfortunately that was still not the end of the matter. By 9 March a patient called on Freud and 'spoke of a lady who had introduced herself to him as [Jung's] mistress, thinking [Freud] would be duly impressed by [Jung] having retained so much freedom'. Completely undeceived, Freud saw through the neurotic compulsions behind the revelation and commented: 'to be slandered and scorched by the love with which we operate – such are the perils of our trade, which we are certainly not going to abandon on their account'.

Then came a dramatic reversal of the whole story. Some weeks later Jung told Freud that Sabina Spielrein had suddenly turned up in person at his new house in Küsnacht, insisted on talking to him, conducted the conversation quite rationally and denied that she had ever circulated the defamatory rumours. Moreover she had now freed herself from the overwhelming transference on Jung, and escaped from her emotional prison with nothing worse than a series of weeping paroxysms.

In a letter of considerable humility, Jung recapitulated some of the details of the affair to Freud and said that he was largely to blame for the 'high-flying hopes of [his] former patient'. Mistakenly he had discussed her desire for a child with her 'in a theoretical manner' but 'Eros was lurking in the background'. Referring to the earlier incident in 1907 when he had suddenly fallen in love with a woman in Abbazia, he said 'the Jewess popped up in another form in the shape of my patient'. Next came this revealing phrase: 'Thus I imputed all the other wishes and hopes entirely to my patient *without seeing the same thing in myself.*' (My italics.) Jung clearly realised that it was not a straightforward case of victimisation by 'the sexual wiles of [his] patient'. Driven by a desperate desire to escape from the net which he, in part, had woven, he finally took the unusual step of writing to Sabina's mother, denying that he had ever had sexual intercourse with her daughter and demanding that she should free him from her unwarranted attentions if not persecution. Overcome with remorse, he asked Freud to write to Sabina telling her of his deep distress about the letter which he had so impetuously written to her mother. His letter to Freud went on: 'I ask your pardon many times for it was my stupidity that drew you into this imbroglio.'

Precisely what the whole episode cost Emma Jung is so far unknown, but these first rumblings were soon to be followed by an earthquake. For the moment Jung was reaffirmed in the solidity and success of his marriage, but the experience had been painful and taken a heavy toll.

The big event early in 1909 was the visit of Jung and his wife to Freud in Vienna on 25 March. A remarkable episode occurred during the visit which remained vividly in the memory of Freud and Jung because it delineated a fundamental difference in their approaches to psychoanalysis and a clash between their temperaments. Busily engaged in arguing about occult experiences in what Freud called his second room at Bergasse 19, Jung suddenly felt 'as if my diaphragm were made of iron and were becoming red hot – a glowing vault'.[8] Immediately afterwards came a loud report from a bookcase which made them jump up in alarm fearing it was going to 'topple over on them'.

Recovering from the shock Jung said to Freud, 'There – that is an example of a so-called catalytic exteriorization phenomenon.' Freud scoffed at Jung. 'Oh, come,' he exclaimed, 'that is sheer nonsense.'

'It is not,' Jung said. 'You are mistaken, Herr Professor. And to prove my point I now predict that in a moment there will be another loud report.'

The second detonation, according to Jung, duly followed from the bookcase. Much later in life Jung commented, 'Freud only stared aghast at me. . . . I do not know what was in his mind or what his look meant. In any case the incident aroused his mistrust of me and I had the feeling that I had done something against him.'[9]

It must have come as a considerable shock to a man like Freud, trained in rational inquisition and the austere discipline of science, to find that his chosen Crown Prince, newly endowed with the right of succession, was capable of interpreting such phenomena in super-natural terms. However, such was Freud's devotion to Jung at this stage, or perhaps his need of a suitable successor, that he re-examined all his presuppositions after Jung had left Vienna and wrote a letter dated 16 April 1909 which said, 'At first I was inclined to accept this as proof if the sound that was so frequent while you were here were not heard again after your departure. But since then I have heard it repeatedly. . . .'

Something else had become clear, Freud said, to rob this experience of all significance for him. 'My credulity or at least my readiness to believe vanished with the magic of your personal presence.'

Occasionally, Jung was said to possess what is referred to as charismatic personality, and while he was there, in the room, passionately expounding his beliefs, he carried Freud along with him, but once he had gone. . . .

'I confront the despiritualised furniture as the poet confronted undeified Nature after the Gods of Greece had passed away.'

Jung received what he regarded as these rationalisations with a smile. By sheer ingenuity, human reason could reduce all experiences to logical terms, but there remained the question: Why did supernatural beliefs arise and could logical explanations of something springing from different roots ever be quite satisfactory to those aware of other dimensions?

Writing to Freud on 2 April, Jung said: 'It seemed to me that my spookery struck you as altogether too stupid and perhaps unpleasant because of the Fliess analogy.' Far more important, 'that last evening with you has most happily freed me inwardly from the oppressive sense of your paternal authority'. This seemed a tremendous admission in their profoundly complicated relationship. If Jung was working through his father fixation with Freud, had he at last escaped from a positive transference powerful enough to create distinct erotic under-tones? In the event the answer seemed to be not yet – and certainly not completely.

When at last arrangements were made for the joint American lecture trip, Freud insisted on Sandor Ferenczi, now a distinguished member of the Vienna circle, accompanying him, and the three men agreed to sail together from Bremen on *George Washington* on 21 April. Almost at the outset an incident occurred which revealed the astonishing intensity of the relations between Freud and Jung.

Two very different accounts of this episode are available. When Jones wrote the first, in his biography of Freud, he did not have at his disposal Jung's personal testimony given to Aniela Jaffé in his eightieth year.

> According to Jung, the three men met in Bremen, where Freud was host at a luncheon party, and Jung turned the conversation to the so-called peat-bog corpses in certain districts of north Germany. These were said to be the bodies of prehistoric men who either drowned in the marshes or were buried there. The bog water contained humic acid which simultaneously tanned the skin of any corpse to a mummified toughness while eating away the bones and preserving the hair. Jung was fascinated by the legend and talked on interminably about it until Freud burst out several times: 'Why are you so concerned with these corpses?'
>
> In Jung's own words Freud was 'inordinately vexed by the whole thing and during one such conversation . . . he suddenly fainted'.[10]

According to Jung, when he came round again, Freud said that he was 'convinced all this chatter about corpses meant I had a death wish towards him. I was more than surprised by this interpretation. I was alarmed by the intensity of his fantasies – so strong that obviously they caused him to faint.'[11]

Many years later, E. A. Bennet discussed this episode with Jung and, according to Bennet, he said: 'I had branded myself in becoming identified with Freud. Why should I want him to die? I had come to learn. He was not standing in my way; he was in Vienna, I was in Zürich.'[12]

On the morning following the fainting fit the three men boarded *George Washington* and Freud settled down to keep a diary of the trip.

The weather held good until they ran into one of those thick midsummer mists which sometimes bedevil ships on the Atlantic and Jung was gripped by the primeval majesty of the ship slipping blindfold through the daylight-darkness like some prehistoric monster wallowing 'towards its objective with regular deep-throated cries from its foghorns'. He spoke to Freud about the sense of slipping back into the primeval past, and Freud confessed some sympathy with the feeling when his cabin window revealed a dank wall of mist, and every sound in the ship seemed muffled and subdued to what he called 'the mating cry of the foghorns'.[13]

In the early stages of the voyage the three men appear to have practised dream interpretation on one another. Freud was the least responsive. Struggling to analyse one of Freud's dreams, Jung pressed him for further information: 'Freud's response to these words was a curious look – a look of the utmost suspicion. Then he said, "But I cannot risk my authority!"' Jung added, 'At that moment he lost it altogether. The sentence burned itself into my memory.'[14]

Freud in turn found Jung's dreams baffling. One dream stood out because it pioneered the formulation of the collective unconscious 'and thus', as Jung wrote, 'formed a kind of prelude to my book *Wandlungen und Symbole der Libido*'. In the dream Jung entered an unfamiliar house which was nonetheless his own home. Descending to the ground floor was like descending from the twentieth century into the fifteenth, the floors being of red brick and the furnishings medieval. The house was completely in darkness, and as Jung groped his way about he 'came upon a heavy door and opened it'. Beyond, a stone stairway led down to the cellar. Descending the stairway he found himself 'in a beautifully vaulted room which looked exceedingly ancient'.[15] The room had traces of Roman architecture with bricks interspersing stone slabs. Suddenly his hand found an iron ring, and heaving at the ring the stone opened to reveal yet another flight of steps falling away into pitch-black darkness. With mounting excitement he felt his way down the stairway and entered a cave cut out of solid rock, but now the growing light revealed some broken bones and pottery scattered around two objects which riveted his attention. They were half-decayed human skulls. As he moved towards them, suddenly he came awake.

Freud paid close attention to Jung's recital of his dream and decided at once that the two skulls crystallised its meaning. Jung seemed evasive about the skulls, and Freud pressed him to search for a wish connected with them. At last Freud bluntly asked, 'Whose skulls are they?'[16] It now became clear that the death wish was dominating Freud's thinking, and Jung 'felt a violent resistance to any such interpretation'. Anxious to placate Freud, eager to learn from him and not wanting to re-open dangerous differences, Jung kept his counsel. If he blurted out the truth he felt sure he would encounter 'incomprehension and vehement resistance'. He did not 'feel up to quarrelling', and feared that he 'might lose his friendship' if he insisted on his own point of view. Presently, he settled on an interesting expedient which he rationalised to some extent in his talks with Aniela Jaffé. He wanted, he said, 'to see what Freud's reactions would be if he deceived him by saying something that suited his theories'. He suggested that the two skulls belonged to his wife and his sister-in-law in order to fit Freud's theory, adding to Aniela Jaffé, 'After all I had to name someone whose death was worth the wishing.'[17] In the event Freud's reaction was disappointing. He simply smiled without comment.

Jung later explained his own interpretation of the dream to Aniela Jaffé: 'The ground floor stood for the first level of consciousness. . . . In the cave I discovered remains of a primitive culture, that is, the world of the primitive man inside myself.' So there it was: the great message of the unconscious within oneself, spelt out by the demons of the dream.

Shortly before Jung's dream occurred he had been analysing the premises on which Freudian psychology was founded and what, if any, were their relations to general historical fact. The dream, he said, now gave him the answers. 'It obviously pointed to the foundations of cultural history – a history of successive layers of consciousness . . . it postulated something of an altogether *impersonal* nature underlying the psyche.'

A conversation took place between Freud and Jung as they both stood watching the towers of New York – clustering thick as a forest – rise out of the horizon. Jung later gave E. A. Bennet an account of what was said. Gazing at the skyline with obvious excitement Freud commented: 'Won't they get a surprise when they hear what we have to say to them!' According to Jones, Freud intended to convey nothing more than the shock which pure-minded American intellectuals would register when Freud and Jung revealed the permeation of sex into so many forms of neurosis. Personal ambition was remote from Freud's mind, but Jung immediately commented: 'How ambitious you are.' Again quoting Bennet: 'Me?' said Freud. 'I'm the most humble of men and the only man who isn't ambitious.' Jung replied: 'That's a big thing to be – the only one.'[18]

Whatever interpretation the two men put on the conversation – its details are recollected by Bennet from Jung's account of the episode – the bustling, raw reality of New York quickly overwhelmed such questions.

Arriving on 27 September, A. A. Brill, a founder member of the first Psycho-Analytic Congress, was there to welcome them and the following morning just one reference appeared in the newspapers to Professor Frend's (*sic*) arrival from Vienna.

The tour of New York which followed had been planned with care, efficiency and a determination not to waste time, but Freud hurried off alone to satisfy a desire which had grown over many years to see the Grecian antiquities of the Metropolitan Museum. Then came a tour of Columbia University where Ernest Jones, newly arrived from London, joined them, followed by a dinner on Hammerstein's roof garden. A hectic day concluded with what the Americans regarded as an obligatory visit to one of those early silent movies where one crazy chase is followed by another comic one.

Jung left a vivid picture of those early American days in a letter to his wife from Clark University, Worcester. 'Last Saturday, there was dreary weather in New York. All three of us were afflicted with diarrhoea and had pretty bad stomach aches. . . . In spite of feeling physically miserable and in spite of not eating anything, I went to the paleontological collection. . . .'[19]

Presently the four men boarded an old-fashioned boat with beautiful white decks and steamed out around the point of Manhattan to make their way up the East River through a tangle of tugs, cargo and ferryboats toward Long Island. Still they were in great discomfort. 'It was damp and chilly, we had bellyaches and diarrhoea and were suffering from hunger besides.' Later that evening there was nothing for it but to crawl into bed.

A depressing beginning to what had promised to be a triumphal procession did not really change until they arrived at Worcester. There Jung found the scenery delightful with 'low hills, a great deal of forest, swamp, small lakes, innumerable huge erratic rocks, tiny villages with wooden houses painted red, green or grey . . . tucked away under large beautiful trees'.[20]

They were booked into the Standish Hotel, and at six the same evening met Professor Stanley Hall. Professor Hall's house was large, comfortable and equipped with innumerable cigar-boxes intended to satisfy what Hall obviously regarded as Freud's insatiable appetite for smoking. Jung described to his wife the two pitch-black negroes who served dinner with 'the extreme of grotesque solemnity'. Later he wrote to Emma: 'Today I had a talk about psycho-analysis with two highly cultivated ladies who proved to be well-informed and free thinking. . . .'[21]

From the outset Jung was alone among the visitors in giving two lectures on his own work which did not mention Freud.[22] By contrast, Ferenczi automatically paid tribute to the Master as a preliminary.

Faithfully maintaining correspondence with his wife, Jung wrote that Freud had delivered his first lectures and received great acclaim. 'We are gaining ground here and our following is growing slowly but surely. . . . I was greatly surprised since I had prepared myself for opposition.'[23]

The anxieties which had troubled him since he set foot in America vanished as he found the Americans responsive and open-minded. They were in fact 'the men of the hour', he wrote to his wife. 'I can feel my libido is gulping it in with vast enjoyment.'

Ernest Jones's *Life of Freud* makes no reference to Jung's generous enjoyment of Freud's success. 'Freud is in his seventh heaven,' Jung wrote, 'and I am glad with all my heart to see him so.' However, Jones did not at that time have access to Jung's letters to Emma.

Now occurred an incident with infinite repercussions. On the point of leaving America, Jones went to bid farewell to Jung, and was startled to hear him say that he no longer 'found it necessary to go into details of unsavoury topics with his patients'. Oblique references were permissible in his view but not blunt confrontation in plain language. The dangers of meeting patients socially at dinner afterwards were too great. Jones commented: 'It seemed to me very different from the blunt way in which he had been dealing with serious matters until then.'[24]

As their visit drew to a close, there were many parties and receptions, and Clark University awarded both men honorary degrees. Meticulously Jung wrote to his wife: 'Last night there was a tremendous amount of ceremony and fancy dress with all sorts of red and black gowns and gold-tasselled square caps.'[25]

Still exhilarated by the sheer dynamism of American life, Jung, by now, was 'enormously looking forward to getting back to sea again'. In a revealing passage he confided to his wife: 'I have, thank God, completely regained my capacity for enjoyment so that I can look forward to everything with zest.'

Analysing America, Jung said 'an ideal potential of life has become a reality' but 'it makes one ponder social evolution deeply'. Perhaps, he said, this great experiment carried 'the germ of the end in itself'.

By 21 September he had shaken the dust of America from his feet 'with a light heart' and an aching head – the result of one particularly lethal champagne-party. Embarked on *Kaiser Wilhelm der Grosse*, the weather quickly worsened but in all the vast heavings and rollings which followed Freud and Jung survived without any threat of sea-sickness. 'In all the cabins round about,' Jung wrote, 'unspeakable groans betrayed the secrets of the menu. I slept like a top.'

The crossing occupied eight full days, and they docked at Bremen on 29 September. They were relieved and glad to be back in Europe once more, and not even the enthusiasm which followed them wherever they went in America could quite obliterate Freud's sense that it was for him an alien land. Jung's reaction was very different. He had his reservations, but something in the cannon pulse of American energy and its openness to new ideas appealed strongly to him. He was destined to return many times.

Chapter 13

Struggles in the Zürich Circle

THE AUTUMN OF 1909 brought many shifts and changes in Jung's life. He was feeling 'in top form', but there seemed to be a temporary dearth of patients: 'So far I have only two thin ones. . . .' Whether from faithfulness to the creed or from stress, Emma was undergoing analysis, and Jung said all was well with the family 'thanks to a lot of dream analysis'. Jung himself carried out her analysis and later added: 'The devil seems to have been beaten at his own game.'

He felt justified in the 'small depravity' of treating so-called normal people as well as neurotics, he said, and 'exploiting the situation financially a bit'. Like Freud, he found the differences between 'normal' and 'sick' people narrow and remarked that normal patients would draw 'a fat profit' from wasting his time, which confirmed his morality in taking their fees. One among these patients, an American, crystallised the mother complex which he believed loomed so large in the American way of life. Exaggerating female dominance in American culture to the point where 'the men . . . become a flock of sheep and the women play the ravening wolves', he arrived at the dubious conclusion that such a national matrix had never existed in the world before.

A gap developed in his correspondence with Freud while he plunged deeply into a mass of mythological and archaeological literature, searching out every possible detail as the significance of symbols became of paramount importance in his reading. He ploughed through the huge mass of Friedrich Creuzer's *Symbolik und Mythologie der alten Volker*, which reactivated his old delight in archaeology. He read Herodotus and found himself faintly shocked by the great man's apparent prudery: 'How could the Greeks have learnt it so early?' Knight's *Essays on the Worship of Priapus* delighted him and replaced in his library Inman's much less reliable work.

When their correspondence opened again, as if to press his claim to priority in all fields, Freud said in his letter of 17 October 1909: 'I'm glad you share my belief that we must conquer the whole field of mythology.' In the same letter Freud first put forward his theory that Leonardo da Vinci was a striking example of a man whose primitive researches into sex at an early age produced a paralysing effect, converting his sexuality into an urge for knowledge. Leonardo found himself unable to finish anything he undertook because 'he was sexually inactive and homosexual'. Unlike Jung at this stage Freud was completely overwhelmed by work: 'I would invent the seventh day if the Lord hadn't done so long ago.'

Every week now, Jung pressed deeper and deeper into the literature of mythology, but it did not prevent his 'positively wallowing in people and social life'. He neglected his correspondence with Freud and wrote an elaborate apology on 15 November 1909 concluding, 'it is a scandalous matter and shall not happen again'. Surprisingly, Freud seemed to suffer from intellectual isolation and needed Jung's letters to compensate for the unsatisfactory company of people like Eitington, described by Jung as enervating and vapid intellectuals.

Jung had, in fact, kept Freud waiting twenty-five days for a reply to one letter, but then came the most revealing statement: 'For me there is no longer any doubt what the oldest and most natural myths are trying to say. They speak quite "naturally" of the nuclear complex of neurosis.' There followed an elaborate analysis of the sexual components in many myths, from Ares returning home to sleep with his mother to the Dionysus festival where women pulled the phallus 'up and down on a string'.

Meanwhile conflicts persisted in Jung which sometimes expressed themselves in extravagant dreams about his wife and work. Injuring his thumb one day, the next night he dreamed that his wife had her 'right arm chopped off', an event open to many interpretations. Once again tensions between himself and his wife were considerable, but 'the Walpurgisnachts of my unconscious do not affect my capacity for work'. However, it was that very work which came under severe self-criticism, creating powerful resistances to writing to Freud. Jung felt that the father complex from which he had been trying to free himself for years still had him in its grip and created an inability to 'come up to' his own expectations. 'One's work is garbage says the devil.' His resistance to writing to Freud he saw as an inverted part of his fixation.[1]

Very much concerned with the mechanism of resistance, he felt that it took different forms in men and women. With men, for instance, Jung found that homosexuality was one of the richest sources of resistance, but with women it frequently, in his view, centred on perversions or variations of sexuality. The power of homosexual resistance in men opened up 'mind boggling possibilities', and there were many reasons for approving homosexual practice if the moral stigma could be removed. First as a contraceptive device, second as a release for those 'inferior' men who seemed to prefer it, third as an escape from enforced marriage. His comments went wider and deeper: 'Because of our short-sightedness we fail to recognise the biological services rendered by homosexual seducers.'[2] In Jung's view, at this time, 'they should be credited with something of the sanctity of monks'. The whole analysis has to be seen in the context of his own homosexual assault as a boy, and his relationship with Freud. It was almost as if he were simultaneously anxious to reconcile the boyhood experience and outdo the Master. Sexual etiology remained the kernel of Freudian doctrine, but not even

Freud had suggested that homosexuality qualified its practitioners for sainthood.

Conveyed to Freud, the sentiments appear to have upset the Master, but we do not know in precisely what way because Freud's reply to Jung is missing. It is clear from the opening of Jung's next letter that 'all sorts of misunderstandings' were in the air. 'How could you have been so mistaken in me? I don't follow.'[3]

Fresh friction arose as the date for the Nuremberg congress of the Second International Psycho-Analytical Congress (30 and 31 March 1910) approached. Jung went off to lecture in America once more. According to Ernest Jones the whole of the arrangements for the Congress had been left in Jung's hands and his sudden disappearance threatened chaos.[4] Aware of the alarm his departure would cause, Jung wrote to Freud *en route* saying, 'Now don't get cross with me for my pranks!' Emma should have written by now, he said, assuring Freud that he would be back in time for the Nuremberg conference, and all arrangements had in any case been made. This included passing over the care of his patients to Johann Jacob Honegger, a psychiatrist who worked at the Burghölzli. Honegger himself was subsequently to come under treatment by Jung, and in the ensuing entanglements to cause Jung great anguish. Freud, more concerned for the moment with the Nuremberg arrangements, wrote to Oscar Pfister, the Protestant pastor of Zürich and a founding member of the Swiss Psycho-Analytic Society: 'I still have not got over your not coming to Nuremberg. Bleuler is not coming either and Jung is in America so that I am trembling about his return.' Then followed the surprising cry, 'What will happen if my Zürichers desert me?'

His fears were unfounded. Jung did return in time for the Congress, gave a contribution which Ernest Jones described as first-class and reassured Freud. Jones wrote: 'Freud was too mistrustful of the average mind to adopt the democratic attitude customary in scientific circles so he wished there to be a prominent leader. . . . Jung seemed admirably suited for it. His research work had made him a man of standing in both experimental psychology and psychiatry where he had already won widespread recognition; he had an academic position and was expected at that time to succeed to the Chair of Psychiatry at the University of Zürich when it should next become vacant. . . .'[5]

Contradicting the struggles and uncertainties which still beset Jung, particularly in his relationship with Freud, Jones found him 'a hearty and confident personality' who inspired 'general esteem', a man 'enthusiastically devoted to the new science'. He added: 'He was young, about thirty-four at the time, forward looking and abounding in energy and ambition.'[6]

Freud had been preoccupied for some time with the idea of tightening the bonds of association between psychoanalysts, and Sandor Ferenczi put the proposition to the Congress with considerable tactlessness. Criticising the Viennese analysts as a second-rate lot, he suggested that the future administration could only be centred on Zürich with Jung as President. In a letter to Freud he stated that 'the psycho-analytical outlook does not lead to democratic equalisation: there should be an élite rather on the lines of Plato's rule of philosophers'.[7] Freud entirely agreed with this approach, but Ferenczi's introductory remarks at the Congress created a storm of protest. The discussion which followed became so acrimonious that it had to be adjourned until the following day. Pioneers like Adler and Stekel in the Viennese Circle furiously opposed the nomination of Swiss analysts to the two key positions of Secretary and President, which ignored their own claims from long and faithful service. Freud wanted to broaden the basis of psychoanalysis from its Viennese Judaic beginnings, and when he heard that Stekel was holding a protest meeting in his hotel-room he went up to join them and made an impassioned appeal for co-operation. 'He laid stress on the virulent hostility that surrounded them and the need for outside support to counter it. Then dramatically throwing back his cloak, he declared "My enemies would be willing to see me starve: they would tear my very coat off my back." '[8]

Replacing impassioned pleas with practical diplomacy, Freud proceeded to devise a compromise which temporarily quietened the storm. He himself retired from the presidency of the Vienna Society, nominating Adler as his successor, and to counterbalance Jung's editorship of the *Jahrbuch* he agreed to launch a new periodical, the monthly *Zentralblatt für Psychoanalyse*, to be edited jointly by Adler and Stekel. In the uneasy calm which followed, the Congress agreed that Jung should become president of the Association and Freud director of the new periodical. Jung appointed Franz Riklin as editor of yet another official publication, the *Correspondenzblatt der Internationalen Psychoanalytischen Vereinigung*.

Writing to Ferenczi after the Congress, Freud said: 'I spent an enjoyable day with Jung in Rothenburg. He is at the top of his form and it is to be hoped he will prove himself.'[9]

Later in the letter came this comment: 'The personal relationships among the Zürich people are much more satisfactory than they are in Vienna where one often has to ask what has become of the ennobling influence of psycho-analysis and its followers.'

Little did he know that within a few months internecine strife at least equivalent to that in Vienna was to recur in Zürich. Meanwhile the theories of psychoanalysis spread across the world, with societies springing up in Germany, the United States and Australia. Brill, an Austrian-born American psychoanalyst, and Putnàm, Professor of Neurology at Harvard, were mainly responsible for developing the interest aroused in the States by Freud and Jung's lectures at Worcester in the previous year. Brill by now had fought his way through considerable opposition to become a leading exponent of psychoanalysis, concentrating mainly on New York. Jones, with astonishing energy and devotion, ranged far and wide from Baltimore to Boston, from Detroit to Washington, and on 2 May 1910 the American Psychopathological Association came into being. Even in far-off Russia, Jung's name was now known through the work of Ossipow, who busied himself translating Freud's *Interpretation of Dreams*. The Australian Medical Congress in 1911 invited Freud, Jung and Havelock Ellis to read papers, and Freud suggested to Jung that they should send a joint paper, but Jung preferred to prepare his independently.

Jung's troubles in the Zürich society centred around the fluctuating role of Bleuler. After the Nuremberg Congress all the existing psychoanalytic groups enrolled as branch societies of the International Association, but Bleuler resigned, ostensibly on the grounds that it was against his principles to belong to an international body. In fact, he had an irritable if not heated preliminary discussion with Jung and expressed very different views. He didn't want, he said, 'to sit down with just anyone' in scientific discussions – a dig at Stekel, his particular *bête noir*. Moreover, the aims of the Society were biased, exclusive and far too narrow.[10] Freud meanwhile wrote to Pfister saying that Bleuler's charges against what he called 'an intolerable sect' were easy to refute: 'The intolerance is really not on our side.' Abraham wrote to Freud on 24 October 1910 stating that he had been in continuous correspondence with Bleuler and 'things are as you say'. Bleuler's arguments, he said, were vague and full of imponderables, but 'I have agreed to go to Zürich . . . if he will give me a chance to compose matters.' Bleuler himself had expressed a wish to discuss their differences personally, and Abraham 'had of course no intention of sacrificing the Society'.[11]

Jung, Freud and Abraham did succeed in modifying Bleuler's point-blank refusal to join the Association for a time, but at the Zürich constituent assembly it was Jung's tactical skills which threatened to outwit Bleuler. Revealing an unexpected political acumen, Jung prearranged the solidarity of a group numbering twelve who did their best to 'unhorse Bleuler'. As the discussion developed it became clear to Jung that Ludwig Frank, a Zürich neurologist, had played the role of the grey eminence working behind Bleuler. Jung allowed the argument to run free until Bleuler and Frank were 'properly cornered' and had to repeat that they simply did not want to 'commit themselves to a confession of faith'. Given an overwhelming majority in favour of joining, Jung still did not press home his victory, basing his tactics on those he had learnt from Freud at Nuremberg, where final decisions on certain issues were postponed until next meeting. Presented with this alternative, Bleuler became more amenable to the point where Jung had high hopes he might eventually surrender. With or without Bleuler, he intended to join the Association, but 'with him would be better'. As for Frank, Jung would happily speed his departure with a 'joyful kick'.

By 5 May, hopes of reconciliation were dashed. By 25 May, Bleuler had definitely decided against joining the Society, and what Jung now regarded as a pyrrhic victory left them in confusion. There was no suitable person to act as President and the stop-gap measure of Riklin and Jung as joint chairmen did not appeal to Jung. Conceding a forum for dissenters, Jung agreed to hold a public meeting where anyone could express his views, but 'Jung's pent up wrath was such' that he would 'take [his] revenge one way or another. I am only waiting for an opportunity. As soon as we are strong enough the whole obstreperous gang can be kicked out.' That would leave at least ten or twelve people on Jung's side, all of them 'young with the exception of Pfister, Binswanger and Maeder'.[12] Jung had, in fact, wanted to make Pfister president, but Binswanger strongly opposed it on what he called objective grounds and Jung those of pure jealousy. The negotiations revealed a considerable power of revenge in Jung which could express itself in terms some considered brutal and others Swiss-blunt. By early June, the Zürich branch society was at last constituted – fifteen members – but still without a president. Bleuler and Maier were still 'hanging back' and Frank 'mercifully' absent, but only two of the younger assistants from the Burghölzli had joined. 'One more such victory . . . ,' Jung wrote.

Jung's workload, very heavy at this time, was shared by his relation Franz Riklin and Johann Honneger. Honneger had written to Jung in June 1909 saying that he wanted to take up psychiatry. Young, very intelligent and subtle-minded, he appealed to Jung to help him because of a 'loss of reality-sense lasting a few days'. Within a short time there was evidently a plan for Jung and Honneger to open a private practice in some sort of collaboration. Among the letters from Honneger to his close friend Walter Gut, a member of the Zürich society, one dated 17 June says: 'May I ask you to help my fiancée find suitable quarters for the firm of Jung-Honneger? The intermediate stage in Küsnacht is now to be skipped after all. . . . We'll need three rooms, unfurnished with telephone.'[13]

Nothing ever came of this, but Jung's association with Honneger ended in tragedy. Within nine months of the proposed partnership Jung broke the news to Freud the Honneger had committed suicide, and added: 'The sole motive was to avoid a psychosis.' Delayed reaction drove Jung to admit three weeks later that the blow had struck home, but 'when I contemplate his fate I cannot but admit that suicide is a thousand times better than sacrificing the most brilliant gifts . . . to the Moloch of neurosis and psychosis'. Seven more weeks passed, and still Honneger's death deeply troubled him. Treating another case of dementia praecox, he said that at all costs 'you have to bring to light the inner world produced by the introversion of libido'. He was succeeding with his current case, he wrote, but had failed to do so with Honneger because 'I had no inkling of it'. 'I tell myself', he added, 'that this lack of knowledge of mine led to his death.'[14]

To show how virulent hostility from the outside could be, about a year before this an old enemy of psychoanalysis had telephoned Freud and managed to penetrate his consulting-room under an assumed name. Calling himself 'Hofrat Schottländer', he presented a card which read 'Hofrat *Fried*länder' and claimed that Freud must have misunderstood him on the phone. He had hardly sat down when he began to denounce all and sundry in the psychoanalytic movement. 'Beelzebub pulled in his horns, emitted his well known stench and went on denouncing,' Freud wrote to Jung. Freud decided to exploit his psychoanalytic skills to draw Friedländer deeper into the morass of his own making. 'Slipping into the father role he was determined to force on me . . . I affected hearty good humour and took advantage of the . . . situation to make the most insulting remarks which produced exactly the desired effect.'

The episode is of interest because it provoked in Jung one of those bursts of invective which he could so readily produce whenever someone incited his full wrath: 'The adventure with Schottländer is marvellous; of course the slimy bastard was lying. I hope you roasted, flayed and impaled the fellow. . . . Since I could read the filth in him from his face I would have gone for his throat. . . . Had I been in your shoes I would have softened up his guttersnipe complex with a sound Swiss thrashing.'[15]

The letter, dated 2 June 1910, was written on new paper headed: 'Dr C. G. Jung, LL.D., Privatdocent der Psychiatrie, 1003 Seestrasse, Küsnacht-Zürich.' The honorary degree given by Clark University Jung underlined with an exclamation mark after it ('*LL.D.!*'). He had now moved to his new house in a rural part of Küsnacht called Im Feld on the lake of Zürich, about half a mile from the village itself and seven miles south-east of Zürich. All houses in the district were subsequently renumbered, and Jung's changed from 1003 Seestrasse to 228 Seestrasse. It was a beautiful house, somewhat in the style of a patrician mansion of the eighteenth century, surrounded by a large garden, with a three-storied tower and turret over the main door. A Latin inscription engraved above the door said: 'Vocatus atque non vocatus Deus aderit' ('Called or not called, God will be there').[16] Sailing, one of Jung's main relaxations, demanded a boathouse, which he duly built, and an observation-pavilion giving a wonderful view of the lake.

Meanwhile the complications which bedevilled the Swiss society in Zürich were more than matched by Freud's difficulties in Vienna, where Adler and Stekel had both become intolerable to him. They 'are so rude . . . personally . . . I'd gladly get rid of them both. . . . I wouldn't mind throwing the *Zentralblatt* after them, then we could enlarge the *Jahrbuch* to handle the rush of material. I hope my tale of woe is a comfort to you in your local difficulties.'[17]

Theoretical exchanges continued between Jung and Freud, and, in one long, technical and beautifully written letter dated 26 June 1910, Jung linked his mythological reading with Freud's incest theories in a way which presaged the troubles to come. He did not, he said, feel satisfied with the paradoxical formulation, 'Sexuality is its own executioner.' There was something typical in the fact that the symbol of fecundity 'the useful and generally accepted *alter ego* of Mithras (the bull) is slain by another sexual symbol'. There was, he believed, an evil necessity in it. 'What it boils down to is a conflict *at the heart of sexuality itself.*' There was only one possible reason, striking at the very source of primitive sexuality, '*the incest prohibition*'. Since the incest taboo frustrated the closest and most convenient outlet for libido, it tended to 'turn it sour'. A long struggle followed during which the libido had to free itself from this repression 'since it must reach its propagative goals'. Mythologically the struggle was represented by the fight between Tishtriya and Apoasha where 'the astral myth' comes 'to the aid of the old Iranians'. Jung spelt out the symbolical meanings: 'Tishtriya = active libido – Apoasha = resistant (incestuous) libido.' The letter continued to analyse mythological correspondences in detail, and commented, 'I must say that my paradoxical dictum about sexuality being its own executioner had some pretty gruesome archaic parallels which must have made a profound impression on man.'

Put in simpler terms Jung was coming to believe that incest 'signified a personal complication only in the rarest cases', and much more frequently contained a 'highly religious aspect for which reason the incest theme [played] a decisive part in almost all cosmogonies and in numerous myths'. It was a mistake to take the literal interpretations of incest when it clearly had spiritual significance as a symbol. This to Freud was explosive thinking.

Late in July 1910 all these profound matters were distanced for Jung by the approach of a holiday which he anticipated with delight. His small cabin-boat was sent off ahead and all communication with Küsnacht cut. Work was going well before he left Zürich, but relations with Bleuler had gone from bad to worse, especially because Jung had 'abjured his faith in abstinence'. For the whole of the next fortnight he was 'gadding about . . . like mad, sailing in and out of the many inlets in the lake', but one link with psychiatric life remained intact. Religiously, every morning, he analysed any dreams which might have occurred the night before.

By 8 August he was back in Zürich waiting to leave again for military service, which he expected to last until the end of the month. Emma was once more pregnant and 'expecting to be confined' in September, but already, on 11 August, Jung was planning another holiday, a two-week bicycle tour to Verona in Italy. A surprising number of short holidays occupied this period. Early in September he set off to London via Paris 'for a consultation' and returned via the Hook of Holland, hoping to see Freud in Holland, but Freud had left on 31 August for a trip to Paris,

Rome and Sicily. Immediately Jung returned to Zürich trouble arose between Sister Moltzer, the daughter of a Netherlands distiller, and Martha Boddinghaus, a woman who later married Hermann Sigg, a Swiss businessman and close friend of Jung. Both women were in love with him, and passionate jealousies developed which led to Sister Moltzer painting the blackest possible picture of Fräulein Boddinghaus. Both consulted Jung, and Sister Moltzer was overcome by remorse at her attacks on Fräulein Boddinghaus. Jung could not tell how much Fräulein Boddinghaus' reputation had suffered from the attacks, but jealous feuds of this kind between the women surrounding him were becoming more frequent.

A third daughter, Marianne, was born to Emma on 30 September 1910, but on this occasion Jung made no mention of the fact to Freud, and within a week he set off on the bicycle tour to Italy with his friend Stockmaier. It turned out to be a great success with 'steady sunshine' and every kind of 'lovely thing' unearthed including a Priapus stele with a snake biting the god's penis. They spent a night at Arona on the lower part of Lake Maggiore, where Jung had a dream which left him with a deep sense of humiliation. His first thought on waking was the paper 'Wandlungen und Symbole der Libido' on which he was working. 'I had', he wrote, 'such intense inferiority feelings . . . that I immediately took the train home in order to get back to work.'

Now came a surprise. 'The event which will interest you most is this,' he wrote to Freud. 'Bleuler has now joined the Society.' He added: 'I bow to your arts.'[18]

Chapter 14

A Love-Affair

Scrutinise the famous Freudian photograph of the Weimar Congress in September 1911, and there, third from the right, in the front row, is a young woman destined to play a most important role in Jung's life. Indeed, personally she was to empassion, delight and disturb many crucial years, and professionally become a close and admired collaborator. She looks, and was, very much younger than the other women, numbering eight out of the fifty-five people, chivalrously granted the distinction of the front row. Not particularly good-looking, with dark waved hair parted at the middle, in the photograph the face has a nervous intensity, and certainly, plunged into such a gallery of celebrated people, a very young woman might have reason to withdraw behind defences. Her name: Antonia Wolff,[1] her age twenty-two, her father Arnold Wolff, a rich businessman, her family one of the oldest Zürich families, tracing its lineage back 300 years. Separated, in the photograph, from Emma Jung by a splendid Walkyrie of a woman wearing a hat equivalent to a ceremonial head-dress, by name von Stack, there were reasons why any closer proximity might have seemed indiscreet.

In the previous year Antonia Wolff had come to Jung as a patient, partly because she failed to adjust to the death of her father and partly from earlier difficulties with her mother Elizabeth Sutz. Her father, twenty years older than her mother, had spent many years in Japan and was said to have traces of Oriental blood in his veins. Born on 18 September 1888, Antonia was the eldest daughter and underwent a typical bourgeois education: primary and secondary school, boarding school for several years, and finally Zürich University where she studied German literature. An essentially lonely person, even in childhood, she decided at a very early stage to stay independent, 'not for the body, but for the soul'. Her heightened sensibilities quickly revealed themselves to a number of perceptive teachers, one of whom encouraged her ability to write poetry. She did this more as a form of self-expression than with any real hope of publication. Conflicts with her teachers and father quickly arose. By the time her father died in 1909 the ground was already prepared for the breakdown which followed.[2]

Exhausting conventional doctors and medical advice, it was inevitable that her mother should think of Dr Carl Gustav Jung, whose reputation was now widely respected – if in some Zürich circles strongly resisted. So, one day early in 1910, Toni Wolff set foot in his consulting-room with the big desk looking out on the lake at Küsnacht and

confronted the handsome young doctor, already the centre of considerable female attention. Physically the very incarnation of a virility
symbol, emotionally passionate, intellectually distinguished, Jung's
personality frequently carried for women – young and middle-aged –
an irresistible charisma. Antonia's intense femininity matched his
masculinity, her emotional responses were as raw as his were powerful,
her brain no less quick and responsive, if it lacked the range, erudition
and depth. Jung, at this stage of his career, gave the impression of a
strong, well-integrated personality capable of coping with almost
anything, but Toni was very disturbed when she came to him. The
surface differences concealed a deeper identity. Within the powerfully
preserved persona immense conflicts were troubling Jung, but he
carried out the prescribed duties of the consultant psychiatrist with
complete propriety.

Already the seeds of the person she was eventually to become, a very
considerable person, were evident in the shy and nervous woman whose
first interview with Jung proceeded uneasily. Tensions produced the
almost stern persona behind which lay the hypersensitive girl, while
genuine pride in her own integrity somehow reconciled itself with deep
humility. Never a person to respond superficially to another human
being, confronted with this man who threatened to break through all
her defences, resistance was strong. It speaks volumes for Jung's skills
that in the first few sessions he managed to bring to life a glimmering of
that fascinating femininity which could melt all her superficial
harshness.

Some time during the years 1911–12 their relationship slowly
escaped its professional restraints, and produced complicated repercussions on Jung's family life. As early as January 1910 he was writing to
Freud, 'This time it was not I who was plagued by the devil but my wife
who lent an ear to the evil spirit and staged a number of jealous scenes,
groundlessly.' (My italics.) If these words applied to Toni Wolff that
would seem to indicate that the affair, in the full sense of the word, had
not yet begun. Moreover, we know that at this time his wife was
pregnant again, 'by design and after mature reflection'. Nonetheless,
this phrase occurred in the same letter to Freud: 'Analysis of one's
spouse is one of the more difficult things unless mutual freedom of
movement is assured.' Then followed the remark we have already
encountered: 'The pre-requisite for a good marriage it seems to me is
the licence to be unfaithful.'[3]

Less than a month before the Weimar Congress, Jung said that the
feminine element would have 'conspicuous representatives' from
Zürich. 'Sister Moltzer [who was also in love with him], Dr Hinkle-
Eastwick, an American charmer, Fräulein Dr Spielrein [who wanted
his child] . . .' then a new discovery, 'Fräulein Antonia Wolff, a
remarkable intellect with an excellent feeling for religion and philosophy'. At the end of the passage came the words 'and last but not least

my wife.'[4] Barbara Hannah in her *Jung: His Life and Work* states: 'I do not know exactly how long Toni's analysis lasted but I think about three years.' Conflicting evidence clouds the inevitable question – did he sleep with her? – but one school accepted it as a *fait accompli*.

Among the women who surrounded Jung, like ladies at a royal court, several were undoubtedly in love with him and the inevitable feuds, jealousies and to some extent back-biting recurred. One in particular grew very jealous in the early days of Antonia Wolff, and at least three versions are given by witnesses of varying reliability of what followed.[5] According to the first witness the jealousy of another woman drove her to reveal to Emma that her husband was sleeping with Antonia. The second witness says that Emma had already divined the truth, and the third that Jung quickly admitted his infidelity to his wife and openly discussed what should be done. That Emma suffered severely comes through even in her letters to Freud, but one witness describes in convincing detail a bitter quarrel between herself and Carl, before she slowly found a way of accommodating what was clearly a threat to the whole foundation of her family life.[6] According to Paul J. Stern in his *C. G. Jung – The Haunted Prophet*, 'Jung's affair with Toni might have been less troublesome if he had not insisted in drawing his mistress into his family life and on having her as a regular guest for Sunday dinner.'

Late in 1911 Emma Jung daringly wrote a letter to Freud in which she said, 'Naturally all the women are in love with him and with the men I am instantly cordoned off as the wife of the father or friend.' She had, she said, a strong need for people, but Carl insisted that she must no longer concentrate on him and the children. 'What on earth am I to do? What with my strong tendency to autoeroticism it is very difficult.' She realised, she said, that she could never hope to compete with Carl, but 'in order to emphasise this I usually have to talk extra stupidly when in company'.[7]

Emma appears to have written confidentially to Freud without telling her husband, and developed an independent correspondence, searching for advice from someone outside the home. Freud always had the greatest respect for Emma. On 21 July he had written to Jung: 'Give your charming, clever and ambitious wife the pleasure of saving you from losing yourself in the business of money making. My wife often says she would be only too proud if she were able to do the same for me.'

Emma, as we know, came from a rich family, but how far they shared family finances or she made her money available is not clear. There were times when his patients dwindled away and he must have needed money to support a family now numbering six. In a letter to Freud dated 14 November, he begins with a reference to Freud as a dangerous rival: 'Yet I think it has to be this way. . . . You dig up the precious stones but I have the "degree of extension".' Then he added, 'At the moment my practice has dwindled to a trickle too, which is fine with me. Riklin hasn't much to do either, which is not so fine. . . .' That would imply that he could always fall back on his wife's money.

As his relationship with Toni Wolff developed, Emma obviously found the situation increasingly difficult but Jung was always against divorce. As he said to Freud: 'I am supposed to analyse Pfister's wife! I shall resist as long and as fiercely as I possibly can. These days I'm getting practically nothing but divorce cases. To hell with them!'

There were now many scattered references to Jung's wife in Freud's letters, and one in particular must have infuriated both. Jung's immense pilgrimage into the literature of symbolism, mythology, religion and the occult was overwhelmingly different and more erudite than Freud's relatively dilettante excursions, but the latter wrote on 1 September: 'I am glad to release you as well as your dear wife, well-known to me as a solver of riddles, from the darkness by informing you that my work in these last few weeks has dealt with the same theme as yours.' To wit, Freud said, the origin of religion. Considering the proposition on which Jung was to break from Freud within a year, the phrases which followed seemed odd, to say the least: 'So you too are aware that the Oedipus complex is at the root of religious feeling. Bravo!' You too! When Jung had clearly preceded and contradicted him. Once again Freud seemed anxious to establish a false priority.

Meanwhile Jung continued to support Freud in his battles with Adler and Stekel. Adler, he said, was becoming a menace, and Stekel utterly irresponsible to 'ally himself with Adler merely because they have the same complexes'.

When Adler wrote referring to a rumour in Vienna that Jung had demanded his removal from the Society, Jung commented: 'He seems to be extending his delusional ideas to me.' No such suggestion had come from Jung. Work at the time overwhelmed him, he was once more longing for a holiday and determined not to allow his practice to swamp his scientific work, but the Freud–Adler–Stekel battles added fresh complications to any free creative thinking.

Between 11 and 16 August, Jung went off to a congress in Brussels but played truant most of the time because the proceedings, in his view, became 'idiotic'. He was 'present, so to speak, only at [his] own lecture'. That lecture, too, led into a comic-opera scene. Each speaker had been granted twenty minutes but Jung, capable when he chose of out-talking most people on any subject, pressed relentlessly on for a whole hour. Van Schuyten, the chairman, then intervened, and Jung agreed to call a halt providing that was the wish of the 200 people present. They promptly greeted 'with acclamation' a further extension of his time. Ten minutes later, the chairman again intervened, and once more Jung appealed to the audience. Again, they pressed him to continue and 'the chairman was hopping mad but had to swallow his rage in silence'. In the end the lecture caused explosive reverberations and people leaving the hall were heard to mutter, 'Vous avez déchainé un orage.' A small handful, only, absorbed what he said sympathetically. 'From now on they will be counted among our silent collaborators,' Jung told Freud.

Exactly one month later Freud, then on holiday in a little village in the Dolomites with his wife and Ferenczi, suddenly decided that here was an opportunity to visit the man who dominated his professional life. He travelled alone to Zürich where he met Jung early on the morning of 16 September. One reason for his spur-of-the-moment decision became clear in a conversation which followed with Emma Jung.[8] Talking almost allegorically Freud said that his children were growing up, his marriage had been 'amortised' and now there was nothing left to do but die. One could not, Emma replied, 'be the child of a great man with impunity', especially when, as with Freud, the man had a strong streak of paternalism. She suggested to Freud that he might overcome the problems which had arisen with his children by analysing their dreams, and Freud replied: ' I don't have time to analyse my children's dreams because I have to earn money so that they can go on dreaming!' Their discussion remained within narrow limits, and if Emma penetrated the surface of Freud's talk with great percipience she kept her counsel at the time, only later divulging to Freud how well she understood its symbolical content. For the rest, we have the briefest reference to Freud's visit in Ernest Jones's *Life*: 'He stopped in Küsnacht for four days before leaving for the Weimar Congress. There were of course seminars, visitors and receptions so it was by no means a pure holiday.'[9]

Since the Weimar Congress took place on 21–2 September, it is reasonable to assume that Freud and Jung travelled up to Weimar together. Emma Jung also accompanied her husband, but whether Antonia Wolff was of the party is uncertain. Jones, Freud and many other current witnesses preserved a discreet silence about Antonia Wolff, but Jones admitted to me that the affair was soon to become a subject of gossip in Vienna as well as in Zürich.

The Weimar Congress recovered the friendly atmosphere which had distinguished the first Salzburg Congress, with no hostility from the Viennese to disrupt proceedings. It also widened the international character of the whole psychoanalytic movement. Bleuler and the Reverends Keller and Pfister came from Switzerland, Magnus Hirshfeld from Berlin, Lou Andreas-Salomé from Gottingen, van Emden from Holland, and at least four representatives from America: James Putnam, A. A. Brill, T. H. Ames and Beatrice Hinkle. According to Jones, 'The papers were of a high order. Among them were several classics of psycho-analytical literature . . . notable papers by Bleuler on Autism and by Jung on symbolism in the psychoses and mythology.' Although Jung clearly dominated many aspects of the Congress, characteristically Jones, whose retrospective hostility toward Jung was strong, put Bleuler first in his list of commendations. The local paper unintentionally satirised the whole proceedings. It gave a short report of the Congress, which said that 'interesting papers were read on nudity and other current topics'.

The story of James Putnam's struggle to overcome American resistance to psychoanalysis had long filtered through to Europe, but now he became something of a hero at the Congress, delivering a paper entitled 'The Importance of Philosophy for the Further Development of Psycho-Analysis'. However, 'his burning plea for the introduction of philosophy – his own Hegelian brand – into psycho-analysis did not meet with much success,' Jones wrote, once more omitting the fact that Jung discussed it sympathetically and at length with Putnam.

Jones also stressed the importance of Freud's paper 'A Postscript to the Schreber Case', in which he made his first reference to the myth-making tendencies of mankind and suggested that the unconscious contained 'not only infantile material but also relics from primitive man'. No attempt was made by Jones to compare it with Jung's paper 'Symbolism in the Psychoses and Mythology', which dealt with closely related matters. Unfortunately, Jung's paper has disappeared except in the form of an abstract by Rank, but Freud in his own 'A Postscript to the Schreber Case' said 'these remarks may serve to show that Jung had excellent grounds for his assertion that the mythopoeic forces of mankind are not extinct but that to this very day they give rise in the neuroses to the same psychical products as in the remotest past ages'. Much of the material contained in Jung's paper later appeared in Part II of *Transformation and Symbols of the Libido*, and there, it was clear, he dealt with the matter in much greater depth than Freud.

By general acclamation, Jung and Riklin were re-elected President and Secretary of the International Association, and it was decided that the *Correspondenzblatt* or *Bulletin*, of which six issues had been published in Zürich, should be incorporated into the *Zentralblatt*.

Freud and Jung were on the best of terms throughout the Congress, and when someone almost within earshot of Jung ventured to say that 'Jung's jokes were rather coarse,' Freud immediately rejoined, 'It's a healthy coarseness.'

Within a few days of his return to Zürich, Jung was swept away once more by his now exasperating military duties. Before he left Küsnacht, he told Freud that all was 'very turbulent at home', which might be read as a reference to the conflicts aroused by Antonia Wolff.

In the barracks at Seestrasse the distinguished consultant psychiatrist became a medical Jack-of-all-trades, treating diarrhoea, sleeplessness, corns, bunions, coughs and colds. 'Luckily I have some time to myself so I am not entirely pulverised by the constant spectacle of odious corporeality.' Never a man to waste time, he made medical observations on the men he had to examine, continued to handle business problems connected with the *Jahrbuch*, and reinforced his new theorising about the unconscious.

From the barracks at St Gallen he sent Freud a condensed account of a development of his symbolistic theories, claiming that these were 'widely disseminated and age-old'. More important, what people assumed to be the earliest memories of childhood – birth, suckling, etc. – turned out on deeper analysis to be not individual memories but phylogenetic ones. These basic recollections from the dim beginnings of the individual psyche were in fact intra-uterine, before the conscious psyche as we knew it had formulated itself. 'I think that we shall find that infinitely more things than we now suppose are phylogenetic memories.' Thus he was underlining another deviation from Freud, a new concept of the unconscious which eventually produced the theory of archetypes.

On 20 October, Jung was suddenly detailed for a mountain exercise 'at the back of beyond'. He returned exhausted, sat down and wrote the briefest letter to Freud explaining his condition. 'Once I am out of the brutalities of military life I shall write you a sensible letter.'

On 30 October, while her husband was still away and Emma alone in the house with the children, she wrote a confidential letter to Freud. It was a surprisingly independent move for a woman in her position. Its contents, too, were surprising. She had to summon up the courage, she said, to write the letter but she was driven by the voice of her unconscious, not by mere presumption. With interesting prescience for what followed she gave as her chief motive a powerful sense that Freud's relationship with her husband was not 'altogether as it should be'. This idea had tormented her ever since Freud's visit before the Weimar Congress, and now she was forced to give voice to it. Unless she was deceiving herself, she said, she believed that Freud did not agree with or accept Jung's *Transformation of Libido*. 'You didn't speak of it at all and yet I think it would do you both so much good if you got down to a thorough discussion. . . .'

Troubled as he was by his own children at the time, Emma divined that Freud's air of resignation referred not only to his 'real children' but 'also to [his] spiritual sons'.

She may not have known the full extent of Freud's feuds within the Viennese circle itself at this time, but signs of theoretical deviation in Jung must have reinforced his sense of disillusion with his own immediate circle. 'My husband', Emma concluded, '. . . knows nothing of this letter and I beg you not to hold him responsible for it or to let any kind of unpleasant effects it may have on you glance on him.'

Anticipating the trouble to come, Emma clearly tried to heal the breach before it occurred. Freud's reply is missing but it must have reassured her because by 6 November she was again writing a long letter thanking him for the goodwill he had shown. She then plunged into a more detailed analysis of the complications which had arisen, revealing that Carl was not only eagerly awaiting Freud's opinion of his Symbols of Transformation, but was also in a state of considerable trepidation: 'He had often said before that he was sure you would not approve of it. . . . Of course this is only a residue of the father (or mother) complex which is probably being resolved in this book.'

By now Emma's understanding of the technicalities of psychoanalysis was considerable and her insights penetrating. What began, for instance, with Jung's attempt to free himself from his father fixation through Freud, a matter of the animus, ended with a struggle to re-adjust elements of his anima – through another woman, Toni Wolff. At least one major aspect of a profound transformation was predicted in Emma's letter of 6 November. When Freud referred to the amortisation of his marriage, Emma said, 'I fancied it was intended just for me because it was meant symbolically . . . and referred to my husband.'

Was this her view of her own marriage now that Toni Wolff had intervened, and was her sudden burst of correspondence with Freud a kind of unprofessional consultation with him? We do not have Freud's letters to determine precisely what advice he may have given her, but she was, in turn, presently in full flood of analytical advice to him. When he spoke of the imperative need to earn money 'in order that his children could go on dreaming', she saw the same urge in Carl as 'only an evasion of something else to which he has resistance'. Overjoyed and honoured as she was that Freud reposed such confidence in Carl, 'it almost seems to me as though you were giving too much'. Then came the most penetrating comment of all. 'Doesn't one often give much because one wants to keep much?'

And there it was. That Freud underwent, consciously or uncon-sciously, a struggle between wanting to surrender his mantle to Jung and keeping it intact is clear. Audaciously perhaps, since Emma was not intellectually of the same calibre as Freud or her husband, she concluded the letter with the same heavy-handed advice: 'Do not think of Carl with a father's feeling . . . but rather as one human being thinks of another, who like you has his own law to fulfil.' Her final salutation read: 'With warm love and veneration'.

Not surprisingly perhaps, the Master appears to have been annoyed by this attempt by a disciple to give him advice about how to cope with his immediate problems. Once again Freud's reply is missing, but its tone can be divined from Emma's next letter dated 14 November. Whether she had yet divulged to her husband that she was conducting a separate and confidential correspondence with Freud is not clear, but Carl had long returned from his military service and was himself exchanging letters with Freud.

'You were really annoyed by my letter weren't you?' her letter began. 'I was too, and now I am cured of my megalomania and am wondering why the devil the unconscious had to make you of all people the victim of this madness.'

Freud had evidently divined that her previous letter was directed at her father image, the substitute she saw in Freud for her real father. 'I thought that knowing the transference side of my father-attitude towards you it would all be quite clear and do me no harm.'

But the unconscious had played a trick on her, she said. She had made a fool of herself in front of the last person in the world she would have chosen for such an indulgence, and 'I can only pray and hope that your judgment will not prove too severe'.

Characteristically sceptical about psychological causes for illness within their own families, the pioneers of psycho-analysis were revealed by Freud as strongly resisting the application of their own doctrines when he reacted powerfully to Emma's suggestion that some psychical condition might underlie his own children's troubles. They were, he protested, 'not doomed to be degenerate'.[10] This took her by surprise. She had not meant anything of the kind. 'Since I have made some very astonishing discoveries in myself on this subject – and do not consider myself excessively degenerate . . . I thought similar phenomena possible with other people.'

More penetrating was her analysis of the unconscious motives now driving Jung into the mutually destructive process of fearing Freud's opinion of his imminent deviations in the *Jahrbuch*,[11] and the self-analysis that implied. 'It seemed out of the question that he could have resistances to his own work; but now it appears that this fear of your opinion was only a pretext for not going on with the self-analysis which this work in fact means.'[12]

Throughout the whole of her brief correspondence with Freud, Emma reveals herself as an intelligent, very perceptive but fundamentally apprehensive and worried person. She concluded her letter to Freud: 'Please write nothing of this to Carl. Things are going badly enough with me as it is.'

The reasons were obvious. Not only emotionally and sexually was a rival threatening to replace her, but professionally, despite Emma's splendid efforts to keep pace, the young, vivid and more intellectual Toni Wolff was about to collaborate with Carl in a manner outside her range. So often when a younger woman appears in the life of an older and intellectually distinguished man he tends to exaggerate her capacities so that she is shown to share many aspects of his life. Jung in fact believed that Toni's poetry was of the same calibre as Goethe's. However, there was no doubt that intellectually Toni Wolff could keep pace with his restless, constantly searching mind.

It all fitted what had now become a theoretical principle anticipated far back in Greek history. There were two types of women. One the 'wife and mother' found fulfilment in her husband, children and domestic life; the other the 'femme inspiratrice' who shared the man's intellectual pursuits and inspired his creative self.[13] Similar distinctions occurred in Athenian society. As with so many aspects of Jung's final model of the psyche this fragment derived directly from his own experience and was indeed seen by some as sheer rationalisation of his affair with Toni. In her anguish Emma had written in her letter of

24 November from which we have already quoted: 'The women are naturally all in love with him. . . . Carl . . . says I should no longer concentrate as before only on him and the children, but what on earth am I to do?' Still afraid that Carl might notice something, by the end of November this fear had disappeared and she wrote: 'he now knows about the exchange of letters as he was astonished to see one of your letters addressed to me'. Nonetheless, she told her husband very little of what she had actually written to Freud.

Chapter 15

Freud–Jung: the Climax

IT IS IMPORTANT to remember that in the labyrinth which now engulfed the leading figures of psychoanalysis Freud, according to some of his own disciples, had one driving purpose. He wanted to re-organise the psychoanalytic movement with a new centre in the heart of Europe under a leader who did not generate the confused love and hate which had grown up around his own person. Above all, he wanted to create conditions which would preserve the purity of psychoanalytic practice as he saw it for the future. This meant accepting a minimum number of basic concepts, without agreement on which men could not, he felt, work together. Since the Viennese Circle was itself in considerable disarray Freud had become doubly sensitive to any suspicious reaction of Jung's. In fact one defection after another in Vienna should have prepared him for the troubles which were rapidly developing in Zürich.

Behind the scenes members of both groups talked about one another in a manner characteristic of any cluster of like-minded men, professionally ambitious in an excitingly new field. The evidence is fragile. Much of it comes from casual statements of group members, or is reported second-hand verbally. Jung was supposed to have told Freud that he regarded Stekel as 'a nuisance to psychoanalysis', and Freud defended Stekel against the charge. On another occasion Adler told Stekel that Jung was such a victim of his conventional upbringing that he could never face the more abandoned implications of Freud's sexual etiology. He then turned and attacked Freud.

Matters now went from bad to worse with Stekel. At one unspecified meeting of the Vienna Psycho-Analytical Society, Victor Frank attacked Stekel and charged him with personally inventing many of the cases he cited to illustrate his hypotheses, and that led to fresh trouble for Freud.

His letters to Jung freely discussed the struggles in Vienna and sometimes feared further defections in Zürich: 'It would be a severe blow to all of us if you were to draw the libido you require for your work from the Association.' Jung admitted the validity of the criticism but added, 'I don't think you need have any apprehension about my protracted and invisible sojourn in the "religious-libidinal clouds".' He would, he said, willingly describe what was 'going on up there' if he could condense it in letter form. 'Essentially it is an elaboration of all the problems that arise out of the mother incest libido or rather the libido cathected mother-image.' By 3 March he was protesting to Freud that his work for psychoanalysis was of far greater importance than his own 'personal awkwardness and nastiness'. In self-critical mood he added, 'I have my work cut out to put up with my own personality without wishing to foist it on you. . . .'

In April talk of Bleuler's retirement from the Burghölzli brought up Jung's name as a possible successor but he was, it seemed, completely out of the running. 'Professorships here mean the end of one's scientific career. You cannot be an official in a madhouse and a scientist at the same time.'

There now ran through the correspondence fresh exchanges about the precise nature of the incest taboo, and with each new reference their differences became more marked. 'We must say', Jung wrote, 'that incest is forbidden *not because it is* desired, but because the free-floating anxiety regressively reactivates infantile material and turns it into a ceremony of atonement.' It was *as if* incest might have been desired but in fact *was not*. This to Freud carried a truly heretical ring.

Something far more serious now supervened. Unknown to Freud, Jung had steadily pressed on with his book *Symbols of Transformation*, and now he approached the chapter called 'The Sacrifice' with a deepening sense that it would cost him his friendship with Freud.

A sustained conflict developed within him. So powerful did it become that he ceased to write and as the tensions increased could not even pick up the fat black fountain pen ever his faithful writing companion. 'Should I keep my thoughts to myself or should I risk the loss of so important a friendship?' If his resistance to provoking a break with Freud were powerful, the conviction beating up from his unconscious that he was right and Freud wrong slowly overwhelmed everything. Once more he took up his pen and plunged into the fatal chapter. As the words multiplied – painfully – he knew for certainty that Freud would never accept the interpretation of incest which they conveyed.

A testing incident occurred shortly afterwards. Freud's old friend Binswanger had to undergo a dangerous operation, and the threat to his life drew Freud away from Vienna to visit him at Kreuzlingen. Since Kreuzlingen was reasonably close to Zürich, Freud wrote to Jung explaining that he would be there for forty-eight hours. Freud duly arrived in Kreuzlingen and stayed from Saturday until Monday, but there was no sign of Jung. Having himself travelled all the way from Vienna to within earshot of Jung, it seemed reasonable that Jung should undertake the much shorter journey to meet him in Kreuzlingen. Several explanations of his absence were possible. Saturated with the material which formed 'The Sacrifice', was Jung too much aware of his 'betrayal' and afraid that whatever he did the truth might burst through to make real the break he both desired and dreaded?

Certainly the word 'Kreuzlingen' took on a special meaning for the two men. Writing once more to Freud, Jung, according to Jones, 'made sarcastic remarks . . . to Freud about "understanding his gesture of Kreuzlingen"'. Freud replied on 13 June: 'I cannot agree with you when you say that my failure to go to Zürich from Constance was motivated by my displeasure at your libido theory. . . .' Following this letter Freud's mode of address began to change. 'Lieber Freund' gradually became 'Lieber Herr Doktor'.

Seldom free from dreams of one kind or another, Jung now experienced a powerfully recurring one which – significantly – took place on the Swiss–Austrian border. Central to the dream, an elderly man dressed as an Imperial Customs Officer, was said to be the disembodied ghost of his former self. Incidental figures appeared in the dream, and one said, 'He is one of those who still couldn't die properly.'

It did not need any great perspicacity to see that this was a dream about Freud, who waited at the border between the conscious and unconscious to check over the new ideas Jung was bringing back from another country. But, like most such dreams, many interpretations were possible.

Jung wrote: 'At that time Freud had lost much of his authority for me. But he still meant to me a superior personality upon whom I projected the Father and at the time of the dream this projection was still far from eliminated.'[1]

The key characteristics of the dream fitted at least one other interpretation. First, the Customs official was really a ghost and, second, he had refused to die properly. If Freud's principle of the death wish meant anything at all, it could not have expressed itself more clearly. Jung refused to accept this interpretation. 'I could find no part of myself that normally might have had such a wish, for I wanted at all costs to be able to work with Freud.'

A second dream followed in which Jung discovered himself walking through a modern Italian city which had ambivalent characteristics drawn from the Swiss town of Basel and the Italian city of Bergamo. As the crowds of contemporary people poured along the streets, suddenly there appeared amongst them a remarkable apparition: a medieval knight in crusading dress. Despite his anachronistic clothing the knight appeared to pass unnoticed. 'It was as though he were completely invisible to everyone but me,' Jung wrote.

Jung regarded the first dream as quite prosaic and the second as 'numinous in the extreme'. 'Interpreting the second dream, Jung related the knight's medieval trappings to the twelfth century, a period when alchemy developed and the quest for the Holy Grail began, both matters of the highest importance to Jung. . . .'[2] He had always believed that the knight's quest for the grail was equivalent to his own search for 'something still unknown which might confer meaning upon the banality of life'.

Another interpretation is self-evident. Freud could easily be seen as a knight whose crusading message was ignored by the press of ordinary people in the streets. Not merely the man in the street but also the greater part of the medical profession forced Freud to fight his own crusade, which indeed he was most bravely accomplishing.

Now came the climax in real life. Jung's famous paper 'Symbols of the Libido' was originally published in two parts in the *Jahrbuch der Psychoanalyse*.[3] When Jones read a proof of the first part, the smell of heresy filled his nostrils and he wrote to Freud sending him a résumé. Freud at once procured a copy of the *Jahrbuch*, read the paper and wrote posthaste to Jones pinpointing the precise page where Jung had – in his view – gone astray: page 174.

Later, in the *Collected Works*, Jung spelt out his position. Incest wishes were not to be taken literally but were symbols of other tendencies. 'The basis of "incestuous" desire is not co-habitation but, as every sun myth shows, the strange idea of becoming a child again . . . of entering into the mother in order to be reborn through her. . . .'[4] There were many rebirth myths. In some a mother substitute recanalised the sexual energy away from the regression toward incest. In others the Hero fought against the lure of the mother and triumphantly transformed it. 'The incest prohibition acts as an obstacle and makes the creative fantasy inventive. . . . In this way the libido becomes imperceptibly spiritualised.'[5]

And then, on 13 June, Freud – no less disturbed than Jung – wrote to say there was no need for theoretical differences to disrupt their personal relations. Temporarily the letter had some effect.

Early in January 1912 the *Neue Zurcher Zeitung* reported a meeting at which Dr Max Kesselring, a specialist in nervous diseases, spoke on 'The Theory and Practice of the Viennese Psychologist Freud', expressing regret that it had met with so much success among the pastors and educators of Zürich.[6] The following day the *Neue Zurcher Zeitung* published a letter from Dr Kesselring stating that he was not a member of the Kepler-Bund, and on 10 January two more letters developed the correspondence. The second letter, signed 'Dr J.', said that to conduct such a discussion as Dr Kesselring's before a lay audience was to commit a crime against good taste and almost equivalent to performing gynaecological examinations in public. Moreover, his lecture contained a number of gross distortions and completely lacked any objectivity.

On 23 January, Jung wrote to Freud apologising for the break in their correspondence and explained the reason. 'We have been the victims of "blackmail" by the newspapers and were publicly reviled though no names were named. I have even consulted a good lawyer with a possible view to bringing a libel action.' However, he had little hope of success 'because the attack was indirect'.

By 27 January the International and Zürich Psycho-Analytic Associations wrote a vigorous protest to the *Neue Zurcher Zeitung*: 'The President of the International and of the Zürich Psychoanalytic

Associations sees himself obliged to energetically reject the insulting and severely disparaging accusations formulated by a layman against medical specialists. The articles signed by F.M. give a completely distorted picture of psychoanalytic treatment owing to the ignorance of their author. No reasonable man would submit himself to such a disgusting method of treatment as depicted by F.M. The tone of these indictments makes any further discussion impossible.'

Psychoanalytic historians have drawn two conclusions from this correspondence. One, that the alleged attacks on sexual concepts in Zürich were fanatical; two, that several objective voices could be heard high above the din, some even embracing the Freud–Jung theories enthusiastically.[7] Certainly, voices like those of Friedlander, Isserlin and Oppenheim, commonly assumed to be 'early opponents', did attempt an objective appraisal.[8] Jung wrote to Freud: 'Zürich is seething. Psychoanalysis the talk of the town. One can see here how worked up people can get.'[9] Just how far this contributed to his continuing drift away from sexual etiology we will see later. Certainly, the pressures of Puritan social sanctions were driving some Swiss analysts into a corner, and the popular press denounced the iniquitous ideas which were pouring into Switzerland from Vienna. Only three Swiss analysts held out against the mounting tide of public opinion, but several followed an ambiguous course which made a qualified loyalty possible.

Jung was in fact under attack from two angles, private and public. Internally, the affairs of the Swiss Society of Psychiatrists were rapidly heading toward a new *impasse*. The winter meeting (25–6 November 1911) had led to fresh frictions if not open hostility between Jung and Bleuler. Ludwig Frank bitterly complained that five out of the seven lectures were on psychoanalysis and protested to Bleuler, who wrote a critical letter to Jung without attempting to talk to him. 'Once again Bleuler has allowed himself to be worked up because of his everlasting opposition to me,' Jung wrote.[10]

Using modern trade union tactics, Ludwig Frank and Bleuler kept the meeting going in the hope of tiring Jung and leaving the field open to their manipulations. Assuming that the main question under debate had been settled, Jung duly fell into the trap, left early and Frank returned suddenly to the motion: That the next meeting of the Swiss Society be held jointly with the International Society for Psychotherapy. Incredibly, in Jung's absence the motion was carried. 'I have no intention of speaking at this joint meeting,' Jung commented, 'for the vulgarity of the International Society disgusts me.'

By the end of November, Freud received a letter from Bleuler notifying him of his resignation, and Freud exclaimed that 'the last trouser button of my patience has snapped'. Possibly, Freud said, Bleuler's masochism was 'only waiting for a good whipping' but 'one cannot put up with abuse for ever'.[11] Inconsistently, Freud added that if

Bleuler still tried to come to terms with Jung and Maeder he hoped that they would do their best to meet him halfway.

Early in February, Jung recorded that since Bleuler had left the Society it was 'blossoming like a rose', but the battle in the *Neue Zurcher Zeitung* had boiled over into the 'carnival newspapers'.

By 1 April, Jung suddenly took off for Lugano 'to be alone with [himself] for a few days before going to Florence with [his] wife'. The weather turned out to be atrocious, raining miserably, but he was alone and unknown, a combination which produced 'the acme of pleasure'. Before he left Zürich strange rumours had circulated at the Burghölzli about Bleuler's retirement, and Freud took up the point three weeks later. The news was of the greatest interest to him, Freud said. 'If he receives an appointment elsewhere or resigns you can imagine how glad I should be for you to exchange your house on the lake for Burghölzli.'

Then came what seemed a remarkable statement in the light of the prolonged and agonised struggles of the last twelve months. Bleuler's withdrawal from the Zürich group, Freud said, had done more harm than he could foresee and 'I would greatly welcome the news that he had re-joined.'

Jung was said to have exploded on receipt of this letter: 'My God – who's now defecting from who?'[12]

Chapter 16

Jung Attacks Freud

IN SEPTEMBER 1912, Jung went off to America once more to lecture at the Extension Course of Fordham University in New York. 'Jesuit!' as Jung commented with an exclamation mark. His enthusiastic reception reaffirmed him in his rapidly developing deviations from Freud. Freud reluctantly approved the expedition, but the date of the 1912 Congress had to be postponed. Against much of the recorded evidence, according to Brill, Jung still did not desire to break away from Freud: 'As I have been in the thick of the movement I can definitely state that Jung would have preferred to have remained in the psycho-analytic fold.'[1] Lectures apart, Jung gave a two-hour seminar every day for a fortnight and found it 'most stimulating'. Under the illusion that he was defending psychoanalysis Jung opened his first lecture with the remark, 'Although it has been pointed out on any number of occasions . . . many people still do not seem to know that the theory of psycho-analysis has changed considerably in the course of the years.'[2]

Certainly Freud constantly refined one after another of his revolutionary concepts in the process of reconstructing major parts of his model, but Jung's remark was ambiguous. It could refer to Freud's theoretical revisions or to his own.

Then came this: 'Now although no fault can be found with Freud's sexual terminology as such, since he logically gives all the stages of sexual development the general name of Sexuality, it has nevertheless led to certain conclusions which in my view are untenable.' Claiming an empirical approach equivalent if not superior to Freud's, Jung said that 'if we judge by what we see', then everywhere in organic nature the life process consisted 'for a long time . . . in the functions of nutrition and growth'. Not only the intra-uterine period, but also the infantile extra-uterine belonged to this stage and it was characterised by 'the absence of any sexual function'.[3] Freud's latency period in sexuality between the age of five and puberty now came under scrutiny and emerged in Jung's view as a very dubious hypothesis. 'What he calls a disappearance is nothing other than a *real beginning of sexuality* everything preceding it being but a preliminary stage to which no real sexual character can be attributed.' Placing the blame squarely on Freud's shoulders, Jung drove home his point: 'The incorrectness of the conception of infantile sexuality' was 'no error of observation . . . the error lies in the conception'.[4]

Nothing could be more explicit. This was unqualified heresy. Turning to the incest fantasy, Jung now claimed that it was 'of secondary and not causal significance, while the primary cause [was] the resistance of human nature to any kind of exertion'.

When, some time later, Freud first heard this proposition he exclaimed to Ernest Jones: 'Idiotic! Everything is explicable in such terms – failure to work – lack of hygiene – malingering – the lot.'[5]

Jung, in his lecture – unaware of any reaction from Freud – pressed home his criticism in some detail. The notion of a boy's sexual tie to his mother should not, he said, substitute the natural need the boy had to be dependent on his mother in many other respects. The mother could obviously be viewed 'as a protective and nourishing figure and not as the object of incestuous wishes'. Jung presented the alternatives as if they were mutually exclusive, whereas, of course, Freud accepted them as complementary, stressing the sexual component because a conspiracy of silence surrounded it.

Continuously paying full tribute to Freud's courage and singlemindedness, the lectures pressed on to qualify his theories further. 'I think there is nothing for it but to abandon the sexual definition of libido or we shall lose what is valuable in libido theory, namely the energic point of view.' Jung felt that it was impossible simply to transfer the libido theory to dementia praecox because this disease shows a 'loss of reality which cannot be explained solely by the loss of erotic interest'.[6]

Libido should be redefined, Jung said, as energic rather than exclusively sexual. In other words, libido was for Jung no longer specifically sexual energy but generalised psychic energy.

Next came a strong resistance to the theory of infantile regression in which a patient fixated at an immature level, lived his adult life, unconsciously, under its conditioning and had to abreact to infantile complexes before he could free himself. This, in Jung's view, was frequently an alibi to avoid facing the true roots of the contemporary conflict. 'It is very suspicious . . . that patients often have a pronounced tendency to account for their ailments by some long past experience ingeniously drawing the analyst's attention away from the present to some false track in the past.' Fully respecting regression, especially to the parental complex, as one of the most powerful mechanisms at work in neurosis, he contradicted Freud once again: 'The cause of the pathogenic conflict lies mainly in the present moment.'[7]

Jung now distinguished three phases in life, the first being the presexual stage, the later years of childhood up to puberty, the pubertal stage, and the adult life from puberty, the maturity stage. Once again this was sharply distinguished from Freud's sexual, latency, puberty and mature periods centred around oral, anal and genital phases.

James Putnam wrote to Ernest Jones from Boston on 24 October 1912, giving an account of his encounters with Jung in America:

I made two attempts to meet Dr Jung in New York and the last one was in so far successful that I heard his address, though unfortunately missing the first part of it; and I had a few words with him afterwards. . . . What Dr Jung said in effect was that while he still held to the importance of the psycho-analytic technique he had come to rate the infantile fixations as of far less importance than formerly as an etiological factor in most cases – though I hardly think he could really maintain this if he were pushed for a positive opinion. At any rate, the point on which he seems now inclined to lay emphasis is the difficulty of meeting new problems and environmental conditions which arise at the time of the actual onset of the neurosis. It seems to me that we all recognise the importance of these influences and I cannot as yet feel that anything is won through minimising the significance of the other factor.[8]

Back in Zürich by 11 November 1912, Jung hastened to give Freud his news, claiming that he was 'able to do a very great deal for the spread of the movement' in America, but he had also made room for those of his views which 'deviate in places from the hitherto existing conceptions'.

The last paragraph of his letter dealt with the difficulties which had arisen with Stekel's editorship of the *Zentralblatt*. Freud had expressed dissatisfaction with Stekel, who refused to accept Freud's proposal that Victor Tausk edit the book reviews. Freud wrote to Abraham that the 'occasion for the split was not a scientific one', but Stekel's presumption in excluding another member of the Society.[9] Jung now said that Stekel should resign from the editorship of the *Zentralblatt*: 'Stekel has done enough damage as it is with his mania for indecent confessions.' Stekel's resignation from the Society had in fact already been predicted.[10]

A quite new note entered Freud's reply to Jung on 14 November. He wrote, he said, no longer affectionately as 'on the last occasion in Nuremberg'.

A meeting which followed in Munich in November seemed superficially to reconcile them. It was a meeting called by Jung himself to transfer the editorship of the *Zentralblatt* to Stekel, while a new *Zeitschrift* was founded to take its place. Jones records a small confusion over the arrangements whereby he almost failed to arrive in time. He was staying in Florence for a month, and Jung not only sent the notification of the meeting to his home in Wales, but actually gave Jones the wrong date, substituting – was the unconscious at work? – 25 November for 24 November. It is conceivable that Jung did not want Jones to be present because Jones was clearly an unquestioning disciple of Freud. When Jones told Freud what had happened, Freud remarked with his usual wit: 'A gentleman should not do such things even unconsciously.' Jones did, in fact, turn up on the correct day, but only because he discovered the date by accident from Vienna.

The meeting began at nine o'clock in the morning when Jung proposed that the changeover of journals be accepted without further discussion, but Freud insisted on giving an account of the difficulties he had encountered with Stekel. Everyone sympathised with Freud, his proposals were accepted, and the meeting ended just after eleven o'clock.

Later, Freud and Jung set off on a long walk together, and now the mystery of the Kreuzlingen gesture became clearer. Jung first complained with some bitterness that he had not received Freud's letter about his visit until Monday, the day on which Freud returned to Vienna. Freud was astonished. Both letters, he protested – one to Binswanger and one to Jung – had been posted simultaneously on the preceding Thursday. He agreed that if his letter to Jung did not arrive until Monday, then he had every excuse for not meeting him, and his own behaviour had been questionable. And then Jung suddenly recalled that he had been away for two days at the weekend which explained why he had not received the letter until Monday.

According to Jones, Freud 'let off steam' and 'did not spare him a good fatherly lecture'. Jones added that Jung accepted all the criticisms and promised to reform.[11]

Luncheon followed, and Freud was in high spirits, believing that once more all their troubles were over, and the Crown Prince had abandoned any idea of abdication. From what followed, it is clear that, whatever his conscious mind believed, unconsciously Freud remained very anxious and unconvinced. Towards the end of the luncheon he turned suddenly to the two Swiss analysts, Jung and Riklin, and asked them why, in recent articles explaining psychoanalysis, they had not mentioned his name. As the unquestioned originator of the whole psychoanalytic movement, Freud certainly had grounds for complaint. Jung rationalised the omission by oblique flattery. It was too well known that Freud had founded psychoanalysis, he said, and there was no longer any need to mention his name in historical recapitulations. This sounded very disingenuous to Freud, who suddenly wondered all over again whether his attempts at *rapprochement* with Jung were doomed to failure.

A dramatic reaction followed. He slid to the floor in a dead faint. This was hysterical transference with a vengeance, but none of the distinguished psychoanalysts who recorded the event described it as such.

The very powerful Jung at once picked Freud up in his arms and 'carried him to a couch in the lounge'. Quickly Freud revived, and his first words as he came round were: 'How sweet it must be to die.' Common-sense interpretation said that he could not face the possibility that Jung was still a traitor and blotted out the thought with unconsciousness. Secondary interpretation said that he had registered Jung's hidden desire to break away from him as a death wish against him and so powerful did it become that momentarily he underwent a kind of death. Beyond these explanations lay many other complexities, one of which Freud himself elaborated to Jones: 'I cannot forget that . . . years ago I suffered from very similar though not such intense symptoms *in the same room of the Park Hotel.*' He had first seen Munich when he visited Fliess there and the town 'acquired a strong connection with my relations with that man'.

Towards the end of 1912 a letter came from Jung destined to lead to the final explosion with Freud. Jung made a fascinating slip in his letter dated 14 December 1912: 'I see from Furtmüller's forthcoming critique in the *Zentralblatt* that the Viennese prophets are wrong about a swing over to Adler. Even Adler's cronies do not regard me as one of yours.[12] It is deplorable that science should still be treated like a profession of faith.' Freud replied on 16 December: '. . . the habit of taking objective statements personally is not only a (regressive) human trait but also a very specific Viennese failing. I shall be very glad if such claims are not made on you. But are you objective enough to consider the following slip without anger. "Even Adler's cronies do not regard me as one of *yours.*"' Jung had obviously meant to write 'one of theirs'. Freud's letter brought an angry reply from Jung:

> May I say a few words to you in earnest? I admit the ambivalence of my feelings towards you, but am inclined to take an honest and absolutely straightforward view of the situation. If you doubt my word, so much the worse for you. I would, however, point out that your technique of treating your pupils like patients is a *blunder*. In that way you produce either slavish sons or impudent puppies (Adler, Stekel and the whole insolent gang now throwing their weight about in Vienna). I am objective enough to see through your little trick. You go around sniffing out all the symptomatic actions in your vicinity, thus reducing everyone to the level of sons and daughters who blushingly admit the existence of their faults. Meanwhile you remain on top as the father sitting pretty. For sheer obsequiousness nobody dares to pluck the prophet by the beard and inquire for once what you would say to a patient with a tendency to analyse the analyst instead of himself. You would certainly ask him – Who's got the neurosis?
>
> You see, my dear Professor, as long as you hand out this stuff I don't give a damn for my symptomatic actions; they shrink to nothing in comparison with the formidable beam in my brother Freud's eye.[13]

Freud told Ernest Jones that he 'felt humiliated at being addressed in such a manner' and wondered what to say in reply. Finally he wrote a letter but did not post it. The letter has since come to light. Among other things, it said:

> I'm sorry my reference to your slip annoyed you so; your reaction seems out of all proportion to the occasion. In regard to your

allegation that since I misuse psychoanalysis to keep my students in a state of infantile dependency I myself am responsible for their infantile behaviour, and to the inferences you draw from this contention, I prefer not to judge because it is hard to judge in matters concerning oneself and such judgements convince no-one. . . . In Vienna I have become accustomed to the opposite reproach, to wit, that I concern myself too little with the analysis of my students.[14]

The letter still ended, 'With cordial regards.'

Chapter 17

The Final Break

JUNG WROTE only one letter to Freud in March of 1913, saying that he had to spend five weeks in America, but all arrangements had been made with Deuticke for publication of the *Jahrbuch*. Travelling by boat from Genoa, Jung stood at the rail as the vessel approached the latitude of Rome, but his hope of seeing Rome was never fulfilled. In America he lectured to the Liberal Club in New York[1] and returned 'unharmed', despite Freud's fears, to Zürich.

On 27 March, Freud wrote to Abraham saying that Jung was once more in America working more for himself than for psycho-analysis. 'I have greatly retreated from him and have no more friendly thoughts for him. His bad theories do not compensate me for his disagreeable character.'

His mood fluctuated widely in the following weeks. On 13 May he wrote arrogantly to Ferenczi: 'We possess the truth; I am as sure of it as fifteen years ago.'

Even as late as 1 June 1913 he wrote to Abraham: 'Jung is crazy but I have no desire for a separation and should like to let him wreck himself first.' By 31 July he said to Abraham that he had received a letter from Jung 'complaining about misunderstandings and making some supercilious remarks that I find difficult to follow'. Remembering the everlasting misunderstandings he only regretted that the Zürichers had 'lost the gift of making themselves intelligible'.

Far into the year, both Freud and Jung were still trying to prevent personal differences from interfering with professional relations and leading to a final break. Freud optimistically believed that formal cooperation was possible even within the bickering which had now become commonplace and wrecked their personal ties. Both men approached the last congress of the International Psycho-Analytical Association in Munich, on 7 September 1913, 'in the expectation that there would be no open break'.

From America, England, Germany, Austria and Hungary eighty-seven members and guests of the still rapidly growing psychoanalytic movement converged on the Bayerischer Hof on 7 September. They quickly fell into different groups with different sympathies and many small 'private meetings' were held to examine the latest developments in the schism which now threatened to break right out into the open. Ferenczi, Freud and Jones were seen together frequently, and Ferenczi was said to have coined the remark which has since re-echoed down the corridors of psychoanalysis: 'The Jung no longer believe in Freud.'

Since Ernest Jones wrote his biography the private journal of Lou Andreas-Salomé has become available and it throws new light on the Munich Congress. Under the date 7–8 September she wrote:

> At the Congress the Zürich members sat at their own table opposite Freud's. Their behaviour towards Freud can.be charac- terised in a word: it is not so much that Jung diverges from Freud, as that he does it in such a way as if he had taken it on himself to rescue Freud and his cause by these divergences. If Freud takes up the lance to defend himself, it is misconstrued to mean that he cannot show scientific tolerance, is dogmatic and so forth. One glance at the two of them tells which is the more dogmatic, the more in love with power. Two years ago Jung's booming laughter gave voice to a kind of robust gaiety and exuberant vitality, but now his earnestness is composed of pure aggression, ambition and intellectual brutality.[2]

She had never felt so close to Freud, she wrote, and she realised that it was only with the greatest difficulty that Freud restrained himself under the conflicting pressures. She and Tausk sat beside Freud, but Freud was still holding Tausk off, although he realised that he represented a wonderful ally in a situation of this kind.

Jones, another eye-witness of the proceedings, merely records that Jung now conducted 'the meetings in such a fashion that it was felt some gesture of protest should be made'. Lou Andreas-Salomé spelt out the difficulty: '. . . at last all political manôeuvring was at an end after a winter when it reigned supreme; one could, one ought, one had the right to thunder. And Tausk knew how. He had to leave again on the second morning after he had done his task. But Jung had improperly shortened the time of our paper.' Freud himself has explained that in his view Jung needlessly restricted the time given to individual speakers and allowed discussion to overwhelm the papers.[3]

Between meetings, considerable lobbying went on behind the scenes, but no one knows how belligerently Jung's supporters worked on his behalf or how far Freud's friends went in stiffening the morale of the faithful.

In the presidential election which followed, Jung accepted re- election with fifty-two votes against twenty-two. Moreover, this was not the result of a free vote. Abraham had suggested that those who disapproved should abstain from voting. Jones abstained, and after- wards Jung came up to him and said, 'I thought you were a Christian.' According to Jones, Jung meant by this that he was not a Jew, but colloquial English allows the more common interpretation that he was not a generous, tolerant person. Jones wondered how far what he called Jung's anti-Semitism conditioned this remark and his whole attitude to Freud, and it will be necessary later to enquire in detail whether Jung was in fact anti-Semitic.

In the midst of many uncertainties, the last international congress drew to an uneasy close and Freud immediately went off to his beloved Rome, where his sister-in-law Minna Bernays joined him.

The final few months of 1913 brought the whole question of the secession of Jung to a new head. Jung wrote to Ferenczi asking him why he had not supported him as President at the Congress, and Ferenczi gave his reply: 'It was only the absolutely improper way in which you as Chairman of the Congress dealt with the suggestions we put forward, the quite one-sided and partial comments you made on all the papers read, and also the personal behaviour on the part of your group, that caused us to protest by voting with blank cards.'[4]

Before Jung received this letter he had already written a final note to Freud saying that he had 'heard from Maeder that [Freud] doubted his "*bona fides*" '. After the reception of such news no further collaboration with Freud was possible, he said, and he forthwith resigned his editorship of the *Jahrbuch*.[5]

What followed revealed that Freud, not Jung, took the initiative in forcing Jung out of the Freudian school. The best way of bringing about the dissolution, Freud wrote to Abraham, was to send the Central Office a resolution signed by the Budapest, Vienna and Berlin groups, calling for a dissolution. If Jung and the Zürichers rejected the proposal, the three groups could withdraw independently and 'promptly form a new organisation'. It would be a tactical mistake, he thought, to 'begin by resigning', because Jung would remain President. 'Similarly, in the event of our resignation, the new organisation would have to elect me as President to put an end to the falsifications of the Zürichers.'

The strain of these last months had taken its toll of Freud. He told Abraham that he was struggling with a severe laryngotracheitis which 'I cannot account for'. Self-diagnosis of psychosomatic symptoms did not come easily in the prolonged struggle with Jung. Early in April, two members of the American group visited Freud and tried to reassure him about the situation in the United States. Jung's influence was small in their own group, they said, but a second group strongly supported him. On 24 April, Freud wrote to Abraham: 'You were certainly just as surprised as I was how meticulously Jung carried out our own intentions; somehow we shall get rid of him and perhaps of the Swiss altogether.'

From the letters which followed it looked very much as though the Freudians were about to deliver a series of attacks on Jung's next book. Certainly a number of very critical reviews appeared in the *Zeitschrift*, but a bigger 'bombshell' had been devised by Freud. It was a powerful polemical essay written by Freud himself. On 25 June, after the essay had at last appeared, Freud wrote to Abraham: 'So the bombshell has now burst. . . . I think we should allow the victims two or three weeks' time to collect themselves and react.'

And then, at last, came the news that Jung had already resigned his presidency, and it was unanimously decided that Abraham should become Acting President until the next congress. In the outer world, international affairs were hurrying implacably towards the nightmare of the First World War, but before hostilities were openly declared Jung announced his withdrawal from the International Association and let it be known that no Swiss analyst from Zürich would attend the next congress, due to meet in Dresden in September.

Interestingly, the *British Medical Journal* for January 1914 gave an account of the split in which it referred to Jung's 'return to a saner view of life'.

Freud himself made a last comment which struck an entirely new and ruthless note. 'So we are at last rid of them,' he wrote to Abraham on 25 July, 'the brutal, sanctimonious Jung and his disciples.'

Both sides have subsequently claimed malicious damage from the other as a result of the final break-up. Jung said that the Freudians circulated rumours about his possible schizophrenia, and so adept and sustained were these rumours that it caused some damage to his practice and 'lost me some of my students'.

In the reminiscences he wrote at the age of eighty, Jung said: 'After the break with Freud all my friends and acquaintances dropped away. My book was declared to be rubbish; I was a mystic and that settled the matter. Riklin and Maeder alone stuck by me.'[6]

Freud later wrote an account of the break-up in his *History of the Psychoanalytic Movement*. He had no idea, he said, that he had chosen a man who could neither tolerate nor wield authority, and 'whose energies were relentlessly devoted to the furtherance of his own interests'.[7] Freudians still maintain that throughout all these struggles Freud did not desire to establish a complete and fixed structure of psychoanalytic dogma, but merely a minimum of agreed concepts without which the working of any team must break down.[8]

Chapter 18

Jung's Breakdown

INTERWOVEN with his personal and professional struggles over the years 1907–13, Jung produced a number of important papers covering three main areas – *Studies in Word Association, Psychophysical Research* and *The Psychogenesis of Mental Disease*. In a different category altogether, *Wandlungen und Symbole der Libido* (1912) not only made the break with Freud inevitable, but also developed his reputation as an original thinker in psychoanalysis. It was a major work, eventually translated into English under the title *The Psychology of the Unconscious*, and for the first time it converted the term 'psychoanalysis' into '*analytic psychology*'. From then on, Jung distinguished his own school from that of Freud by the term 'analytical psychology'.

Despite the impact it made in psychological circles, and the revolutionary ideas it proposed, Jung never felt happy about the book. 'It was written at top speed amid the rush and press of my medical practice without regard to time or method.'[1] He literally flung the material together because the 'whole thing came upon [him] like a landslide' which could not be stopped. Admitting the urgency which drove him on to write the book, his claim that 'it was the explosion of all those psychic contents which could find no . . . breathing space in the constricting atmosphere of Freudian psychology' concealed deeper and much more disturbing forces.

The opening chapter analysed two kinds of thinking, one intensive, deliberate or directed, which dealt in words and expressed itself in disciplines like science, the other thinking in images, symbols and myths which expressed itself in dreaming and mythology. The spirit of antiquity created not science but mythology, and its world of subjective fantasies seemed to Jung to resemble in many ways the child mind today. Infantile thinking and dreams tended to re-echo the ancient – even the prehistoric – experience, and myths could be seen as the crystallisation of the mass dreams of a whole people.

The second chapter analysed the fantasy material of an unknown young American woman pseudonymously called Miss Miller. Miss Miller had unusual suggestibility, and was so capable of identifying herself with others, including long-dead figures, that she could literally feel in her own breast 'a truly piercing pain at that place where [Christian de Neuvillette in *Cyrano*] received the deadly blow'. Jung had not only witnessed the same capacity in Hélène Preiswerk, his fifteen-year-old cousin, but had also realised just how far the contents of unconscious fantasies could be removed from 'those which a girl of that age would be expected to have experienced'. In the same sense that Hélène Preiswerk became in her split-off fantasies 'the race mother of uncounted peoples', so Miss Miller could range from identification with Rostand's *Cyrano* to characters in Milton's *Paradise Lost*. Jung showed that creative fantasy could reach far beyond personal sources or those of literature to re-activate and draw upon 'the forgotten and long buried primitive mind with its host of images which are to be found in the mythologies of all ages and all peoples'. They could, he argued, arise spontaneously and flow across all boundaries to reveal remarkable identities 'not only in all corners of the wide earth but at all times'.

Carrying these reflections into analytical psychology, Jung suggested that 'The sum of these images constitutes the collective unconscious which is potentially present in every individual. It is the psychic correlative of the differentiation of the human brain.'

If the 'soul' possessed in some degree historical strata, then its oldest stratum would correspond to the unconscious. Psychologically, 'an introversion occurring in later life' would first seize upon regressive infantile memories of the *individual* past and then with stronger introversion, repression and regression penetrate tracts of 'an archaic mental kind which under certain circumstances might go as far as to re-echo a once manifest archaic mental product'.

Jung's work in the original German version abounds with un-translated Greek, Latin, French and English quotations and long etymologies copied from dictionaries. One tidal wave of learning after another submerges the reader in references to the Gilgamesh epic and the Odyssey, to the Bible and the Upanishad, to Goethe, Nietzsche and a score of other philosophers, to poets ranging from Longfellow to Heine in many languages, to a wealth of mythological scholars like Creuzer and Steinthal, to archaeologists, historians, psychologists and psycho-analysts, automatically embracing modern analysts like Freud and Adler. It is an awe-inspiring experience to try to enter the immense forest of his learning, and the average reader retreats after a number of attempts to trace the tortuous paths sometimes obliterated by sheer cross-fertilisation.

Any attempt accurately to represent the detailed complexities of Jung's *Psychology of the Unconscious* would require a scrupulous re-capitulation of the whole book, and the interested reader is recommended to read Volume 7 of the *Collected Works*. It is not my purpose to give detailed expositions, book by book, of Jung's work, but to adumbrate the developing frame of his thinking and finally bring together a critical analysis of his completed model of the human psyche.

After the break with Freud, Jung acknowledged that 'a period of inner uncertainty began . . . which it would be no exaggeration to call . . . a state of disorientation'. Indeed, he admitted feeling literally as if he were suspended in mid-air and had, so to speak, lost his footing. The question – by what myth do you live? – persisted continuously at the back of his mind, but his close scrutiny of possible answers left him so uncomfortable that he at last abandoned the quest. 'I had', he finally wrote, 'reached a dead end.' Simultaneously, he set out for a four-day cruise on Lake Zürich with Albert Oeri and three younger friends, during which Oeri fell into the habit of reading aloud the Nekyia episode of Homer's *Odyssey*, the journey of Ulysses to the Sojourn of the Dead. It was significant because Jung now approached perhaps the most shattering experience of his life, and later frequently referred to it as his own Nekyia.[2] In the same year he abandoned his academic career by withdrawing from his lecturing as a privat docent[3] at the University after eight continuous years.

Internal conflicts were now so intense that he could no longer lecture coherently. Anthony Storr commented: 'Jung told me he knew what sacrifice meant because of this abandonment of an academic career. I am sure it meant a great deal to him.'[4]

Innumerable dreams and fantasies now began to harass him which – not unexpectedly because he was slipping from the role of psychiatrist into the role of patient – he failed to interpret with any verisimilitude. One such dream involved a dove which spoke with a human voice and said that only when the male dove was absorbed with the twelve dead could the female convert herself into a human being.

Jung awoke from the dream in great perturbation, but all his immense analytical skills failed to find a satisfactory interpretation of the phrase 'the twelve dead'. Did they represent the twelve Apostles, the twelve months of the year or the signs of the Zodiac? When no interpretation presented itself 'there was nothing for me to do but . . . to go on with my life and pay close attention to my fantasies'.

One dream now crowded upon another fantasy, but time and again they centred around corpses, or involved something present which was dead, yet not quite dead, until one very powerful dream seemed to crystallise many others. In the region of Alyscamps near Arles the local authorities preserve a number of sarcophagi which can be traced back to Merovingian times, and Jung dreamt that he was walking down a long row of tombs in a closely similar situation. Instead of being hewn out of stone they were mummified and wearing antique clothes, but when Jung scrutinised one such mummy closely it was as if its gaze became animated, causing the corpse to move and come to life. Something similar happened with a second mummy, but as he proceeded down the row he came at last to a twelfth-century crusader in chain mail, and this time it seemed that he was immutably dead. As Jung's scrutiny persisted his gaze intensified, and then at last just a finger of the crusader's left hand began to stir.

Preoccupied with his profound incursion into the literature of symbols, mythology and religion, Jung automatically looked for some archaic explanation which would nonetheless 'link with the living'.

Surprisingly he overlooked one obvious explanation. Did the twelve dead represent the psychoanalytic apostles who had one after another deserted the Master, and was his account of Judas in the *Psychology of the Unconscious* concerned with someone living who was guilty of betraying another Master? More profoundly, in breaking away from Freud had the son, symbolically, murdered the father and now, overwhelmed with guilt, dreamt of corpses he was driven to try to resurrect? Coming to the oldest crusader of them all – Freud himself – did he merely succeed in stirring signs of life in one finger of his left hand? The death wish which Freud claimed Jung directed against him was reinforced by innumerable corpses strewn through his dreams, but he had psychologically murdered the father and, already searching for atonement, desperately sought to resurrect the corpse. The ambivalence of wishing Freud alive and wishing him dead was clear in the dream.

So intense did these fantasies become that Jung at last felt – what he might long ago have suspected – that 'there was some psychic disturbance in himself'. Practising analysts are frequently blind to psychic origins in their own conflicts, as happened with Freud on several occasions.

Like Freud, however, Jung now began what amounted to a self-analysis which was to lead him, devastatingly, into the deepest and most volcanic regions of his psyche and carry his theories into quite new and brilliantly original fields. Jung had urged on Freud that all future analysts should be analysed, a requirement which has since become standard practice. Whether the initial steps in his self-analysis were deliberately taken or whether, like many another mentally disturbed person, he regressed involuntarily needs close examination. Jung claims that 'I twice went over all the details of my life paying special attention to childhood memories',[5] but deliberate retrospection appears to have led him nowhere. He then decided to yield himself up to the dark undertow of the unconscious without knowing where it might carry him and deliberately provoked the upsurge by first writing down his dreams every morning. His reminiscences apart, Jung's journey through the unconscious is known in considerable detail from a series of private seminars he gave in 1925,[6] which dates the beginning of the exploration from 12 December 1913. Just how far deliberation entered into the process, and to what degree pathological forces carried him involuntarily back to his beginnings is difficult to establish. In anyone else the straightforward term 'breakdown' would describe the general, non-technical characteristics of what took place, but with a psyche so complex, rich and powerful every conceivable complication cross-fertilised the process until the rationally willed was indistinguishable from the compulsively inescapable.

The first recollection thrown up by the past revealed Jung as a child playing passionately with building-blocks to create an array of castles, temples and houses. Astonishingly once more in an analyst, he seemed surprised when this memory was 'accompanied by a good deal of emotion'. The idea that he could only bridge the gap between the man of thirty-six and the boy of eleven by once more playing childish games seemed so repugnant to him that he could not voluntarily submit. The very fact that he put up 'endless resistances' and only succumbed in the end 'with resignation' indicates that neurotic compulsions certainly played an important part in driving him back down those painful and with each recessive step more disturbing paths.

There was indeed something grotesque to anyone but an analyst in the picture of one of the most distinguished psychiatric consultants of the century walking along the lake shore gathering suitable stones in order to begin building first cottages, then a castle and finally a whole village, reproducing with alarming accuracy his childhood playtime habits. A village required a church, and he proceeded to add 'a square building with a hexagonal drum on top of it and a dome'. Detailed almost to the point of preciosity, the church now demanded an altar and, walking along the lake one day, he suddenly caught sight of a red stone, 'a four-sided pyramid about an inch and a half high'. Instantly he knew that he had found his substitute altar, but now the abreactive forces went to work to reactivate not merely childhood games but the much more powerful and disturbing dream of the underground chamber with its gigantic phallus which had occurred in his fourth year.

His precise reactions are difficult to determine. In his reminiscences he wrote, 'This connection gave me a feeling of satisfaction,' but he admitted to Lancelot Whyte, the physicist philosopher, that 'something erupted at the recollection which I found difficult to control'.[7]

His application to playing games became even more passionate. Immediately after lunch he would hurry back to the shore and continue to build his 'miniature village, or begin a quite new structure'. He 'continued to do so until the patients arrived; and if [he] was finished with [his] work early enough in the evening [he] went back to building'.[8]

Continuously the question recurred – what exactly was he doing and why, and as consistently back came the answer – 'discovering my own myth', but the building game proved itself only the beginning of what was to become a whole multitude of self-revealing fantasies. Slowly the stream mounted until 'I stood helpless before an alien world' and the inner tensions multiplied. There came a time when he felt as if 'gigantic blocks of stone were tumbling down upon' him and one colossal thunderstorm followed on the heels of the last. 'My enduring these storms was a question of brute strength,' he wrote, but a driving purpose to discover what it all meant also contributed to his survival. Above all, while he 'endured these assaults of the unconscious' he had 'an unswerving conviction that' he was 'obeying a higher will'.

Technical control of any analysis may become a prerequisite of successful treatment, and he now found himself so wrought up that he had to do certain Yoga exercises to hold his emotions in check. Thus it was that in the late summer of 1913 he fulfilled the classic pattern of some deeply disturbed persons by resisting further withdrawal into himself and beginning to feel the pressures moving outwards into external life again. He knew only too well the terrifying possibilities of becoming completely split off from reality, but now when he sought to return to that reality 'the atmosphere actually seemed to me darker than it had been before'. Alarmingly, he became convinced that the 'oppression no longer came from an inner psychic situation but from external reality'.[9]

The struggle swayed to and fro. Sometimes the contents of his unconscious threatened to overwhelm all attempts at transmutation, sometimes he regained surface control and came to a kind of compromise with reality. Once conscious control was restored he would deliberately abandon it again and 'allow the images and inner voices to speak afresh'.

Clearly he had at this stage gained deliberate control over the analysis.

The autumn of 1913 brought one rich, monstrous, overpowering vision. Travelling alone on some unspecified journey, the railway track was invaded by a great flood of water which slowly overwhelmed the 'low-lying lands between the North Sea and the Alps' and roared on to threaten Switzerland itself, but as the tide ran across the outer boundaries the mountains seemed to climb higher and higher into the sky as if to escape the flood. Jung, too, retreated from the tide, but presently he saw with horror that its mighty yellow waves carried the debris of buildings, floating rubble, thousands of drowned corpses, the remnants of a collapsed civilisation. Finally the whole vision was invaded by a lurid colour which turned the sea into blood. Unlike many fantasies, this one persisted for at least an hour and left Jung 'perplexed . . . nauseated and ashamed of [his] weakness'.

Two weeks later the fantasy repeated itself with renewed intensity, and this time the blood seemed even more brilliant in colour. Simultaneously a voice spoke to Jung: 'Look at it well: it is wholly real and it will be so. . . .'[10]

Shortly afterwards a friend asked Jung what he thought the future held for Europe, and Jung admitted that he 'saw rivers of blood'. Analysing the vision in greater depth, he came to the conclusion that it represented the threat of his own inner disintegration in the form of a psychosis.

His failure to identify the First World War with his dream did not undermine a belief which subsequently came to dominate his thinking: that many creative people were vessels through which new and superior insights were made manifest. Later he saw himself as one such person and formulated the theory of synchronicity. For the rest, his personal

struggle was too intense – indeed, devastating – to permit any prolonged self-examination of universal roles at that point.

Continuously he wrote down many of the fantasies in the high
rhetoric suggested by the unconscious, and frequently it seemed to
amount to automatic writing as if dictated by the unconscious itself.
The rhetoric he found distasteful – as indeed were many of the fantasies
which seemed to become a 'diabolical mixture of the sublime and the
ridiculous'.

His suffering was immense. Insomnia, stomach trouble and a
continuous sense of being almost 'possessed' reduced him to states of
withdrawal which deeply worried Emma, Toni Wolff and many
friends. Among the women, some vied with one another in their efforts
to help him, but the results were equivocal.

Rooted in a form of conventional stability by his wife and family,
there was no doubt that this sheet anchor held firm against the terrifying
pressures which continually tried to overthrow his reason, but part of
the cause of those storms can be traced to the appearance of Toni Wolff
and the discovery that his nature did not easily surrender to the
austerities of monogamy. Toni Wolff became, in the end, the person
who reconciled his maladjusted anima, but for the moment her role
remained ambivalent. Combine the internal and external forces and his
near-breakdown is easily explicable. Freud as a father had not merely
absorbed all Jung's craving for a surrogate, but re-activated his
homosexual experience as a boy, reinforcing the emotional and
intellectual ties with sexual libido. The intensity of the positive
transference was matched by the power of the final negative transference, and this was no ordinary break between father and son. 'I had
foreseen my isolation and harboured no illusion about reactions of my
so-called friends.' Torn out of a professional context which had
nurtured him for six years, he found himself alone in Zürich with no one
comparable with Freud. His last abusive letters were equivalent to a
sustained attack aimed at silencing the Master once and for all. In
psychological terms, when one person speaks of murdering another it is
nothing more than a 'happening' with no necessary physical correlative. However, psychological reactions with all their attendant
grief, guilt, horror and loneliness hit Jung with considerable force.
Simultaneously the sheet anchor of his family had shifted under the
stress of his affair with Toni Wolff, the moral principles by which he
lived were severely tested, and his struggle to plumb the deepest caverns
of his own psyche threatened to tear him apart. All unaware he had
lived out one of the oldest myths of all – parricide – and, if one accepts
Toni's anima role, his enactment of several details of the myth
reinforced the conclusions he was about to draw.

In the forest of motives which sustained his self-analysis, Jung
persuaded himself that he could not ask his patients to do something
which he dared not do himself. 'Dared not' became a very operative

phrase, because he had now reached a stage where he either had to 'plummet right down' into the fantasies he had activated or try to retreat from what threatened to become an all-engulfing maelstrom. Knowing too well what would happen if he lost control and surrendered completely, violent resistance arose to any further self-investigation. Again the knowledge that his patients under treatment would confront a similar fear and could not be expected to overcome it if he himself failed, drove him on.

One other big factor underlay everything, a factor not mentioned in his reminiscences. As we have seen, in a letter to Ewald Jung on 30 December 1959 he revealed that his great-grandmother Sophie Ziegler had suffered from 'a mental illness'. Her handwriting, he wrote, 'shows no schizophrenic traits but rather, for all its character an emotional ravagement, such as can be observed in psychogenic melancholias'.

Were hereditary factors at work in his illness? Whatever the explanation, he now wrote: 'It was during Advent of 1913 – 12th Dec. to be exact – that I resolved upon the decisive step.' As if it were a physical reality he suddenly, in his own phrase, let himself drop. The ground appeared literally to collapse under his feet, and he 'plunged down into dark depths'. As he fell, panic overtook him because he felt that he might have plunged into a bottomless pit, and then, to his immense relief, something checked his fall – 'a soft sticky mess'. He was in darkness, but as his eyes grew accustomed to the gloom he saw the entrance to a cave filled by a mummified dwarf. Forcing his way past the dwarf he waded through cold water to the opposite end of the cave where he encountered a crystal formation, glowing red. Lifting the stone supporting the crystal, he found a smaller cave underneath through which water ran, and in the water floated the corpse of a youth with a wound in his head. A huge black scarab then appeared, followed by a blood-red sun rising out of the depths of the second cave. The brilliant light blinded him, and he tried to replace the stone over the corpse, the water and the sun, but suddenly a thick jet of blood spurted upward and continued pouring its crimson radiance over everything.

'I was stunned by the vision,' he wrote. Obsessed with his new mythological theories, he translated the myth as 'a drama of death and renewal, the re-birth symbolised by the Egyptian scarab'. Immediately a difficulty arose. Instead of a new day dawning an 'intolerable outpouring of blood' followed. Association with his earlier fantasy of the blood-red flood overwhelming the world occurred to him, but he remained dissatisfied with this interpretation.

Within a few days a new dream developed, and again Jung read it mythologically. He saw, in vivid detail, a bare rocky landscape slowly illumined by dawn and there, armed with rifles, were two men, one in his own likeness, the other a brown-skinned savage. When a horn sang out across the landscape Jung was suddenly seized with the conviction that they had to destroy the approaching hero Siegfried. Dramatically poised high up on the crest of the mountain, illumined by the rising sun, Siegfried appeared driving a 'chariot made of the bones of the dead' and came crashing down a precipitous path at breakneck speed. As the chariot turned towards the two waiting men, ruthlessly they shot him down.

Overwhelmed by horror and remorse, they rushed away, afraid that 'the murder might be discovered'. The landscape suddenly darkened, rain began to fall and with the rain came relief because it would remove all traces of their crime. 'Life could go on but an unbearable feeling of guilt remained.'

Coming awake, full of apprehension, Jung examined the dream from many angles and failed to understand it. On the verge of falling asleep again, an inner voice told him that he must understand the dream because if he did not, only one alternative remained – to shoot himself.

The weapon was in fact at hand; Jung always kept his service revolver loaded in the drawer of what he called his night table. Concentrating once more on the details of the dream suddenly, he claimed, the meaning dawned on him. The dream projected the problem then being played out in the external world of Europe. Siegfried represented the rising military might of Germany and her desire to impose her will on the world. Jung, too, had once cherished a similar ambition and therefore identified with Siegfried, but the hero's attitude no longer suited him and he had to be destroyed. Commingled with his compassion for the dead was an overpowering sense that in destroying Siegfried he had also destroyed himself. Not until he reached the end of his account did Jung reveal that the brown-skinned savage in the dream really initiated the murder. He now saw him as an 'embodiment' of what he was later to call his shadow self. Carefully analysing all the elements of the dream, Jung drew the conclusion that he must abandon his ideals and reformulate his aims in life.

Consider these two dreams from a quite different approach – his recent traumatic break with Freud. Jung was six feet, Freud five feet seven, one relatively a dwarf to the other, and there, in the first dream, the entrance to the cave was blocked by a mummified dwarf. The dead Freud checked Jung's struggle towards rebirth so powerfully that when the sun of a new day arose in the cave it suddenly obliterated everything with a bursting jet of blood, simultaneously symbolising rebirth and death.

As for the dream of Siegfried riding so splendidly down in a chariot of bones, identification with Freud was clearly possible and his deliberate destruction literally admitted as an act of murder; but now, searching for expiation, Jung saddled the little brown savage with the crime. A clinching detail occurred in his admission that by destroying Siegfried he had destroyed himself.

Jung set out on this prolonged self-analysis in the belief that it was a voluntary confrontation with his unconscious no less experimental than those he had frequently undertaken with patients, but by now dynamic forces within the process had taken charge and spontaneously forced him deeper and deeper into what might easily become a bottomless abyss. In fact the material which overwhelmed him was indistinguishable from the chaotic images sometimes thrown up by psychotics and even the insane.

Anthony Storr has pointed out, in an excellent short account of Jung's theories,[11] that 'normal', 'mad' and 'schizophrenic' are relative not absolute terms. All three types had myths by which they lived, and those millions who accepted and lived by the Christian myth would be outraged at the suggestion that they were anything other than normal. In one person the material thrown up by the unconscious fatally confused his mind and he became schizophrenic, in another the material emerged as the 'matrix of a mythopoeic imagination which had vanished from our rational age'.[12]

The unconscious was charged with infinite potential, but modern man considered it too dangerous to entrust himself to the hazardous paths, haunted by demons capable of human embodiment, which led into its more profound depths. It had become 'the path of error, of equivocation and misunderstanding'.

Jung was now slowly formulating a quite different theory in which the widespread neurosis harassing modern man might be seen as the result of alienation 'from the myth-creating substratum of the mind which was shared both by the normal person and by the psychotic'.[13] Later in life Jung quoted Goethe: 'Now let me dare to open wide the gate/Past which men's steps have ever-flinching trod.'[14] Faust was to Jung far more than a literary exercise. He became a link in the Golden Chain of alchemy where the great wise men, beginning with Hermes Trismegistos, finally conjoined earth and heaven.

Such mythological figures now came to his aid in the terrifying turmoil which persisted for another year. One of the worst moments occurred when he felt that he had entered a deep crater without life of any kind. Suddenly in the crater he encountered two figures, one a beautiful young girl, the other an old man with a white beard. The girl, to Jung's astonishment, called herself Salome and the man, equally a surprise, explained that he was Elijah.

Jung reminded himself that many similar encounters had occurred in mythology. According to the Gnostic tradition, Simon Magus went about with a young girl whom he had picked up in a brothel, Lao-tzu became involved with a dancing girl and Klingsor accompanied a woman called Kundry. A third figure, much more significant to his subsequent theories, now separated out from Elijah, a figure called Philemon. This figure brought with him 'an Egypto-Hellenic atmosphere with Gnostic colourations'.

Baffled by the vision, Jung decided to paint a portrait of Philemon, and this practice became part of the therapeutic process which reinforced his crumbling psyche. The contents of his fantasies were written down in what he called his Black Book and then suitably elaborated with paintings and drawings. The Black Book, which still exists, consists of six black-bound leather notebooks and the Red Book, bound in red leather, contains similar fantasies set down in medieval script.

It was the Philemon fantasy which reinforced his growing belief that elements in the psyche could arise from sources completely independent of personal experience. Jung held extensive conversations with what seemed to be the separate embodiment of Philemon giving utterance to thoughts which did not belong to his own consciousness.

Personified to the point where Philemon became a living personality, Jung walked up and down the garden talking with him, and such a scene in anyone else would certainly have conveyed the impression of a madman listening to his voices. Half-aware of this, Jung feared that Philemon might give place to an alter ego, a third embodiment, and so successfully reproduce a line of merging figures ending in a luminous cloud of non-being. 'My ego felt devalued – although the successes I had been having in worldly affairs might have reassured me.'

A new element now intervened. One day in the middle of a fantasy he said to himself, 'Has what I am doing anything to do with science?' and was on the point of answering, 'No,' when to his amazement he heard an unmistakably feminine voice saying, 'It is art.' This interpretation surprised him – he had never dreamt of being an artist – but that it should be formulated by a woman was even more remarkable. As the dialogue continued, he thought he detected a familiar note in the voice and quickly identified a patient, 'a talented psychopath who had a strong transference' to him. The alarming question arose: had she lodged herself like a living parasite in his mind, or was some other much more subtle process at work?

Challenging his invisible companion, he said that the irrational processes taking place in his mind 'had nothing to do with art' and waited for an answer. None came. When he continued to write his experiences in the Black Book, the flow of his thoughts was suddenly interrupted again by the voice which reasserted, 'That is art!' Determined not to be outwitted, he immediately retaliated, 'No – it is not art because it is nature!' Again he waited for the reply, but once more nothing materialised.

His account of what followed is paradoxical. On the one hand the voice within had already communicated in simple Swiss German, but now when she did not answer he explained it away by saying, 'She does not have my speech centres.' Compounding the paradox he suggested that she now communicate through his own speech centres, which could be seen as differentiating the animus from the anima. There follows in the reminiscences this unsatisfactory summing-up: 'She did so and came through with a long statement.' Until we have the full text of the Black Book we do not know what that statement was, nor do we know whether he ever recorded it in detail. In the mill-race of his mind, Jung now formulated the hypothesis that 'the voice' must represent the soul 'or the primitive sense', and immediately asked 'why the name anima was given to the soul'. This led into a classic fragment of his model of the psyche – the anima – a name finally given to that 'inner feminine figure which plays a typical or archetypal role in the unconscious of man'.

The voice, or anima, had negative and positive aspects. Coping with the initial sense of awe produced by the negative aspects led him to prolonged periods of writing in the belief that if he responded passionately enough he would receive more from this invisible presence. It was, he wrote, rather like 'a patient in analysis with a ghost and a woman!' Technically he perfected the process of personifying unconscious voices, and later argued that the degree of autonomy which they achieved made this comparatively simple. A further paradox now occurred when he claimed that personification of unconscious contents 'stripped them of their power' because it was the crux of his anima–animus theory that such power must be *creatively assimilated*.

The written record of his breakdown and simultaneous self-analysis is rambling, perhaps for this reason it conveys most vividly the almost incoherent upsurge of potentially destructive material. The whole tumultuous outpouring carefully avoids any mention of Antonia Wolff. An intellectual woman in one sense she epitomised the mythopoeic approach to life in another. Was it possibly her voice speaking from Jung's unconscious because his guilt had repressed her constantly recurring image and she now represented the ideal anima with all those attributes he desired in a woman? Or had he projected his internal anima figure on to her, readjusted it in the process and at last reflected back the image in a new orientation of his own tormented self? Jung had a very powerful and unruly anima,[15] and in the poetic sense of the word it was almost as if Toni tamed it. In a quite different sense she was his *'femme inspiratrice'*. Emma Jung told a friend of Laurens van der Post: 'I shall always be grateful to Toni for doing for my husband what I or anyone else could not have done at a most critical time.'[16]

Jung's reminiscences frankly admit how near he came at this period to madness, but justifiably claim that his family kept him sane. He did in fact repeat to himself for reassurance, 'I have a medical diploma from a Swiss university . . . I have a wife and five children, I live at 228 Seestrasse, Küsnacht.' These facts and the demands made on him by his patients convinced him, when his physical reality seemed about to dissolve into nothingness, that he did continue to exist as an independent human being. Nietzsche had undergone a similar experience but finally lost touch with reality and disappeared into his inner world, a collapse which Jung succeeded in avoiding only by the most sustained

and exhausting effort. In the end his breakdown became a creative
illness and from it emerged a new man.[17]

Signs of recovery became apparent early in 1916, when he felt a
recurrent urge to 'give shape to something'. The first premonitions were
surrounded by an atmosphere in which he came to think that his house
at Küsnacht was haunted. Odd supernatural effects were produced,
and they did not at first happen directly to Jung himself but involved his
family. His eldest daughter woke one night in great alarm when she
thought she saw a ghostly white presence moving in her bedroom. His
second daughter, unaware of her sister's experience, told Jung that
twice in the same night the blanket had been snatched away from her
bed. His nine-year-old son also woke from an 'anxiety dream' and the
following day drew a picture which he called 'The Picture of the
Fisherman'. It was perfectly possible for one daughter to imagine a
ghostly presence, something experienced by millions of people, and for
another to interpret a slipped blanket during a restless night as the work
of supernatural powers. The boy's dream and his need to convert it into
pictures could also have occurred in rationally explicable circumstances.

But when around five o'clock the following afternoon, a Sunday, the
front-door bell of the house began a prolonged peal and no one could be
seen ringing it Jung began to sense that mysterious forces were
preparing the ground for a new development in his psychic odyssey. It
was a beautiful summer day, two maids had the front porch in full view
and although they could see the bell moving and hear it ringing, no
human agency was evident. The whole family looked uneasily at one
another and Jung knew that 'something had to happen'. It was, he
wrote, as if 'a crowd were present' and the whole house 'crammed full of
spirits. They were packed deep right up to the door and the air was so
thick it was scarcely possible to breathe.'

Jung records in his reminiscences that the spirits 'cried out in chorus'
the words, 'We have come back from Jerusalem where we found not
what we sought.' No explanation is given of this cabbalistic message but
from that moment there began to flow from his pen that remarkable
book *Septem Sermones*. At the moment of picking up his pen the spirits
which had invaded the house vanished and he wrote obsessionally over
the course of three evenings to complete the work. Symbolically the
purging of the house was the purging of his near-madness. In one sense
the demons had been exorcised; in another, his encounter with the
archaic materials of the collective unconscious had at last been
assimilated in a new harmony.

We have seen how the mummified dwarf in the mouth of the cave
combined to symbolise the psychological murder and Jung's desperate
struggle to be reborn as a completely independent analytical psychologist. That struggle invoked, over several years, all the mythopoeic

figures we have encountered which can be read clinically in several ways. Was it that he had never faced up to what his wife, Toni Wolff, Freud, Salome, Elijah, Philemon, God the Father and all the interlocking figures, real and fantastic, actually meant to him? At a deeper level had he all his life avoided confrontation with his true self, the person skilfully camouflaged behind the masks created by primary and secondary processes? As he lifted one corner of the veils on his true self, did the shock of the first revelations drive him to drop it hastily in place once more? Was he forced to return again and again to encounter, overcome and assimilate so many aspects of himself, superficially known but not fully acknowledged at the deeper level of individuation? One revelation led to another. Slowly the reasonably 'normal', conventionally faithful married man, believing in one form of God, had been revealed as a person with bi-sexual potential, committing adultery, unreconciled to the personal God of Christianity and capable of murdering his own father at one remove. A shattering metamorphosis.

At another level had he also come face to face with the person, presented by some witnesses, who took his wife's devotion for granted, insisted on incorporating his mistress into the family and showed very little interest in his children? Seen in technical terms Jung was a cyclothymic personality who suffered a manic-depressive psychosis. He did not collapse into schizophrenia.[18]

Chapter 19

Recovery, and Work Resumed

THE DAILY ROUTINE of family life, work and patients continued at his beautiful lakeside house at Küsnacht, but with many variations. Self-analysis disturbed both work and family life, and between the years 1913–16 he not only found himself 'incapable of reading a scientific book', but also, according to Aniela Jaffé, wrote very little. This is not entirely true. Forty years later the manuscript of *The Transcendent Function* was discovered and published for the first time.[1]

This was written, like many passages in the Black Books, in a special study built into the large library at Küsnacht, where the windows, darkened by panes of coloured glass, created the atmosphere of an intellectual cave. Before he could concentrate fully, his temperament demanded that he be cut off in a small room dimly lit with no 'extraverted view' outside. A considerable library surrounded him. Its earliest acquisitions included all those medical, psychiatric and psychological writings which had enlightened the beginning of his career. Thus, inside the small study were the works of Sigmund Freud and his school, the writings of Darwin, Stohr, Strumpell and Zeigler, and many volumes of religious history and mythology.

Some of his more profound visionary experiences took place in this cave-like study. He demanded absolute silence when he was writing, with children banished and the domestic routine not allowed to intrude. Entry to the study was forbidden to anyone lacking the excuse of a grave emergency.[2] Summoning him to a meal was sometimes a difficult operation.

Two more children had been born, Marianne (10 September 1910) and Emma (18 March 1914), to enlarge the family to five. Gret Baumann-Jung, his daughter, recalls that in the games they played he was not a good loser. Quite capable of cheating at deck tennis, in his excitement he once collapsed into the water. He could shout in anger, and she was very apprehensive of his outbursts. Sometimes she felt as if he resented her even being alive.[3]

Jung's relationship with his wife had changed. Her struggles to keep pace with him intellectually never really succeeded, but now her efforts were seriously handicapped by having to cope with a large family, and Toni Wolff. Being civilised women, they had come to an uneasy accommodation of their mutually distressing situation, but occasionally the strain was too much for both of them. There is some evidence to show that Jung insisted on Toni becoming almost a part of the family on many occasions. There was also the occasion when Carl woke in the middle of the night to find his youngest daughter crying, and felt that she was disturbed by his own distressed state. Silently, he dressed and went out into the night and sought the solace of Antonia's company.[4] He seemed to feel that Antonia could help to prevent emanations from his anima upsetting the family, and this could be seen as an ironic inversion of the whole situation. One precipitating cause of his emotional troubles was Antonia, and removing rather than encouraging her presence the conventional imperative of social morality, but theoretically at least, Jung did not subscribe to the accepted conventions.

Just how far he carried this doctrine is not clear, but several women surrounded him idolatrously, and they in turn were torn by jealousies. Struggles for his favours were now commonplace. As the years went by the number of women increased rather than decreased, but the inner circle seemed to include a certain proportion of spinsters and some lesbians.

At least one amongst them talked freely about Jung as a man and lover, but only under a cloak of heavy anonymity and with nothing more than corroborative verbal evidence from similar sources.[5] It is a mistake to put too much reliability on such sources, but a witness who knew the situation intimately described him as not a great lover. His sexuality was very straightforward, and all the mythopoeic talk vanished in a cloud of uncomplicated passion. But it 'varied according to his mood and the events of the day. Given a summer's evening, a private place looking out on the lake and he would quote something in that deep resonant voice of his and look at a woman like a young girl he had just fallen in love with on a spring day.'[6]

Emma and Toni were different women with different outlooks. Emma, conventionally correct, believed in the eternal verities and could not follow the higher flights of Carl's intellect. She did become an analyst and applied his psychotherapeutic method, but it was largely in an attempt to understand her husband's psychology.[7] However, it would be a mistake to underestimate her. People who worked with her in analysis found her extremely helpful and understanding.[8] She was also a tower of strength in the family. As for Toni, she wanted to live a life free from moral or other inhibitions, brought the true intellectual's scepticism to accepted values and collaborated with Jung to the point where she pioneered new ground in her own right. She elaborated Jung's four functions with a description of four typologies in woman: the woman as Mother and Wife, the woman as Hetaera or companion and friend to Man, the woman as Amazon with a calling of her own, and the woman as Medium or mediator between the conscious and unconscious. Toni was both the inspired Hetaera and the Medium.

In his reminiscences Jung claimed that two events contributed to his 'emergence from the darkness'. First, he broke with a woman who had tried to convince him that his 'fantasies had artistic value' and, second, he first encountered and began to understand the nature of the mandala.[9] As early as 1916 he had painted his first mandala, unaware how deep an influence it was to have on his theories. Regarded by now as the high priest of a new and still developing psychological school, a much-sought-after therapist, he had undergone an interior metamorphosis not completely assimilated until the meaning of the mandala became clear to him.

A brief period as Commandant de la Région Anglaise des Internés de Guerre at the Château d'Oex gave him the leisure to sketch every day and triggered off the new experience. One morning Jung found himself spontaneously sketching a circular symbol and immediately the strongest conviction overtook him that it represented 'in some living way' his 'inner situation'. T. S. Eliot would have regarded it as an objective correlative, and Jung described it as a mandala. Many of these drawings, made day by day, revealed to Jung the psychic transformation he underwent. When, for instance, the person described as an 'aesthetic lady' insisted that his sketches had artistic talent, he became so annoyed that his mandala 'burst open'. Whether the 'aesthetic lady' was in fact Toni Wolff I have been unable to establish, but that certainly described one aspect of her personality. Following his first mandala discovery, Jung gave many descriptions of mandalas' meaning: 'The psychological expression of the totality of the self';[10] 'Formation, Transformation, Eternal Mind's recreation';[11] 'Cryptograms concerning the state of the self',[12] In the *Collected Works* he gives a fuller definition:

> 'Mandalas' . . . usually appear in situations of psychic confusion and disorientation. The archetype thereby constellated represents a pattern of order which, like a psychological 'view-finger' marked with a cross or circle divided into four, is superimposed on the psychic chaos so that each content falls into place and the weltering confusion is held together by a protective circle. . . . At the same time they are *yantas*, instruments with whose help the order is brought into being.[13]

Professor Maurice Carstairs once exhibited a collection of schizophrenic drawings which undoubtedly revealed *aspects* of the inner states of mad people, but Jung was now making more comprehensive claims for the innumerable mandalas he conveyed to paper. They represented the *totality* of the inner self and became part of the therapeutic process which finally brought him back to mental health. The prolonged pilgrimage into the deepest places of the individual and collective unconscious had thrown up mandalas which fused elements of both with his conscious self and thus initiated the process later to be called individuation. As Ellenberger puts it, 'Toward the end of World War I Jung discovered that a decisive advance in individuation was often marked by the occurrence of a specific quadratic figure in his dream more or less similar to the mandala of India and Tibet.'[14] Thus, when primal forces drove Jung's mind and hand to convey mandalas to paper they liberated psychic energy in such a way as to help redress the balance of his whole psyche. 'I knew', he wrote, 'that in finding the mandala I had attained what was for me the ultimate.'

Not unexpectedly in such a man, his creative illness was followed by a state of near-euphoria. Those who knew him recall the absolute conviction with which he began to speak of the collective unconscious, the anima, the self and individuation. Ellenberger commented, 'It is another characteristic of those who have lived through such a spiritual adventure to attribute a universal value to their own personal experience.'

During his Nekyia, Jung applied the same elucidation of symbols with the help of comparative mythology that he had employed in interpreting Miss Miller's fantasies. From the whole long, painful experience emerged several of his most important concepts including individuation, the transcendant function, the anima and the self. An article published in December 1916[15] outlined a number of ways of coping with the powers of the unconscious including attempts at repression, exhaustion through reductive analysis, and the uncontrolled release of those powers.

By far the best method, Jung said, was a dangerous but transforming fight against the contents of the unconscious which finally subdued them. Similar experiences were represented in those myths which unfolded the hero's fight against a monster, leading to the recovery of an invincible weapon, and the whole process had the deepest roots in mythology and the history of man.

The supposition that Jung's mental breakdown overwhelmed his work between 1913 and 1918 is qualified by the appearance of *Psychological Types* in 1921, part of the research for which appears to fall within those dates, and *The Transcendent Function*. From the first beginnings of *Metamorphoses and Symbols of Libido* (1911–12) he slowly developed his equally important work, *Psychological Types*. Scattered through its 700 pages are references to Antisthenes, Diogenes, Tertullian, Origen, Spitteler, Schiller, William James and a hundred more figures ranging from Chinese philosophers, Fathers of the Church and medieval theologians to Greek mythologists and modern psychoanalysts. The overwhelming weight of references makes the book difficult to read and a long arduous road has to be followed before the crucial chapter, 'A Psychological Theory of Types', is reached.

Romantic, sanguine, choleric, classic – all these types are examined in detail, and fierce divergences between people like St Augustine and Pelagius, Tertullian and Origen, Luther and Zwingli derived from introverted and extraverted attitudes.

Jung himself wrote: 'The work sprang originally from my need to

define the ways in which my outlook differed from Freud's or Adler's.'
This led him to believe that 'It is one's psychological type which from
the outset determines and limits a person's judgment.'

Any short account of Jung's theory of psychological types, like most
aspects of his work, runs the danger of distortion, and nothing can
replace reading the arduous Chapter X of the book itself. In broad
outline, introverts are people who derive their motivations from
internal sources and subjective factors, and extraverts those drawing
inspiration from the external world and outside factors. The two types
are not mutually exclusive, and in the same sense that one individual
may be 'more or less introvert or extravert' he or she can change, as the
rhythms of life develop, from one to the other. However, in many people
one attitude frequently predominates, and then the typology becomes
much more clear-cut. Jung characterised introversion as 'a hesitant,
reflective, retiring nature that keeps itself to itself, shrinks from objects,
is always slightly on the defensive and prefers to hide behind mistrustful
scrutiny'. The extravert by contrast has 'an outgoing, candid and
accommodating nature that adapts easily to a given situation, quickly
forms attachments and, setting aside possible misgivings, will often
venture forth with careless confidence into unknown situations'.[16] Since
there were so many intermediate types, any clear-cut classification
became difficult, and as Jung put it 'every individual is an exception to
the rule'. Indeed, a complementary mechanism tended to arise in the
unconscious of the introverted person and compensatory extraverted
pressures could be called into operation at any time. Infinitely subtle in
its final formulations, Jung's theory allowed for those individuals who
despite an introverted nature yet have an extraverted view of the world
which explained the paradox of happy marriages between introverts
and extraverts.

Derivative as his typology was from the Gnostic philosophy and
many other sources, he carried their formulation into much more
complex and penetrating fields. The Gnostics believed that there were
three types corresponding to three basic psychological functions –
thinking, feeling and sensation. The *peumatikoi* could be correlated to
thinking, the *pychikoi* to feeling and the *hylikoi* to sensation. Jung
subdivided his introvert and extravert categories into four similar
functions of the conscious psyche. Involving two pairs of opposite
functions, they comprised the two rational functions of thinking and
feeling, and two irrational functions of sensations and intuition. It has to
be stressed that in Jungian terminology the word 'irrational' does not
imply 'anti-rational', but means being beyond what is normally
considered rational. 'Un-rational' would be a better term. Multiplying
complexities, like a genealogical tree, introversion, extraversion and the
four functions were further elaborated by eight subsidiary psychological
types, of which, in turn, four were introverted and four extraverted.
Pressing into still more speculative areas, Jung attempted to relate

specific characteristics, like 'sociable, pleasure-loving, dogmatic, mag-nanimous', with the sub-divisions of his types. These detailed extensions of his definitions began to make them suspect. In proportion as he speculated on specific characteristics scepticism multiplied.

Wittily illustrating the behaviour of Jung's psychological types at an imaginary dinner-party, Ania Teilhard[17] described the (feeling extrav-erted) perfect hostess receiving the guests with a husband (sensation introverted) whose mild manner is matched by an aesthetic sense which makes him an art collector and a specialist in Classical painting. A lawyer first rings the doorbell (thinking extraverted) followed by a well-known businessman (sensation extraverted) with his musician wife whose manner is somewhat taciturn (feeling introverted). Next to arrive is a distinguished scholar (thinking introverted) unaccompanied by his wife, a one-time cook (feeling extraverted). The dinner-party proceeds happily despite the fact that one of the guests, a poet (intuitive introverted) has failed to arrive because his psychological type makes him liable to forget invitations or misplace dates.

Serious criticism underlies the irony running through this picture but, whatever qualifications one has about a pioneering work, by 1950 the Swiss edition had gone through seven reprints, totalling 15,000 copies.

Chapter 20
Some Case-Histories

MANY NEW AND DISTINGUISHED patients consulted Jung between 1917 and 1920, among them Mrs Harold McCormick (Edith Rockefeller), James Joyce's daughter and Sir Montagu Norman, the Governor of the Bank of England. By the fortune of war, Zürich developed into one of the most important theatrical centres between 1914 and 1918, with Sir Max Reinhardt dominating the scene. Lenin, the Dadaists and James Joyce all concentrated wildly contradictory talents among a proliferation of wealth which enraged Lenin, fascinated James Joyce and amused the Dadaists.

Joyce had already written his play *Exiles*, but failed to find a backer. His friend Jules Martin then organised an amateur cast which included himself in the role of Richard and his friend Mrs Harold McCormick, who was reputed to be the wealthiest woman in Zürich, as Bertha. 'Her embonpoint, dresses, furs and diamonds . . . would make her perfect for the role.'[1] Sensing something slightly ridiculous in the undertaking, Mrs McCormick point blank refused to take part[2] but, on 27 February 1918, Joyce suddenly received a letter from the managing director of the Eidgenossiche Bank in Zürich asking him to call on a highly confidential matter. Borrowing a black suit, obligatory for anyone visiting a Zürich banker, he entered the splendid offices to receive a warm welcome. 'A client of this bank who has followed your work with increasing interest and knows you are hard up, wants to provide you with a kind of fellowship,' the manager said. 'It will be paid at the rate of one thousand francs a month.'[3] Joyce immediately tried to identify his benefactor and at last discovered that it was Mrs Harold McCormick who, according to Richard Ellmann, 'besides patronising writers and musicians . . . heavily endowed the psychologist Jung'.[4] Remembering Emma's wealth and Jung's successful practice, this would seem the supreme act of supererogation. Joyce now met his benefactress, and Mrs McCormick rapidly came to the conclusion that Joyce was a very odd man indeed, badly in need of analysis by her close friend and adviser Carl Gustav. A capricious woman, when Joyce described such an undertaking as 'unthinkable', she reacted strongly. Prepared to introduce him personally to Jung and bear the cost of analysis, she was very annoyed at the vehemence of his rejection.

On 1 October 1919, Joyce called at the bank to collect the monthly stipend only to be told curtly, 'Der kredit ist erschopft' ('Your credit is stopped'). Searching around for the cause, Joyce first traced a conspiracy between his old friend Ottocaro Weiss, who knew Jung, and

Mrs McCormick. 'Weiss protested his innocence but Joyce did not swerve from his conviction.'

At this stage Jung had not met Joyce, but reports of the 'wildly original' work *Ulysses* failed to impress him and Joyce came to believe that Jung may have influenced Mrs McCormick to withdraw his allowance on the grounds of his heavy drinking and 'inability to write well'.[5] According to Joyce, Jung said that '*Ulysses* could be read backwards or forwards in *Finnegans Wake*', which did not please him. Retaliating, Joyce wrote: 'We grisly old Sykos who have done our unsmiling bit on alices when they were yung and easily freudened . . . the law of the jungerl.'[6] Joyce came to believe that Jung had 'successfully cured' another recipient of Mrs McCormick's patronage, Wolff-Ferrari, by urging her to withdraw her subsidy because of his dissipation. W.-F. was, of course, one of the patients heavily disguised in Jung's reminiscences, and Joyce's scepticism misplaced. Wolff-Ferrari had in fact begun to compose music again when Mrs McCormick withdrew her subsidy.

It was Joyce's daughter who finally brought her father close to Jung and led to further complications. A very disturbed person, she had been treated by Dr Florel at Les Rives de Prangins in Montreux. When her condition did not improve she was finally taken off to the Burghölzli, where Professor Maier diagnosed her as catatonic. Joyce then remembered the suggestion of a friend of his, Mrs Jolas, who had recommended placing his daughter in the care of Dr Jung. Talking the matter over with Professor Giedion,[7] Joyce said: 'I wouldn't go to him [myself] but maybe he can help her.' On 28 September, Lucia took another step in her long, depressing pilgrimage and passed into the private sanatorium of Dr Brunner at Küsnacht, where Jung was the chief consultant. Since she had already been seen by twenty doctors without improvement, it came as a surprise to Joyce that Jung quickly penetrated her catatonic trance and persuaded her to talk to him. From the patient's history, this was remarkable, and a letter from Joyce shows that Lucia proceeded to gain weight and seemed happier.[8] In his struggle to sustain communication, Jung suggested that he would have more room for manoeuvre if Joyce left Zürich for the time being. He clearly saw that fierce complications in the relationship with her father underlay her slowly increasing madness. When Joyce told his daughter that he intended to leave Zürich for a month, she was very upset and in the end he spent far more money that he could afford remaining, in a state of deep depression, at the Carlton Élite Hotel.

The first positive transference to Jung was quickly followed by negative reactions. Long afterwards Jung admitted to Richard Ellmann that Lucia resented 'a big fat materialistic Swiss man' trying 'to get hold of [her] soul!'

Joyce now went to see Jung, but no detailed record remains of their meetings except from the interview granted by Jung to Richard

Ellmann. Ellmann, quoting from that interview, said: 'When the psychologist pointed out schizoid elements in poems Lucia had written, Joyce remembering Jung's comments on *Ulysses* insisted that they were anticipations of new literature and said his daughter was an innovator not yet understood.'

According to Jung, Lucia and her father were 'like two people going to the bottom of a river, one falling and the other diving', implying that one was unsuccessfully trying to rescue the other. 'The relationship of father and daughter Jung thought to be a kind of mystical identity or participation.' Joyce seems to have sat listening to Jung's comments on his daughter in silence. 'Jung took his manner to indicate that he had no emotional rapport with others when in fact he had no emotional rapport with the Reverend Doctor Jung,' Ellmann commented.

Ellmann strongly resisted Jung's interpretation of Joyce as a 'latent schizoid who used drinking to control his schizoidal tendencies'. He did not understand, Ellmann said, that Joyce was 'abstemious during the day and drank only at night . . . with a nice combination of purpose and relaxation'.

Much more revealing was a final comment from Patricia Hutchins:[9] 'I received a long letter from Jung asking me whether I knew anything of his Anima theory because if I did here was a prize example of it.' The letter said: 'She [Lucia] was definitely his *"femme inspiratrice"* which explains his obstinate reluctance to have her certified. His own anima . . . was so solidly identified with her that to have her certified would have been as much as an admission that he himself had a latent psychosis.'[10]

Jung had by now developed his therapeutic practice as well as theory in contrast to Freud's. Unlike Freud's patients, Jung's did not lie on a couch but sat in a chair and the length and frequency of sessions varied. 'I don't want to put the patient to bed,' he commented to Ruth Bailey, later to become his housekeeper.[11] He himself might sit looking out on the lake with the patient in any position he or she pleased. Sometimes he even treated patients on board his boat, and on one occasion went careering around the lake in a high wind, singing, as part of the therapy. The patient was expected actively to collaborate with Jung, the present life situation stressed, and Freudian concepts of negative and positive transference modified. Transference in Jungian terms was developing into a collaborative process between patient and analyst with a confrontation of their mutual findings. Simultaneously, the progressing synthesis of conscious and unconscious material sophisticated the process to become known as individuation and the therapist, when necessary, reached the unconscious through dream analysis. However, there were many cases where the first dreams clearly indicated those aspects of the psyche rejected by the patient, and this alone might indicate treatment and prognosis. Understanding and assimilating what he later called the shadow self became an important part of his new technique.

Another patient roughly coincidental with Lucia Joyce was a young woman of eighteen whose basic medical diagnosis – anorexia nervosa – involved many other symptoms. She could not sleep, she had lost her powers of concentration, and there were signs of an incipient lesbianism which greatly alarmed her mother. Daughter of a rich London businessman, money was no object to her parents, and having exhausted all conventional consultants they turned to Jung. The case is particularly interesting because Jung developed his new – mythological – analysis with this patient.

'Anna Maria'[12] – now a lady of seventy who insists on anonymity – found Jung at first meeting intimidating.

> He gave the impression of great power and insight and I was altogether shattered at the idea that he could see right through me, even into the sexual fantasies which were tormenting me. Torment-ing is not altogether true; I also derived great pleasure from them. But he overcame my shyness by the sheer informality of his manner. He talked to me – casually – like a friend – I don't even remember him making a note – not even writing down my name. It was all very informal, and I liked that. Everyone else I had seen – and by now they seemed legion – had been so stiff, correct, professional. He conveyed the feeling of an open-minded man warmly sympathetic to me in my dilemma. . . . Slowly my shyness vanished. . . .

It quickly became apparent to Jung that he was dealing with a case of mother fixation, but from the outset he suspected many complications. He asked Anna Maria to keep notes of her dreams over a period of some weeks and then analysed them as a single related system. She was disturbed to find that he immediately uncovered one of her main weaknesses which she had tried to mask by an elaborate system of bluff. Taking decisions had become such a nightmare to her that the issue of which dress she should wear on what day sometimes occupied her the whole morning, while she walked around in her dressing-gown smoking cigarette after cigarette. Deceiving herself into believing that she had taken the final decision, it was invariably her mother who made the choice. An intricate network of minor interlocking indecisions had her trapped in its power, and at the centre of the web, always sending out the final instructions, was her mother.

In fact a recurring dream frequently represented a female spider sitting at the centre of the web directing what appeared to be the traffic pouring down its silken threads with signals flashing on and off as her huge eye opened and shut.

> 'When he made me see that I was really in the power of my mother it came as a great shock because I thought I loved her more than

anything else in the world. . . . But it released something. I felt as if
a barrier had broken and my emotional life began to flow again.
But my mother didn't like it because as I recovered a little I
became that much more independent. Doctor Jung then pointed
out to me that my mother was fighting back to keep power over me
and prolong unnaturally the biological tie between us. He advised
me to insist on having a room of my own at the hotel – which I did.
It cost me a great effort but I had made up my own mind on a
major point for the first time in years, and that made me very
exhilarated. My mother was furious and wanted to take me away
from treatment but I had begun eating again, and she could not
deny an improvement.

There followed a period of regression due, Jung thought, to the
renewed conflict of wills between mother and daughter, but also to a
much deeper-rooted cause closely related to his mythological theories.

As Anna Maria slowly recovered again, she had the feeling that
something deep inside her which belonged to the very core of her viscera
had been disturbed and a new and much more powerful dream
occurred. It was the dream of a monstrous mountain in the shape of two
huge female breasts which slowly opened and engulfed her, and she
woke screaming so loudly that the other guests in the hotel reported the
matter to the night porter. He came to investigate and found her sound
asleep, but in the morning she hurried off to Küsnacht and poured out
the dream to Jung.

He saw it at once as a dream of the Earth Mother and asked her
whether she had ever read any mythology or knew of the Earth Mother
myth. She did not. By now a new and so far undetected symptom had
pushed into consciousness. 'It was a deep, deep sense of longing – of
emptiness – of craving for something I could not identify.' First she
imagined it must be a longing for food, but by now she was eating
reasonably well.

The Earth Mother dream recurred and when, against her own
inclination, Jung persuaded her to encourage the dream 'an extraordinary thing happened. Three nights in one week the same dream
recurred but it was different. First a sense of being engulfed, then of
being embraced and then of being reborn between those beautiful, soft,
huge breasts.' She now formulated the question herself – was she being
reborn under Jung's treatment?

In the end Anna Maria put on weight, her mother-angst diminished,
she was able to take up her study of English literature again and back in
London asserted her independence by moving into a flat with another
girl. 'But it was really due to a kind of alchemy Jung exerted which
activated something in me from a long dead past – a past to which I
belonged, but wasn't really mine.' The words vividly illustrated Jung's
mythological theory.

Far more dramatic was the case of a woman who sometimes turned up in his consulting-room with a loaded gun concealed in her handbag. Seduced by her brother at the age of fifteen, and then by a school-friend, she retreated into herself and within a year reached a typical catatonic state. Coping with psychotics needs enormous stamina, and it is too often forgotten that Jung was not only a pioneer in the field but also had a remarkable gift for dissolving the formidable defences built by such patients. Growing steadily worse, by the time she was seventeen this young woman continually listened to her inner voices, could no longer eat and never spoke herself.

As in the case of Lucia, Jung slowly infiltrated the prison she had elaborately erected and very soon she confessed to him the disconcerting fact that she lived on the moon. During her sojourn there a tremendous drama had taken place. Lunar society was so organised that the women lived below ground to protect themselves from a terrible vampire who came down from the high mountains to kidnap and kill, threatening the population with total extinction. The patient conspired to trap the vampire and kept a brave and lonely vigil on a watchtower erected to warn the lunar people of its approach. Several nights passed before she saw a monstrous bird darkening the sky with multiple wings and such a magnificent array of feathers that its head and figure were entirely masked. Finally confronting the bird with a long sacrificial knife in her hand, she wondered what manner of person was hidden by the feathers and at that moment the wings opened and 'a man of unearthly beauty stood before her'. His wings then closed in on her, gripping her with such power that the knife was useless in her hand and exerting all his strength he lifted her from the earth and flew away.

Symbolically representing the childhood experiences she had undergone, their re-enactment released her distorted energies and she began to talk freely. Jung realised from her outpourings that the moon represented to her a life rich in meaning compared with the blackness and poverty of earth, but before he could act on this interpretation she had a relapse. Devastatingly, from the patient's point of view, Jung had stopped her returning to the moon, and the relapse was so bad that she had to be sent to a sanatorium.

After two months, Jung began to rebuild his relationship with her and now he tried to get her to see that life on this earth was inescapable, but when she finally confronted the reality she collapsed once more and had to be sent back to the sanatorium. Jung visited her and once again attempted to reconcile her to the cold realities of earth. A dramatic improvement led to her taking a job as a nurse in a mental home, but when a young doctor made 'a somewhat rash approach to her' she promptly drew the revolver from her handbag and shot him. Luckily the wound turned out to be superficial. It now transpired that she carried the loaded revolver in her handbag wherever she went, and made no exception of her visits to Jung.

.

Convincing the girl that she felt 'humiliated in the eyes of the world but elevated in the realm of fantasy' was a difficult process. Mythological explanations were even more complicated. Incest, frequently the prerogative of royalty, had carried her into the realm of the mythic, where dark monsters and beautiful birds held sway. Surrendering to the bird-man of unearthly beauty, a figure symbolic of all those forces waiting to rush up from the collective unconscious, she had been overwhelmed by him, but now this earth-figure Jung threatened to drag her down to the mundane world again. She projected the evil aspect of the winged demon on to Jung and wished to destroy it with earth weapons, a commonplace revolver, but she had also betrayed her attachment to the beauty and power of the demon by revealing his story to Jung. In his reminiscences Jung omits an aspect of the case which he revealed to Lancelot Whyte.[13] The girl did arrive one day bent on destruction and placed the revolver on his desk, almost equidistant between them. 'It was as if she were asking – which of us is to shoot the other? When her hand moved out towards the gun I must say I felt distinctly uneasy . . .,' Jung said, 'but she merely put the weapon back in her handbag.'

In the end, Jung's treatment made it possible for her to talk and work again, but the last interview had a dramatic climax. The girl produced the gun once more, handed it to Jung and said, 'I would have shot you down if you had failed me!'

This case, according to Jung, was a long-term success. The girl married, had three children and 'survived two world wars in the East without ever again suffering a relapse'.

It is difficult to establish his actual success or failure rate with any degree of accuracy for two reasons. First, because hardly any records covering the years before the First World War seem to have survived[14] and, second, because criteria of success or failure vary so widely. If the patient before treatment could not work, found difficulty in sleeping and failed to reach a reasonably satisfactory relationship with a member of the opposite sex, and after treatment achieved all three, that was certainly one form of success. The difficulty lay in the third qualification. How to define such a relationship without disappearing into an infinite recession of further qualifications? However, Jung certainly including the gun-toting lady among his successes.

For the rest he did once give statistics, but when asked by Lancelot Whyte what they revealed said: 'I can't recall the figures exactly but I would say at least a third were – cured – another third I drew a blank with – and the remaining third was certainly much better.'[15] Roughly, this is a claim made by a number of psychiatrists.

Fully aware of the need for follow-up studies, Jung commented that the 'improved cases were the hardest to judge' because that category of patient did not realise until years afterwards what the treatment was all about. In Volume 16 of the *Collected Works* Jung wrote: 'The clinical material at my disposal is of a peculiar composition: new cases are decidedly in the minority. Most of them already have some form of psychotherapeutic treatment behind them. About a third of my cases are not suffering from any clinically definable neurosis, but from the senselessness and aimlessness of their lives. I should not object if this were called the general neurosis of our age.'[16]

One classic case of failure involved no less a person than Sir Montagu Norman, then Governor of the Bank of England. It began as far back as 1911 when, as Norman put it in his diaries, an apparently harmless attack of eczema foreshadowed a complete breakdown which drove him to abandon directing the Bank. A travelling holiday recommended by the doctors took him to the Caribbean, Central America and Panama. The manager of a bank in Panama revealed unusually sympathetic understanding of his troubles and recommended consulting a Swiss doctor who had a clinic in Zürich.[17]

Wasting no time, Norman telegraphed Jung and without waiting for a reply left for Lausanne, accompanied by his sister-in-law. On 15 April he saw Jung for the first time and somewhat to Norman's surprise Jung ordered a blood and spinal test to be carried out, which laid Norman low for several days. On 21 April another long session with Jung led to a diagnosis which shattered Sir Montagu. As Andrew Boyle says: 'Precisely what Jung said is not recorded because Norman's case history was not kept among Jung's private papers,'[18] but 'in Jung's considered opinion Norman was suffering from general paralysis of the insane, an incurable by-product of syphilis, tell-tale signs of which were the delusions of grandeur unmistakably betrayed by the patient'.[19]

Incapable of facing such an appalling truth, Norman failed to record the diagnosis in his diary. Instead he wrote: '. . . shall go through Jung's treatment which takes weeks or months according to individual'.[20]

Without the testimony of Sir Montagu's brother Ronald, the details of the case might remain suspect, but Ronald, urgently summoned from London, heard the verdict 'with indignant incredulity' and immediately determined to verify the facts with Jung himself. Courteous but firm, Jung simply repeated his diagnosis and Ronald returned to his brother, painfully bewildered.

Later he spelt out what had taken place: 'When I saw Jung he told me that Monty would be dead in a few months. It was a cruel wicked thing to suggest and I have never forgiven him. The following days were among the most miserable I've ever spent. My brother was in great pain and tragically depressed.'[21]

Andrew Boyle lays the blame directly at Jung's door, but we do not have the pathologist's report of the blood and spinal tests which might give full authority for his fatally wrong diagnosis. It seems incredible that Jung would not check out 'delusions of grandeur' with psychological as well as physiological causes, but one reason is possible. Although the blood serum and spinal fluid reports were said to be negative, Wassermann tests had only recently been introduced and were not universally accepted as foolproof. Moreover, delusions of grandeur unerringly pointed, for many doctors of the day, to G.P.I. What Sir Montagu Norman did not know was that 1913 marked the beginning of Jung's own psychological breakdown, and it was more than possible that the powerful demons pursuing him distracted his attention from an occasional patient, if indeed they did not undermine his judgment.

Dr Vittoz of Lausanne took over the case, and within a few weeks Norman's condition began to improve. It became apparent that he was 'subject to alternating cycles of despondency and euphoria', in other words a manic depressive. Periods of sleeplessness and 'intolerable pains in the head' would paralyse him for several weeks, only to relent and allow him to recover his joy in living.

All psychiatrists have failures. This was a serious one for Jung. Meanwhile his international reputation continued to grow.

Chapter 21

Travels Abroad

THE PRECISE DATE of Jung's recovery from his breakdown is obscured by fluctuating states of mind and conflicting evidence, but by 1919 he was living a full-scale life again professionally and privately. Indeed, as we have seen, during 1918–19 he became commandant of a camp for interred British soldiers at Château d'Oex (Canton Vaud). It was also during this year that he first used the term 'archetype' in *Instinct and the Unconscious* (*Collected Works*, Volume 8).

Invited to visit England by the Psychiatric Section of the Royal Society of Medicine, in July 1919 Jung came to London with a sense of relief and exhilaration. Trapped in Switzerland throughout the war years, his breakdown had dominated everything, but now at last the world was open again. Throughout his life Jung found a *rapport* with the English which frequently expressed itself in a state of early-morning euphoria when staying with friends in London. On this first post-war visit he delivered a paper, 'The Problems of Psychogenesis in Mental Disease', for which William McDougall took the chair. The dour old Scot was said to have remarked afterwards, 'Well, Switzerland has at last justified her existence.'[1] The highly successful London visit was the forerunner of many such visits as analytical psychology steadily increased its disciples in England.

On the evidence of his son Franz, he continued to bring up his family on liberal lines.[2] Locally, an austere version of Christian doctrine, originally laid down by the sixteenth-century theologian Huldreich Zwingli, prevailed, and at the age of ten the question arose: should Franz go to the Sunday School? Jung had already given his son a brief outline of alternative religions, attempting to preserve an open mind. Now the local pastors pressed Jung to send his son to Sunday School, and Franz Jung vividly remembers the discussion in which his father analysed the pros and cons, and said the final decision must rest with him. The boy decided against Sunday School, with the result that he suffered at the hands of his schoolfellows but felt that he had preserved his integrity. When the local pastors pressed his father, he simply replied, 'It is the boy's decision, not mine.' In due course the question of confirmation arose, and once again many pressures were brought to bear, but Jung told his son to make up his own mind. In the embalmed correctness of Zwingli Christianity such liberality could lead to ostracism. However, Franz Jung has no regrets about his decision not to be confirmed.

Emma Jung, Franz recalls, ran the household on a tight rein, insisting on correct behaviour at the dinner table, while his father was liable to throw off his coat and, if he felt like it, sing.[3] Emma was calm, sensible, balanced; Carl spontaneous, unpredictable, but he could also on occasion be very withdrawn.

His daughter Gret Baumann-Jung recalls that her father did not like shop talk at table and frowned heavily on anyone breaking into an account of his or her dreams. Until she reached fifteen Jung would join them for meals and disappear into his study, and she had no sense of real contact with her father. In all those years she had the impression of a severe father-figure. Then, when he had recovered from his break with Freud, 'suddenly he was there', and he even began to join in the games of the children.[4] 'In the 1920s it was not unusual for him to see eight or nine patients a day. In common with most Swiss he would see his first patient about 7.30 or 8 a.m. He never sat with a patient more than 60 minutes and usually they were seen three times a week. . . . Patients would be greeted at the front door and escorted up a staircase which led to a smallish book-lined room that Jung used as his consulting-room. A door from this led to a larger room heavily lined with books which was his study.'[5]

Patients apart, he had the knack of getting on with people – when he chose – at all levels. He could put the postman, the stonemason or the gardener at ease in a few minutes, and the tradespeople liked talking to him about food. Students would turn up at his house and, if he liked them, he would see them at once. He was delighted when the village postmaster wanted to ask him something about *Psychology and Alchemy*, which he had read.[6]

Jung frequently took his children on camping expeditions, and sometimes embarrassed them by the clothes he wore. He saw nothing unusual in walking about the garden clad in a tattered pair of shorts which shocked the neighbours. A visitor searching for the great man was introduced to what he took to be the Italian gardener and found it hard to believe this was Carl Gustav Jung. He was, as one witness said, a bull of a man who had to find relaxation in hard, physical work – building walls, refitting boats, sailing and mountaineering. Sometimes he took out his repressed aggression on physical objects, sometimes on people. Frequently he had the overwhelming impulse to get away from 'people, patients, everything'. One patient in the latter part of 1919 was greeted with the words, 'Oh, no. I can't stand the sight of another one. Just go home and cure yourself today!' Summing up his father at this time, Franz Jung said, 'He was maddening and marvellous.'

Jung's relationship with Antonia Wolff had now entered a new phase. Much of the evidence is verbal and needs sceptical scrutiny. According to Paul J. Stern (*C. G. Jung – The Haunted Prophet*) the relationship between Toni and Emma underwent many changes. At one stage they invoked analytic techniques to explore their situation and arranged regular meetings with Jung's assistant Carl A. Meier in which they analysed one another.

Psychotherapy did not prevent Toni from breaking out of her assigned role at another period. According to Stern, 'She began to demand forcefully . . . that Jung divorce Emma and marry her. Her offensive took the form of a massive direct interference in Jung's family life which Emma could not ignore and to which Jung's children reacted by becoming even more hostile and mocking towards Aunt Toni than before.'

As far back as 1915, Antonia had conceived the idea of founding the Analytical Psychology Club, and a number of Jungian organisations developed in Zürich, accompanied by those personal frictions inseparable from pioneering schools. Sometime between 1917 and 1918 serious troubles split the Analytical Psychology Club, and Antonia withdrew, but she rejoined in 1926 and finally became President. Her work was continuous and widespread, her quick, vivacious mind made her a good lecturer, and the paradox of her integrated personality was partly explained if Jung remained her lover. She also became a trained analyst and when, eventually, the C. G. Jung Institute was formed, entered with zest into its activities. A correspondence had taken place between Antonia and Carl over the years, and the letters included many love-letters which her family returned to Jung on her death. Unfortunately, he decided to destroy them.

Overwhelmed by the attentions of many adoring women, Jung decided early in 1920 to break out of the elaborate net his fame, personality and charm had woven in Zürich. Another equally powerful motive drove him to explore primitive cultures, hoping that he might find confirmation of his mythological theories in lands and peoples far removed from the European. It may have been that by the early part of 1920 the intensity of his relationship with Antonia had diminished, or perhaps when Hermann Sigg, a Swiss businessman, asked Jung to accompany him on a trip to Tunis the opportunity was quite simply too good to miss. Whatever the reason, he immediately accepted. If he had taken Antonia with him, 'tongues would have wagged', but it is debatable whether he wanted her to go.

All unaware, his travels were to initiate yet another relationship with a woman which continued until the end of his life, but, for the moment, he set out for Algiers one March day in 1920, free from family, wife, mistress and patients.

From Algiers they proceeded to Tunis and quickly pushed on to Sousse where Jung parted company with Hermann Sigg. A new sense of exhilaration took hold of him. He was alone at last in a non-European country.

On Monday, 15 March he wrote to his wife from Sousse: '*This Africa is incredible. . . .* Unfortunately I cannot write coherently to you for it is all too much. . . .' It had taken thirty hours to reach Tunis by train, he said, with the 'African soil towering up the the noble and spreading shapes of the great Atlas range . . .'. Then came Sousse with its 'white walls and towers, the harbour below; beyond the harbour wall the deep blue sea and in the port lies the sailing ship with two lateen sails which I once painted!' Roman remains were everywhere, and he had already dug, accidentally, 'a piece of Roman pottery out of the ground'. But this letter, he said, was miserable stuttering which completely failed to match up to his experiences. 'I do not know what Africa is really saying to me but it speaks. . . . In the markets you can still buy the amphorae of antiquity – things like that – and the moon!!!'

Having no Arabic, Jung sat for hours in coffee-houses listening to conversations he could not understand but observing Arab reactions to this alien 'monster' in their midst. Physically such reactions were understandable. As one Arab put it through an interpreter, 'You are so big and strong you could carry the sky.'[7] Trying to translate what was said through gestures, Jung quickly registered the subtle change in manner which overtook everyone when they spoke to Europeans. 'What the Europeans regard as Oriental calm and apathy seemed to me a mask: behind it I sensed a restlessness, a degree of agitation which I could not explain.'[8] One impression constantly haunted him, indicating that he was not so free from the fantasies of his breakdown as he imagined. He could not understand, he said, why the Moorish soil seemed to smell so queer, and even when he identified the smell as that of blood it still baffled him. The impression grew stronger until it was as if 'the soil were soaked with blood'. This strip of land surrounding Sousse had seen the rise and fall of three civilisations – Carthaginian, Roman, Christian – and the overwhelming power of the past responded to the smallest imaginative effort, but that did not seem to him a satisfactory explanation of the blood-dominated scene. Aware that he was searching for answers to very profound questions, he pushed on south to Sfax, from there entered the Sahara and reached the small oasis-city of Tozeur.

When he first saw it, the scene enchanted him. A green, gold and white paradise with its towering date-palms, brilliant white buildings, peach- and apricot-trees, profusion of vividly green alfalfa, and kingfishers flitting like jewels through the foliage. Sparkling springs bubbled up everywhere, a spirit of joy breaking through the earth's crust to give life to a vegetation richer by contrast with the surrounding desert.

Strolling in the shade of the date-palms, Jung quickly discovered that most of the white-clad figures were men, among them many couples 'holding one another in close embrace' and his dragoman confirmed what they made self-evident – homosexuality was taken for granted. As for women, only a few could be seen in public, and if not heavily veiled were probably prostitutes. It was, Jung reflected, like stepping back to fifth-century Athens, where a society of socially free men produced a man-dominated society and all its attendant simplifications.

'I felt cast back many centuries to an infinitely more naïve world of adolescents' preparing to emerge from the ancient tradition of an almost twilight world to challenge the slow inroads of European technology and culture. Glancing at his pocket-watch became a symbol of a time-dominated world which did not exist here, and punctuality, he discovered, was certainly not one of the higher virtues.

Hiring mules, Jung and his dragoman pressed on again toward another oasis, at Nefta, and the deeper he penetrated into the Sahara the more his sense of time diminished. Shimmering heat-waves rising from the desert gave an ethereal quality to the vast sweep of sands, and as they approached the oasis there suddenly appeared out of the haze a dramatic white-clad figure 'mounted on a black mule whose harness was . . . studded with silver'. Very proud in bearing, distant in mien and unrelated to time, he passed without offering any greeting as if he were a ghost-figure from centuries ago who dressed and rode exactly like his descendants. Jung found him a most impressive figure, lacking that 'faint note of foolishness which clings to Europeans'.

Constant comparisons recurred between Arabic culture and his own. The illusion of European man's triumph over nature was reinforced by his technological marvels, but he had lost touch, Jung thought, with instinctual roots reaching right back to the beginnings of mankind, revealed here in the heart of a desert where time stood still. They spent the night in the equivalent of a country inn with Moorish pillars and open courtyards, burnished the following morning by a sun of blazing brilliance. A great commotion arose in the village square and brought Jung abruptly out of sleep. Scores of wild-looking desert tribesmen poured into the square dragging unwilling camels, groaning mules and donkeys, villagers screamed and gesticulated, and a passage was made through the throng for a man of distinction – the marabout, or administrator of poor relief. He owned a number of fields near the oasis and had hired the tribesmen for two days to dig the necessary irrigation-canals.

With a roll of drums and a dramatic unfolding of a great green flag, the milling mass became an untidy procession, and out of the cloud of dust their ghost-figures, carrying hoes and baskets, formed up behind the white-bearded marabout. Sitting astride his mule, very upright and commanding, he led the wildly dancing men out into the oasis 'as if going to battle'.

There followed a scene which Jung deliberately witnessed at a distance, so threatening did it become. Converted into a frantic anthill, the whole area was alive with men hacking the ground 'at a furious rate', carrying heavy baskets of earth and literally dancing to the deep rhythms of a series of drums. Through the tumult of clashing hoes, cries, drums and dancing men the marabout rode on his white mule, totally unmoved and calmly directing everything. From dawn to dusk the frenzied ritual continued, and then exhaustion overwhelmed everything, men dropped instantaneously asleep beside their camels and, as the last howling of the pack of dogs died away, utter stillness obliterated all movement and sound. 'Until at the first rays of the rising sun the invocation to the muezzin – which always deeply stirred me – summoned the people to their morning prayer.'[9]

The scene left a profound impression on Jung. Recollected in tranquillity, he analysed its significance. These people lacked the will to direct their individual efforts but drew their being from 'affects' or emotions, sustaining an intensity missing in many ego-directed Europeans. There was something hypnotic in their ritualised work, and if Jung successfully resisted its spell he claimed that he 'had been psychically infected' when acute enteritis attacked him the following day. The scene had, in fact, reactivated a struggle within himself between his Europeanised conscious and his 'primitive' unconscious. Once again it expressed itself in a dream. In times of stress, fantasies, dreams, symbols crowded in upon him. Throughout his life, even into those years when the whole house became full of spirits, the conclusion could be drawn that the intensity of these 'visitations' indicated a continuous subterranean threat from the forces which had so recently led to a breakdown. Alternatively, spontaneous use of the language of dream and symbol came so naturally to him that it simply marked a temperament different from its more logical equivalents. This would explain his capacity to tap the power of the mandala.

Back once more in Tunis, about to embark for Marseilles, the dream occurred with the vivid detail which characterised his almost total recall of such experiences. Imagine an Arab city in the middle of a plain with a casbah surrounded, unexpectedly, by a wide moat, at one side of which Jung stood on a wooden bridge, facing a horseshoe-shaped doorway at the other. Striding over the bridge, eagerly expectant of what the casbah would reveal, Jung was halfway across when a splendidly regal Arab wearing a white burnous emerged from the horseshoe gate, walked swiftly forward, grappled with Jung and tried to throw him into the moat. Physically very powerful, Jung easily contained the attack, but in the struggle both crashed through the protecting hand-rail and plunged into the water. His opponent at once tried to 'push [his] head under water'. That, Jung wrote, was 'going too far' and he retaliated in kind. No desire to kill his assailant drove him, but a need to render the Arab incapable of further aggression.

Subduing his opponent, the scene changed dramatically. Transported to an octagonal room in the inner citadel where low divans stood against marble walls, the Arab, now revealed as a prince, sat beside Jung gazing at a big book which lay open before him revealing 'a magnificent calligraphy on milky-white parchment'. Unaware of its contents, Jung yet knew that this was 'his book' and the reward of his victory was to force the prince to read it.

Suddenly Jung realised that the Arab in the dream corresponded to the strange austere figure on a silver-studded horse who had ridden past them in the desert a few days before with royal indifference. Another flash of insight revealed the casbah from which he emerged as a perfect mandala symbol: 'a citadel surrounded by a square wall with four gates'. So here, he concluded, was a 'messenger or emissary of the self'. Digging deeper for an explanation, Jung found echoes of biblical mythology in Jacob's struggle with the angel, but any detailed correspondence became obscure.

What remained clear was the clash between his European consciousness and reverberations of African culture forcing their way through with primal power. The evocation of forces in himself which could co-operate with African life came as a surprise, and a battle ensued which the dream symbolised. The European consciousness, alarmed at the danger of surrendering to primal African affects, fought to maintain its supremacy. The wholly different Arab way of life had awakened 'archetypal memory of an only too well-known historic past which' he had entirely forgotten.

Time and again this conflict arose in Jung's life, always to be reconciled by his own theories as if he were the living proof of so much that he wrote. Indeed, there is a sense in which his model of the psyche is an autobiographical journey around his own rich and complex person, a journey constantly renewed but mapping closely similar territory. Not that he was aware of these interpretations in 1920. Only later did he formulate what he regarded as the true meaning of this first African trip. For the moment, as he left that great continent, one wish dominated all others – to return as soon as possible.

Chapter 22

Bollingen and New Mexico

IT WAS IN THE YEAR 1920 that Jung began to experiment with the technique described in the famous *Book of Mutations – I Ching*. That summer he decided to make 'an all-out attack on the meaning of [the] book'. Sitting beneath a hundred-year-old pear-tree in the garden of Bollingen, he cut himself a bunch of reeds, in place of the traditional yarrow-stalks, and divided them up arbitrarily 'at a single swoop'. The 'player', he wrote, 'does not know how many stalks are contained in each bundle and yet the result depends upon their numerical relationship'. The division of the sticks apart, no other act of the human will intervened. 'If a psychic causal connection is present at all it can only consist in the chance division of the bundles.'[1] The sticks were a kind of oracle which gave answers in the form of hexagrams, each hexagram having its own meaning. In the *I Ching* the hexagrams consisted of a number of lines in different patterns which spelt out a special code. Experimenting with a patient one day, Jung asked him to 'cast' the reeds and began to translate the answers from the code. This young man had a strong mother-complex and wanted to marry a girl he had recently met, but feared that he might burden himself with yet another mother. Jung wrote: 'The text of his hexagram read: "The maiden is powerful. One should not marry such a maiden."'

The mind boggles at the implications of this. Some psychic 'influence' passes between the complex life-situation of a young man and a bunch of casually distributed reeds by which his problem is understood, examined and commented upon in rational terms. The animate invokes processes in the inanimate equivalent to human insight and produces oracular answers to human problems.

Jung sat for hours beneath the old pear-tree on summer days, casting and recasting the reed sticks. 'All sorts of undeniably remarkable results emerged – meaningful connections with my own thought processes which I could not explain to myself.' Time and again Jung also encountered remarkable coincidences between the message of the reeds and external events 'which seemed to suggest an a-causal parallelism'. During the whole of his summer holidays he examined this possibility with mounting excitement. On one occasion the hexagram implied that illness was imminent, and with somewhat suspicious alacrity he promptly developed a serious bout of flu. If the growing body of evidence were true, what was the explanation of the correspondence between psychic and physical events? The process, he argued, must contradict all known forms of rational communication and fall into the extra-sensory class, but it was not what people called telekinesis or telepathy. After long experiment and thought he finally named the process synchronicity. It was not mere coincidence but the result of a mysterious a-causal connection between, say, a dream and its realisation in fact. One big problem with synchronicity, Jung later wrote to Professor J. B. Rhine, 'is that one thinks of it as being produced by the subject while I think it is rather in the nature of objective events'. Thus, when one 'cast' the yarrow sticks an a-causal distribution achieved a meaningful relationship with the psychic reality of the person involved.

Throughout his writings Jung makes several attempts to analyse synchronicity especially in Volume 8 of the *Collected Works*, *The Structure and Dynamics of the Psyche*. His description of the phenomenon is much more successful than his attempts to explain its origin. He writes like a man struggling to explain the inexplicable. At one moment he implies that the psyche can organise matter which by natural extension might include events. 'Either there are physical processes which cause psychic happenings or there is a pre-existent psyche which organises matter.' What appears to the average person an accidental coincidence brought about by chance becomes for Jung a meaningful coincidence produced by a-causal laws. Normal cause and effect is replaced by parallelism, the simultaneous occurrence of psychic and physical events. He postulates at one point a 'nervous substrate' separate from the cerebrum which can think and perceive differently from normal consciousness. 'The archetype *is* the introspectively recognisable form of a priori orderedness. If an external synchronistic process now associates itself with it, it falls into the same basic pattern – in other words it too, is ordered. . . . the forms of psychic orderedness are *acts of creation in time*.' Innumerable examples of synchronicity are scattered through his work which according to his analysis have less than a million to one chance of happening by accident.

Later Jung met the Chinese philosopher Hu Shih, and asked him what he thought of the principle of the *I Ching*. At first Hu Shih dismissed the book with the remark, 'Oh, that's nothing but an old collection of magic spells without significance,' but pressed further he told the story of a friend involved in an unhappy love-affair. They were passing a Taoist temple together one day when he said to his friend, 'Why not consult the oracle?' 'And was the oracle correct?' Jung asked. 'Oh yes,' came the reply. 'Of course it was.'

Shortly after Jung's first experiments Richard Wilhelm published a translation of the book with a commentary which so stimulated Jung that he immediately determined to meet him. In 1922, Wilhelm visited Zürich and called on Jung. It was the first of several meetings. 'What I had to tell him about the results of my investigation of the unconscious caused him no little surprise, for he recognised in them things he had considered to be the exclusive possession of the Chinese philosophical tradition.'[2]

There was an occasion when the two men stayed up all night playing with the *I Ching*[3] and before Jung fell asleep from sheer exhaustion the oracle proclaimed: 'Beware tomorrow – and do not take it too seriously.' That was the day when his old friend Oeri was nearly killed in a road accident. Jung held Wilhelm in great respect and never failed to praise him for going to China on a Christian mission and failing to baptise a single Christian. Jung found him completely orientalised in thought, manner and speaking. Wilhelm gave a talk on the *I Ching* at the Psychology Club in Zürich in 1923 which deeply impressed everyone.

The precise dates of Jung's recovery from his breakdown are considerably confused by his comments about the Taoist–alchemical treatise entitled *The Secret of the Golden Flower*, a document closely related to the *I Ching*. It put forward, among other propositions, one which said that any event is immortally endowed with characteristics belonging – and *only* belonging – to the moment of its occurrence. As late as 1928 he one day painted a mandala with a golden castle at the centre. Puzzled by its Chinese ambience, Jung suddenly received a copy of the *Golden Flower* from Wilhelm, who asked him to write a commentary on the manuscript. In remembrance of yet another example of synchronicity Jung wrote beneath his mandala, 'In 1928 when I was painting this picture showing the golden well fortified castle, Richard Wilhelm . . . sent me the thousand-year-old Chinese text on the yellow castle.' The following year he collaborated with Wilhelm in writing the commentary and said: 'It was only after I had reached the central point in my thinking and in my researches namely the concept of the Self, that I once more found my way back to the world.' That radically changes one's ideas about the duration of his breakdown. If it did extend into 1929, it must have lasted twelve or thirteen years. But the evidence is contradictory.

Richard Wilhelm and Jung remained close friends, with a special kind of understanding, for many years, and it was while staying with Jung at Küsnacht that Wilhelm suffered a recurrence of amoebic dysentery. Returning to the Chinese Institute in Frankfurt am Main, his condition grew worse over the next few months. When they carried him off to hospital, Jung went to visit him and found him 'a very sick man'. The doctors were not very hopeful, but Wilhelm continued to speak of his plans for the future, which filled Jung with foreboding.

Communication broke down over the following months, and then one night as Jung was about to fall asleep he had what he described as a vision. 'At my bed stood a Chinese in a dark blue gown, hands crossed in the sleeves. He bowed low before me as if he wished to give me a message. I knew what it signified. . . .' A few weeks later Wilhelm died. It was yet another example of Jung's powers which interwove with his theories of the *I Ching*. Wilhelm's death was a great loss to him. He went for the last time to Frankfurt to read the funeral oration. 'He was deeply moved,' one witness said.

After the African trip Jung was seized by a new urge. 'Gradually through my scientific work I was able to put my fantasies and the contents of the unconscious on a solid footing,' he wrote, but now something even more tangible became desirable. He wanted to 'achieve a kind of representation in stone of [his] innermost thoughts' and thus began the project of building the Tower at Bollingen which occupied several years.

His strong predilection for living beside water played a major part in selecting the site which eventually centred on the area of St Meinrad on the upper lake of Zürich. When his eldest daughter came to see the site, she immediately exclaimed, 'What – are you still going to build there – how can that be – corpses will be found at this spot!' Jung brushed the idea aside, but not very long afterwards they did discover a skeleton buried in a deep grave. From a rifle bullet in the elbow Jung concluded that the soldier's body must have been in an advanced stage of decay before they buried him, and further researches established that scores of French soldiers were drowned in the vicinity in 1799 when the Austrians blew up the bridge at Grynau which the French were storming. Moved by his encounter with the skeleton and very aware of reverberations coming up from the past, Jung carried out an elaborate reburial service, erecting a headstone and having a gun fired three times over the grave. From this experience he came to believe that his daughter had inherited powers of psychic insight from his grandmother which included sensing the presence of the dead.

At the outset Jung planned a one-storey structure to be built in a circle encompassing a central hearth with bunks along the walls. The idea came from the huts he had seen in Africa, where the whole life of the family revolved around a central fire in a circular hut. This plan had to be abandoned as too primitive for modern Swiss life, and a two-storey house slowly began to take shape, but in the form of a tower. 'So . . . the first round house was built and when it was finished I saw that it had become a suitable dwelling tower.'

Suitable? Well, it had no running water, electricity or gas, fuel came from chopped wood, heat for cooking from oil and light from oil-lamps. Whatever concessions he made to modern living, they did not extend far, but from the first day he went to stay in the house he felt a marvellous sense of repose and renewal. Once again it was as if he had stripped away a too self-conscious ego, softened and distorted by technology, to recover the instinctual grace of living at close quarters with nature. Romantic elements were present in this view. Jung admitted the point. 'I refused to wear a bearskin,' he told Lancelot Whyte, roaring with laughter.[4]

Gradually over the years he developed the house. A sense that it incompletely expressed what he wanted to say drove him to add a central structure with 'a tower-like annexe'. In turn, some years later, completely reversing his original approach, the building suddenly seemed too primitive and he developed the tower-like annexe. He wanted 'a room in this tower' where he could 'exist for [himself] alone'. This idea derived once more from Indian houses he had seen in which a curtained-off area was used as a place of withdrawal, for meditation and Yoga exercises.

He developed the habit of carrying the key of his withdrawal room everywhere he went, and no one else was allowed to enter the room without his permission. It became an oasis, cut off from everything, where he achieved a degree of spiritual concentration not possible under any other circumstances. Alone in that room he sometimes fell to painting on the walls, expressing in symbols what could not be said in words and demonstrating his faith in all those images which carried him 'out of the present into timelessness'.[5]

Sometimes the depth of his concentration in the second tower became so great that when a woman, later to become his companion housekeeper, summoned him to meals, 'it was like summoning the dead'.[6] Sometimes he locked the door behind him and sat gazing out on the lake in a fakir's trance, pantheistically surrendered to the lake, the countryside and sky in what he described as 'sheer poetry of the spirit'.[7]

He seemed not to notice close similarities between this experience and the boy of eleven withdrawing to the loft of his father's house. Many times in adult life he regressed to modes of infantile sanctuary, re-creating psychic states resembling those of his boyhood. Whether these were minor relapses into mental illness or attempts to cure his psychotic potential is difficult to determine. In his reminiscences Jung made no reference to the fact that Bollingen also helped to divide off his extra-marital from his marital life. His wife and family would remain at Küsnacht while he occasionally spent weekends at Bollingen with Antonia Wolff. There was a sense in which the house symbolised, among other and more enduring aspects, the split in his marriage and a desire to realise a side of himself not acceptable to a correct and very conventional Swiss family.

While the original simplicity of Bollingen steadily became more complex, a desire grew in Jung to penetrate a 'still lower cultural level'. The need to travel backward in time and culture became a growing preoccupation until he once more set out on a long journey, not back to Africa, but to New Mexico and the Pueblo Indians.

He was accompanied this time by Fowler McCormick, the son of Mr and Mrs Harold McCormick who had been very active in helping to found the Zürich Psychological Club in 1916, and George Porter, a frequent visitor to Zürich psychological circles. The third member of the party, Xaime de Angulo, had the obvious advantage of familiarity with the Indians of New Mexico.

Among the villages where 'the crowded houses piled one atop the other' in New Mexico, Jung had the good fortune to encounter the chief of the Taos Pueblos, romantically named Ochwiay Biano. A man of forty or fifty with a quite different vision of the world from the European, talking to Ochwiay Biano was a free floating experience on 'deep alien seas'.

'Look', the chief said, 'at the cruelty in the faces of white men with their sharp noses, thin lips, staring eyes and furrowed brows. They are restless, always seeking, always wanting faces, and the Indians have no idea what it is they worry about wanting so much!' They did not understand the white man's cravings and could only regard him as 'mad'.

Asked why they were mad he replied: 'They say what they think with their heads.' Jung thereupon asked Biano what he thought with, and he replied, with his hand on his heart, 'We think here.'

Now, this might seem to the European a fully predictable explanation from an earlier people, unacquainted with modern knowledge of brain anatomy, but Jung gave it the weight of a revelation. 'The Indian had struck our vulnerable spot, unveiled a truth to which we are blind.'

His conversation with Ochwiay Biano took place on the fifth-storey roof of a building in New Mexico, seven thousand feet above sea level. Beneath them the immense plateau of Taos stretched away to the horizon, interrupted by vast conical peaks reaching twelve thousand feet into the sky and, dominating everything, half an hour's journey up-river, a single, mighty mountain, the mountain which by ancient tradition and out of religious awe had no name. Immediately surrounding the main building where Jung sat were low-built square houses constructed from adobe with ladders leading directly from the ground to the roof, a survival from the days when attack made it necessary to draw up the ladders and seal off the inhabitants.

The Pueblos carried the stereotype of the taciturn Indian to the point of inaccessibility whenever the subject of religion arose. Self-controlled and dignified, they preserved a 'fatalistic equanimity', but when Jung at last succeeded in drawing limited comments about their religion the profundity of their concealed emotion sometimes moved them to tears. Religion to them, Jung said, 'was not a series of dogma or theoretical concepts but a living reality directly connected with the eternal facts'.

Sitting on the fifth-floor roof watching blanket-clad Indians lost in contemplation of the sun, Jung became aware that it had a special significance and, approaching the question with infinite subtlety, received the following answer from Ochwiay Biano: 'Is not he who moves there our father? . . . How can there be another God? . . . Nothing can be without the sun.' Momentarily drawn out of his contemplative isolation, Biano drove home his point with the words: 'A man cannot even build his fire without him.' Jung's tactful suggestion that perhaps the sun was a ball of fiery material miraculously created by a different God did not make a favourable impression. 'The sun is God. Everyone can see that.'

Later that day Jung began to feel 'rising within [him] like a shapeless mist something unknown and deeply familiar'. From this mist materialised a series of fantasies which paralleled those of some of his patients: Roman legions smashing into the cities of Gaul, St Augustine trying to convert the early Britons, Charlemagne murderously enforcing his conversions, crusading armies burning and sacking, a whole tumultuous outpouring of historical recollection and identification which culminated with the Conquistadors coming 'with fire, torture and Christianity down upon even these remote Pueblos dreaming peacefully in the Sun their father'.

The visions vanished as quickly as they had arisen. And then one morning, looking up at the immense height of the mountain reflecting that he stood on 'the roof of the American continent' a deep voice spoke almost in his ear: 'Do you not think that all life comes from the mountain?' An Indian had come up beside him, silent in his mocassins, and now stood following the majestic lines of the river falling in its splendid arc from an invisible source. As usual the word 'mountain' in the mouth of an Indian carried undertones, because religious rites performed on cloud-capped peaks by specially selected members of the community were wrapped in mystery which no foreigner was ever allowed to penetrate. Carried away by the conviction in the old man's voice, Jung answered, 'Yes – of course you speak the truth.'

If religious rites were never revealed to strangers, the word 'Americans' set flowing a tide of criticism and abuse. Living as they did on the 'roof of the world' closest to the sun god, the Indians believed that their contemplation helped the 'great ball of fire' in its daily journey across the sky. 'If we were to cease practising our religion in ten years the sun would no longer rise,' they said. Since the world would then he plunged into eternal darkness, how could these strange white people want to destroy the Indian religion? Why did they raise objections when children were taken from school to the Kiva where a much more profound communication with the sun god became possible? The Indians did nothing to harm the Americans. Their practices benefited the whole world. Why, then, did they harass them, forbid their dances, try to interfere with their traditional way of life?

Believing that their own efforts gave fresh impetus to the sun's journey across the sky instilled a cosmological meaning into the life of the Indians and was for Jung the explanation of their marvellous composure. They were the sons of the sun and they not only held the equivalent of Holy Communion with him every day, but also actually affected his magnificent passage across the Empyrean.

The absurdity of the notion that a handful of Indians could affect what we Europeans know to be the immutable path of the planets lost some of its force, Jung said, when one remembered that Christians hoped to influence the reactions of God by offering up prayers and carrying through Holy Communion. Jung did not draw the conclusion that both achieved a false harmony by living an illusion. Instead he said: 'Out of sheer envy we are obliged to smile at the Indians' naïveté . . . for otherwise we would discover how impoverished and down at heel we are.'

There was some confusion here. If Christian and sun god rituals were expected to have similar effects, then both peoples drew – as indeed many Christians certainly did – a spiritual balance if not composure from the experience.

Jung's experiences with the Pueblo Indians deepened his belief in a non-rational relationship between the conscious forces of modern man and his archaic roots which could be refined by the process of individuation into something resembling the composure he had encountered in the mountains of Mexico. Certainly his self-analysis, travels and elaboration of mythological theories could be seen as a search for a means of achieving that composure.

In September 1902 something happened which put any such aim at risk. Another very disturbing dream presaged, according to Jung, the death of a person who really played a deeper role in his life even than his father – his mother. For almost twenty-six years the image of his father had been exorcised from his dreams, but now one night he reappeared with fresh vividness as a new and rejuvenated figure. In the dream Jung escorted him into his library, anxious to introduce his father to his books and his wife, and to discuss with him his work on psychological types. His father had other preoccupations. Jung became aware that he 'wanted something from me' and slowly it emerged that his father desired to consult him about 'marital psychology'. On the point of launching into a lengthy lecture, Jung suddenly came awake. Unaware at the time what the dream meant, within a year he was able to give an ingenious if somewhat odd interpretation. Since his father's marriage had been full of trials and tribulations and was not a happy one he had, according to Jung, returned to earth to discover the latest insights into marriage problems because he knew that his wife would soon resume her relationship with him. The logic appeared bizarre. It implied that marriage continued after death, and that we on earth had more up-to-date solutions than those available in – Heaven? It also appeared that, without earthly advice, the renewed heavenly marriage might turn out to be equally disastrous.

Interpreting the dream, Jung gave a warning to 'weak and suggestible' minds that they must not 'hypostatise mere phantasms', a process which he himself simultaneously indulged. It is possible, of course, to see the dream as Jung's search for a better understanding of his own marital troubles, which had by now reached a fresh stage. There is in fact some dispute about the troubles. Barbara Hannah claims that he did not have family troubles[8] since everyone accommodated themselves to the pattern he desired.

A much more clearly related dream occurred at the time of his mother's death in January 1923 while he was staying in Tessin. . . . The dream submerged Jung in a primeval forest with huge rocks interspersed between giant trees locked together by thick lianas. Suddenly a preliminary whistle became a roar which resounded through the whole forest, filling him with fear. His knees shook, his breath came in gasps, and then 'a gigantic wolfhound with a fearful gaping maw burst forth'. Petrified with fear, Jung knew, as if it were certainty, that 'the Wild Huntsman had commanded it to carry away a human soul'. Waking in sweating terror, he found great difficulty in getting to sleep again. The following morning he received the news of his mother's death the night before.

After the first shock – her death was quite unexpected – his reaction became savagely ambivalent. Returning home on the night train from Tessin there was no disguising great distress, but another quite different mood intruded. Throughout the journey 'dance music, laughter and jollity as though a wedding were being celebrated' constantly recurred. Two waves of emotion met and clashed, one temporarily overwhelming the other, only in turn to be replaced by its opposite. The great emptiness of grief filled with anguish had to give place to dance music and laughter which slowly yielded once more to grief.

It was explicable in terms of his own theory of the anima, but later in life Jung gave a different explanation. Seen from the viewpoint of the anima, his mother's death removed an irreplaceable person, but from the viewpoint of the self it was 'a wedding, a *mysterium coniunctionis*' in which the soul attained 'its missing half' and thus achieved 'wholeness'. Summoning many legendary precedents, Jung spoke of the pious Cabbalist Rabbi, Simon ben Jochai, whose friends said that he celebrated a wedding when he died. He reminded his readers that All Souls' Day saw many a picnic taking place on graves.

Interpreted in terms of his own doctrines, his mother's death had removed one personal source of his anima and reduced its power. Toni had met and readjusted that image during his breakdown, but now he was moving towards an even wider freedom and on the verge of becoming entirely himself. First his father, then his mother had died, and his relationship with his wife changed to admit the presence of Antonia; but now that relationship, too, was settling into a different pattern.

Chapter 23
Middle Age and Africa

AT FIFTY a change had overtaken Jung. Earlier photographs present a tight-lipped man, with small intense eyes behind rimless spectacles, whose drain-pipe collar, shorn hair and austere countenance could have belonged to a Prussian military officer neurotically concerned with committing his army to battle.

Moods, of course, changed his face as well as his personality, dramatically. Caught off guard, the camera recorded many different impressions, but inevitably during his breakdown his persona did not have the full-blooded response which frequently characterised him in his fifties. Contradictions remained, but in a different sense. One moment the extravert, vociferously bawling commands at an imaginary crew in his boat on the lake, or bursting into roars of laughter at the idiosyncrasies of colleagues, a man still capable of drinking a deep stein of beer and yodelling with a voice somewhat more cracked than before. At another, a benign, relaxed middle-aged man still with a touch of the peasant somewhere about him, who wore a soft collar in place of the stiff one, smoked a pipe with self-evident enjoyment, and exuded tremendous reassurance to his patients.

In the complexity of his many-sided self Jung could play any number of roles. At fifty he was more mellow, less intense, more active, less shut away. He spoke fluent English in the same forceful and explosive manner, still had trouble converting *w*s into *v*s and could commit himself to full-blooded anger in a way which alarmed those who did not know him.

It was the explosive person who said one day to his wife, 'If I get another perfectly normal adult malingering as a sick patient I'll have him certified!' And to George Beckwith, his American friend, 'I'm sometimes driven to the conclusion that boring people need treatment more urgently than mad people.' Witty on some occasions, he commented to one of his assistants, 'Show me a sane person and I'll cure him for you.'[1] Anthony Storr records the comment, possibly apocryphal: 'The penis is nothing more than a phallic symbol.'[2]

He continued to bring up his family upon liberal lines. Discussing his future career with his father, Franz Jung found him very open-minded. 'He did not', Franz said, 'wish to influence me in one direction or another. My career – as always – was a difficult decision. Since I had a grandfather who was a doctor I decided to study medicine first, but I gave that up. Then an aunt suggested – like another relative – I might try architecture. I had always been interested in building – I helped my father build Bollingen – but he wasn't really building. He was playing with sand castles.'[3]

H. G. Wells went to visit Jung about this time and came away with very mixed impressions.[4] Many years later I met Wells in his Hanover Terrace house and brought the conversation round to Jung.[5] 'We had a talk once,' Wells said in that combative way of his. 'I didn't get the hang of too much of it. . . . But he seemed to speak of that Old Man of his as if he were a kind of Collective Human Being we were all in touch with in one way or another. Sounded suspiciously like God to me. Never understood why he side-stepped the word so often. And look at that stuff about the Anima. I've always known I had a beautiful young girl trying to break out from inside me!'

Uncompromising when bored, Jung was quite capable of breaking away in the middle of a dinner party and leaving his wife to cope with all the guests. During one birthday party a stranger broke in on them and said, 'Are you Mr Jung?' and Jung abandoned the celebrations to go off and talk with him. His daughter Gret Baumann-Jung said she stopped praying at twelve because it did not please her father. He seemed to her the most Godless kind of man, and to please him she did not go to church on Sunday.[6]

In the early summer of 1925, Jung returned once more to London to visit the Wembley Exhibition, where Imperialist Britain could still shamelessly reproduce a survey of tribes under British rule which deeply impressed Jung and set him yearning to see Africa again. By the autumn, the second African trip had been arranged. On the eve of his departure he decided to consult the *I Ching* and now he threw the hexagram No. 53 with a nine in the third place. As Barbara Hannah told me this included the words 'the man goes forth and does not return'. He read this as meaning that, although the unconscious favoured the trip, he might even have to pay for it with his life. The apparent threat did not deter him.

Passing through London *en route* to Malaga, he was joined by H. G. Baynes and George Beckwith, his rich American patient-friend. From Malaga they proceeded to Marseille and Genoa, and from there to Egypt where they arrived in Port Said on 7 November. Once more his skill in writing letters scaled down to the minds of young people revealed itself in a long detailed account which he sent, interestingly, not to one of his own children but to Hans Kuhn, the sixteen-year-old boy he had met by chance on the upper lake at Zürich.[7]

It so happened that, when Jung set out for Africa, Ruth Bailey, an English woman, had booked a passage on the same boat *en route* to Nairobi where her sister was about to be married. The ship, she remembers, carried many Englishmen travelling to civil service appointments with such a sense of destiny that it qualified the gaiety of shipboard life.[8] Some were government officials, some settlers, some looking for adventure, and Jung made no particular mark among them.

Gradually, the passengers thinned out as the voyage went on, and by the time they reached Mombasa the three men and Ruth Bailey were isolated, waiting for the night train to Nairobi. Mombasa remained in Jung's memory as 'a humidly hot, European, Indian and Negro settlement hidden in a forest of palms and mango trees . . . an extremely picturesque setting . . . with an old Portuguese fort towering over it'.

Shortly afterwards Ruth Bailey boarded the train which 'almost immediately plunged into the tropical night'. Following the coastline, Miss Bailey remembers the chain of Negro village fires where people sat around talking, but as the train began to climb, the settlements ceased and a total velvety darkness which seemed almost tangible engulfed the whole train. Farther up the train Jung, relaxing as the air grew cooler, slowly fell asleep but awoke abruptly again as the 'first ray of sunlight announced the onset of day'.[9]

He then looked out on a remarkable sight. Surrounded by a cloud of red dust, the train twisted round a steep cliff and there, starkly outlined against the brilliant blue sky, standing on a jagged rock, was a Masai leaning on a spear with 'a gigantic candelabrum cactus' towering over him. 'It was a picture', Jung wrote, 'of something utterly alien and outside my experience but on the other hand a most intense *sentiment du déjà vu.*'

Impressed by the splendour of such spectacles, Ruth Bailey was equally concerned to get the long exhausting journey over and join her sister. The reunion which followed pleased her and she met her brother-in-law-to-be, who had come in from the country for the great occasion. Ruth Bailey and Jung stayed at the New Stanley Hotel, where shortly after their arrival a fancy-dress dance took place. Despite the fact that only twenty-five per cent of the guests turned out in fancy dress, it was a successful party, but while the engaged couple constantly danced Ruth Bailey decided that she could not go on 'sitting out' alone. 'I'll go over there and sit with Dr Jung,' she said to her sister. 'He was on the boat.' A bold, strong-minded person, she walked across the floor and said to Jung, 'Do you mind if I sit there? I won't disturb you.' Whereupon Jung looked up from the map he was studying but did not immediately speak.[10] A few minutes later he said, 'Are you interested in maps?' Miss Bailey admitted that she was, and he spread the map across their two laps. 'I'll show you where we are going. We're going to camp out here,' he said, pointing to Mount Elgon. 'We'll find out a lot more about this country than ever you will in an hotel like this.'

Shortly afterwards they all went to bed, and when Ruth Bailey came down next morning Jung said, 'Why don't you have breakfast with us?' Over breakfast Jung remarked, 'Come shopping with me; but we'd better be careful – you can't have two wives even in Africa.'[11]

They hired a rickshaw, set off for the bazaar and almost at once Ruth Bailey's fearlessly honest comments had him laughing. In the course of the next few days they saw one another frequently, and something about the 'total naturalness' of Miss Bailey 'freed from the sophistications and shams of polite urban society' appealed even more to him. 'You should come with us,' he said to her one day, 'but I don't know what as.'

Miss Bailey's sister was married, several parties followed, and at last Ruth decided to move on towards Lake Wilden. Then one day a runner arrived with a message from Jung which said: 'We are in camp – come and join us and bring a bottle of whisky and brandy.' Her brother-in-law was flatly against her doing any such thing, and Captain Torr, her host, strongly objected. However, an engineer travelling in the direction of Jung's camp on Mount Elgon agreed to accompany Ruth Bailey, and they set out together. Arriving at a native village they suddenly saw the bizarre sight of an askari with a water-bottle on his back carrying the name C. G. Jung. The askari took over the role of guide, and Ruth Bailey set out on the last long trek to Mount Elgon. It must have needed immense stamina to march across miles of wild African bush accompanied by an African whose sole preoccupation seemed to be to get the job over as quickly as possible. Her guide spoke no English, but Miss Bailey had learnt one useful word in Swahili: *poli, poli*. It meant 'slowly, slowly'. Travelling along wild tracks beset by lions, through glorious stretches of forest with huge rock escarpments and occasional encampments of monkeys, when she tried to exploit the single word at her disposal – '*poli, poli*' – he seemed to regard it as an invitation to suicide.

Jung, meanwhile, had undergone a series of experiences which would leave a lasting impression. Unlike Ruth Bailey, he had set out from Nairobi in a Ford car to visit a game reserve where magnificent rolling prospects stretched away to a far horizon dotted with herds of zebra, antelope and gazelle. 'There was scarcely any sound save the melancholy cry of a bird of prey. This was the stillness of the eternal beginning.'[12]

Deliberately walking away from his companions, Jung further isolated himself and savoured what he described as the extraordinary feeling of re-creating the world – for himself. 'In an invisible act of creation', he put the 'stamp of perfection on the world by giving it objective existence'.[13] His old Pueblo friend who helped the sun to journey across the sky came into his mind. Now Jung went beyond that experience to become 'the second creator of the world'.

There were those who complained later in life that Jung could fall into the role of the great guru 'with a hot line exclusively to God'.[14] He had always believed that specially selected people were vessels of grace through which certain revelations were conveyed to enrich the lives of ordinary human beings. Perhaps his self-aggrandisement in the savannah that day reached a point where only his disciples could follow him with tolerance. God-Jung, one man complained, 'believed in his own divinity'.[15] But many a poet before him had elevated pantheistic visions into lyrical outpourings where man re-created the beauty of nature claiming nothing more for himself than the inspiration of the poet. There was a great deal of the artist in Jung and his words could easily be misunderstood.

From Nairobi, Jung and his party took the Uganda railway, then under construction, to its temporary terminus, called Sixty-Four. There the party of eight piled their luggage into two big cars and set off into no man's land. After several hours' bumping over back-breaking tracks they were caught in a tropical thunderstorm, which at its height released a cloudburst, engulfing everything. Not until 12.30 did they arrive at the tiny outpost of empire known as Kakamegas, where a makeshift hospital, and a garrison of African Rifles adjoined, incredibly, a small madhouse. Stepping into the drawing-room of the District Commissioner's house, with a wood fire burning in an open grate, a large table carrying English magazines, and some very English armchairs, Jung might have entered a country house in the heart of Sussex. The fire, whisky and food restored the party's desperately tired spirits and at last they summoned the energy to pitch their tents.

Rounding up the bearers the following day, they set off on foot, accompanied by three askaris, toward Mount Elgon towering 14,000 feet above the landscape. Vivid details of their life in the next few days can be extracted from the letter he wrote to the young boy Hans Kuhn. They marched for five days now with forty-eight bearers, four black servants and a cook, reaching 'huge . . . impenetrable forests'. Every night lions, leopards and hyenas prowled around the camp, with great eagles which came soaring down from the mountain to steal the meat of slaughtered oxen. They had to keep their guns close to hand and on one occasion killed three big poisonous snakes.[16]

For a man of fifty it must have been an exacting trek. Whatever mental troubles overwhelmed him, Jung was physically very tough and in all the long years which presaged middle-age bouts of flu appear to have been his main trouble. Of those virile young empire-builders who first set sail for Mombasa with him, several died of amoebic dysentery, tropical malaria and pneumonia, but Jung, pursued by all the alien bugs of Africa, emerged unscathed.

Danger became his constant companion. Rest-houses were scattered along the track – earthen, grass-roofed constructions with lanterns at each doorway waiting to be lit against any intruder. Highly trained by the Swiss Army, Jung knew exactly how to handle the 9mm Mannlicher rifle which he carried, and twice it was snatched up during the trek ready for use. First because the remnants of a splendid meal prepared by the cook from a five-shilling sheep attracted menacing packs of hyenas who eventually surrounded them on all sides but were easily dispersed by a few gunshots. Second when the cook came rushing, panic-stricken, out of his hut one night convinced that a *fizi* or hyena had broken in and was about to kill him.

The African bearers quickly nicknamed the three mad Europeans who had no apparent need to face the hazards of the Great Mountain. Grey-haired Jung was called *mzee* ('old man'), Beckwith, because of his elaborate wardrobe, *bwana maredadi* ('the dapper gentleman') and Baynes 'Red Neck' – a characteristic automatically expected by Africans of anyone English. Already they were travelling territory not under white control and the askaris, two privates and a corporal, stood guard, on rota at night, for which Jung – who had no heroics about the hazards of the trip – was duly appreciative. The jungle slowly became richer, more profligate and colourful. Full of every possible variety of life, a ceaseless orchestra of animals, insects and birds enlivened the forests of red-blossomed flame-trees. Constantly looming larger as it came into the foreground the huge peaks of Mount Elgon remained silent, formidable and beckoning. Another ever-present reality was the heat. Overpowering, suffocating heat in the day turning to cooler nights with all the abruptness of the tropics. Exhausted at the end of each day's trek, bitten by giant insects, threatened by snakes and many varieties of carnivore, Jung said that 'it was a paradisal world'.[17]

On the lower slopes of Mount Elgon, they at last encountered a man on the first horse they had seen, who turned out to be Chief of the Elgoni and son of the local medicine-man. He brought with him a letter from the Governor of Uganda asking Jung's expedition to take into their care 'a lady who was on her way back to Egypt via the Sudan'.

This, of course, was Ruth Bailey, who takes up the story.[18] She arrived with her single askari to receive a splendid welcome from the big, bronzed, handsome man who strode about the camp, laughing, joking, in the highest of spirits. 'What a man he seemed to me on meeting him again,' she said. 'They were camped in big tents with canvas floors half way up the sides, thousands of feet above sea level in mountain air with no miasma. The people of the village hadn't seen white people before, and that pleased Jung immensely. Someone told him he would never get to talk to the natives but by the time I joined them Jung had learnt some Swahili and was already talking away with the witch doctor.'

'He impressed me even more than when I first met him. I remember him – the second day I arrived – talking to a man and woman living in a cave with nothing more than a stone axe and giving them – on the spur of the moment – a modern metal axe which astonished and delighted the gent. Somehow he managed to talk to the man and broke down all his suspicion.'

According to Jung, Ruth Bailey's arrival sufficed to produce 'an unconscious or fated constellation: the archetype of the triad which calls for the fourth to complete it'.

Ruth Bailey was an important asset for many reasons. Beckwith went down with a bad case of malaria, and it was Ruth Bailey, trained during the First World War, who nursed him. Today, Jung's general reaction to women would be regarded as male chauvinist. The relationship between Ruth Bailey and Jung was 'very decent indeed. Somehow we managed – with the pool at the bottom of a waterfall which became our bath – to remain very correct in our behaviour – which was quite a feat under those circumstances – believe me!'

Extraordinarily, there was only one occasion during the whole trip when Jung spoke to an African woman, partly because it was required by the mores of the different tribes that men should not speak to women. 'As in Southern Europe men speak to men, women to women. Anything else signifies love making,' Jung later recorded. The division of roles among the Eligoni was clear-cut and met with Jung's approval; the men did the hunting and tended the cattle while the women 'were identified with the *shamba*' – in other words, the fields containing the maize, sweet potato and banana crops. Each partner had his or her part in the social economy from which, according to Jung, their natural dignity flowed, even if the wife in addition to tending the crops had to care for and accommodate children, goats and chickens all in the same hut. He believed that 'the concept of equal rights for women is the product of an age in which such partnership has lost its meaning'. Primitive societies like the Eligoni were regulated by 'an unconscious egoism and altruism'. It is difficult to spell that out against modern doctrines of emancipation in any way which makes sense, but one strikingly handsome youth introduced Jung to his sister to illustrate the point.

Emerging from her hut she revealed herself as already middle-aged although only thirty, a good-looking woman who greeted Jung with 'utter naturalness'. Eighty yards away stood another hut occupied by the woman with whom she shared a husband, though they lived separate domestic lives with their own children. At the apex of a triangle stood a third hut, the husband's, but there was no sign of him and it quickly became evident that the first wife was not very concerned about his movements or whereabouts. Jung saw her as a self-assured gracious woman full of confidence because the wholeness of her world, combining husband, children, house and livestock – even though she shared her husband – gave her a definite and respected place in society. It is ironic that he wrote as if his own life was far removed from any such arrangement when in fact there were close resemblances. He, Antonia and Emma had reached a similar accommodation. His conviction that the past held a message for the present which we ignored at our peril made him ask 'whether the growing masculinisation of the white woman [was] not connected with the loss of her natural wholeness (shamba, children, livestock, house of her own . . .) and whether the feminising of the white man [was] not a further consequence'.

Characteristically with those who seek to justify a system, Jung manipulated the facts to make them fit his doctrine, as indeed, on other occasions, he conveniently overlooked awkward discrepancies in the interests of a strained consistency.

Deeply concerned to preserve the distinction between the sexes, he could easily write: 'the worst sight . . . is the women parading in trousers . . . I often thought if only they knew how mercilessly ugly they looked'.[19] Women, he complained, plunged into a process called co-education, trying to make the sexes equal instead of emphasising their differences. 'They belonged usually to a very decent type of middle class and were not smart at all, but only touched by the . . . raging hermaphroditosis.'[20]

Certainly Africans divided men and women in the most decisive way, as Jung found when he came to join a palaver initiated by his head man Ibrahim. No woman ever came near the circle of the palaver, at the centre of which Jung was grandly ensconced on a mahogany stool belonging to a chieftain. With the use of a dictionary, regarded as magic by the Africans, pidgin Swahili, and a great deal of gesture, Jung discussed many matters for over an hour, though communication frequently collapsed in laughing incomprehensibility. The high point was a specially arranged encounter with the *laibon*, or medicine-man, who arrived for the occasion splendidly arrayed in a blue cloak made from the skins of monkeys. Still researching the world of dreams, Jung had tried to draw out a number of Africans on dream imagery without much success. Now, using freshly acquired gambits, he asked whether the *laibon* ever dreamt? Tears came into the old man's eyes as he replied: 'In the old days the *laibons* had dreams, and knew whether there is war or sickness or whether rain comes and where the herds should be driven.' But now the English, who knew everything, had made dreams and their predictions superfluous. The *laibon*, also, had become superfluous, as embodied in this old gentleman so easily moved to tears about his lost role and the powers which went with it.

One ritual which Jung related to its Western equivalent he unravelled only after sustained enquiry. Each morning at sunrise the Africans would spit on their hands and hold them up to the burning sun. When asked what the ritual meant, they simply replied that it was an age-old custom without any special significance, but under further questioning it became clear that all the tribes 'as far as the eye could see' treated the sun at the moment of rising as *mungu*, or God.

Spittle, in the eyes of the Elgoni, contained every man's personal *mana*, or spirit, and exposing the spittle-wet palms was an intimate offering to the sun god. As Jung wrote: 'The act was therefore saying: I offer my living soul. It was a wordless, acted-out prayer which might equally well be rendered: "Lord, into thy hands I commend my spirit." '

The Elgoni believed, again with Christian echoes, that all things created by their god were good and beautiful, and when asked about the predators which killed their cattle replied, 'The lion is good and beautiful.' As for illness, and disease, 'You lie in the sun and it is good.'

These were daylight attitudes sustained by the power of the sun god, but when darkness came swiftly down positive turned to negative, security to insecurity, optimism to pessimism. The all-encompassing velvety blackness was the living presence of *avik*, full of evil forces which had to be countered with magic rites.

Once again Jung seemed to strain the evidence to make it fit a pattern for which he had strong predilections. 'It was', he wrote, 'a profoundly stirring experience for me to find at the sources of the Nile this reminder of the ancient Egyptian conception of the two acolytes Osiris Horus and Set.' The link appeared to be a somewhat vague connection between the principles of light and darkness in both examples, which of course also belonged to the ancient Persian Manichaean philosophy. Jung wrote: 'Here evidently was a primordial African experience that had flowed down to the coasts of the Mediterranean along with the sacred waters of the Nile.' Did the Persians also acquire it from the Africans? Clearly day passing into night was a primordial inevitability experienced by all peoples everywhere, and sun-worship entered spontaneously into many religions. Jung concentrated on the relationship between his African experience and Egyptian mythology, finally linking both with modern man. This aspect of his trip inspired a description of an African dawn which revealed considerable literary powers and conveyed the African scene more vividly than many a professional writer:

> The horizon . . . became radiantly white. . . . Gradually the swelling light seemed to penetrate into the very structure of objects which became illuminated from within until at last they shone translucently like bits of coloured glass. Everything turned to flaming crystal. The cry of the bell bird rang round the horizon. At such moments I felt as if I were inside a temple. It was the most sacred hour of the day. I drank in this glory with insatiable delight . . . in a timeless ecstasy.[21]

At last their sojourn on Mount Elgon came to a close, regretfully they struck camp and set out on the enormous trek back to civilisation. Ruth Bailey records:

> We had to walk scores of miles across terrible country in blinding heat with only a very occasional resthouse consisting of a roof with four uprights. We used to begin at 5.30, to avoid the heat of the sun. The first day we trekked seventeen miles. The next day I think we also did about seventeen miles, but we were tiring. On the third day the heat really beat us into the ground and we gave up after ten miles. Jung was certainly feeling the strain but he remained a tower of strength. When I was resting by the track on one occasion he looked down at me and said, 'You can't die here, Bailey. We'd have to leave you at the roadside.'[22]

As they entered the territory of the Bugishu the Africans seemed to grow blacker, bigger and clumsier beside the graceful Masai, and the strain of the trek continued to take its toll. Jung began to lose weight, and Baynes said one day, 'Don't carry it too far. You'll become one of your disembodied spirits.' By the time they reached Mbala, Jung had lost twenty pounds, and Ruth Bailey said, 'I wasn't exactly the plumpiest and prettiest girl in the kingdom.'

The most dramatic moment came when a tall native chieftain on the way to Regaf in the Sudan invited them at dusk to witness a *n'goma*, or dance. Exhausted from their long day's trek, suspicious of these tribesmen and supported by no more than three askaris, each possessing only three cartridges, they agreed with the utmost reluctance. There followed a quite unexpected scene with sixty tribesmen, all carrying swords, clubs and lances, gathering round a huge fire where an inner ring of women and children crouched, waiting and watching. Swinging their legs left and right, the men began to sing warlike songs, and as the singing and dancing increased in tempo the drums beat out powerful rhythms. The warriors moved in towards the fire, only to come dancing back once more with increasing ferocity. Ruth Bailey looked around anxiously for the three askaris and their bearers. They had all vanished.

The crimson glow of the fire, the huge yellow moon lighting the landscape and the glitter of innumerable weapons swinging in all directions quickly gave the scene sinister overtones. Hoping sympathetic magic would work, Jung and Baynes decided that the only thing to do was to join the dances. They swung in amongst them, dancing vigorously, with Jung cracking his rhinoceros whip. The Africans beamed approval and redoubled their efforts as they 'stamped, sang, shouted, sweating profusely'. Still the pace and passion mounted until the dancers seemed to become possessed. Jung and Baynes decided the time had come to disengage themselves and rejoin Ruth Bailey. She later described what happened as follows:

> The dancing grew even wilder and they began waving their spears even more fiercely . . . until suddenly they moved in on us once more. My god – it was quite a moment, I can tell you. 'Hold it, Bailey,' Jung said to me, 'here they come.' And then his great voice boomed out at them, telling them to calm down. It was all right for a bit, but they began again – just one more – the chief kept saying – just one more. I must say Jung showed amazing courage, to stand up unarmed and start trying to control a horde of wild tribesmen overcome with a kind of orgy of dancing – it was quite something to see. I didn't feel exactly at home in it all myself.

To reinforce his words Jung swung his rhinoceros whip threateningly, and then on the inspiration of the moment he burst into a flood of Swiss German swearing – enough, as he later said, 'to send anyone home to bed'.[23] Simultaneously he distributed cigarettes amongst them and made a gesture of sleeping. In the end it worked. The savage singing gave place to laughter and the Bugishu began to disperse, but everyone was uneasy as the drums went on beating, rising and falling, now close, now far off, far into the night.

According to Ruth Bailey:

> We cheated over the last part of our trek. C.G. was getting exhausted and we were tending to stay in the shelter part of the day because it was too hot – only setting out again in the early evening. So when a man appeared with an ancient lorry and said he was looking for a German scientist, we were very happy to be found. On the way back we stayed for a time with a District Commissioner who asked me whether I was a psychologist and Jung said – no I found her in Africa. When we told the District Commissioner about the war dance, he said 'Are you people mad – we lost two of our men up there recently – and you worked them up in these dances!' Jung was a bit shaken when he heard about the deaths of two other men.[24]

While they were staying with the District Commissioner, Jung dreamt of a Negro holding 'a tremendous red hot curling iron to [his] head' obviously trying to give it that kink which would convert him into an African. Something familiar about the Negro's face at last identified him with a Negro barber who had dressed Jung's hair on his last lecture tour in America. Immediately he saw the significance of the dream. His unconscious had invoked the memory of the Negro barber to warn him of the dangers of being sucked back into the primal life of the African continent and becoming, symbolically, a Negro himself.

It now dawned on Jung that his African adventure was not only an investigation into a way of life alien to Europeans, but also yet another excursion into his own unconscious. It became clear to him that this trip had been '. . . an intensely personal one' in which he was even prepared to risk the age-old danger of 'going native'.

Gliding peacefully down the Nile, still in company with Baynes, Beckwith and Bailey, he developed a new phase in his self-analysis, but the root causes went much deeper than he admitted. His father had suffered all his life from a wound which would not heal and, still under his father's influence, Jung could be shown to be undergoing a similar fate. Jung, like his father, had lost any faith in orthodox religion, rejecting the dogma of the Church, and now his new model of the human psyche showed signs of becoming a substitute for faith. Moreover, each new refinement of theory was challenged by diminishing outbreaks of psychological disturbances based on the wound that would not heal. The wound and the bow, the sickness that was creative, the occasionally crippled oracle who uttered words of wisdom because his suffering gave him special insights.

The recurring demons receded again as the party entered Egypt, and Ruth Bailey records:

> We had a marvellous time. Baynes was very helpful because he had been in the Camel Corps in Baghdad and we went – splendidly – up the Valley of Kings on camels. C.G. was so sore after riding the camels that he had to retreat into an open carriage. When we came to the Coptic Monastery in the Valley of the Kings I wanted to enter it too – but only men were allowed in – so C.G. dressed me as a man and we got away with it. . . . But I'll tell you something. When it came to travel arrangements it was no use expecting Jung to arrange anything for you – you had to help yourself. It was Beckwith who found me a cabin on the boat – not Jung.

Returning to England, Ruth Bailey received an invitation from Emma Jung to spend a week with the family in Küsnacht. 'Every year after that I went to Küsnacht for a holiday in the summer. . . . In the years of the late '20s Emma and Dr Jung also stayed with us at Lawton Mere, our family house in Cheshire. . . .'[25]

It was the beginning of a long and devoted friendship which ran on into Jung's very last days.

Chapter 24

Eranos

RETURNING to Switzerland in April 1926, Jung plunged into an overwhelming backlog of work which 'sometimes seemed to lack . . . meaning any more so vividly fresh in my mind were my African experiences'.[1] A mass of letters awaited him, as usual, but most of his replies seem to have vanished. If the *Collected Letters* is in any way representative of the years 1920–6, then the correspondence Jung maintained with so many people throughout his life dwindled away to a trickle. There are only ten such letters and most of them reveal nothing significant. One, to a New York psychiatrist, Dr London, said that rumours he (London) had heard about Jung's successes with dementia praecox cases were exaggerated. As a matter of fact he had only treated 'a limited number of cases and these were all what one might call in a liquid condition'.[2] A letter to Christiana Morgan revealed a new attitude to patients. Jung had used part of Christiana Morgan's analytical material in his seminars at the Psychological Club in Zürich,[3] and now he wrote telling her that she should not think he had forgotten her. 'It is all due to overwork . . . there is just too much to do.' Her face had haunted him for a while, he said, and 'you are always a living reality . . . whereas other former patients fade away into oblivion becoming unreal shadows in Hades'. If he didn't write again, he said, it was simply because of the 'hell of letters and patients and papers'.

Another person who came and went in the 1920s on a very casual basis – 'I never saw him make a note about me' – was Margaret Flinters, a would-be writer whose hated father and failed marriage had led to severe psychological disturbance.[4] She was alienated from her husband, her family, her work and indeed the world, which she frequently saw as a globe floating in space around which she circulated as a kind of zombie satellite. 'Bringing me down to earth', she said,

> was literally the problem and he succeeded brilliantly. I don't know how he did it quite. First of all I think it was his own peasant solidity which gave me the feeling I was in touch with a real man for the first time in my life. All the others were wraiths. Second – I suppose – he made me see that I had a ghost somewhere inside me, directing me. It was what he later called the animus – a sort of archetypal animus-figure of the father of all nature. My own father – who was a perfectionist – wouldn't have any truck with anything which didn't match up to the best standards. That was

part of my trouble too. My husband fell short of my ideal. My writing was not perfect. I was afraid of having a child in case it wasn't brilliant. I don't clearly understand transference – but something like that took place – Jung becoming a much more tolerant, much less exacting father figure – and of course the repressed love I had for my father burst out all over him and he found it – I know – damned inconvenient. It must have been a terrible trial to him. But the funny thing is I can never remember receiving a bill from him.

Another person who first became interested in Jung's work at this time was Miss A. I. Allenby.

I first wrote to him after the second World War. I was preparing a thesis on the psychology of religion at the time and – without knowing me at all – Jung took the trouble to send me an unpublished version of an article of his on the Trinity. When I made my first visit to him . . . I was very apprehensive – but no sooner had I entered his presence than I felt completely at ease. And everyone I have known since who met him told me the same story. We talked at different times about parapsychology – synchronicity – the occult – and I would go home in the evening and see him sitting there – the chair, his feet, clothes, hands – and I would know it was not a memory image but communication with reality. . . . You see, he had an uncanny gift of being able to talk to the person inside me who refused to come out.

On one occasion he illustrated to me what happens when you distrust your own feelings and refuse to act on them by telling me a story about a dog – he was very fond of dogs. 'You see my boathouse out there down by the lake,' he said. 'Well, a few days ago I went for a swim and then lay on the balcony to sun myself. The lake comes up very high sometimes and completely surrounds the boathouse. Well, this dog of mine – I frequently walk beside the lake with him – came in search of me but he was confronted by this water – and he doesn't like water. First one paw went into the water and then the other. He repeated the process several times but he was too much a coward to risk it. Then I deliberately made a noise to stimulate him, and all at once he rushed into the water, reached the boathouse and came clambering up the steps. You see, the dog is conditioned by instinct and has no will-power of its own – but a small sign from his master can release that will-power.'[5]

Miss Allenby read this to mean 'that a person who mistrusts his own feelings or thoughts and does not utilise his will to put them to the test is hardly distinguishable from an animal'. In later discussions with her, Jung said, 'Our needs and desires are always active. . . . Trouble occurs only if they are active in the unconscious and we do not take them consciously in hand to give them definite form and direction. If we refuse to do this we are dragged along by them and become their victim. . . .'

The story of the dog had theoretical analogies which he was to repeat endlessly to the point where one colleague exclaimed, *sotto voce*, at a seminar: 'Not that dreary old cliché again.'

It was in the 1920s that Frau Olga Froebe-Kapteyn built a hall in the grounds of her residence at the northern end of Lago Maggiore near Ascona in Switzerland for the express purpose of creating a discussion group between eastern and western philosophies. A terraced garden with a commanding view of the lake and the mountains separated the hall from her beautiful villa Casa Gabriella. Searching for a title, Professor Rudolf Otto of the University of Marburg suggested the Greek word *eranos* – a meal to which everyone contributed – since the name evoked 'the convivial spirit of an unsystematic interchange'.[6]

Frau Froebe's first invitation-list included Dr Heinrich Zimmer, Professor of Sanskrit at the University of Heidelberg, Mrs Rhys Davids of London, President of the Pali Text Society, Dr Erwin Rousselle, Director of the Ching Institute, and Dr Carl Gustav Jung. The lectures were delivered in German, English and Italian 'from the contrasting standpoints of the several speakers' on the common theme of Yoga and Meditation in East and West.

'Conviviality then broke out' as Jung put it to Professor Inkermann. Everyone adjourned to cafés in Ascona where a shared feast was laced with coffee and wine. 'In the course of the first decade, the interest of the participants shifted from the meeting of East and West to Europe's meeting with the multiple aspects of its own destiny.'[7] For many years the sense of continuity was due partly to the guidance of Frau Froebe but also to the 'continuous presence and genial spirit of Dr C. G. Jung'.[8]

Lancelot Whyte, the physicist philosopher, told me: 'Yes – I certainly talked to Jung at Eranos on more than one occasion. For the oracle he had become he certainly had the patience of a good listener – I suppose you can't avoid that if people buy your time as a professional psychiatrist.'[9]

Whyte, who had lectured widely in America, was surprised to find that Jung kept up to date with new data in physics through his American friend Professor Wolfgang Pauli. He had an *au courant* view of the latest theory of elementary particles and could draw out not so much the scientific details as the philosophic implications brilliantly. 'And talking of drawing out – that was another gift. He knew every turn of phrase which would draw a person out. He did it with me. Towards the end of one talk that quizzical smile of his came over his face, "Do you realise how many times you have used the phrase 'One should'?" he said, and I acknowledged the weakness. Then he added, "Why *don't* you?" It summed up my problem in three words.'[10]

Aniela Jaffé was another frequent visitor to Eranos. The predominance of women among his audience led to sardonic comments about his Jungfrauen and maenads, but it was a price they 'were quite willing to pay', Aniela Jaffé said. Later Miss Jaffé began an analysis with Jung and recalls his idiosyncratic method. She arrived burning to discuss a new dream one day only to find that he, too, had a preoccupation he wished to work through, and once launched into it there was no stopping him. 'A good deal of strength was needed to interrupt him in sessions like these and trot out one's own affair, which of course he did not take amiss.' She in fact never had the necessary nerve to interrupt the great man but a remarkable characteristic frequently became apparent in his outpourings. If the patient 'swam along' with them 'without giving a thought to the advancing hand of the clock', it slowly became apparent that they were coming round to the very thing about which the patient wished to talk. As one Englishman told Miss Jaffé, 'He has terrific intuition.' On Miss Jaffé's own testimony, patients 'got the answer without having posed the question'.[11] 'But his technique was likely to be different with each patient,' she continued. 'Sometimes he spoke of parents – but not with me. I tried once to tell him about my mother, and he said: "Don't waste your time." '[12]

Aniela Jaffé described the lecture-hall at Eranos: 'It opened on to a terrace separated from the garden and the lake by a low stone wall. In the half-hour interval during each lecture and again when the lecture was over Jung used to sit on this wall and in a flash we were clustering round him like bees round a honey pot.'[13] This annoyed other participants, but the maenads were not to be denied the brief glory of their idolatry. 'These wall sessions', Aniela Jaffé wrote, 'were the unforgettable highlights of the summer. They acquired a different character when Erich Neumann of Tel-Aviv was there for then a dialogue developed between the two and we listened.'[14]

In the early days Jung stayed in Casa Semiramis at Verita, but when the walk to Moscia became tiring Olga Froebe-Kapetyn gave Jung the small flat above the lecture-hall. There he would invite a few disciples, and special seminars took place.

The night came, famous now in memories of Eranos, when what Jaffé described as a 'nocturnal celebration on the terrace . . .' developed into a party where 'merrymaking resounded far over the lake'. Such a pitch did the party reach that neighbours 'far and wide' sent in complaints to Mrs Froebe who, herself lost in the spirit of the moment, simply ignored them. As for Jung, like everyone else he grew tipsy on wine, and moved among the throng encouraging those who hesitated to dip deeper into Dionysus. 'It was', as one woman present said, 'the nearest I ever came to wicked abandonment in my life.' And Aniela Jaffé later recorded:

'Jung was here there and everywhere bubbling over with wit mockery and drunken spirit. Only a poet could describe this gay and abandoned "night-sea journey".'[15]

Chapter 25

The Anti-Semitic Legend

THE EARLY 1930s saw the beginning of a tormented period in Jung's life, the roots of which can be traced to Hitler's dramatic rise to power in Germany and an article Jung wrote in the *Zentralblatt für Psychotherapie*.

In his book *The Solution of the German Problem*, Wilhelm Röpke claimed that when the famous Professor Kretschmer 'found himself unable to continue his function as President of the German Association for Psycho-therapy and as editor of the leading periodical, Professor Jung obligingly filled the vacancy left by his honest German colleague and accepted the Nazi invitation to take over his function'.

Röpke's account continues:

> After the *Gleichschaltung* [literally, 'bringing into step'] of the Association and its periodical, the first number of the Nazified paper (*Zentralblatt für Psychotherapie*) was opened by a solemn introduction written by Professor Jung underlining the necessity of distinguishing thenceforward a Germanic and a Jewish psychology, while in the same number the new *Reichsführer* of the psycho-therapists, Professor M. H. Göring,[1] pledged the members of the new association to Adolf Hitler's fundamental book *Mein Kampf*. In order to make it perfectly clear what the obliging attitude of Professor Jung meant, a few pages later (p. 142) the *Reichsführer* declared: 'Thanks to the fact that Dr C. G. Jung accepted the presidency . . . it has been possible to continue the scientific activity of the Association and of its periodical.'

We need to turn to the *Zentralblatt für Psychotherapie* to discover the real roots of these charges.[2] Jung had written:

> The Aryan unconscious has a higher potential than the Jewish; this is the advantage and the disadvantage of a youthfulness not yet fully escaped from barbarism. In my opinion it has been a great mistake of all previous medical psychology to apply Jewish categories which are not even binding for all Jews, indiscriminately to Christians, Germans or Slavs. In so doing, medical psychology has declared the most precious secret of the Germanic peoples – the creatively prophetic depths of soul – to be a childishly banal morass, while for decades my warning voice has been suspected of anti-semitism. The source of this suspicion is Freud. He did not know the Germanic soul any more than did all his Germanic imitators. . . . Has the mighty apparition of National

Socialism which the whole world watches with astonished eyes taught them something better?

Written one year after Hitler came to power in Germany, this somewhat obscure passage is open to several interpretations. Threading through the qualifications, three statements appear. The higher potential of the Aryan unconscious has advantages and disadvantages; there is a difference between Jewish and Aryan psychology; the mighty apparition of National Socialism has something better to teach us.

Taken together these statements do not amount to anti-Semitism. In December of the previous year (1933) Jung had discriminated sharply between Jew and Gentile in the *Zentralblatt für Psychotherapie*: 'The factual differences between Germanic and Jewish psychology which have long been known to intelligent people shall no longer be wiped out and that can only be helpful to science.' In any normal atmosphere these words were innocuous enough, but seen against the blazing context of Nazi anti-Semitism and the proclaimed intention of Hitler to obliterate the Jews, they could be distorted to endorse philosophic assumptions of a dangerous kind. However, the statement that Germanic and Jewish psychology were different did not ask for any form of Jewish discrimination or persecution.

On 27 February 1934, the *Neue Züricher Zeitung* carried an article on German psychotherapy by Dr Gustav Bally, a Swiss psychiatrist. He wrote:

> The General German Society for Psycho-therapy had to cease publication of the *Zentralblatt für Psychotherapie* in February 1933. Almost a year later, the periodical has appeared again [issue December 1933]. Dr C. G. Jung makes himself known as editor of this co-ordinated periodical. So we find a Swiss citizen editing the official organ of a society which, according to the statement of one of its leading members, Dr M. H. Göring, requires of all its actively writing and speaking members that they shall have studied Adolf Hitler's fundamental book *Mein Kampf* with full scientific thoroughness and shall recognize it as the basis of their activity.

Jung could not ignore this challenge. On 13 March 1934 he replied with the first of two articles:

> I found myself faced with a moral conflict . . . should I as a prudent neutral withdraw into security on this side of the frontier, live and wash my hands in innocence, or should I – as I was well aware – lay myself open to attack and the unavoidable misunderstanding which no one can escape who, out of a higher necessity, has to come to terms with the political powers that be in Germany? Should I sacrifice the interests of science, of loyalty to my colleagues, of the friendship which binds me to many German physicians, and the living community of German language and

intellectual culture, to my egotistic comfort and different political outlook? . . . So I had no alternative but to lend the weight of my name and of my independent position for the benefit of my friends. . . .

In the last paragraph of his second article, Jung wrote: 'I have no hesitation in admitting that it is a highly unfortunate and confusing coincidence that my scientific programme *should have been superimposed without my co-operation and against my express wish, on a political manifesto.*' (My italics.)

Under the eyes of his Nazi sponsors these were bold words. He took the risk of causing grave offence whether they had deliberately deceived him or not.

Letters which have since come to light reaffirm Jung's defence. Writing to Dr Olaf Brüel, a Danish psychotherapist and co-founder of the International General Medical Society for Psychotherapy, he said, 'Thus Göring's manifesto which it was agreed would appear in a special German issue had been printed in the *Zentralblatt* under his name. This is against my express demand that the special German issue should be signed by Göring and not by me.'[3] He would, he concluded, try every possible means in future to eliminate politics from the *Zentralblatt*. On the same day he wrote to Walter Cimbal, the honorary secretary of the General Medical Society for Psychotherapy, protesting against the confusion which had arisen.

But one flaw remains. When Jung had discovered this first piece of duplicity, why did he not resign at once? Part of the answer appears in his letter to Walter Cimbal: 'I would however urgently request you to make the *Zentralblatt* intended for foreign circulation unpolitical in every respect otherwise it is quite impossible for foreign subscribers to join the Society.'

On 19 March he wrote reaffirming this to Olaf Brüel.

Nonetheless the storm grew. Writing to E. Beit von Speyer, a German analytical psychologist, he said that he had fallen foul of contemporary history. It was impossible any longer to have any kind of association with Germany without 'becoming politically suspect on one side or the other'. Indeed, it had reached a stage where he personally was regarded as 'a blood-boltered anti-Semite' because he had 'helped the German doctors to consolidate their Psychotherapeutic Society'.[4]

By 21 December 1935 the Dutch group of the International Society for Psychotherapy withdrew an offer to hold a congress in Holland because of the prevailing political views in Germany. Jung challenged this, pointing out that a congress held outside Germany would be neutral, need not exclude Jews and should subscribe to free speech. He emphasised that their German psychiatric colleagues were not responsible for the Nazi revolution, its politics or persecutions.

Similar difficulties had arisen in Denmark and Sweden. Jung

concluded his letter to the Praesidium of the Dutch group with the words: 'The logical outcome of this is that I tender my resignation as president of the International Society.'[5] In fact, at this stage, he did not resign.

By March 1938, Jung had become even more vociferous in his defence of Jewish participation. Writing to Eric Benjamin Strauss, an English psychiatrist, he said: 'As you know pars 2, 3 and 4 of our regulations allow the participation of everyone quite apart from his political or religious conviction.'[6] Then came the assurance: 'I cannot and shall not exclude non-Aryan speakers.' One qualification followed. He would insist on tactfulness from Aryans and non-Aryans alike. They should avoid remarks liable to 'arouse the political psychosis of the day'.

In September of the following year came the catastrophe of the Second World War and with it Jung's realisation that what he referred to as the Nazi psychosis had reached its climax. Not until October of the following year did he make 'his resignation final'. He wrote to Z. H. van der Hoope of the Dutch group that Professor Göring gladly accepted his decision. The first part of the long-drawn-out saga of Jung's alleged anti-Semitism came to an end with his resignation, but this was only the beginning of a sustained persecution which burst out afresh after the war.

All these years Jung had been without a regular secretary, although his wife and his third daughter Marianne frequently stepped in to organise his correspondence, lectures, patients and bills. Barbara Hannah told me: 'I always seemed to get bills for the wrong amount – usually in my favour.' Then, in 1932, Jung's old friend Dr Hans Schmid died unexpectedly and his eldest daughter Marie-Jeanne, a trained secretary, volunteered to help Jung. For the following twenty years she served him faithfully, bringing order into what sometimes threatened to become chaos.

From 1933 onward Jung was busy writing a number of papers elaborating two of the main principles of his psychological model – the archetypes and their correlate the collective unconscious. He had first mentioned the archetypes as far back as 1919 (*Instinct and the Unconscious*), but now, in a lecture delivered to the Eranos Society, he defined them as 'archaic or . . . primordial . . . with universal images that have existed since the remotest times'. One expression of such archetypes could be found, he said, in myths and fairy tales, but these were not original archetypes since they had received shape and form and been handed down through the ages. The term 'archetypes' applied only 'to those psychic contents which [had] not yet been submitted to conscious elaborations and [were] therefore an immediate datum of psychic experience'. In other words, the archetypes were the undifferentiated raw material from which their correlatives, like myths and fairy tales, might be distilled.

The archetypes were part of the dynamic structure of the collective unconscious which had to be carefully distinguished from the personal unconscious. For several years Jung had dealt with the personal unconscious, but he did not, like Freud, assign purely regressive characteristics to that concept. 'While the personal unconscious is made up essentially of contents which have at one time been conscious but which have disappeared from consciousness . . . having been forgotten or repressed', the contents of the collective unconscious had never entered consciousness and were not individually acquired from life experience. They were in fact exclusively inherited. 'Whereas the personal unconscious consists for the most part of complexes, the contents of the collective unconscious is made up essentially of archetypes.'[7]

Jung's general approach to the unconscious differed from Freud's in three ways. First, the unconscious, in his view, followed an autonomous course of development; second, it was the source of archetypes or universal primordial images; and, third, it was complementary to and not conflicting with consciousness. One of the earliest cases which led to the archetypes concerned a very old schizophrenic patient subject to elaborate hallucinations day and night. The unfortunate Dr Honneger, who committed suicide, happened to be the physician in charge when the patient declared one day that he now knew the secret of the origin of the wind. He had observed, he said, that the sun had a phallus, and the movements of this phallus corresponded with the creation of the wind. Amused, at first, by the sexual ingenuity of the idea, Jung stumbled on a recent book by the historian Albrecht Dieterich which dealt with the liturgy of the Mithraic religion.[8] Based on a hitherto unpublished Greek papyrus, the text mentioned the idea of the wind originating from a tube hanging from the sun.

Excited by the coincidence, Jung ruled out the possibility that the patient had read such a recently discovered text, particularly since there was no copy of the work in the Burghölzli library.[9] The episode seemed open to a number of interpretations. First, that the patient's hallucinations derived from his preoccupation with the penis symbol and had a straightforward sexual meaning. Second, that the proximity of the anus might connect the imagery with the creation of wind. Third, that there existed a correlation between the delusions of psychotic patients and the universal symbols which recur in religious myths. In fact, although Jung failed to mention it, the symbol of the phallic sun appeared in Friedrich Creuzer's *Symbolik und Mythologie der alten Völker*, a book he had read. Jung now concluded that the individual unconscious could draw on the deeper pool of the collective unconscious and find correspondences at the mythic level of which a patient might be totally unaware.

In this early paper Jung was still struggling towards a clearer formulation of several vital concepts, one of them the anima archetype.

He drew a vivid picture of a man seeing his own image mirrored in the water with unexpected creatures looming up 'presumably harmless dwellers of the deep – harmless if only the lake were not haunted'. Sometimes a 'nixie', a female, half-human fish, swam into the fisherman's net. 'The nixie is an even more instinctive version of a magical feminine being whom I call the anima.' This was the female aspect of the male unconscious. Embodiments of the anima, Jung said, could be found in Rider Haggard's *She*, Benoit's *Queen of Atlantis* and *Helen of Troy*.

Jung's critics were already busy repeating what he regarded as ill-informed attacks on such concepts. They were, his critics claimed, nothing more than part of the mythology he invoked. They had no existence in reality. Jung came back strongly: 'I must emphasise that the concept of the anima is a purely empirical concept whose sole purpose is to give a name to a group of related or analogous psychic phenomena.'

Never one to be easily dismayed, Jung pressed on with the difficult task of assembling the final components of his rapidly growing model. One element in that model – individuation – he now illustrated with the case-history of a woman first encountered as early as 1920. Miss X was fifty-five years old and a student of psychology. Intellectually animated, very cultured, and unmarried, she 'lived with the unconscious equivalent of a human partner, namely the animus (the personification of everything masculine in women)'.

This, Jung quickly discovered, was the result of a father complex which produced its inevitable conflict with the mother. Such powerful personification of the animus sometimes generated intolerance, but Miss X was open-minded and quickly saw that certain disrupting incidents indicated a critical phase in her life amounting to a psychological *impasse*.

Scandinavian on her mother's side, she travelled to Zürich via Denmark where she stayed for a time fully conscious of the fact that she was 'turning back to her own origins and . . . setting out to re-activate a portion of her childhood that was bound up with the mother'.[10]

Associating landscape with Mother Earth, one of the most profound archetypes, she felt the urge to capture the Danish countryside on canvas and began painting. Tensions relaxed, an approximation to contentment overtook her and, as the paintings multiplied, a sense of new life inspired her to fresh efforts.

Arrived in Zürich she continued painting, and on the very day preceding her visit to Jung she was suddenly possessed by the 'memory' of a different landscape which she at once tried to paint. In full flood of recollection a fantasy image suddenly disrupted her work and deeply disturbed her. The fantasy, terrifying in its vividness, took place on a beach beside the sea, and there she saw herself 'with the lower half of her body in the earth stuck fast in a block of rock'. Trapped, helpless and utterly dismayed, she suddenly saw approaching a medieval sorcerer, but as the figure drew nearer she realised that this was none other than the man she had to see – Carl Gustav Jung. Jung heard her call for help, turned towards the rock, 'touched it with a magic wand and the stone instantly burst open as she stepped out uninjured'. Scrapping the second landscape painting, she now tried to capture the details of the fantasy. Extraordinarily, until she arrived in Denmark she had displayed no marked capacity to paint, but now the picture was aesthetically effective.

The following day she hurried off to show Jung the completed painting. There was a happy reunion – he had known her well in the United States – and then Jung studied the painting in detail. Aided by Miss X's associations, he began interpretation. Jung believed that subliminal fantasies frequently forced themselves into patients' paintings and created technical difficulties. Thus the big boulders on the beach would not transcribe accurately to canvas, but underwent distortions until some of them looked like 'hard-boiled eggs cut in two with the yolk in the middle'. Another boulder reached up like a minor pyramid in which her body was partially trapped with the wind ruffling the sea and sending her hair streaming out behind her.

It was easy enough to see the trapped state of body and mind represented by the picture, but the interpretation which followed was later attacked by Edward Glover as a typical example of Jung forcing the patient's evidence into theories derived from his own life experience.[11] According to Jung, Miss X was not only trapped by the earth but also by the Earth Mother, one of the most powerful archetypal images. Then came the following sentence: 'Psychologically this state means being caught in the unconscious.' Elaborating the point, Jung said: 'Her inadequate relation to her mother had left behind something dark and in need of development.'[12]

Jung did not trouble to interpret the obvious sexual symbolism of the first picture – a girl drawing a cone toward her body with divided eggs like an ovum waiting to be fertilised. Jung claimed that such sexual symbolism 'was for naïve minds' and 'had no significance' in the case of Miss X.

Her second painting repeated the boulders of the first, but now what once looked like eggs had become circular and one of the 'round forms had been blasted out of place by a golden flash of lightning'. This could be seen as an ecstatic flash of passion fertilising the egg, but Jung had other interpretations.

He remarked that the lightning had released a spherical form from the rock as if in liberation, and in the same sense that the magician in the first had been replaced by the lightning in the second, 'so the patient had been replaced with the sphere'.

Her artistic limitations had driven her to use spheres as substitutes for human beings, but it was her unconscious which brought about the change in technique. Communication between the conscious and unconscious had been activated in a new sense. 'Reason always wanted to make the picture as it . . . ought to be; but the eyes held fast to their vision and finally forced the picture to come out as it did.' The beginnings of cross-fertilisation between conscious, unconscious and collective unconscious implied an attempt at wholeness, represented by the sphere, while Jung the therapist was reduced to a flash of lightning.

Brilliant insights and enormous ingenuity distinguish Jung's elaborate analysis of the remaining twenty-two pictures drawn by Miss X, concluding with a beautiful flowering mandala which could easily be seen as the beginnings of a new harmony. Freudians, of course, would point to striking resemblances to the vagina in the pictures, stress the constant repetition of snake motifs and the fact that they were drawn by a fifty-five-year-old unmarried woman.

Jung would have none of this. He saw the beautiful elaboration of one picture after another as an interlocking series representing 'the initial stages of the way to individuation'.

Chapter 26
The Visit to India

BETWEEN 1929 AND 1935 the number of devoted disciples surrounding Jung grew, and women continued to predominate. Some came as patients and remained as friends, some met him socially and surendered to a combination of charisma, charm and sheer exuberance. Within his own developing theories among the four functions he appeared to be a strong *intuitive* type, but his *sensations* were powerfully primitive and his *feelings* not so strong. He imagined himself to belong to the type called Logos- or thinking-dominated man, but in fact the intuitive-sensation functions came first and the Logos last.

Barbara Hannah consulted him as a patient, and within a very short time the intuitive-sensation functions drove him to exclaim, 'Oh my God, you bore me.' Jung quickly passed Miss Hannah over to his wife, who had now begun to handle patients in her own right. Briefly treated by Mrs Jung, Barbara Hannah then passed into the hands of Toni Wolff, also a practising analyst. 'She was still amateur enough', Barbara Hannah said, 'to extend her sessions beyond the normal fifty or sixty minutes.'[1] Barbara Hannah finally returned once more to Jung and told him that she had experienced a most powerful dream which all took place in a ditch. 'Ah,' Jung roared at her, 'you've ditched both of them [Emma and Toni] and now, you hell cat, you want to get me in the ditch.'[2] Primitive sensation with a vengeance! 'I knew you were a hell cat from the start,' he added. 'That's why I passed you on. But I tell you what I will do. I will take you on again on the understanding that, if you get me in the ditch too, it's up to you to get me out again!'

Asked whether she ever lay on a couch Barbara Hannah replied: 'No, we sat in very comfortable armchairs. He sat by his desk, and if he could walk up and down he did. He used to say, "I never get any exercise, so I'm very glad to walk up and down." '[3] Mary Briner developed the description. The leather armchair in which she sat had one spring broken, and Jung either used the swivel chair at his desk, or drew another armchair very close to the patient.[4]

'He could be kind,' Barbara Hannah said, 'but also frightfully ruthless. He could wipe the floor with one. He did something to me which was apparently very disloyal and very unkind. Somehow I managed to swallow it, and that helped me more than any kindness he ever did for me. I said that to him. "Yes, I know," he said, "I never do it on purpose – the unconscious does it through me." '[5] He had in fact asked her to prepare a translation of two of his books and then accepted an alternative translation by someone else.[6]

Another witness said that in his more extreme moods Jung would apply a kind of shock treatment when he fell back on blunt language to rouse a patient from self-deception, hypocrisy or time-wasting. 'You want to f— this priest don't you?' he would say. 'Come on – be frank about it – tell me the real truth of the matter.' Or to a patient exploiting vacillation as a delaying tactic: 'Stop buggering about and wasting my time. Go away and think your way through . . . then come back again.'

Dr Liliane Frey-Rohn was another who joined the circle in these days. Attending an Eranos meeting, one day she suddenly felt a big strong hand descend on her shoulder and begin to knead it. As she turned to confront the stranger, his deep voice suddenly said, 'Ah, you have a cramp here, haven't you?' It was, of course, Jung, and Dr Frey-Rohn found it a wonderful example of his intuitive powers because she certainly did have a cramp, psychic or otherwise. One flash of insight followed another; she was father-fixated. 'Then I am right for you,' Jung said, and she became his patient. Dr Frey-Rohn's father was instrumental in Jung's becoming Professor of Psychology at the Swiss Federal Polytechnic in 1935, a significant appointment since his academic career had never prospered. Like many of these early patient-friends, Frey-Rohn became a practising therapist and brought to light one remarkable fact about Jung. Legend had it that he grossly overworked, but Dr Frey-Rohn made a study of his work-schedule for one year only to discover that at least twenty-six weeks of that year were spent at Bollingen where he went to relax.[7] Of course, this was not entirely true; he did a considerable amount of writing at Bollingen. Frey-Rohn also made an interesting study of his handwriting over the years. 'He wrote in a crabbed small hand when he was a dry scientific writer, expanding into a much more open work style as he gathered confidence in his theories and later using on occasion a beautiful exact Gothic script like a medieval manuscript.'[8]

'He always seemed to be troubled by minor illnesses – colds and flu,' she recalled. He also spoke freely about Toni Wolff and, as we have seen, regarded her as a poet equal to Goethe!

Barbara Hannah found that Toni was completely frank about her relationship with Jung: 'She talked quite openly – indeed, why shouldn't she?' If Toni and Carl pursued closely similar paths, they also shared mutual blank spots. Both were unmusical, both could quickly tire of company, both had the capacity for deep withdrawal. But Jung's admiration of Toni was not unqualified. He complained on one occasion, 'Toni behaved this morning as if she really were a re-incarnated goddess.'[9] And when she moved to a new flat: 'Only Toni would have gone to live in a place with marble pillars and a study like Mussolini's.'[10] They both liked dogs but Jung was so devoted to one dog after another, including a particularly splendid British bulldog, that the death of a dog seemed to matter out of all proportion. Indeed, he carved and erected a replica of his boyhood mannikin over the grave of his favourite dog. The ritual went deep. He had lost the talisman of his boyhood and found reassurance by resurrecting it in his garden as a monument to animal-psychic life.

There was a human death in 1935 which might have had profound effects on Jung if his sister had not remained a background figure all her life. He commented on his sister's death: 'A few days before [she] died her face wore an expression of such inhuman sublimity that I was profoundly frightened.' Later he added: 'What happens after death is so unspeakably glorious that our imagination and feelings do not suffice to form even an approximate conception of it.'[11]

Between 1935 and 1938 Jung travelled widely. In London he gave a course of five lectures in English at the Tavistock Clinic to a large and critical group of doctors. 'From the start Jung held the audience as in a spell,' Dr E. A. Bennet wrote. 'There was complete silence. . . . He was entirely at ease, totally free from shyness or stiffness in manner, and spoke for an hour or more out of his own experience . . . salted here and there with a nice sense of humour.'[12]

Checking some of his references, Jung paid a visit to the Reading Room in the British Museum, only to discover that he needed a ticket. 'Who are you?' the clerk in the director's office asked. 'I am a Swiss doctor. . . . My name is Jung,' he replied. 'Not Freud, Jung and Adler?' the assistant asked eagerly. 'Oh, no,' Jung answered. 'Just Jung.' Whereupon he was granted entrance.[13]

In September he went on to America to lecture at the Harvard Tercentenary Conference of Arts and Sciences. Returning to Zürich once more, he wrote to Jolande Jacobi that it had all been so gruelling that he intended to restrict his work the following winter to concentrate on a single book.[14]

However, by 1937 he was again in America to give the Yale Terry Lectures with considerable success. An incident occurred during one lecture which vividly illustrated the charismatic aspect of his personality. Accustomed to lecture in small halls in England, he had asked for similar facilities at Yale, but his American host said that he would prefer him to begin in a large hall and migrate to a smaller one as the initial crowds dwindled away. This, he assured Jung, always happened no matter how brilliant the visiting lecturer. Exactly the reverse transpired. 'With a seating capacity of 3000 and the hall two-thirds empty Jung confronted his first audience of 700 people with some dismay, but when he insisted on using the smaller one for the second [lecture] he was told the larger one was already full to overflowing.'[15] Then came the third lecture, again to a packed audience, and an incident with the Professor's wife. 'He was invited to tea at the Professor's house after the lecture, only to find the Professor's wife in tears when he arrived. Asked whether she was in trouble she replied "No". Asked why she was crying, she said: "I didn't understand a word of your lecture, but I *felt* it – oh, so deeply. It was your voice, your manner, the way you said things. I felt the absolute truth of what you said. That's why I'm upset. It was beautiful." [16]

There emerged from these Terry Lectures another important work, *Psychology and Religion*, which became part of Volume 11 of the *Collected Works*. Since his boyhood Jung had been preoccupied with the problem of religion. His illness between 1913 and 1918 changed his attitude, and he came to speak of 'the natural function of religion' ascribing 'numinous' characteristics to religious archetypes. Rudolf Otto's *The Idea of the Holy* reaffirmed his new approach when it first appeared and was hailed as a considerable contribution to the psychology of religion.

The term 'religion' no longer meant to Jung a creed but 'a careful and scrupulous observation of what Rudolf Otto aptly termed the numinosum'. This, in turn, meant 'a dynamic agency or effect not caused by an arbitrary will'.[17] Struggling to clarify the concept, Jung said that the numinosum 'was the influence of an invisible presence that causes a peculiar alteration in consciousness'.

Jung took over the term 'numinous' but gave it a much more phylogenetic meaning. Whereas Otto tended to limit numinous experience to exceptional people like religious leaders, mystics and prophets, Jung identified certain aspects of the numinous with the archetypes. The total experience of the numinous as described by Otto was not transferred complete to the archetypes but, as Ellenberger put it, 'certain features . . . accompany the manifestations of the archetype'. Once again the archetypes were the powerhouse from which derived the religious 'impulse', expressing itself in rites and dogmas.

The first three chapters of *Psychology and Religion* are full of erudite references which constantly return to the concept of the archetype. Nothing short of a sustained scrutiny of several hundred pages will accurately abstract the detailed subtlety of Jung's approach to religious experience, but the unwary reader must be warned that he may emerge more confused than when he began.

Certainly Jung regarded man as 'naturally' religious and the religious function no less powerful than the instincts of sex and aggression. He went farther and suggested that those of his patients who were over thirty-five or forty always came to him with a religious problem in the foreground. As for religious archetypes they could be as destructive on occasion as they were creative. Paul, on the road to Damascus experiencing the vision which finally converted him, exemplified the religious archetype seizing a human subject creatively. The Swiss mystic Nicholas von der Elüe, on the other hand, experienced a vision of the Holy Trinity so shattering that his face underwent a physical change and he himself became a frightening person. The archetype from which sprang the most profound religious experience could also manifest itself in the delusions of schizophrenics.

Psychology and Religion first appeared in 1938, and in April of the same year Jung wrote to Erich Neumann that he was leaving almost at once for India.[18] The British Government had invited him, he said, to take part in the twenty-fifth-anniversary celebrations of the Indian Science Congress Association in Calcutta.

By now deeply involved in the alchemical studies which were to play such an important part in his later work, he set sail for India with, among other books, the first volume of the *Theatrum Chemicum* (1602) which included several papers on the thinking of Gerardus Dorneus. If Jung was right about the collective unconscious, then it should override all national boundaries and offer a common pool of psychic inheritance which people of all creeds and races would share. He approached India bearing this in mind.

During the voyage the sight of women parading the decks in trousers reinforced his dislike of women wearing men's clothing.[19] 'It is a sad truth but the European woman and particularly her hopelessly wrong dress have no show at all when compared to the dignity of the Indian woman and her costume.'[20] Even fat Indian women, in his view, could be made attractive by saris, whereas in Europe 'they [could] only starve themselves to death'.

Arrived in India, he was also critical of men's clothes: 'There is something effeminate or babyish about it. You simply cannot imagine a soldier with such garlands of cloth between his legs.' Revealing the depth of his European indoctrination, he added: 'It is quaint but not very masculine.' Even worse in his view: 'A real fight in such a contrivance is well-nigh impossible.'

On the very first day an experience occurred which further unsettled his immediate impressions. He hired a car and drove out into the dusty fields, with their native huts, sickly palms and great weird banyan trees, where everything moved to a tempo he could only describe as 'hasty leisure'. Then, driving through a strip of jungle, he emerged into a clearing, but 'instead of running over a lurking tiger we were in the midst of a native movie scene'.[21] There it all was just like a European re-creation of India in some Hollywood studio – men excitedly walking about in shirt-sleeves, megaphones bawling, cameras turning and a *white girl* dressed up as a *dompteuse* escaped from a circus. The shock was sufficient to drive him straight back to the city from which he had just fled.

In the next few days, observing the effects of British rule, he remarked that the lineaments of India's majestic face had survived the Mogul and Aryan invaders and would also survive the British. The aim of Indian culture he found had little to do with what Europeans regarded as moral perfection. Indeed, the concepts of good and evil interlocked in a quite different sense and were not concepts. The Christian drive towards 'the good' frequently succumbed to 'evil', whereas the Indian felt himself to be outside good and evil and aimed not at moral perfection but *nirdvandva*. Surrendering to an elaborate process of withdrawal, meditation and self-annihilation, the Indian sought to escape the common clay of everyday experience, to find an inner peace of imageless emptiness. This philosophy did not appeal to Jung. He had no desire whatever to be freed from nature, human beings or himself. On the contrary, all such 'phenomena' appeared to him capable of enriching his life and could only be suppressed at the cost of great impoverishment. 'To me,' he wrote, 'the supreme meaning of Being can consist only in the fact that it *is*, not that it is *not*.'

Never a man to put too much store by socio-economic factors, he underestimated the power of poverty and malnutrition from which the least ingenious culture might have retreated in self-annihilating rituals. A rich man himself, Jung never interpreted cultures through economic determinism. Nor did he fully appreciate that spiritual flights into higher realms of self-abnegation could compensate for the intolerable realities of those who lived on the brink of starvation.

The self-liberating rituals of the Yogi were equally uncongenial to him. 'Real liberation becomes possible for me only when I have done all that I was able to do . . . a man who has not passed through the inferno of his passions has not overcome them.'[22]

Accompanied by a pandit, Jung visited a pagoda in Konarik Orissa, where the walls were covered with what he described as 'exquisitely obscene sculptures'. The pandit claimed that they were a means to spiritual experience, and when Jung objected that the open-mouthed peasants gaping at the multiple patterns of intercourse were scarcely experiencing spiritualisation, he replied, 'But that is just the point. How can they ever become spiritualised if they do not first fulfil their Karma?'

Two seductive dancing girls guarded the entrance to the pagoda, and again they were explained away in similar terms: 'Naturally,' the pandit added, 'that does not apply to people like you and me, for we have attained to a level of consciousness which is above this sort of thing.'

Then came the supreme moment of naïveté. Walking down a lane away from the temple, they encountered a number of stones, and the pandit said, 'I will tell you a great secret about them. . . . These stones are a man's private parts.' Jung looked at him dumbfounded, only to see him nod self-importantly as if to say, 'You would never have realised that, would you!'

Travelling with the British delegation to the Indian Science Congress in Calcutta he was entertained at many dinners and receptions and had his first opportunity to talk to educated Indian women. He left no record of the impact they made, but simply said, 'Their costume characterises them as women.' No less than three doctorates were granted him – from Allahabad representing Islam, from Benares Hinduism, and Calcutta British Indian medicine and science.

Jung felt that there was nothing in India which had not 'lived a hundred thousand times before', a remark which could apply to any civilisation thousands of years old. He also observed that the unique figure of Buddha was not in fact unique but had been preceded by a score of other Buddhas. In Jung's view, Christ was an embodiment of the Self, but one foredoomed to sacrifice, and conjoined with God, while Buddha remained a historical person not necessarily committed to suffering.

When Jung visited the *stupas* of Sanchi where Buddha had delivered his first sermon, the spirit of India really gripped him for the first time. Overcome by the spell of the holy site, he 'took leave of [his] companion and submerged [himself] in the overpowering mood of the place'. One suffocatingly hot night he witnessed a Kathakali dance with its 'demonically clever and incessant drumming that shakes up the ever dormant plexus solaris of the European'.[23] A score of different nuances from the sentimental to the obscene, from the monstrous to the blood-curdling, arose in the dance and would have become grotesque but for the insistent rising and falling of the drums which drew upon mysterious powers and created 'a new reality rising from the bowels'.

Far removed from such experiences were the many lectures and ceremonials which combined to produce a hectic routine until suddenly, in Calcutta, Jung was hit by dysentery, which carried him into hospital for ten days. It was 'a blessed island' in a 'wild sea of new impressions' and he lay in bed trying to give order to the multitudinous turmoil of his thoughts.

Then came, inevitably, the dream. At every crucial point in his life a dream developed which not merely crystallised his current situation but frequently indicated some new direction which must be taken. The current dream involved him in a search for the Holy Grail. Recapturing the details with remarkable vividness at the age of eighty, he built up a picture of an unknown island 'presumably situated not far off the coast of southern England', where he and a group of Zürich friends were standing in the courtyard of a medieval castle. One wall of the castle was decorated by a black iron trelliswork, and at regular intervals the branches carried small metal bird-houses. Suddenly he saw 'a tiny hooded gnome, a cucullatus, scurrying from one little house to the next.' Among the assembled company was a professor, and as Jung drew his attention to the hooded gnome the dream changed abruptly.

It now became clear that an urgent search had begun for the Holy Grail because they were due to celebrate its discovery that same evening in the castle. A long and strenuous trek developed leading to the narrowest part of the island where it was split by the sea. There they set up camp, and darkness came down on the desolate landscape. As his companions one by one fell asleep Jung came to the conclusion that there was only one thing left to be done – he alone must swim across the channel and recover the Grail. As he was taking off his clothes to plunge into the icy water, he woke up.

The message rang clear. India had a significant part to play in his continuous search for the equivalent of the Holy Grail, but the real discoveries were to be made in Europe not India. England became the focal point for his return because there the myth of the Grail was still pursued as a living reality. Then occurred a link with his alchemical studies which occupied the few idle periods of his stay in India. 'This fact . . . impressed me all the more when I realised the concordance between this poetic myth and what alchemy had to say about the *unum vas*, the *una medicina* and the *una lapis*.' Jung believed that certain powerful figures 'which consciousness reduced to banality' were 'recognised again by the poets and prophetically revived'. They could also be recognised in 'changed form' by the thoughtful person. In other words the great ones of the past could be resurrected in new form by alchemical processes similar to those which 'inspired' the Holy Grail.

But the *message* of the dream was much more urgent. Waste no more time on India – significant though that vast subcontinent would remain – but concentrate on your own goal. Thus at sixty-three he was still searching for what he later described as 'the healing vessel, the *servator mundi*'.

It was a particularly beautiful spring day when he set out on the homeward voyage from India, and now, obsessed with his Latin alchemical texts, he had plunged so deeply into reading that when they arrived at Bombay he decided not to waste time going ashore.

His alchemical studies produced two papers published in the *Eranos Jahrbuch* – 'Traumsymbole des Individuations Prozesses' and 'Die Erlösungsvorstellungen in der Alchemie' – which became the basis for his famous Volume 12 of the *Collected Works, Psychology and Alchemy*. He opened the chapter 'The Psychic Nature of Alchemical Work' with the words: 'The alchemical opus deals in the main not just with chemical experiments as such but with something resembling psychic processes expressed in pseudo-chemical language.' He then quoted from Evola: 'The spiritual constitution of man in the pre-modern cycles of culture was such that each physical perception had simultaneously a psychic component which "animated" it adding a special "significance" to the bare image.'[24]

Jung's original alchemical lectures lacked the elaborate illustrations which eventually adorned Volume 12 and expressed in images what the alchemists could not express in words. Jung found many of these images more illuminating than clumsy philosophical concepts but something much more important distinguished them. 'Between such images and those spontaneously produced by patients undergoing "psychological" treatment, there is, for the expert, a striking similarity both in form and content.'

It was a momentous discovery. As he later wrote in his reminiscences: 'I had stumbled upon the historical counterpart of my psychology of the unconscious. The possibility of a comparison with alchemy, and the uninterrupted intellectual chain back to Gnosticism gave substance to my psychology.'[25] The theory that his patients transmuted their dreams and fantasies in mandalas was paralleled by the alchemists, who achieved a different kind of individuation in pseudo-chemical operations. It explained, Jung argued, why so many visions occur in alchemical writings.

Chapter 27

The Second World War

WHEN THE SECOND WORLD WAR broke out Jung saw it as the climax of what he had long referred to as the Nazi psychosis. Travelling to Basel he observed that people seemed to be carrying on as usual and reflected that the closer people were to the really big issues the calmer they became. Standing at a point on the frontier between the French and German lines he could see their rival fortifications, but here, too, all was quiet and peaceful: 'no noise, and no shots: all the villages are evacuated and nothing stirs'.[1]

By October family relations were already beginning to be disrupted. His married daughter living in Paris had come to Zürich with her children, his son and sons-in-law – with one exception – were all called up in the Army. In the very early days of the war, returning home from Bollingen to Küsnacht he tried to concentrate on reading a book, but a strange image kept forming at the back of his mind until he realised that it was the image of someone drowning. An interruption like this had once occurred while he was on military service, but now nothing seemed to expunge the recurring image. Reaching Küsnacht he entered the garden to see his second daughter's children looking very upset. When he asked what had happened they said that Adrian, his grandson, had fallen into the deep water beneath the boathouse and had almost drowned. 'His elder brother had fished him out. This had taken place at exactly the time I had been assailed by that memory on the train.' Once again the theory of synchronicity was reaffirmed.

Within a few weeks a new and surprising twist threatened to change the direction of Jung's career. Now one of the most distinguished citizens of Zürich, he was asked to stand for Parliament by a group of people who believed his psychological understanding could contribute something new to politics. When he protested that he was no politician they argued that they wanted to bring him in precisely for that reason. Under Swiss law, if elected he would be expected to attend sessions of a fortnight's duration five or six times a year, and Jung foresaw an immense blanket of boredom coming down on him. He had no great faith in the power of legislation to change the lot of man. The whole of his philosophy was an inner philosophy conceived in terms of self-realisation and, although socio-economic factors could play an important role, Jung felt that in the final analysis they were ineffectual if the psyche remained at odds with itself. 'By great good luck', he wrote to 'My dear Mrs N.',[2] 'it might be that I can say something reasonable. I'm told that people want representatives who mean spiritual values.

It's an interesting sign of the times.'

Jung insisted on placing his name at the bottom of the list of candidates and privately hoped he would not be elected. Unable to concentrate on writing, and too old for active service, politics offered a combination of roles which might relieve his sense of helplessness in the face of war. The scene in Zürich was very disturbed, withdrawal impossible, the atmosphere 'entirely apocalyptic'. God had allowed Satan to roam the earth again, Jung wrote, but the Germans were 'partially terrified and partially drunk with blood and victory'. As for Hitler, he was clearly half-crazy.[3]

Within a month Jung had plunged into the political arena, addressing a forceful letter to Gottlieb Duttweiler, a Swiss politician and founder of Migros, the first Swiss co-operative retail trading society. Jung argued that something must be done for the dependants of conscripted men. Thousands of families lost their breadwinner when fathers and sons were called to arms but others, including foreigners, continued to maintain their standard of living, causing considerable unrest. In Jung's view mobilisation should become absolute and 'every Swiss citizen between the ages of 18 and 60 counted as mobilised whether he was liable for military service or not'.[4]

Without naming any specific sum Jung pressed for every citizen to be put on the state payroll while 'everything earned over and beyond . . . would be used for the public good'. An almost identical letter went to his old friend Albert Oeri, now editor of the *Basler Nachrichten* and a member of the National Council, with one extra stipulation. Any surplus funds from special earnings should be made available to the 'distressed families of . . . conscripts'. There was an ironic element in these letters coming from a rich man who hated socialism and regarded communism as anti-Christ. Rejecting Jung's method, the Swiss Wages and Income Compensation Order nonetheless adopted his idea. Then came the anticlimax. Jung stood as a candidate for Landesring der Unabhängigen but was not elected.

Over the next few weeks tension mounted throughout Europe as the German armies took up strategic positions for the attack in the west. Writing to Dr Lauchenauer, Jung referred to the 'exquisite bestiality of the young German fighters during the Blitzkrieg in Poland', and described collective-man as nothing more than beast-man. Once the voice of the individual was stifled in any country, he said, mankind ran the risk of degenerating into a vast subhuman monster.

Four months later the Germans launched their stupendous attack on France through the Netherlands, Belgium and Luxembourg, and suddenly Switzerland seemed in imminent danger of invasion. An American friend, Mrs Goodrich, wrote at once to Jung suggesting that he bring his family over to California for the duration of the war, and the letter caused him much heart-searching. It would have been easy to opt out of the nightmare while he still had time, but he had no desire to desert the country of his birth. 'Your very kind letter has touched me profoundly,' he replied to Mrs Goodrich. 'I hope I have not to avail myself of your most generous proposition.' Already many Swiss families had abandoned eastern Switzerland for a redoubt in central Switzerland – known as Saanen. There, very soon, Jung's whole family, now including eleven grandchildren, took refuge in the mountains. His practice became erratic, visitors from abroad dwindled away, and Switzerland, in a state of siege, gave a corresponding impression of 'sitting on a box full of dynamite that might go off [at] the next moment'.[5] Temporarily in Saanen himself, Jung remarked that despite the imminent threat of total destruction everyone appeared quiet – because 'it [was] a great fatality'. Several letters at this time showed considerable prescience, as when he remarked, 'It looks as if Italy prefers an undisturbed Switzerland,' and 'even the dictators mistrust each other'. Assuming that England and France lost the war, he said, then the reign of anti-Christ would begin, 'but we Swiss cling to our soil and we share its fate'.[6]

As we know, in the autumn of 1913 Jung had dreamt 'an overpowering vision' of 'a monstrous flood covering all the northern . . . lands between the North Sea and the Alps' which subsequently turned to blood. Another dream concerned fire falling like rain from heaven and consuming the cities of Germany, with a strong intimation that this would happen in 1940.[7]

Another example of near-synchronicity occurred in an interview Jung gave about this time to the American journalist H. R. Knickerbocker in Randolph Hearst's *International Cosmopolitan*.[8] Jung suggested to Knickerbocker that the only way to stop Hitler making war on the west was to turn his aggressive libido toward Russia.

On 19 June, Jung wrote to Mrs Mary Mellon indicating that his letter would be the last one until the war was over, but that proved to be false. Correspondence continued with America. Between 1939 and 1940 Mrs Mary Mellon, the first wife of Paul Mellon, the American philanthropist, had undergone psychotherapeutic treatment with Jung for asthma, but the war broke into it and she had returned to America. The close friendship which developed between them led to her establishing the Bollingen Foundation responsible for the publication of his *Collected Works* and many other Jungian projects.

Jung quickly began to feel in wartime Zürich as if he were imprisoned, with the newspapers full of doubtful information and the censor busily excising even the least suspicious remark from letters sent abroad. He frequently complained to English friends that if Chamberlain had read his interview in *Cosmopolitan* he might have saved the west from the mad slaughter which had overtaken it. Grandiose claim though that might seem, it did contain a grain of truth.

The sense of being old and useless in the next few months was qualified by the need for civilian doctors since all the young ones had been called up into the Army. Defensively, Jung began to feel happily estranged from a horrible world where he loathed the new style, the new art, the new music, literature, politics and, above all, the new man. 'It's the old beast that has not changed since the troglodytes,' he said, and concluded a letter to his friend 'Peter' Baynes with the words: 'My dear Peter, I am with you and with old England.'[9]

By October his depression had deepened. He felt physically unwell and overwhelmed by the preparation of lectures on the individuation process in the Middle Ages. Despite the fact that people were still moving about Zürich, the trains running as usual and food – though much more expensive – still available, cars had almost vanished from the streets and Zürich become a somnambulistic city going through its daily routines without zest. By January 1941 the miscalculation of a flight of British raiders underlined the idiocy of war by dropping bombs near the main station of Zürich with many houses destroyed and a few people killed. 'Nobody minds because all our sympathies are on the British side.'[10]

By April he was once more enmeshed in multiple activities from lectures and meetings to patients and correspondence, but still feeling very depressed and 'missing the great world and travelling therein. Why in the hell is man unable to grow up? The Lord of this world is surely the Devil.'[11]

Soon food was rationed, petrol unobtainable, and Jung, feeling at times 'old and rotten', found consolation in planting potatoes and beans in his garden. His heart had begun to trouble him, he felt his age whenever tired, and four days of black depression descended on him when the Japanese attacked Pearl Harbor. Many letters still emerged from Küsnacht, one to an anonymous Dr N. who received elaborate professional advice through the post. Another to Mrs Alice Lewisham Crowley said: 'If they are going to send you to Poland you can only suicide yourself.' A third letter went to Jolande Jacobi, who received a subtle disquisition on the projection of the Jewish anima in Jewesses.

Preparing his lecture 'Der Geist Mercurius' (*Eranos Jahrbúch*, 1942), Jung said that the material suddenly seized hold of him, transformed him into Mercury and gave him 'a remarkably miserable fortnight'. He had first dreamt of Mercury as the Arab prince who tried to push him under water, and now many dreams connected with Mercury recurred. 'I dreamt of an Eastern prophet, followed by a woman who was almost hypnotised by his prophetic stammerings.' Clearly his anima had been 'completely fascinated' by his shadow 'which was seized by the spirit of life (Mercury!)'. As Dr Gerhard Adler has said: 'Mercurius is the most elusive and paradoxical figure in alchemy with innumerable significations for which reason he was called Mercurius duplex and was sometimes regarded as an hermaphrodite. He symbolises both the lowest prima materia and the highest lapis philosophorum as well as the chthonic god of revelation and transformation (Hermes). Psychologically he represents the collective unconscious.'[12]

In another letter Jung wrote: 'For the time being I am still immersed in Mercury who, as he will always try to, has dissolved me almost and just failed to separate me limb from limb.'[13]

The twelfth volume of the *Collected Work*, *Psychology and Alchemy*, is once again an immense monument to the industry, erudition and insight of Jung, opening with a long essay, 'Introduction to the Religious and Psychological Problems of Alchemy'. Jung wrote 'the archetypes of the unconscious can be shown empirically to be the equivalents of religious dogmas'. He saw the Christ image as consonant with 'the most highly developed and differential symbol of the self'. He quoted from the alchemist Maria Prophetissa: 'One becomes two, two becomes three and out of the third comes the one as the fourth.' Outlining analogies between this and the analytical process which reconciled opposites, created a new awareness and finally a transcendant self, Jung claimed that alchemy ran like an undercurrent to Christianity and psychology. Christianity ruled on the surface and it was 'to this surface as the dream was to consciousness and just as the dream compensates the conflicts of the conscious mind so alchemy endeavours to fill the gaps left by the Christian tensions of opposites'.

Straining to develop psychological analogies Jung invoked another alchemical work, the *Rosarium Philosophorum*: 'Who knows the salt and its solution knows the hidden secret of the wise men of old. Therefore turn your mind upon the salt, for in it alone [i.e., the mind] is the science concealed and the most excellent and most hidden secret of all the ancient philosophers.'

The square brackets are Jung's and seem to mis-read the sentence. The phrase 'it alone' clearly refers to salt and not mind, but Jung attempts to defend his interpretation. 'As a matter of fact "mind" and "salt" are close cousins – cum grano salis!'

Doubt does break in on page 246. 'If it really did dawn on the alchemists that their work was somehow connected with the human psyche and its functions. . . .' On page 258 Jung claimed that alchemy had a double face: 'on the one hand the practical chemical work . . . on the other the psychological process in part consciously psychic, in part unconsciously projected . . .'.

Jung came to believe that alchemists projected their own unconscious images and processes into the 'chemical events' they analysed. He found and demonstrated close resemblances between the dreams and fantasies of his patients and the elaborate alchemical iconography. Deepening his researches he found common elements between a range of motifs in alchemy and archetypal equivalents in the dreams of patients who had no knowledge of alchemical literature.

In short *Psychology and Alchemy* was intended to defeat the idea that alchemy merely anticipated chemistry and stood in a living relationship with the most recent discoveries of the psychology of the unconscious. 'Not only does this modern psychological discipline give us the key to the secrets of alchemy but conversely alchemy provides the psychology of the unconscious with a meaningful historical basis.'[14] Alchemists realised that the first process in their 'art', separation and analysis, had to be matched by its counterpart, synthesis and consolidation. These terms equally applied to analytical psychology. Similarly the initial stages where opposing tendencies had to be brought back into harmony characterised both alchemy and psychotherapy.[15]

Extrapolation from one 'discipline' to another is always hazardous. We have seen the ethologists relate truths found in rats to human beings with all the multiple differences of speech, nervous systems and transmitted culture patterns. Jung's Volume 12 was open to a similar criticism. There were fundamental differences which could not be reconciled. Was he, in fact, in search of further reaffirmation of his model by *himself projecting* its elements into alchemy, consciously or unconsciously?

Psychology and Alchemy (Volume 12) received mixed reviews, but unexpectedly an excellent one appeared in *Schweizer Monatshefte* by the once hostile Arnold Künzli.[16] For editorial reasons it was published in an abbreviated form, which drove Jung to comment, 'This is yet another reminder of the fact that I have to be presented to my contemporaries only as a third-class passenger.'[17]

In August 1942, Jung gave up his lectures at the Swiss Federal Polytechnic in Zürich because of ill health which presaged a much more serious collapse two years later. Toward the end of the same year food shortages in Switzerland were beginning to bite deeper, and when Aniela Jaffé sent him 'an edible present' Jung accepted it as 'most opportune, especially here in Bollingen where one is a bit pinched'.[18] It was not a pleasant situation, he wrote to Alice Crowley, when food reigned supreme, but at least they were self-sufficient in fuel. In one day they had felled three trees, working at last by the light of a lantern.

Some acid letters went to a number of people, among them one to Arnold Künzli, then a student at Basel University, who had questioned the validity of his claim to be a scientist. 'I would be sincerely grateful to you if you could enlighten me how it comes that the conception of science prevalent in Germany, England, America and India by virtue of which I was awarded degrees as a *scientist* does not satisfy the scientific and theoretical requirements of the Philosophical Faculty of Zürich.' Jung went on to enumerate an overwhelming array of honours: Honorary Member of the Academy of German Scientists and Physicians, Fellow of the Royal Society,[19] Doctor Scientiae of Oxford and Harvard universities, with honorary degrees from the universities of Benares, Allahabad and Calcutta.

Angrily rejecting the term 'romantic', he denied any direct connection with philosophy and claimed categorically that he was an empiricist. He did not *postulate* the unconscious. It was a *nomen* which 'covered empirical facts' and could be verified at any time. Whether his methodology satisfied the rigorous requirements of the hard sciences was a matter much debated at that time among those members of the Swiss scientific circles who were not much more preoccupied with the grim realities of war. A number came up with the answer that it did not. Others supported him on alternative grounds.

Jung dealt with a different kind of evidence from that available to the hard sciences but he seemed desperately anxious to equate the two in an effort to acquire the bedrock reality of scientific fact. It was a mistaken undertaking. Until we know the precise *physical* nature of those millions of cells which make up the human brain any form of psychological investigation cannot satisfy the requirements of science, but since the verification principle itself is now in question and Popper's 'falsifiability' widely accepted, the constructs of science are equally suspect. All this became a continuous ferment surrounding Jung's findings and the penultimate paragraph of his reply to Arnold Künzli did at last throw the whole question back at him. 'People can only prove to me that certain facts do *not* exist. But I am still waiting for that proof.'

Another letter directed at no less a person than Heidegger revived Jung's power of invective. It began on a relatively quiet note: 'Heidegger bristles with [prejudices] trying in vain to hide behind a blown-up language.' Jung then quoted Brinkmann's lecture at the SGPP and contrasted Brinkmann's 'normal language' with 'the twaddle he read out from Heidegger' which was 'positively comic'.[20] In the next line Heidegger's words had become 'unutterably trashy and banal' and then followed a description of Heidegger's method. His '*modus philosophandi* is neurotic through and through and is ultimately rooted in his psychic crankiness'. Next an attack on his personality: 'His kindred spirits close or distant are sitting in lunatic asylums, some as patients and some as psychiatrists on a philosophical rampage. . . . For all its mistakes the nineteenth century deserves better than to have Heidegger counted as its ultimate representative.' Jung was in full flood now, and a few more champions of German philosophy had to be felled. 'Hegel is fit to bust with presumption and vanity, Nietzsche drips with outraged sexuality and so on. . . .' Then came the clinching phrase: 'it is a pisspot of unconscious devils'.

In September 1943, Jung was still wrestling with the problem of the coniunctio, 'which I must now work up as the introduction to Aurora Consurgens', he wrote to Aniela Jaffé. 'It is incredibly difficult.' His letter contained some baffling statements which it is difficult to spell out in lucid terms, perhaps indicating the preliminary confusions before he broke through with the vastly expanded account in Volume 14 of the *Collected Works*.

Coniunctio was an alchemical term for the union of opposites that

THE SECOND WORLD WAR

'confront one another in enmity or attract one another in love'. The search for a synthesis which would reconcile opposites remained one of the driving forces in Jung's life and work. In one sense derived from his own inner conflict, coniunctio made universal what had been personal in his breakdown. His disorder became a basic disorder of the universe with a common cure. The magic nostrum which reconciled the alchemist's chemistry had its equivalent in curing his psychic wound.

Jung quoted Gerard Dorn, a medieval alchemist, to illustrate the three steps in coniunctionis. The first step, *unio mentalis*, was intellectual and attempted to liberate a chemical element corresponding to the soul from matter. Medieval man could easily conceive of the same *veritas* existing in man, matter and God, subject to similar laws. Next the liberated spirit had to be reunited with matter in a new and higher synthesis. Rich symbolical representations of this 'chymical marriage' were given from a dragon embracing a woman in her grave, to a king dissolving in water.

In psychotherapy, Jung wrote, the second stage of conjunction 'therefore consists in making a reality of the man who has acquired some knowledge of his paradoxical wholeness. The great difficulty here however is that no-one knows how the paradoxical wholeness of man can ever be realised. That is the crux of individuation.'

The third stage was an attempt to create a new and transforming union with *unus mundus*. This Jung regarded not as the external world but as the primal essence of life from which all creation sprang. It was as if he suggested reuniting the individual soul with the timeless flux of the beginnings of creation.

Jung wrote: 'The thought Dorn expresses by the third degree of conjunction is universal; it is the relation or identity of the personal with the supra-personal atman and of the individual tao with the universal tao.'

Today Volume 14 of the *Collected Works* is regarded by many as Jung's *magnum opus*. There are others who think that his lofty language overwhelms an old theme repeated down the centuries in simpler terms – man must reconcile conflicting aspects of his nature with ancient and universal wellsprings.

Chapter 28

A Serious Illness

THE YEAR 1944 began very badly. Taking his usual daily walk on the ice-covered road near Küsnacht he slipped, fell and broke his ankle. In great pain he managed to get to his feet, limp to a nearby house and telephone for his car. Everything would have pursued a normal course but for the plaster on his ankle necessitating several days' complete rest.[1] This led, suddenly and unexpectedly, to an embolism which caused a severe heart attack. Carried off to hospital he hovered between life and death for three weeks and the doctors frequently had recourse to oxygen.

Extraordinary visions overtook him while he hung on the edge of life, and he came close in his own terms to having a glimpse of the other world. His nurse told him that his face gave the remarkable impression that 'it was surrounded by a bright glow'. In his own words, he 'had reached the outermost limit' and did not know whether he 'was in a dream or in ecstasy'.

It was almost as if some insubstantial part of him, freed from the clay of the flesh, had ascended the heavens and, looking down, saw the vast curve of the earth with seas and continents bathed in a 'gloriously blue light'.[2]

It was, according to Jung, the most wonderful vision. 'Later,' he wrote, 'I discovered how high in space one would have to be to have so extensive a view – approximately a thousand miles!'[3]

Whether Jung retrospectively injected into these visions the reactions of a rationally aware self, or whether at the time he genuinely experienced a soaring sense of impossible grandeur, is difficult to determine. What followed was even more incredible. It could be seen as a beautiful allegory of a soul ascending to heaven suddenly confronted in some other world by the whole long story of its physical embodiment and asked the embarrassing question: What was it all worth?

For, as Jung turned (in his flight?) from the north to the south, suddenly an enormous block of dark stone like some vast meteorite came into his field of vision. Invested with miraculous powers he had no difficulty in slipping across the Empyrean, entering a gate carved in the stone and confronting a black Hindu sitting silently in the lotus position. As he did so he had the extraordinary feeling that the 'whole phantasmagoria of earthly existence' was stripped away from him – 'an extremely painful process'. The Hindu obviously expected him, and now he was led to the gate of an inner temple where 'innumerable tiny niches' were filled with burning wicks, the whole door wreathed in their light. It closely resembled the Temple of the Holy Tooth which he had visited in Ceylon, but as he approached a new premonition overtook him. He felt sure that he was about to meet all those people 'to whom he belonged in reality' and at last he would discover the true perspective of his life. 'I would know what had been before me, why I had come into being and where my life was flowing.'[4]

Clearly undergoing the recapitulatory process said to characterise people at the point of death, Jung never seems to have taken the fatal step into the temple which, symbolically, would have extinguished his life. Instead, from somewhere in the area which encompassed Europe, an image closely resembling his doctor floated into view. In practical terms his fevered delirium was subsiding and the reality of his doctor taking shape through the haze. However, Dr H. did not materialise in any normal sense. 'Aha,' Jung said to himself, 'this is my doctor', but not in his everyday physical embodiment. Instead he comes as a basileus of Kos, or 'the temporal embodiment of the primal form' which had existed from the beginning. Basileus was, in fact, equivalent to King and Kos the site of the temple of Asklepios, the birthplace of Hippocrates.

One witness present at the time of his illness says that Dr H. had certainly spoken some encouraging words to Jung because his condition had at last shown an improvement, but Jung gave a different interpretation. His family, he said, delegated Dr H. to express 'a protest against [Jung's] going away', saying that 'he had no right to leave and must return'.

Dr Frey-Rohn, a very close friend, also recalls a dream unrecorded in his reminiscences. It was a dream that, while he floated in the Empyrean, no less than thirty women were clamouring for his return to earth. 'He had to take their protestations very seriously.'[5]

At this stage of Jung's illness so critical had his condition become that Emma moved into the hospital and slept there constantly in touch with the doctors and nurses.[6]

Now came the turning-point. The will to live flickered weakly over the next ten days and all food repelled him. There followed another series of 'visions' when he came to believe that the view from his window was like a 'tattered sheet of newspaper full of photographs that meant nothing'.

Disliking the idea of returning to life he continued to resist his doctor's encouragement. Simultaneously a new and even more disturbing idea developed. When people attained their primal form, as with Dr H., it meant that they were going to die. The idea crystallised with terrifying force that Dr H. had been selected to die in place of himself. Struggling up from his pillows, he tried desperately to warn Dr H., but the doctor failed to understand, and this drove Jung into a dangerous rage. Emma, who nursed him faithfully throughout the long illness, reproved him for being what she saw as hostile to the doctor. 'Damn it all,' Jung said to himself, the doctor 'ought to watch his step. He has no right to be so reckless!'

What followed in Dr H.'s life not only confirmed Jung's synchronistic powers but, if taken literally, also granted him demonic abilities to transpose death from himself to someone else. Reference to special powers is a falsification of Jung's theory. The formulation of synchronicity avoided the concept of power. Within such experiences it meant possessing what appeared to be 'magical' a-causal potential to put oneself inside someone else.[7]

April 4, 1944 was the first day when Jung had sufficiently recovered to sit up in bed and *on that very day* Dr H. duly fell ill and took to his bed. A fever attacked him, and within a very short time he died, his death certificate giving the cause as septicaemia. As if to underline the close connection between the two events, Jung was Dr H.'s last patient.

If Jung's illness can be measured by the gap in his correspondence, it ran on for nearly six months, but very soon afterwards a burst of renewed activity began which was to produce several important works. However, as late as 1 February 1945, he wrote to Kristine Mann, an American analytical psychologist, who was dying of cancer, that the 'angel of death' had struck him down too 'and almost succeeded in wiping [him] off the slate'. He had been 'practically an invalid ever since' and his recovery was very slow. Fortunately, his mind had not been affected and his scientific work continued.

Late in 1944 he placed more and more emphasis on the scientific character of that work and in September wrote a very long and powerful apologia for his approach to analytical psychology. It was in reply to a Catholic theologian Herr Irminger, who claimed that Catholic doctrine completed and perfected Jung's psychological writings. It also made Jung's failure to return to the bosom of the Church incomprehensible. Jung replied that he had once corresponded with an alchemist who believed in the medieval art of gold-making and claimed that if only Jung understood the true nature of alchemy he would avow a similar faith. Likewise in India the philosophers assured him that their enlightenment was much greater than his, and no doubt a Persian Sufi would find his comments on Chadis very jejeune.[8]

'My dear sir!' Jung continued, driven at last to pontificate, 'My pursuit is *science*, not apologetics and not philosophy. . . .' Since science and evangelism were mutually exclusive their two opposite viewpoints made any further discussion impossible. Whereupon Jung forcefully, and with great polemical skill, continued to discuss it in eloquent detail. Science, he said, sought the truth – being fully aware that it did not possess it – while the Church *possessed* the truth and had no need for any further search. But what, Jung asked, was Herr Irminger's fundamental aim in writing to him? 'With commendable patience and undoubted good will . . . and despite my . . . obdurate folly you want to bring me to the goal and consummation of my life's work . . .', to that very spot 'from which I started, namely, to that still medieval Christianity which failed not only four hundred years ago but is now more of a failure than ever and in the most terrible way'. Clinching his whole argument, Jung said, the German Army consisted mainly of Christians and 'the larger half of it Catholics at that', and what were they engaged in at this very moment? Wholesale slaughter.[9]

Several pastors and theologians were now attacking Jung, some because they feared he might offer a substitute form of religion to those who could no longer swallow an anthropomorphic God. Jung wrote to Pastor Max Frischknecht, 'Your opinion that I am an atheist is pretty bold to say the least.' If the learned pastor had formed the 'peculiar notion' that Jung aimed to create a new religion, then that was due to his 'ignorance of psychotherapeutic methods'.[10]

In 1945 Jung was pleased that 'the Germans were getting it in the neck', but when at last the Allies finally overwhelmed the German armies, Hitler committed suicide and Europe lay in smoking ruins his elation was heavily qualified. 'Psychological collective guilt is a *tragic fate*,' he wrote. 'It hits everybody just and unjust alike, everybody who was anywhere near the place where the terrible thing happened.'[11] Writing his long and penetrating essay 'After the Catastrophe' Jung found himself 'very churned up' and had the utmost difficulty in trying to reach 'anything approaching a moderate and relatively calm point of view'. Moral indignation insisted on revulsion from the German people, but 'we are, on the whole, much more deeply involved in the recent events in Germany than we like to admit'. No article had ever given him so much trouble to write because his 'inner identity or *participation mystique*' made him realise afresh how painfully wide 'was the scope of *collective guilt*'.[12] It involved not only the whole German nation, but also European culture and in particular the 'Christian Church should put ashes on her head and rend her garments on account of the guilt of her children'.[13]

Not unexpectedly, a wonderful sense of liberation drove him to travel soon after the war. His six years' incarceration in Switzerland gave tremendous zest to a visit to London where he broadcast a remarkable talk for the B.B.C.'s Third Programme. 'As early as 1918,' he said, 'I noticed peculiar disturbances in the unconscious of my German patients which could not be ascribed to their personal psychology.' These he attributed to mythological motifs realised from the archetypes. Then came this astonishing statement: 'There was a disturbance of the collective unconscious *in every single one of* my German patients.' (My italics.) Moreover, each one expressed 'primitivity, violence and cruelty'. Modern psychology would require a control group of equal numbers selected from other races to see that statement in perspective. The unqualified uniformity of Jung's unscientific sample made it automatically suspect, but the experience led Jung to believe that 'the "blond beast" was stirring in an uneasy slumber, and that an outburst was not impossible'.[14]

Observing the coming German holocaust in the test tube of the individual, Jung did not know at that time 'whether there were enough of them in Germany to make a general explosion inevitable'.[15] However, he believed that a tide arose in the collective unconscious after the First World War which reflected itself in dreams and mythological symbols among his *German* patients. When such symbols occurred in large numbers without being understood they drew 'these individuals together as if by magnetic force of an avalanche'. Thus the failure to bring the creative powers of the collective unconscious into a proper relation with the personal unconscious gave the destructive elements their head, and the full horror of the Second World War was let loose upon the world.

There were those who found his analysis completely convincing, others who wondered whether the Japanese were any different from the Germans, and some who believed that the application of his model to world war overstretched its powers. His most adamant critics found the theory ridiculous.

Very soon after the war the campaign against Jung's alleged anti-Semitism blew up again and drove him to write a long letter to Dr Michael Fordham[16] claiming that the story of his Nazi sympathies originated with the Holy Father himself – meaning Freud. When Jung quarrelled with him, Freud had to find a reason for his incomprehensible behaviour and decided that he must be anti-Semitic. The new smear campaign was savagely sustained in America, where one man in particular wrote letters, reprinted articles and caused scenes at psychoanalytic meetings. Jung's reply to these attacks said that during the Second World War his book *Psychology and Religion* sold out five impressions in America, and his enemies could find nothing pro-Nazi in that book because he severely criticised the Nazis; yet they constantly returned to the year 1934. What were the facts about that year? Threatened with suppression, the German psychotherapists sought for somebody non-Jewish to prove that their work was not exclusively Jewish, and no better figure could be found than the German-speaking Jung with his reputation for independent thinking. There remained quite a number of Jews among the psychotherapists, and Jung thought that he could help to protect them by accepting the presidency of the International Society for Psychotherapy. Jung also claimed, in his letter, that he was on the Nazi blacklist, but I have not been able to confirm this. If the Germans had invaded Switzerland, he said, he would have been one of the first to be shot.

His letter to Dr Fordham seemed to strain in search of redeeming detail and pointed out that he had never had any particular sympathy with Germany, choosing to study as a young man in Paris and not Berlin like so many of his friends. Similarly, living for twenty years on the Alsatian border, he had come to understand the true nature of the Germans. The whole story of his pro-Nazi – anti-Semitic sentiments was, he went on, absolute nonsense, a cheap attempt to discredit a man who had refused to accept the Freudian party line. A counter-charge of an extraordinary character now disfigured the attempted logic of the letter. These unscrupulous Freudians, Jung said, had not even stopped at the mutilation of his photograph to represent him as a two-headed monster. In Calcutta University a photograph of himself had come into his hands, distorted by the addition of pince-nez and an emphasised nose which caricatured, what he regarded as, the worst kind of Jew.

The final word came in a letter written to Mrs Aniela Jaffé by Gershom Scholem, a member of the Eranos meetings. It concerned Leo Baeck, a rabbi and professor of religion, who was deported to Theresienstadt concentration camp in 1943: 'As you are so interested in the story of Baeck and Jung, I will write it down for your benefit and have no objection to being cited by you in this matter,' Scholem wrote.

Scholem met Baeck in 1947 and asked him whether he should accept an invitation to Eranos, remembering the rumours of Jung's anti-Semitism. 'You must go – absolutely!' Baeck said, and told the following story. After his release from Theresienstadt in 1946 he returned to Switzerland but refused to call on Jung. Jung sent a message begging Baeck to visit him, but once again Baeck declined. 'Whereupon Jung came to his hotel and they had an extremely lively talk lasting two hours.' Suddenly Jung said, 'Well, I slipped up,' referring to his phrase that National Socialism might have something to teach the world. 'Baeck said that in this talk they cleared up everything and . . . they parted . . . reconciled.' As a result, when Jung issued a second invitation for Scholem to visit Eranos he accepted.[17]

Chapter 29

Growing Old

SEE JUNG sitting at his desk in the small inner study at Küsnacht early in 1945 and it is difficult to believe from the photograph that he is a man of seventy. Undoubtedly handsome, apparently full of vigour, lost in purposeful concentration he looks much younger. There were those who visited him in his seventieth year and found all these characteristics, briefly, true. One at least fell in love with him on sight 'because he was so fantastically handsome and emanated a kind of radiance'.[1]

Jung himself qualified this image in his letters. He wrote to Professor J. B. Rhine, 'During the war my health wasn't too good. As a matter of fact I was seriously ill and having reached the biblical age of 70 I'm none too efficient any more. . . .'[2] And to his anonymous correspondent Mrs N.: 'The moment peace came a real avalanche of letters descended upon me. . . . Now I am in the frying pan particularly so since my 70th birthday when the flood of letters became even worse. Ever since my illness I can never get through with my correspondence and I suffer from a chronic bad conscience.'[3]

Mary Briner became his patient after his illness and described how they sat opposite each other in armchairs in the most informal way. He explained to her his technique for coping with a too powerful countertransference. Moving away from the patient to the window he stared out at the lake, examining his own reactions until he came to understand the nature of this upsurge from the unconscious and brought it under control again.[4]

On one occasion he played it much more dangerously. Another colleague recalled the patient who fell in love with him and proposed marriage. At first Jung said, 'I am already married – this cannot be'; but when the patient persisted he began to humour her. For some considerable time he no longer refused the marriage proposal but, to all intents and purposes, went along with her desire. Continuing to prepare for the marriage the patient issued invitation-cards, and still Jung did not disillusion her. Not until the day before the marriage was due to take place did an express letter arrive saying that the previous night God had revealed to her that, unhappily, the marriage would never be consummated. The powerful fantasy-transference deserved to be treated as a reality and Jung took the risk that the unconscious would spontaneously find a solution, which on this occasion it did.[5]

Women had much stronger transferences to him than men. 'I wouldn't have discovered my psychology without you women,' he once said. There were those who believed he literally made use of women in

his work and reserved his deeper relationships for men. The older he got
the younger the women tended to become. 'The end-of-term party at
the Institute brought many American students crowding in and he
usually sat next to the prettiest among them.[6]

There were many celebrations on his seventieth birthday, among
them a special edition of the *Eranos Jahrbuch* under the title *Studienzum
Problem des Archetypischen*. He still found relaxation in sailing on the lake
at Bollingen and nothing was more calculated to restore his serenity
than 'the lapping of water against the bow and the gentle breeze of the
mornings'.[7] However, his angry explosions were, if anything, more
choleric. Astrologically a Leo, Aniela Jaffé claimed that the extreme
sensitivity which enriched and burdened his life was due to his
temperament. Jung himself enlarged on the delights and dangers which
hypersensitivity engendered. It had tormented him, he said, from his
early youth, 'encumbered him in his relationships . . . made him
unsure of himself', and given him a sense of shame, but interwoven with
the pain went a heightened perception which opened a world of beauty
unknown to most other people. Moreover, now that he was old, he did
not hesitate to give full vent to it in joy, sorrow and anger. Especially, it
seems, in anger.

Multiplying the contradictions, he frequently quoted from the old
alchemists phrases like 'In patentia vestra habetis animam vestram'
('In your patience you have your soul') or 'Omnis festinatio a parte
diaboli est' ('All haste is of the Devil'). Even the card-game 'Patience'
made him impatient; it was a game he very much enjoyed, but when the
cards refused to fall out right 'he had no compunction . . . in helping
fate a little by switching the cards around. The game had to come out
[right] damn it!' Even when uninitiated friends caught him cheating
and were duly scandalised, he remained completely unabashed and
even, secretly, enjoyed shocking them.

Reading detective stories was another pastime, and now in his
seventies they lay around everywhere literally accumulating in piles on
the top floor of the house. Ruth Bailey found that if the cover of a new one
appeared too lurid it was wise to shroud it in a more correct wrapper
before placing it, innocuously, on the slate table in the library. 'For
Jung,' Miss Jaffé said, 'the figure of the detective was a modern version
of the alchemical Mercurius, solver of riddles and he was entertained by
his heroic deeds.'

A special shed had been built near the tower at Bollingen which
became his stone-carving 'den', and this was another but deeper form of
relaxation. Indeed, he would emerge from the shed 'spiritually
renewed'. Some years before he had made a stone monument to express
what the tower at Bollingen meant to him. Ordering a triangular stone
from the quarry, when it arrived he found that they had sent a square
block by mistake. The mason was furious and wanted the bargeman to
take it straight back, but Jung suddenly said, 'No, that is my stone. I

must have it.' The next day, going to work with his chisel the Latin verse of the alchemist Annaldus de Villanova occurred to him, and he engraved into the stone:

> Here stands the mean uncomely stone
> 'Tis very cheap in price!
> The more it is despised by fools
>   The more loved by the wise.

The words described the alchemist's stone, the *lapis*, which was rejected and despised He himself was sometimes possessed by the same sense of rejection. The natural surface of the stone on its front face suggested to Jung an eye constantly regarding him, and he converted this into a tiny homunculus which for him corresponded to the reflected image seen by one person in the pupil of another's eye. 'On the third face – the one facing the lake – I let the stone speak as it were in a Latin inscription.' The inscription began, 'I am an orphan alone: nevertheless I am found everywhere. . . .' Jung's final description of the meaning of the stone read: 'The stone stands outside the Tower and is like an explanation of it. It is a manifestation of the occupant, but one which remains incomprehensible to others.'

Jung was, of course, what McLuhan would call a Gutenberg Galaxy man, a person at ease with the printed word and books, but those who thought him completely unmusical were mistaken. If music did not play an important part in his life, he experienced great pleasure from Mozart, Bach and Handel, and could surrender to the mood of a Negro spiritual. Very occasionally someone performed on the grand piano at Küsnacht, and when the Russian pianist Ania Dorfmaan played one evening the two men responded warmly to each other at the musical level.

There was a brief but very unenlightening correspondence between them. Jung could, if necessary, carry on a correspondence in three languages, but mostly he used English and German. 'Ordinarily,' Aniela Jaffé said, 'Jung spoke in Basel German which to my ears accustomed to High German, sounded like a merry warbling', but it delighted him when he met someone who could use the Basel dialect. Replying to some correspondents he peppered High German with English words, and his English was better than his French. Latin and Greek texts he could read with ease.

Gerhard Adler, Michael Fordham, Edward Bennet and Jolande Jacobi all had close contact with Jung during his sixties or seventies. Jacobi told the story of a long-standing patient who arrived one morning ten minutes late to find that Jung had gone off sailing on the lake. Mr X was furious, immediately hired a boat and instructed the navigator to find Jung as quickly as possible. When they sighted him, Mr X used the equivalent of a loud hailer to bawl at Jung, 'Where the hell are you? I've been waiting at your house.' Without answering, Jung simply sailed away as fast as he could on a zig-zag course. Mr X gave chase. No sooner did Mr X overtake and confront his quarry than Jung made off again until at last coming up once more within hailing distance Jung shouted: 'Go away – you bore me!' Some considerable time elapsed before patient and analyst at last came to terms again.

Dr Michael Fordham first met Jung in Zürich in the Institute building in 1935. The circumstances which led to the meeting were distressing to Dr Fordham. H. G. Baynes had suggested that Fordham should go to Zürich with a view to being analysed by the master; 'accordingly I wrote to Jung . . . stating that it would be necessary to find work in Switzerland because I had no money'. Jung replied saying yes, Fordham should come out to see him. In the interview which followed Jung simply stated that Fordham's proposition was quite impossible and he could not undertake to analyse him. At the time, such was Fordham's respect for what Baynes described as a giant of a man that, although he was smarting under his rejection, he did not take it too badly. Much later he recorded: 'It was most inconsiderate to bring out to Zürich a young man who had no money and to tell him that what he wanted was out of the question; could he not have written that my wishes were impossible to realise?'[8]

In the following years he saw many aspects of Jung's character and said that if Jung could ride roughshod over people he was also capable of great flexibility. 'On one occasion Jolande Jacobi was seen coming down the stairs on her bottom after Jung had thrown her out of his room, and on another Jung spent a considerable time listening to a student because the student was in great personal distress.' Among his patients, when Fordham knew him, was a person referred to as the Princess. Jung strongly criticised her habit of bringing her dreams recorded on dirty bits of paper. She must, he insisted, get herself a new book and keep the record, so to say, clean. The Princess arrived for the next session with yet another collection of bits of paper, whereupon Jung simply ejected her. 'He had a tendency', Fordham said, 'in acting out the transference to overdetermine the counter-transference!'[9]

According to a London Jungian, Mrs Jacobi claimed that Jung was under-sexed. The Jungian commented, 'Presumably *she* hadn't been his mistress anyway. As for his homosexual component, 'it was quite well integrated'.[10] By implication it might appear that Jung had other mistresses apart from Toni Wolff.

On the last occasion Fordham met him, disillusion set in. 'Suddenly I saw him in a new perspective. I had believed before that he was not an ordinary human being. Now, suddenly, he seemed nothing more than an ageing man with arteriosclerosis. It was the end of his being a Mahatma for me.'

Gerhard Adler, now President of the International Association for Analytical Psychology, underwent a training analysis with Jung. 'In the beginning it was disappointing because Jung talked in what seemed to me such general terms, but in the end it turned out to be highly particular.'[11] Adler attended Jung's Wednesday-morning seminars and discovered a new refinement of his own experience. 'Each member of the seminar felt that Jung's general remarks perfectly fitted their own case!' It was interesting that Jung replaced Freud's Wednesday-evening circle with a Wednesday-morning one. Now a man of seventy and a distinguished living member of the Jungian Old Guard, Gerhard Adler represents that aspect of the schism in Jungian analysis which uses the transference as an important part of treatment, but according to Fordham he did not introduce it to the London school.

A. I. Allenby, who knew Jung from the end of the Second World War onward, elaborated thus: 'London broke away from the Zürich school. . . . They argued that reductive analysis had been neglected. London Jungians tended to assimilate certain aspects of Freudian and Kleinian concepts.'[12] Several conflicting accounts are given of the differences between Zürich and London in which Michael Fordham played an important role.

Many distinguished women still formed a coterie of analysts around Jung, partly at the Jungian Institute founded in 1948 and partly in private practice. Barbara Hannah, Marie Louise von Franz, Jolande Jacobi and Liliane Frey-Rohn were all very active members. Many stories are told of rivalries between other women in the circle and some whose passionate commitment to Jung as a man and master led into fresh feuds.

Consulted by Marie Louise von Franz on one occasion about a patient she was treating he said: 'Perhaps you are driving too hard. Perhaps it is her right to be psychotic.'[13] He also believed that there were occasions when suicide was justified.

E. A. Bennet recalled that Eranos resembled a Chinese court with the great man surrounded by courtiers, many of them elderly, and Anthony Storr remembers that, when Jung came down to breakfast in the morning, if he had experienced a dream the night before they all gathered round to hear it like a revelation.[14] On Storr's first meeting, 'he spoke for one and a half hours and assumed the mantle of the Great Man'. He had a kind of conceit on occasion, as when he spoke of his duty in writing *Job*: 'this is pure poison but I owe it to my people'. 'And on another occasion with lowered voice and very serious mien he leant towards me and said, "You know, with dreams, there is always a chance of the Eucharist every night." In a very real sense I think he believed that he had a hot-line to God. Perhaps he occasionally saw himself as the personification of the Wise Old Man he had invoked in his theories.' There were undoubtedly many who now regarded him as the Oracle of an entirely new and fundamentally religious creed in whom lineaments of the Messiah could be detected.

In November of 1946 the Messiah suffered another threat to his life. On the afternoon of 2 November he had addressed a discussion group of his closest pupils and, although tired, seemed to Barbara Hannah in very good health. 'It was therefore a completely unexpected shock to hear two days later that he had had another heart attack the night before and was again very ill.' Refusing to go to hospital, two nurses were engaged to watch over him night and day. This time it took him three months to recover but once more his splendid constitution pulled him through.

Despite his illness during the years 1946–52 a renewed burst of intellectual activity produced four more important works: *On the Nature of the Psyche, Aion, Answer to Job* and *Synchronicity: An Acausal Connecting Principle.* The series culminated in the two volumes of *Mysterium Coniunctionis*, which he described as his last book.

When Jung published *Aion* in 1951 the religious among his disciples felt that his ambiguities about God had reached a new stage of complexity if not obscurity. 'My investigation seeks with the help of Christian Gnostic and alchemical symbols to throw light on the change of psychic situation within the "Christian aeon".'[15] Christ, he wrote, was manifested at a predetermined moment when the point of Spring entered the zodiacal sign of the Fishes, and Jung seemed to identify Christ with the archetype of the self.

The self was the most central of all the archetypes. There is no English word which conveys the real meaning of the German word *Selbst* ('the itself'). Combining the conscious and the unconscious it was the invisible unconscious centre of personality, a psychic totality. Freud's conscious ego could not be confused with Jung's self. Normally submerged and unconscious, the self could manifest itself in dreams, or fantasies, or by means of projection. Above all, any attempt to delineate the self could only be attempted through the process of individuation.

In the following year *Answer to Job*, regarded by many as his most controversial book, appeared. Writing to 'Dear Dr H.' on 30 August 1951, he said: 'You must pardon my long silence. In the spring I was plagued by my liver and had often to stay in bed and in the midst of this misère wrote a little essay (c.a. 100 typed pages) whose publication is causing me some trouble.' He was afraid, he said, of stirring up a hornet's nest. He wanted to compile a satisfactory portrait of the phenomenon called 'Christ' in psychological terms and this became the book *Answer to Job*.

Throughout his life the intractable problem of God allowing evil to permeate the world had troubled Jung, and in this book he tried to get to fresh grips with it. If God could allow Adam to be trapped by the serpent in the Garden of Eden, permit Satan to torment Job and demand Abraham's son as a sacrifice, how could he escape the charge of being evil himself? 'I hope to act', he wrote in *Answer to Job*, 'as a voice of many who feel the same way as I do and to give expression to the shattering emotion which the unvarnished spectacle of divine savagery and ruthlessness produces in us.'[16] Writing to Henry Corbin, he said the 'book came to me during the fever of an illness. It was as if accompanied by the great music of a Bach or Handel. I don't belong to the auditory type. . . . I just had the feeling of listening to a great composition. . . .'[17] Was it conceivable, Jung asked in the book, that God had attributes of evil as well as good which must be 'worked through' before they could be reconciled?

If one understands Jung's thesis correctly, Job reveals a hubris which involves a higher form of justice than God himself and the challenge is met by the incarnation of Christ. In this interpretation Christ appears as a deliberate attempt to set right the balance between good and evil, to redeem the injustice God has committed toward Man. This perfection of God is achieved by union with Divine Wisdom or Sophia, the feminine counterpart of the Holy Spirit which reappears under the image of the Virgin Mary. Thus for Jung the most significant religious event since the Reformation was the Papal pronouncement in 1950 of the dogma of the Assumption of the Blessed Virgin. This he saw as an expression of the collective unconscious. When one considered, Jung wrote, that 'evil was originally slipped into the scheme of things and is still there' would it not have been much simpler if Yaweh had called this ' "practical joker" severely to account', getting rid of his pernicious influence and thus eliminating 'the root of all evil'. There would then have been no need for 'the elaborate arrangement of a Special Incarnation with all the unforeseeable consequences which this entails'.

There were those who felt that *Answer to Job* simultaneously committed the sins of blasphemy and arrogance: blasphemy that he should attempt to unravel the metamorphoses of the Holy Spirit in the manner of a neo-Gnostic and arrogance in making it conform to his own theories. Fierce controversy followed, with one school reading the book simply as a psychological explanation of Man's conception of God, while others recoiled from the notion that any imperfection had ever appeared in the Holy Spirit. Ellenberger believed that the book could also be understood 'as a cry of existential anguish from a man desperately seeking for the solution of the greatest of all philosophical riddles, the problem of evil'.

There remained a hostile handful who claimed that Jung had now appointed himself psychiatrist to God, diagnosed a divine sickness and successfully cured the Patient by applying his own theories. Eric Neumann, his old friend in Israel, wrote on 5 December 1951, '[*Answer to Job*] is a book that grips me profoundly. I find it the most beautiful and deepest of your books. In a certain sense it is a dispute with God similar to Abraham's when he pleaded with God on account of the destruction of Sodom. In particular it is for me – for me personally – also a book against God who let 6 million of his people be killed, for Job is really Israel too.'

Jung replied that nothing compared with the arrogance he had to summon 'in order to be able to insult God'. God had become for him 'a contradiction in terms . . . an ailment man has to cure'.[18]

Confronted with the question 'Do you believe in God?' Jung still tended to be evasive. Talking to H. G. Wells on one occasion he seemed to refer to his Old Wise Man as if the whole of humanity were in touch with this God-like personification of the collective unconscious. However, in 1955 he returned to more direct affirmation. In two interviews, one with Frederic Sands and the other with John Freeman, the ambiguities disappeared. Speaking to Sands, he described God as the inexplicability of fate and the voice of conscience. 'All that I have learned has led me step by step to an unshakeable conviction of the existence of God. . . . I do not take His existence on belief – I know that He exists.'[19]

In December of the same year a Mr Leonard wrote to him out of the blue about his interview with John Freeman and Jung replied: 'Mr Freeman in his characteristic manner fired the question . . . in a somewhat surprising way, so that I was perplexed and had to say the next thing which came into my mind.' No sooner had the answer left his lips, he added, than he knew he had 'said something controversial, puzzling or even ambigous'.[20] He was therefore just waiting for a spate of letters like Mr Leonard's. Any attempt to elaborate the answer simply came down to this: 'I do know that I am obviously confronted with a factor unknown in itself which I call God.' As for his idea of the Devil, he wrote to Professor Hilty: ' "Devil" is a very apt name for certain autonomous powers in the structure of the human psyche. As such the devil seems to me to be a real figure.'

Constant minor illnesses now troubled him. He wrote again to Neumann on 28 February 1952: 'I have been banished to bed again with flu. At 77 this is no light matter.'[21] And to Father Victor White in the spring of 1952 from Locarno: 'I had a pretty miserable time throughout March on account of a grippe. I came down here to pick up again. Although we are in the sun the air is still pretty cold and windy.'

Father Victor White had first reacted enthusiastically to *Answer to Job* – 'the most exciting and moving book I have read in years and somehow it arouses tremendous bonds of sympathy between us'. Within a very short time enthusiasm gave place to qualification, qualification to criticism and then a prolonged and sometimes bitter argument followed White almost into the grave.[22] It concerned the same old problem of *privatio boni* or the question of whether evil is a thing in itself or simply the absence of good. On 30 June 1952, Jung wrote a long letter to Victor White in which he argued that if Good was 'a moral judgment and not substantial in itself', then its opposite Evil was no less non-substantial. 'If however you assume that Good is Being then Evil can be nothing else than Non-Being.' Between 17 and 27 July 1952, White spent ten days in Bollingen arguing continuously about *privatio boni* without reaching any agreement.

On 28 July, Jung wrote to an unidentified correspondent: 'My birthday, though celebrated modestly in the family circle was rather exhausting on account of too many letters and telegrams.' He was, he added, only 'picking up slowly'. And to Barbara Robb, 19 November: 'Unfortunately my illness has nothing to do with the weather or only indirectly inasmuch as a brilliant summer seduced me into an activity surpassing my actual strength.' He was slowly recovering from what really amounted to prostration, he said.

Chapter 30

Death of Toni and Emma

ONE PERSON steadily loomed larger in Jung's life – Ruth Bailey, the Englishwoman who accompanied him on his second trip to Africa and remained a close family friend over the years. Every year from 1946 onwards she went to stay with the Jungs in Zürich, slowly becoming almost a part of the family. She carried about her an air of stalwart common sense, and her forthright treatment of Jung pleased him. 'You're an old humbug,' she would say to him when he seemed to contradict himself, and he would roar with laughter and answer, 'You're quite right.' A very relaxed person herself, she found some members of the family stuffy and formal, but she had the greatest respect for Mrs Jung and liked Toni Wolff.

> As I came more and more into the picture Toni seemed to be fading. She was unlucky. She had very bad arthritis – it made her fingers fat. . . . She was getting on for sixty. . . . There were times when Jung deliberately avoided her. He would say to me, 'Toni is coming today – I hope she doesn't stay very long.'[1]

Ruth Bailey found Toni elegant, quick-witted and sometimes sad. If she knew Toni was coming to tea she would say to Jung, 'I'll leave you' – but Jung would insist that she stayed.

The day still began with a relatively early breakfast, work running on through the morning, and the afternoon remaining relatively free. Sometimes in the evening Ruth and Jung would spend long relaxed hours with Emma, everybody reading. Jung's favourite leisure literature, detective stories, included all the popular authors from Agatha Christie to Simenon, and he had an insatiable appetite. He would sit there sucking away at his water-cooled pipe, oblivious to everything except the search for whodunnit. He commented, 'It was so nice to have someone else solve the problems in a way which was entertaining and sent you to sleep instead of boring you and driving you mad.' Given a good night's sleep Jung was always cheerful at breakfast the next morning.

Early in 1950 Emma was still recovering from a fall in the corridor said to be due to having slipped on a rug. As Jung wrote to Father Victor White, she 'broke her right arm in the shoulder – a nasty fracture' and was 'in the hospital for two months. . . . Then I myself was laid up with gastric grippe and a troublesome liver.'[2] His illness dragged on for some time. Writing to Dr Maurice Nicoll, 30 July 1950, Emma said that Jung had given up 'practising' because he found it too exhausting.

And then in 1952 came the death of Toni Wolff. For some it was quite unexpected, among them Jung himself. Toni had become more withdrawn as the years advanced, partly from crippling arthritis and another mysterious illness which no one seemed able to explain. Characteristically, in this analytic circle no one gave it a psychological name, but she was still unmarried, she must have suffered from Jung's diminished attentions, and deep psychological stresses seemed inevitable. There had been a time when Jung and Toni saw one another frequently, when love illumined every day they spent together and it was difficult to differentiate between his and her work. Towards the end she was a disillusioned woman who transcended her suffering in a form of spiritual reconciliation which was very exacting. She became an inveterate smoker, sometimes running through forty cigarettes a day. Her attempts to give it up always failed. Jung collaborated with her shortly before her death and succeeded in freeing himself from the smoking habit only to surrender once more in a very short time. It worried Toni that he was subject to attacks of paroxysmal tachycardia – bursts of rapid pulse-movement – which could be very distressing.[3]

Dr Gerhard Adler went to see her two days before her death and found her talkative, vital, alive. She commented to him: 'How marvellous it is to have someone arrive in Zürich who is not neurotic.'[4] Dr and Mrs Adler were just off to spend the weekend in the mountains, but when they came back a friend slipped a letter into their door saying that Toni had died on Friday night.

According to Barbara Hannah,[5] Toni suddenly felt ill in the middle of treating a patient on 20 March, and immediately afterwards she went to see her doctor. He reassured her, but the maid was distressed to find that she could not eat any supper. She went to bed early, leaving her maid still more worried because she could not recall her mistress ever having refused food before going to bed. Circumstantially, it seemed that she left her bed, went to the bathroom and collapsed on the floor from a heart attack.[6] Her sister, Frau Erna Naeff, said, 'We really did not know what she died of.'[7]

Many distinguished people attended the funeral service with the remarkable exception of Jung himself. Some said he was ill at the time, others that he could not face it, others that he simply refused to go. The true explanation according to Barbara Hannah was that he disliked funerals on principle and never went to them.[8] Did that imply a fear of the presence of death? Certainly he wrote from Bollingen on 28 May 1953: 'On the day of her death even before I received the news I suffered a relapse and had a bad attack of tachycardia.' They had met only two days before, he said, both of them completely unaware of any threat to her life. 'The Hades dream . . . related entirely to myself because nothing pointed to Toni Wolff. . . .'

Many members of the Jung Institute, analysts, friends, family and, interestingly, Emma Jung went to the memorial service. What Emma felt as she sat listening to the long-drawn-out and justified homage paid to a remarkable woman few people know and they are not prepared to say. The voice of the orator rolled on: 'She never gave in to human relations quickly, but when the ice was broken there was no legitimate claim which she wouldn't answer with self-sacrifice. . . . Despite her arthritis she worked until the end. . . . The doctors did not know anything about her [other] illness. Ordinary medicine could not deal with the phenomena of the spirit. . . .'[9]

On 4 February of the following year (1953), Emma was writing to Dr Maurice Nicoll that Jung had been unwell the whole winter with recurring attacks of tachycardia.

By the spring Jung was writing to Father Victor White, 'My wife and myself are tired, though . . . active but in a very restricted way.'[10] Still his attempts to give up smoking persisted. As a result of a dream he had completely laid off smoking. 'At present I am still in a foul mood. What would the gods do without smoke offerings?'[11]

Suddenly Emma fell ill, and in the summer of 1955 Jung wrote to Father Victor White: 'The serious illness of my wife has consumed all my spare time. She has undergone an operation so far successfully, but it has left her in a feeble state needing careful nursing for several weeks to come.'[12]

A letter to Aniela Jaffé said: 'I can walk only for a quarter hour at most. . . . Everything you do, whether watching a cloud or cooking soup, is done on the edge of eternity . . . it is meaningful and futile at once.'[13]

He now plunged into an elaborate correspondence about *Answer to Job*, defining and redefining Christ Jesus and the meaning of the book. There were many combative exchanges. Staunchly, eloquently, he defended his position and refused to recant or apologise. Astonishingly his American publishers refused to publish *Answer to Job*. It was too shocking for their religious susceptibilities. Writing to J. B. Priestley he said, 'Your succour comes at a time when it is badly needed; soon a little book of mine will be published in England which my publishers in USA did not dare to print.'[14] Nonetheless, he was still 'a dyed in the wool protestant'.

At this time Aniela Jaffé recorded: 'Because of his wife's . . . illness, the atmosphere in the house was muted and it touched me to see how Jung took over the function of the master [*sic*]. A new cook had just been engaged and Jung dictated to me the luncheon and dinner menus for every day of the week.'[15]

Jung thought his wife was well enough to allow himself a respite from all the stresses by spending a week at Bollingen. He did not think she was any longer seriously ill. Then came the news of a relapse. The cancer had affected the brain and brought on a stroke. He hurried back to Küsnacht. It was distressing to see her now. He found it difficult even to look at her. 'We had come through so much together,' he said, 'and there she was – ruined. It was appalling.' The end came five days later. For much of the time she was unconscious, and her final passing peaceful and painless.

Writing to Erich Neumann, Jung said the shock he had experienced was 'so great' that he could 'neither concentrate nor recover [his] power of speech'. He continued, 'I would have liked to tell the heart you have opened to me in friendship that two days before the death of my wife I had what one can only call a great illumination. . . .'

Comparing the experience to a flash of lightning which lit up a secret rooted in the centuries but embodied in his wife he did not elucidate its details. 'I can only suppose that the illumination came from my wife who was then mostly in a coma, and that the tremendous lighting up and release of insight had a retroactive effect upon her, and was one reason why she could die such a painless and royal death.'[16]

'I was with the family', Ruth Bailey recalls, 'when his wife died. Jung was very distressed – all white and tense – and not speaking. I remember shortly afterwards he came striding through the room in which all the family sat – silent, knitting, all afraid to say a word to him. I got up and went after him and succeeded in getting him out of himself.'[17]

There was an elaborate funeral with Küsnacht Church full to overflowing, and as the organ began to play Jung came in from a side door looking slightly bent and frail, followed by five children and nineteen grandchildren. An almost feudal atmosphere distinguished the ceremony, and no one could question the splendour of this going down of a patient, tolerant, wise woman who had shared every kind of experience with him over half a century.

There was a dramatic collapse after the ceremony. Jung retired to his study to be alone, and there Dr Fordham and his wife Frieda found him literally sobbing. It revealed a side of his character which has not appeared in this biography. There were long stretches of Jung's life when he was an ordinary likeable man easy to get on with and without any special charisma. But he could burst into childish tantrums and literally become the child demanding attention on occasion. Sometimes in these moments he had been accustomed to fall into his wife's arms. Now, without them, he broke down like a child once more and sobbed, 'She was a queen! She was a queen!'[18]

A much more profound change overtook him as the days slipped away. Liliane Frey-Rohn recalls, 'He became a different man after the death of his wife.'[19] His four daughters and his daughter-in-law, each the centre of a large family, now took it in turns to stay with him for short periods. Writing to his daughter Marianne he said it was 'a joy to be together with you for a while. . . . Mamma's death has left a gap for me that cannot be filled. So it is good if you have something you want to carry out, and can turn to when the emptiness spreads about you too menacingly.'[20]

Two dreams now came to haunt Jung. One demonstrated to him the objective cognition of real coniunctio, the other the evolution of the soul after death. The first had characteristics of a vision more than a dream, in which his wife materialised in her prime at the age of thirty 'wearing the dress which had been made for her many years before by my cousin the medium'.[21] It was a very beautiful dress and she stood there appraising him frankly in all the coolness of objective wisdom. A special dimension in the vision made Jung realise that it was not his wife in spiritual or physical reality but a portrait especially commissioned by his wife for him. It concentrated their lifespan together, crystallising fifty-three years of marriage up to her death. 'Face to face with such wholeness one remains speechless for it can scarcely be comprehended,' he wrote.

It was as if approaching his eightieth year he had not only escaped the emotional ties with Toni and his wife but also achieved a degree of objectivity which was an essential prerequisite of true individuation. This was the final objective coniunctio of his psychotherapy which had to occur before the birth of the true Self.

The second dream came some time later. He suddenly woke in the middle of the night full of the sense of his wife's presence and realised that he had 'spent an entire day with her in Provence'. In her last years Frau Jung had concentrated on a study of the Holy Grail which she had left unfinished. Close friends said she immersed herself in this search because perfection had failed to materialise in her life. Now Jung wrote as if activities common to this life were continued in the next. 'She was engaged on studies of the Grail there.' It signified to him on the subjective level that 'my anima had not yet finished with the work she had to do', and on the objective the knowledge that his wife continued her spiritual development struck him as 'meaningful and held a measure of reassurance'.

In his reminiscences, recollection of this dream led Jung into abstruse speculations about the correlation between amplified dreams and elaborate mathematical equations. Dreams gave a wrong impression because they were equivalent to constructing a four-dimensional model out of a three-dimensional body. Mathematics, on the other hand, had developed a means of expressing relationships 'which pass empirical comprehension'. It was ironic to find Jung in old age invoking the very discipline which he had so much despised in his youth and could not practise with even elementary accomplishment.

Chapter 31

Old Age

IT WAS IN 1955 that Jung finally invited Miss Bailey to become his companion-housekeeper, but Miss Bailey hesitated before making a decision which would revolutionise her life. 'Come and see me out,' Jung persuaded her. 'You are good at seeing people out.'[1]

Once Ruth Bailey had made up her mind, what appeared to be a relatively simple arrangement quickly became enmeshed in Swiss bureaucracy. When she applied for the necessary papers the police began to ask awkward questions. Why did the Professor with such a large family need anyone from outside to run his household? Jung's daughter Marianne explained that all his family were married with children and had family responsibilities. It was some time before the necessary work permit arrived from the Town Hall.

At the outset Jung said to Miss Bailey: 'Now there's one thing you must understand. I am a man who can get into great rages. Take no notice of them. They don't mean anything. And I soon get out of them.' His 'terrible temper' quickly became evident. Preparing a meal of minced meat at Bollingen one day she placed two tomatoes in the pan and Jung exploded: 'Don't do that!' He continued carping about the tomatoes and then stormed out of the kitchen. He remained angry all that morning until at last Ruth Bailey said to him: 'Look here. If I'm not worth two tomatoes to you, I'm going.' 'Don't do that,' Jung said at once. 'You mustn't take any notice of my explosions. I told you they didn't mean anything.' When calm was restored, he said: 'All you have to remember is not to do anything to make me angry.' A remarkable request remembering how quickly he could react and take offence. Jung was a very good cook. Ruth Bailey would prepare all the food ready for Jung to do the cooking. In restaurants, too, whenever they dined out he was a great gourmet making a minute scrutiny of the menu before reaching his decisions.

It took Ruth Bailey some time to adjust to oil-lamps, wood-fires, and water brought from the pump. They alternated between Küsnacht and Bollingen. The houses were twenty miles apart but they represented 'two different worlds'. Many long serene evenings were spent at Bollingen looking out on the lake, and Jung said on one such occasion, 'Ruth, you have learnt a marvellous gift – the gift of silence.'

Two days before his eightieth birthday Jung had his first experience of mass-media electronics which he professed to despise. It needed considerable pressure to bring him before the B.B.C.'s microphone, and he felt uneasy throughout the whole process. Dr Stephen Black, a medical research worker well known as a forthright interviewer, put some searching questions. He began by repeating the Latin translation of the Greek quotation carved in stone over the door of Küsnacht – 'Invoked or not invoked the God will be present' – and asked, 'Why did you choose this to put over your front door?' Jung replied, 'Because I wanted to express the fact that I always feel unsafe, as if I'm in the presence of superior possibilities.' It was a revealing remark. After all those years of experience, character-building, suffering, philosophic reflection and survival, he still shared something of the common man's sense of *angst*.

Black came to a crucial question: 'What do you think will be the effect upon the world of living under the threat of the hydrogen bomb?' Jung replied: 'I think the West is more affected by it than the East because the East has a very different attitude to death and destruction. Think for instance of the fact that practically the whole of India believes in reincarnation.'[2]

Jung's eightieth birthday was a great occasion which began at his home in Küsnacht, reached into several Zürich receptions, and embraced London, New York, San Francisco and Calcutta. An International Congress of Psychiatry in Zürich invited him to speak on the psychology of schizophrenia. The private party at Küsnacht brought together no less than forty close relatives and two 'outsiders', E. A. Bennet and Ruth Bailey. On his arrival at the party Jung said to Bennet, 'You will have to be a member of the Jung family for the day.'[3] It was a merry and moving occasion from which Jung emerged exhausted. As part of the formal recognition of his birthday Jung received a two-volume *Festschrift* with articles from thirty-two contributors.[4] The C. G. Jung Institute in Zürich also presented him with an original papyrus, now known as the Jung Codex, the four books of which included the *Gospel of Truth* by Valentinus himself. These were considered to be the writings of the Gnostic School founded by Valentinus in the second century. Delighted though he was with the gift, Jung felt that the papyrus should be restored to the Egyptian Government, and it now rests in the Coptic Museum in Cairo.

Jung's eightieth anniversary was marred by the renewal of anti-Semitic accusations,[5] but now a group of Jewish disciples published a powerful protest against his attackers.[6]

In May 1957, Jung wrote to Gustav Schmaltz saying that solitude was for him 'a fount of healing' which made life still worth living.[7] 'Talking is often a torment for me and I need many days of silence to recover from the futility of words.' He had, he said, received 'his marching orders and only [looked] back when there's nothing else to do'.

A few days later he completely contradicted his withdrawal by a strong attack on Martin Buber. 'He overlooks the existence of the individual psyche. He also thinks he can override all other ideas of God by assuming that his God image is *the* God image.'[8]

By December of the same year the streak of gullibility which began with his belief in Hélène Preiswerk's séances, persisted with ghosts, and gave scientific validity to some aspects of astrology now insisted that he dare not contradict statements about the physical reality of flying saucers.[9]

Throughout his last years Ruth Bailey was in close attendance upon Jung and gives an interesting account of their relationship. A continuous flow of famous people came to consult the oracle, and his reactions were sometimes unpredictable. The novelist Hugo Charteris left a vivid picture of his visit.

He took the road which was nothing more than a track leading to the black door set in the wall of Bollingen, and when the door opened 'a woman enjoying – physically – an Indian summer [Ruth Bailey] introduced [him] to an open courtyard stacked . . . with neat bundles of firewood piled against the wall. At one side there [was] a platform like a miniature theatre with a roof supported by two columns and on it a table set for two, a fireplace and a sculptured ceiling newly painted in . . . traditional style. Another door [opened] and there at the water's edge [sat] a tall old man with snow-white hair . . . dressed in a gardener's apron and open shirt. . . . Jars of different tobaccos surrounded his chair and in between talking he puffed away with that gentle rhythm which is to be seen in the tail of a stationary fish. . . .'

Charteris was surprised to find himself 'looking into slightly elongated and slanted eyes . . .'. Old age encroached unpleasantly in some respects: 'Mr Jung's hands [were] getting bulbous jointed with rheumatism, he [could not] stand for long periods. . . . When he laughed, he laughed completely like a hippo waiting for a bun. No dentures. Only four eye teeth ground to needle sharpness and gums like hard wet wood.'

Many subjects came and went. Of China, 'What has happened there is unspeakable.' Of Americans, 'Wurl – they're on roller skates.' Of Africa, 'What a pity that we could not have left it alone. . . .' Of Freud, 'He said to me – "I thought it – so it must be true" – imagine. . . . But his wife's younger sister. She appreciated the old man.' Jung laughed mischievously and then said more soberly: 'I don't know what happened. Once I think . . . I think he slept with her once . . . he told me.' His voice trailed off.[10]

Another person who remained close to Jung was, of course, Aniela Jaffé. When a group of Jungians founded the C. G. Jung Institute in Zürich, Aniela Jaffé became its secretary, and Jung began to delegate various tasks to her – research, letters, reports, manuscripts. They were 'piled mountain high in his library'. In 1950 she prepared a psychological study 'Bilder und Symbole aus E. T. A. Hoffmanns Märchen Der Goldene Topf' which Jung regarded highly enough to include in his volume of essays *Gestaltungen des Unbewussten*. Then in 1955 she became his secretary, and first confronted Jung as an employer.

Jung's office at Küsnacht was on the ground floor between the kitchen and the large dining-room with a window opening on to the gardens and the lake. Aniela Jaffé on her very first morning sat beside the window reading copies of his letters while she waited for him to arrive. Suddenly she heard his 'slow rather dragging step as he passed through the hallway'. After that 'I must confess . . . the approach of the old magician never lost its excitement. With my inner ear I still hear it till this day.' Work that first morning began at ten and lasted until midday. There were two things she had to do: take in dictation the menus for every day of the following week, a considerable feat involving every variety of food, and accompany him upstairs to the library to witness the ceremony of opening the safe, which he called his cache. On this occasion he took out the four fragments of the breadknife which had exploded so dramatically all those years ago while his mother was still alive and asked her to have them mounted as a single exhibit.[11] Almost at once he repeated the warnings given to Ruth Bailey. She must never under any circumstances allow herself to be upset by his angry outbursts or by his great roarings and cursings. 'I was further expected not to try to make myself indispensable. In Jung's eyes this well-known female aim was nothing but a secret demand for power, and the conscious or unconscious craving for power was for him the dark shadow, the root of countless evils above all in human relationships.'

She quickly discovered that 'he was satisfied . . . he had said everything it had been given him to say. . . . Only those who knew him well could detect a slight tone of resignation behind his words.'[12] Externally his tall figure gave the impression of fragility, but this 'paled beside the massive strength, the powerfulness that radiated from him'. Any idea that he derived this strength from arrogance – as some suggested – Miss Jaffé flatly rebuts: 'He was too good natured . . . too kindly . . . too outgoing . . . and his humour was infectious.'[13]

Jung's correspondence grew rather than diminished with age, and letters played a role beyond the normal in his life. As he ceased to write books he poured refinements of his theories into letters, and they became a multifarious link with a world from which he had slowly withdrawn. He also admitted to Aniela Jaffé that he needed to receive letters because they made him feel that his work was still being analysed and discussed.

It was surprising in a person of Jung's stature that he should still be vain enough to worry about the world's reactions, since he had already been given by his disciples the semi-divine elevation of an oracle. As Aniela Jaffé said: 'When – trying to be considerate – I forwarded too little post while he was on holiday – he became quite angry.'

Aniela Jaffé believed that he needed reassurance because in a scientific age he was still considered by many as non-scientific.

On 25 February 1960 he wrote to Eugen Bohler: 'On January 23rd I had a slight embolism followed by not too severe heart cramps.' He was under house arrest for a month and forbidden all mental activity. Against all orders he carried out a prolonged rereading of the Buddhist texts. Thanks to his isolation, he said, he had spent long hours slipping away from the world and conversing with 'voices long past'.

The Mother Prioress of a Contemplative Order wrote to say that his old friend and critic Father Victor White had a malignant tumour and was likely to die. Part of Jung's distress arose from the fact that his prolonged 'quarrel' with White had tapered off into silence for many years. A dream presaged White's fatal illness, and Jung wrote: 'Synchronistic phenomena occur for the most part in emotional situations – death, sickness, accident – we observe them relatively frequently at moments of heightened emotional tension which need not be conscious.'

In April he wrote again to the Mother Prioress saying that he was sorry the news about Victor White was so bad and the end apparently near. Concerned that their quarrel should be reconciled in death, he added: 'If you have any chance to let him know about myself I should be much obliged if you would tell him that I am at peace with him and that he should not worry any more.'[14]

By August 1960 he was suffering from blood pressure, and the doctor was still against too much mental work, but he continued his correspondence. In one letter he tried to convince Sir Herbert Read that Picasso was simply 'catering to the morbidity of his time – as he himself admits'.

The profile drawn at the beginning of this book of a wise old man who had come to terms with 'natural life' and the collective unconscious is now subject to severe qualification. Vanity still troubled the Master, what the world thought of him concerned him deeply, and whether he meticulously replied to every letter because it was another power-point from which he could influence the outside world, or whether an obsessional courtesy demanded detailed attention was a question put to Aniela Jaffé: 'Oh, it was a matter of courtesy. . . . A distinguishing mark of his correspondence was that many of the people were unknown to him.'[15]

Among the people who wrote to him, some were clearly mad, others eccentric, others again relentless in their persistence. A continuous flow of letters came from a seventy-year-old spinster he had once diagnosed as a senile schizophrenic. Written on cheap lined paper in a bold childish hand the letters invariably contained an *I Ching* hexagram with a commentary linking it to her current condition.[16] Her letters multiplied so thick and fast that it became an impossible task to reply to them all, but out of respect for the old lady Jung preserved them in a mahogany cupboard. Suddenly, one week the letters ceased to arrive, and three days later Aniela Jaffé read in the newspaper that she had died. Turning to the cupboard, she opened the last letter and found drawn on the first page a hexagram with the word 'peace' beside it. According to Aniela Jaffé, Jung had deliberately preserved her letters as a symbolic gesture. 'We simply do not know', she commented, 'the effect it may have when somebody's spirit is accepted without any concrete reaction and merely through an act of empathy.' The final footnote was touching. Even when she was known to be dead Jung left her letters undisturbed in the cupboard.

Ruth Bailey found that he was a very economical man constantly switching off electric lights in the house, and he fitted Freud's anal erotic category with his obsessional punctuality and tidiness.

Inanimate objects sometimes had for him a kind of malignancy. 'Things take their revenge!' he once exploded to Jaffé when she had mislaid a ruler. 'Things' shared the aura of the person who owned them, and from the splitting of the table to the splitting of the knife there was plenty of evidence that inanimate objects could not resist the powerful charisma of Jung! Psychic elements were constantly invoked. When, for instance, any item was lost in the big house, Jung spoke as if it had been bewitched. 'The blue tobacco jar has been magicked away again,' he would say, quoting the phrase used by a schizophrenic. Looking for missing objects was a pointless intervention with Fate since they would in due course be magicked back again. 'Don't interfere' was one of his guiding principles. If Jung never claimed to be a consistent man, Aniela Jaffé said that 'anyone who followed [him persistently] would discover immanent laws that held the apparent contradictions together'. There were some elements in his day-to-day life difficult to reconcile with any such comment.

His views on sensitivity, for instance. In her work as Jung's secretary, Aniela Jaffé was constantly on tenterhooks as she put the finished letters before him for signature. 'Every typing mistake was reproachfully and copiously commented on.' His sensitivity to error, his inability to overlook any mistake, however trivial, led him to look for further errors, and once his scrutiny began there was the danger of finding what literally did not exist. Then he 'went too far and found *himself* in error!' At this stage she could easily turn the tables on him by making him laugh, but 'when the tempest had really broken . . . this weapon no longer worked' Despite his warnings, when a simple mistake led to grumbling throughout the whole day it was anything but easy to carry out his advice and ignore his explosion.

Observing his own weaknesses reflected in others he could not bear them. 'Once he gave me a violent scolding for my sensitiveness and accused me of a secret lust for power.'[17] Flatly contradicting his own behaviour he claimed that such sensitivity was demanding and tyrannical.

*

In 1956, during the Eranos Conference in Ascona, the publisher Kurt Wolf had expressed a wish to publish Jung's autobiography, but at first Jung did not take kindly to the idea. There were many episodes in his life that he did not want opened to the prying public gaze. There followed a long period of doubt, self-examination and indecision. At last he surrendered. 'I have . . . weighed the matter,' he wrote to a friend of his student days, 'and come to the conclusion that I shall fend off other obligations long enough to take up the very first beginnings of my life and consider them in an objective fashion.'

Jung knew with some degree of certainty now that he was approaching the end of his life, and inevitably thoughts of a possible hereafter occupied the penultimate chapter of his reminiscences. 'It is not that I wish we had a life after death. In fact I would prefer not to foster such ideas. Still I must state and give reality its due . . . thoughts of this nature move about within me.' Asked whether immortality were true or false he refused to commit himself. However, the romantic notion of a serene paradise where spirits bathed in eternal bliss spent their days trying to re-establish contact with lost husbands or wives on earth did not have much appeal for him. Reincarnation in one form or another also seemed a dubious proposition, but he did not deny the possibility of communication between the living and the dead which seemed to imply some form of immortality. Jung also noticed the curious anomaly that spirits living outside time and space frequently invoked the help of earthly mortals instead of revealing what their superior 'life' might have to teach us here on earth.

Still ambiguous, he claimed that there must, in his view, be anguish and suffering in the other world, and he supposed some kind of evolution as on earth, but he did not pretend to understand what must remain infinitely mysterious. Life on earth might be an assignment set 'from without' or, in his own terminology, 'the incarnation of an archetype', a temporary projection of a permanent self. Certainly there were indications that at least part of the psyche was not subject to the laws of space and time, Jung said, and quoted the experiments of Professor J. B. Rhine as scientific proof. Examples of foreknowledge and extrasensory perception convinced him that some aspect of the psyche contradicted the laws of spatio-temporal causality. The Totality of the phenomenon could only be explained by postulating another dimension as yet unknown to us. An experience of the evolution of the soul after death had been his encounter with his dead wife when he awoke convinced that he had spent a day with her in the south of France and found her still engaged on her studies of the Holy Grail. This introduced further complications. In the last analysis the main problem of the individual was to discover whether he or she embraced the vast and complex notion of the infinite in such a way that real individuation delivered one from the fear of death. Certainly he seemed to have no fear of death. His final conclusion: 'We must hold clearly in mind that there is no possible way for us to attain certainty concerning things which pass our understanding.'

In old age he still liked to take car trips through Switzerland with his old American friend Fowler McCormick, who drove, and Ruth Bailey, who played the part of nurse. Returning from one of these trips he stumbled on a bunch of letters he considered indiscreet and solemnly carried out what had become something of a ritual – consigning them to the flames of the beautiful green-tiled stove which stood in the library. Toni Wolff's love-letters had already suffered the same fate. 'Once,' Aniela Jaffé said, 'with the fire roaring he smote the side of the stove with the flat of his hand as though clapping an old friend on the shoulder and remarked, laughing: "This fellow is my discretion." '[18]

One of his last smaller works was *Flying Saucers: A Modern Myth of Things Seen in the Skies*, based upon a whole archive of books, photographs and cuttings, prepared by Aniela Jaffé. It snowballed over into six large files and several bookshelves before Jung finally went to work on the material. The finished work led many people to argue that Jung believed in flying saucers as a physical reality. In part, he saw them as satisfying the need for a modern myth, but did not finally dismiss their possible reality.

The actual room in which he worked in old age varied according to mood and season. Two rings on the bell to Aniela Jaffé meant he was waiting in the library. Sometimes she arrived to find him taking the bowl and stem of his water-cooled pipe apart, and it was some minutes before he had reassembled and lit it with, surprisingly perhaps, a mechanical lighter. Lunch was usually followed by a Brazilian cigar.

While Emma was alive Ruth Bailey had slept on the floor above Jung, but now as he grew older and frailer she moved down to be next to him in what was once Emma's bedroom with the interconnecting door. Someone had to be within constant call in case he felt unwell or suffered the small accidents familiar to ageing people.

Bollingen had no telephone – he hated the instrument – and there came the day when he suddenly fainted and Ruth Bailey propped him up on the couch and rushed off a whole mile to get the doctor. His doctor came hurrying over, examined his patient and heard him say, 'I think I'm going,' but the doctor would have none of it. 'You're O.K.,' he said, and the next morning Jung had recovered.

Bored on another occasion he suddenly expressed a wish to see the mountains and the old familiar passes at close quarters again. It was far too dangerous an undertaking for an old man with a weak heart, but Ruth took the risk, packed brandy and medicaments in the car and set off to follow his old beloved tracks once more. High up in the mountains, lost in their desolation, with snowy peaks stretching away above and nothing but the sky marking the horizon, he climbed slowly out of the car and sniffed the mountain air. Later to an old friend he said, 'I think that's the last time I shall meet the mountains.' There were tears in his eyes.

Jung's eighty-fifth birthday brought a deluge of greetings from all over the world, and many celebrations were carefully spread over several weeks so as not to tire him too much. On the actual day he entertained his children, grandchildren and great-grandchildren – now numbering ten – to a splendid party. The following day the Town Council invited him to a banquet at the town hall where he sat under a full-length portrait of his grandfather. He was elected Erenburgher or Freeman of the Town, a distinction only granted twice in the previous 150 years. 'He almost had to leave during the meal,' Ruth Bailey said. 'He felt so ill.'

Chapter 32

The Last Year

IN HIS EIGHTY-FIFTH YEAR there was a marked deterioration in his physical condition. When he slept, he slept deeper, when he tried to work, he tired more easily, when he walked, his steps were sometimes faltering, and he made careful use of his stick. He carefully harboured his strength for distinguished visitors, to 'put on a good show'. As he wrote to Hugo Charteris: 'With existentialism our words come to an end in complete meaninglessness and our art in total inexpressivity and our world has acquired the means to blast us into cosmic dust.'[1] He concluded the letter: 'To hell with the Ego world! Listen to the voice of your daimonion.'

'The older I become,' he now wrote, 'the less I have understood or had insight into or known about myself.' For a man who had spent most of his life investigating his psyche, it was tantamount to an admission of failure. 'And so I am disappointed and not disappointed. I cannot form any final judgement.' Still he quoted Lao-tzu with evident relish and self-application – 'All are clear; I alone am clouded.' He commented to Charteris: 'That's exactly as I feel in advanced old age. Once I was alienated from the world. Now it is transferred to my inner world. I have a very surprising unfamiliarity with myself.'[2]

He told Charteris: 'I suppose it is possible a kind of Karma has been acquired by me from the long line of my ancestors' lives. It might take the form of an impersonal archetype which has taken a particular grip on me. . . . It might – crystallise centuries of development of the triad. . . . Put another way, if I had another incarnation in another century – I might have found problems to which there was then no answer. I had to be born again because now there are some answers to these problems.'

The summing-up came in his reminiscences. While the man who dies in the belief that he will not survive after death 'marches towards nothingness, the one who has placed his faith in the archetype follows the tracks of life and lives right on to his death. Both, to be sure, remain in uncertainty but the one lives against his instincts the other with them.'

On 10 May 1961, Miguel Serrano, a new friend, telephoned Ruth Bailey hoping to call on Jung. 'He is seriously ill in bed,' she said, 'but come over to tea with me.'

Serrano believed that he was 'the last foreign friend' to see Jung before he died. Miss Bailey said to Serrano over tea, 'You know he has

271

been very busy these past few days writing an essay called "Man and His Symbols" for an American publication. The work has exhausted him. . . . He writes it all by hand and has now completed eighty pages. He is writing directly in English because he is afraid that German syntax may confuse his meaning and hopes that it will be more clear in English.'[3]

When Serrano at last climbed the stairs to Jung's room he found Jung, to his surprise, out of bed sitting in a chair looking out on to the lake. 'He was dressed in a Japanese ceremonial gown, so that in the light of late afternoon he looked like the magician of some ancient cult. When I entered the room Jung tried to rise from his chair but I hurriedly prevented him from doing so.' The Japanese gown, the hollow cheeks, the carefully measured speech all contributed to the sense of an oracle still striving to marry Eastern and Western thinking and not quite succeeding.

Dr Michael Fordham recalls: 'My last meeting with Jung was a sad one. Shortly before his death a mutual friend brought me a letter from Jung over which he was very much upset. It was written in a shaky hand and was full of complaining despair; nobody understood him and his work had been a failure. . . . I decided therefore to go out to Zürich and see him in the hope of being able to relieve his distress by telling him something of the extent that he had been studied in England. . . . I arrived and Jung was there in his dressing gown and a skull cap. I told him about the letter and delivered my message. He looked at me as if I were a poor fool and did not know a thing. . . . He eventually became confused and distressed, and I asked him what was the matter. He did not speak for a minute or two and then he said "You had better go" and regretfully I did so.'[4]

He was now very near the end. Ruth Bailey wrote: 'He was so very tired and weak. On May 17th after a very happy and peaceful day . . . he had an embolism, a blood-clot on the brain, and it affected his speech. . . . You can imagine this was a great shock to me, it happened at breakfast time. But after a few days he began to pick up again and his speech improved very well – but he could not read so well and I spent much time reading to him.'[5] Barbara Hannah went to visit him but found his blurred speech too distressing.

Ruth Bailey continues: 'May 30th . . . a very peaceful and happy day we were sitting in the library window having tea when he had a collapse and that was the last time he was in the library, afterwards he was in his room. From this time onwards he got weaker and weaker and for two days before he died he was away in some far country and he saw wonderful and beautiful things, I am sure of that. He smiled often and was happy.'[6]

'I think I knew he was going to die but I pushed the knowledge aside because I might not be able to do what I had to do for him. I stayed with him now day and night.'[7]

His last words to Ruth Bailey were: 'Let's have a really good red wine tonight', and with that he despatched her to the cellars.

There was a prolonged coma with his family surrounding him. And then at 4 p.m. on 6 June 1961 he drifted off quietly, his heart simply ceasing to beat from old age.[8]

According to several reliable witnesses, two hours after his death a violent thunderstorm broke, and lightning struck the very poplar tree beside the lake where he was accustomed to sit. Sizzling along the trunk into the ground, it was powerful enough to dislodge the heavy stones of a low parapet. Aniela Jaffé said: 'From the open wound it had burned into the bark I cut out a strip of bast. Then the gardener stopped up the wound with pitch and the tree is still alive today.'

What one witness described as 'a hushed assembly' came to the Protestant church in Küsnacht where the pastor celebrated his passing as a prophet who had stemmed the flood of rationalism 'and given man the courage to have a soul again'. Some sat through the ceremony unperturbed, but there were several who had difficulty in controlling their grief and others who openly wept. The body was cremated. The ashes now lie in the family grave alongside the remains of his father, mother, sister and wife. Jung himself had designed the grave and decorated it with his coat of arms.

Epilogue

In 1975 I revisited the Burghölzli Hospital in Zürich, Jung's home at Küsnacht, the Jung Institute and many other places linked with his name. It came as a surprise to find no plaque in the three rooms which he had occupied for seven years in the Burghölzli. The wide staircases, the broad landings, the discreet doors with their metal scrollwork led into the same rooms looking out on the spacious grounds and distant hills. Did they still accept his theories or practise his therapy? The young man who now held the job of Oberarzt once held by Jung, smiled sadly. 'A prophet is honoured in his own land,' he said, 'but we use every theory at our disposal. This is a public hospital and we cannot afford to handle public patients as Jung handled private ones.' At the University it was the same story. A half-regretful smile and, in one instance at least, amusement that one should still take the man and his theories seriously.

Walking down the long, tree-lined path to the double green doors of his house at Küsnacht, every step was charged with memories of my pilgrimage into his life. My steps merged with his, and I felt his gaze over my shoulder as I stared up at the central tower, the big green shutters and iron trellises over the windows. I pulled the long, brass-handled bell, and there was the same wide lobby with the wash-basin, but a new dog lay sprawled asleep on the rug. Most startling of all, there was Jung standing in the doorway – tall, broad-shouldered, blue-eyed – reincarnated in his son Franz.

We entered the sitting-room, lofty, panelled, still proudly proclaiming his grandfather's portrait, but a room less shadowed by the trees which his son had cut down. The boat-house remained, but the study had changed, no longer bearing much resemblance to its old organisation. New relatives were occupying familiar rooms. I walked down the shallow wooden steps almost into the lake and sat staring out across its restless surface. Jung had sat there scores of times. Even in his own home the old familiar surroundings had begun to crumble, and the power of his presence diminished.

Later in the same year a contradiction arose. It was the centenary of Jung's birth, and an exhibition of the man and his work in Zürich drew 20,000 visitors, radio and television celebrated the occasion, there were many lectures and ceremonies, and the Jungian initiates in Zürich reaffirmed their faith. Throughout the world – in London, Berlin, New York and elsewhere – the occasion was honoured in many and diverse ways. If the steps of the Master had seemed to me to falter during my previous visit, they recovered their old confidence and purpose in the summer of the same year.

Appendix I

Jung's Model of the Psyche

IT IS NOW POSSIBLE to attempt a recapitulation of Jung's theories in the form of a résumé of his model of the psyche. This is a hazardous undertaking. No one Jungian theoretician gives the same reading of the Old Testament as another. Immense controversies are generated and it is a brave man who ventures into the battle. Clearly any attempt to condense the complex mountain of Jung's thinking into a miniature model is fraught with dangers. Nothing short of a separate 100,000-word volume would give the right weight and balance to different parts of the system or embrace the details in sufficient subtlety. For a fully satisfying account of Jung's work there is no alternative but to read the eighteen volumes yourself and make your own interpretation. This brief résumé is the result of my own reading of the work and cannot by its nature be comprehensive.

Jung describes the ego as 'a complex of ideas which constitutes the centre of my field of consciousness and appears to possess a high degree of continuity and identity'.[1] Consciousness becomes for him the activity which maintains the relation of the psychic contents with the ego. The concept of Self 'is not meant to take the place of the one that has always been known as the *ego* but includes it in a supraordinate concept'.[2] Moreover, it is not just a constant form but involves a dynamic process. The Collective Unconscious is 'the deposit of mankind's typical reactions since primordial times to universal situations such as fear, danger, the struggle against superior power . . . love, birth and death . . .'.[3] The conscious and the unconscious are not separate entities but part of a compensatory whole.

The psyche operates through the four functions of thinking, feeling, sensation and intuition. 'Thus thinking is the function which seeks to apprehend the world and adjust to it by way of thought or cognition i.e. logical inferences. The function of feeling on the other hand apprehends the world through an evaluation based on the feelings of pleasant or unpleasant acceptance or rejection.'[4]

Sensation and intuition fall into irrational or non-rational categories since sensation reacts directly to experience without evaluation and intuition invokes the inherent potentiality of what can loosely be referred to as 'things'. One of the four functions usually predominates and creates the particular 'quality' of a given personality. In the neurotic either the expression of the 'natural' dominant function has been blocked or the constitutional position of the second or third function artificially elevated. A man may have achieved great success in life by exploiting one function and neglecting the remaining three. To become a fully integrated person the neglected functions have to be readjusted in proper balance.

The two broad types, extravert and introvert, have biological bases and are more clearly determined from birth than the function type. The desired goal relates the typology to the functions and the unconscious to the conscious in such a way as to achieve conscious individuation. Having extracted – with brutal short cuts – a miniature model from its huge and complex matrix, let us now examine the original in greater detail.

That part of the psyche which is centralised in the conscious ego Jung envisages as situated between the interior or psychic world and the exterior or spatio-temporal world. The ego is surrounded like a planet by satellite sub-personalities, but the cosmic analogy collapses when the sub-personalities are seen to change their orbit, place and power according to laws quite different from gravitation. Named, variously, the Self, the Archetype of the Spirit, the Anima, Animus and the Shadow, they are subject to qualification by the Persona. As we know, in Latin the word *persona* meant 'mask', and in analytical psychology it describes the external personality projected according to a person's race, creed, class, occupation and a number of other conditioning factors. Jung says: 'The persona . . . is a compromise between individual and society as to what a man should appear to be.' Pouring considerable psychic energy into the persona, some people come to believe that the projected image is the real Self and in consequence lose contact with the actual Self-as-it-is.

Whereas the Persona deliberately externalises itself, the Shadow is the sum of those characteristics we wish to conceal not only from the world but also especially from ourselves. Possessing considerable manipulative power, the Shadow can project itself on to other people, while the Self rejects responsibility for its behaviour. These reactions may produce a Jekyll and Hyde effect as when the Shadow, breaking free from control of the conscious personality, carries out actions which would be regarded as evil by the Self. Lurking deeply embedded in the negative aspect of the personality, the Shadow is not a result of psychic repression but of *unawareness*. A Christian gentleman may live an apparently blameless life, showing every consideration for others, without realising that he has exploited his wife at home, his colleagues in his profession, and may even have become a tyrant. Rationalising outrageous conduct, safe in the false assumption that all his motives are lofty, he refuses to become aware of the Shadow directing so much of his life.

The Persona and the Shadow belong to relatively shallow levels of the individual's psyche, but the archetypes of the soul (the Anima or Animus), the archetypes of the Spirit (the Old Wise Man, the Magna Mater) and the most central of all archetypes (the Self) belong to that part of the model designated the Collective Unconscious.

The archetype of the Soul takes the form of a feminine figure in man –
the anima, and in a woman a masculine counterpart – the animus.
Psychological residues of the woman remain in the man, and of the
man in the woman, owing to their complementary nature, and both
hold in their unconscious 'a representation of the other sex'. 'Every man
carries within him', Jung wrote, 'the eternal image of woman, not the
image of this or that particular woman but a definitive feminine image.
This image is fundamentally unconscious, an hereditary factor of
primordial origin engraved in the living organic system of the man, an
imprint or "archetype" of all the . . . impressions ever made by
woman. . . .'[5]

The glossary in Jung's reminiscences attempted to give this genetic
justification, claiming that psychological bisexuality reflected the
presence of male or female genes which determined sex, the smaller
number of contrasexual genes producing a 'corresponding contrasexual
character which usually remains unconscious'.

Modern liberationists would be horrified by the claim that in women
Eros (the function of relationship) 'is an expression of their true nature
while their Logos is often only a regrettable accident'.[6] Jung first fully
realised the power of the anima, as we know, when the woman's voice
spoke to him at a turning-point in his self-analysis, but subsequently he
identified anima images in mythology, literature, and his patients'
dreams and fantasies. Manifestation of the anima can result in a
distorted view of the women a man encounters – whether his sister, wife-
to-be or sister-in-law – and explains the apparent idiocy of a man falling
in love with a totally unsuitable woman. A combination of narcissistic
love, mother imago and other influences, its power is exemplified in
Thomas Hardy's novel *The Well-Beloved*. There the protagonist falls in
love with three women – one when he is young, another in middle-age
and a third as he is approaching sixty. None reciprocates his love to the
point where they will marry him, but with a symmetry too perfect to be
convincing, one becomes the mother of his second love and she in turn of
his third. The slowly accumulating details at last force on him the
realisation that he has been trying to marry women closely resembling
one another all his life.

At a different level the anima becomes a personification of male erotic
desire, an image projected upon a real woman who may not reflect it,
but beyond erotic seduction the anima possesses a kind of age-old
wisdom. Epitomised in Rider Haggard's *She* – much quoted by Jung –
she is not only beautiful but an immortal priestess with access to arcane
knowledge. In therapeutic practice a schizoid intellectual alienated
from emotion and instinct may be led back to a form of sanity by an
erotically attractive woman. This happens in Herman Hesse's *Step-
penwolf*. Hesse was a writer Jung knew and analysed. In the novel the
alienated protagonist meets a commonplace young woman, who takes

pity on him, seduces him and initiates a process of psychological readjustment which realises his true Self.[7]

Jung expended less exposition on the Animus, the archetype of the Soul in woman, than he did on the Anima, and there was no balancing opposite *single* figure. The Animus expressed itself in a plurality of male figures from an older woman's infatuation with a substitute for her son to the young girl's surrender to a surrogate father. Distortions very similar to those produced by the Anima occur with the Animus as when it projects upon a husband someone quite different from the living reality. Correlative to the Animus a rigid system of ideas or opinions may render any conciliatory discussion between husband and wife a dangerous undertaking.

'Whereas', Jung wrote, 'the man has floating before him in clear outlines the significant form of a Circe or Calypso, the animus is better expressed as a bevy of Flying Dutchmen or unknown wanderers from over the sea, never quite clearly grasped, protean, given to persistent and violent motion. These expressions appear especially in dreams though in concrete reality they can be famous tenors, boxing champions or great men in faraway unknown cities.'[8]

Brilliantly realised in Ibsen's *Lady from the Sea*, Ellida's animus is so powerfully projected on the mysterious stranger, briefly encountered aboard ship, that she can no longer derive any real satisfaction from her husband. During the brief and enchanted meeting with the stranger they consummate their encounter by throwing rings into the sea, a ceremony Jung might well have endowed with the sacred quality of the Mysterium Coniunctionis. The climax of the play comes when the stranger reappears from the sea once more and Ellida has to make a choice between demon lover and husband, a confrontation of animus projection and reality frequently part of Jungian analysis.[9]

Not until a woman understands and out-faces those personifications of subjective desire and emotion generated by the animus do they cease to distort the conscious will and disappear as autonomous beings. Once Ellida confronts the true nature of the stranger from the sea he loses his magical powers, and at last her relationship with her husband is free to develop in 'true maturity'. Thus, among their other powers, the proper adjustment of the animus and anima creates a harmonious reformulation of relationships with the opposite sex.

The Personal Unconscious Jung saw as the repository of all those aspects of the life experience of which the conscious psyche was unaware, but he did not emphasise the repressive elements. Within it he found all varieties of what he had named the complex, from lesser conflicts to fully fledged dual personalities. As we know, he defined a complex as psychic entities that have escaped from the control of consciousness and split off from it, whence they may at any time hinder or help the conscious performance.[10]

As we have seen, all other components of Jung's model were

subserved by the Collective Unconscious represented as a part of nature, morally and intellectually neutral, but crystallising an infinite recession of human experience as if it were a psychic function handed down by generations as a phylogenetic substructure of the modern mind. Unlike Freud's concept of the Unconscious, the Collective Unconscious remained autonomous but complementary to consciousness and the seat of the universal primordial images, the archetypes.

The whole model was driven by something referred to as 'psychic energy' of which modern brain neurologists can find no trace. In keeping with his model of energetics, Jung assumed that the ruling principles of physical energy were reproduced in psychic energy, making it possible to speak of conservation, transformation and degradation in both cases. The precise relationship between psychic and physical energy cannot be demonstrated, but, like Janet, Jung assumed that such a relationship existed.

Although, as in physics, the quantity of energy available remained constant, psychic energy arose in the instincts and could be transferred from one to another. Jung also believed that when psychic energy seemed to disappear it was in reality carefully stored in the unconscious and could be recovered and redirected to many purposes.

In *The Structure and Dynamics of the Psyche*, Jung gave an elaborate analysis of the concept of psychic energy. The nuclear element in a complex, he argued, was characterised by the intensity of affect as when in word-association tests a patient underwent considerable stress reacting to a disturbing word. 'The constellatery power of the nuclear element corresponds to its value intensity, i.e. to its energy.' Exact quantitative measurement of physical energy had become a reality, but Jung argued that if only an *estimate* of such energy were possible it would 'still be [reasonable] to consider psychical events as forms of energy'. Precisely this formulation of *estimating* psychic energy was one of his principles for demonstrating its existence. Even the principle of entropy – taken from physics – had some equivalents, he claimed, in psychoanalytic experience. Entropy – the equal distribution of energy over a whole system to the point of inertia – could be found in some schizophrenic patients who remained motionless and mutistic within their interior world.

Following the example of Janet, Jung spoke of higher and lower psychic levels, but formulated a new principle of progression or regression. Progression used up psychic energy in adjusting to the demands of the external world, and, if that failed, stagnation or regression took place, finally involving the reactivation of unconscious conflicts. Unlike Freud, regression was not necessarily pejorative to Jung. When a man or woman lost touch with the deepest levels of the unconscious a temporary regression might bring about a necessary reconciliation between the frustrated archaic material and the possibly impoverished conscious self. It was at this point in the fascinating interconnections of his whole psychic system that symbols became creative transformers of psychic energy. The process had been beautifully exemplified in the successful outcome of Jung's self-analysis.

Turn now to the Superior and Inferior Functions of the model as a whole. Superior did not mean more effective or morally better, but simply predominating, while Inferior was not worse or lacking in desirable qualities, but simply unexercised. The Superior and Inferior Functions comprised not only thinking, feeling, intuition and sensation, but in the case of the Inferior also embraced those functions which have through neglect disappeared and become inactive in the Collective Unconscious.

The Collective Unconscious was, as we have seen, the source of the archetypes. Jung distinguishes between the archetypes in essence which are unconscious or latent, and archetypal images by which the raw material of the archetypes are brought into consciousness. If hierarchical importance is given to the archetypes, next to that of the Soul-Image (anima or animus) comes the archetype of the Spirit. This may find symbolic embodiment in many forms from the figure of the Old Wise Man to the medicine man of primitive peoples. Converted into a wizard the spirit-archetype becomes a figure capable of evil which can project on to the psychotherapist transforming him into a destructive magician. Nietzsche epitomised identification with the Old Wise Man in the figure of Zarathustra, and in his psychotic days experienced appropriate delusions of grandeur.

As we have seen, the kernel of the whole model, the most fundamental of the Archetypes, was the Self, much better conveyed by the German word *Selbst* – 'the itself' – a psychic totality resulting from the merging of many levels of the conscious and unconscious.

Given such a model how did his psychotherapy work? There were four methods. The association method, symptom analysis, anamnestic analysis and analysis of the unconscious. Reconstruction of the historical development of the neurosis played a vital part. At the outset the psychotherapist had to determine whether the anamnesis justified reductive-analytic treatment as practised by Freud, or Jung's synthetic-hermeneutic method. Conceding that reductive-analytic techniques sometimes brought good results, Jung claimed that progress often came to a halt when the patient experienced dreams of an archetypal character. Thus, he preferred the synthetic-hermeneutic technique, but there was no doubt that it best suited those patients in the second half of life whose condition involved religious, moral or philosophical problems. 'As a rule it is only in the second half of life that [the] opposition of functions and of conscious and unconscious attitudes is exacerbated to the point of conflict,' Jolande Jacobi wrote.[11]

Surprisingly, as we have seen, Jung claimed that among all his middle-aged patients the problem of religion was predominant. If that seemed to some to project his own lifelong struggle with Christianity, he also believed that returning to Mother Church might be part of a cure for, say, lapsed Catholics.

Unlike Freud, Jung placed more emphasis on contemporary situations, and brought the patient to full awareness of his present psychic state. Time and again Jung found that patients were living in artificial worlds where they converted reality into acceptable substitutes and failed to face the moral consequences of their actions. Although the analogy was false at several points, he liked to retell the story of the protagonist in Alphonse Daudet's *Tartarin sur les Alpes*. Tartarin believed that the Swiss Alps had been honeycombed with tunnels and galleries which removed the hazards from mountaineering. Full of false courage, as a result of this delusion, he daringly dashed halfway up the Jungfrau only to find no tunnels or galleries, and was duly overcome by terror. Thus, Jung said, many people at different stages of life suddenly become aware that they are living a lie because they have failed to face up to reality. The first step was to confront such patients with their reality situation and even to make them aware of its moral implications. It was, for instance, in Jung's view, immoral for one young patient to live on the earnings of an older woman teacher simply because she was in love with him. Freud, of course, would have abhorred any such moral judgements.

The second step in psychotherapy uncovered what Jung referred to as the pathogenic secret. An example of this was the case, familiar to the reader, of the young woman who felt that a man she desperately wanted to marry failed to reciprocate her love. Having married a second, far less satisfactory person, she proceeded to poison one of his children – only to discover that the first man had, in fact, been in love with her all the time. Slowly, skilfully, Jung unearthed and made her face up to the pathogenic secret which she had kept carefully locked away from even the most prying eyes.

Early in the psychotherapeutic process Jung encouraged active collaboration from the patient, and he might assign a variety of books to read or tasks to perform. Coping with the inevitable development of transference in a manner different from Freud's, Jung saw it as a collaboration with the patient leading to a confrontation of their mutual findings. Jung regarded Freud's negative and positive transference as unnecessary artefacts liable to prolong treatment, a kind of degrading bondage which could hinder more than help the analyst. But transference and countertransference certainly played a powerful role in many cases.

Dealing, initially, with the persona and shadow of the patient, the first dreams usually indicated what line the treatment should follow in the early stages. The shadow had to be assimilated into consciousness without continuing to accept the shadow's behaviour and motives. It had, in effect, to be met, contained and disarmed. Usually, spontaneous manifestations of the anima and animus followed in which, with a man, various personifications of a woman appeared in dreams and he came to recognise her as his anima. Brought, step by step, to overcome his anima projection, he at last saw women as they really were, and his relations with the opposite sex underwent a corresponding change. Similarly, the animus appeared in a woman's dreams and underwent modification.

There are two schools of thought about the 'transference principle' among Jungian psychotherapists today. In Zürich they tend to remain strictly Old Testament. In London positive and negative transference are accepted by many analysts. This has led to something of a schism between the two cities. In fact, of course, elaborate refinements of both schools are now practised in different parts of the world. Some Freudian analysts, for instance have abandoned dream analysis, whereas it remains of the utmost importance to Jungians in penetrating the 'pathogenic secrets'. Jung rejected Freud's distinction between the manifest and latent contents of dreams, accepting the first recollections of the dream at their surface value, but rather than exclude he developed symbols of interpretation. Moreover, Jung tended to allow a series of dreams to accumulate before risking interpretations, and, instead of Freud's free association, he employed amplification by means of active imagination. Above all, archetypal dreams were of the utmost significance.

Following the persona, the shadow, anima and animus came the archetypes of the Old Wise Man and the Magna Mater. These images appeared in dreams, fantasies and drawings, and had to be assimilated before finally confronting the archetype of the Self. The Magna Mater could roughly be interpreted as the primordial image of the Great Mother, and the Old Wise Man as representing 'certain motifs and contents of the collective unconscious'.[12] Detachment from the mother was one of the most important and delicate problems in the development of personality.

All these steps contributed to the realisation of the transcendent function, which was the progressive synthesis of conscious and unconscious 'material' leading to the process known as individuation. Put very briefly, individuation meant the harmonious unification of many differing aspects in the human personality. Individuation frequently began through the emergence of archetypal images of the Self, among them possibly the quaternity, the mandala and the divine child. Sometimes it was a matter of completing a triadic figure with a fourth term, thus making it into a quaternity. A series of 400 dreams published by Jung brought up the quaternity symbol no less than seventy-one times.[13] However, individuation was not a matter of progression but of deepening introversion toward the unconscious. 'The quaternity', Jung wrote, 'is an archetype of almost universal occurrence.' Thus, if you needed to describe the horizon, you were forced to name the four quarters of heaven, and if you desired to reorient the psyche, there were four aspects which had to be taken into account. 'We must have a function which ascertains that something is there (sensation): a second function which establishes *what* it is (thinking): a third function which states whether it suits us or not . . . (feeling) and a fourth function which indicates where it came from and where it is going (intuition).'[14]

Penetrating deeper into the unconscious, the patient elaborated some dreams in drawings, and others in paintings. It was legitimate to help the patient by means of *directed* association of dream images and the introduction of parallels from mythology or religion.

During the long and painful journey, the patient would experience enantiodromia, or the return of the opposite, as when Dante and Virgil reached the furthest depths of hell and at last began the opposite journey back toward purgatory and heaven. In a sense, the Collective Unconscious with its inexhaustible store of energy and potential wisdom had to be vanquished and brought to life again in a new guise, namely the concept of a transcendental Self.

Jolande Jacobi gives a clear recapitulation of the stages of therapy: 'The dark side has been made conscious, the contra-sexual element in us has been differentiated, our relation to spirit and primordial nature has been clarified. . . . We have penetrated deep into the unconscious, we have brought a good deal of its contents to light and we have learned to orient ourselves in its primordial world.'[15]

Life to Jung was a series of metamorphoses from the time the child emerged from the Collective Unconscious to the realisation of the totality of the Self through individuation. Perhaps the most important stage occurred at the turning-point (*lebenswende*) between the ages of thirty-two and thirty-eight when profound changes overtook the human psyche, adolescence and immaturity had to be abandoned and confrontation with the archetype of the Spirit and the Self begun.

The pretensions of the ego were assimilated by the Self, harmony replaced *angst*, and the individual no longer feared the inevitability of death. According to Jung's disciples, 'the natural end of life is not senility but wisdom' – a saying he frequently used but never printed to demonstrate the ultimate aim of psychotherapy. In itself something of a cliché, it belonged to the class of exhortation which desperately needed practical elaboration.

Over the years Jung refined many parts of his therapy. 'We should not try to "get rid of" a neurosis but rather to experience what it means, what it has to teach. . . . We should even learn to be thankful for it, otherwise we pass it and miss the opportunity of getting to know ourselves as we really are. . . . We do not cure it . . . it cures us. A man is ill but the illness is nature's attempt to heal him.'[16] Similarly he came to content himself with a maximum of four consultations a week, slowly reduced to one or two hours, because the patient 'must learn to stand on his own feet'.[17] He also believed in breaking off treatment every ten weeks or so 'in order to throw [the patient] back on his normal milieu. In this way he is not alienated from his world – for he really suffers from his tendency to live at another's expense. . . .'[18] There were many other refinements of his system and practice over the years.

Comparative analysis of different psychological systems involves three main factors – the constitutional, the predisposing and the precipitating. Jung's Collective Unconscious belonged to the constitutional, one of the most difficult to counter with scientific arguments because it emphasised pre-structural elements in psychic development which could not be checked by direct scientific examination. Precisely the same objection could be brought against most metapsychology, including Freud's, but Jung's was particularly susceptible since it dealt in phrases like numinous, synchronicity, antinodromia, and the Old Wise Man. There was a sense in which Jung's model of the human psyche converted autobiography into psychotherapy. He had experienced every detail of his model, and it was as if he had elevated an elaborate process of self-analysis into abstract theory convinced that it had universal application.

There was another sense in which many high-flown labels in Jung's model described relatively commonplace phenomena. If fear stimulates the adrenal glands and a reflex action takes place, or hunger reactivates primal drives, or love and hate evoke primordial emotions, that roughly describes the relationship between instinct, emotion and the endocrine system underlying much of Jung's psychology. Extrapolate from such a biological base exact psychological formulations like the archetypes, and one runs the risk of forcing the evidence into preconceived patterns. In the same sense that elaborate psychological details of Freudian or Jungian models can be reduced to primary and secondary processes, models of the Collective Unconscious are susceptible to a similar reductive methodology.

Whereas the Personal Unconscious carries some conviction, a Collective Unconscious seems to entail inheriting acquired characteristics – not a popular position among biologists today. Are the brain imprints of the archetype already inbuilt into the brain cells, or are they genetically coded to develop as the baby grows into the child? In either case there should exist a gene or part of a gene conditioning the brain's Collective Unconscious, which seems unlikely. In a letter to Michael Fordham (14 June 1958) Jung said: 'The assumption therefore that the (psychoid) archetypes are inherited is for many reasons far more probable than that they are handed down by tradition.'

It seems to the present writer more likely that many constituents of the gene pool retain over billions of years part of their old instinctual coding, which gives rise to irrational drives and primordial reaction formations. The pool of such conflicting reaction formations has acquired the lofty label Collective Unconscious. Thus, it is possible to reduce Jung's model of the Collective Unconscious to what were once called primary process and thereby strip it of many pretensions. But no self-respecting Jungian would do that. There were many other qualifications if not objections.

Implicitly the Collective Unconscious was the repository of archaic forms of racial experience crystallised in the Old Wise Man, but the very earliest brains from which ours were derivative should have – so to say – less unconscious from which to inherit. The earliest beginnings of the racial Unconscious should be relatively impoverished in Jungian terms, and the deeper one went back the more impoverished they should become.

If this appears to introduce chronology into a timeless process, irrespective of time, a deepening of imprint must have occurred as successive waves of experience reinforced their initial impact. Assuming that imprints have any scientific validity, being relatively weak and unstructured in the beginning an imprint would not have the power and structure of its full-blown counterpart. Edward Glover developed this approach: 'So far from being particularly wise the archetypes are of a predominantly superstitious and animistic nature. The forms of symbolism are also archaic, naïve and from the point of view of reality function profoundly obscurantist.'[19]

There were those who believed that Jung, instead of creatively using myths, drew his strength from one of the most easily exploded myths of all, the Myth of the Noble Savage. The fact that the transcendental Self could only be reached in the second half of life because the first half was unsuitable for the arduous process of Individuation, also troubled many people.

There were many other qualifications if not objections. So many Jungian categories were imprecise in modern psychological terms, such as his four functions – sensation, thinking, feeling and intuition. Irreconcilable differences arose between dreams unfolding in *pictures* and highly organised *mandalas* expressing psychic states. Precisely how the mandala corresponded to the totality of certain psychic states remained obscure, and it was difficult to grasp the process by which symbols were transmuted from the Collective Unconscious into rejuvenating forces.

As for the concept of the Shadow, poetically satisfactory though the 'dark and light' side might be, even when spelt out they lacked the precision required by modern academic psychology. The process of dream amplification also aroused suspicion. Whenever a dream appeared to originate from the collective unconscious, it became of special interest to Jung, but patients could not be expected to have *personal* associations with such dreams, and Jung did not hesitate to fill the gap by drawing on his knowledge of mythology, comparative religion and alchemy. In *Psychology and Alchemy*, Jung examined 400 dreams of a patient he saw only once before passing him on to a colleague, and of the 400 only forty-five occurred 'under direct observation'. Dreams concerning the patient's personal life were excluded for reasons of discretion, and left the impression that the patient encountered almost exclusively 'collective dreams'. Moreover, many of the dreams would remain very obscure, if not incomprehensible, but for Jung's technique of amplification by which he himself supplied the necessary analogies. As Anthony Storr said in his brilliant little study of Jung, 'Jung was . . . inclined to see collective material in dreams which could equally well be looked upon as merely personal. Like every creative person he sometimes oversold his own creative discoveries.'[20]

Interpersonal relations played a lesser part in Jung's model than in Freud's. The realisation of the Potential Self was all-important and open to the charge of selfishness since so much concentration on the individual's psyche endangered consideration for the psyche of others. Jungians believed that the proper realisation of Self automatically improved relations with others, but this could be seen as a rationalisation.

In his book *Freud or Jung*, Edward Glover developed such criticisms to the point of invective. According to which school you embraced, his attack was the result of Freudian jealousy, or convincing at a dismaying number of points. 'It would be absurd to suggest that any psychological system can be condensed to a few paragraphs without doing some violence to its outline: nor for that matter is it possible to indicate by a few quotations the immense lather of verbosity in which Jung's concepts are smothered. From the point of view of scientific exposition, Jung is at the best of times a confused writer apparently unable to call a spade a spade and to keep on calling it a spade.' Easily said, but the fact remains that the foundation on which Jung's model rests carries logical conviction if the personification of its parts and the powers disposed by the Collective Unconscious cannot be verified. Archaic material in the mind, repressed experience in the personal unconscious, bisexual elements in men and women, an experiential sense of self and a projected image of that self, all form the malleable raw material of a psyche whose primary and secondary processes are highly probable. Whether they can be satisfactorily assimilated in the elaborations of Jung's model is open to question. There is a sense in which his model becomes too symmetrically patterned to be satisfactory. The categories are too neatly interlocking. His insistence on reality correspondence to many if not all details of the model also made arbitrary what should have remained heuristic. For the rest, alleged scientific fact sometimes becomes aesthetically satisfying poetic imagery.

A recent edition of *The New Outline of Modern Knowledge*[21] removed Jung's work from the section on science to that on religion and the arts. As Michael Fordham commented: 'This change marks a trend to be found inside as well as outside the ranks of analytical psychology.'[22] In 1958 Michael Fordham set out to counteract that trend.

Appendix II
Jung's Sources

OVER THE YEARS Jung's interests gradually transferred from psychiatry through psychoanalysis to analytical psychology, from the theory of archetypes to the psychology of religious motifs and Eastern–Western philosophy.

The psychiatric sources of Jung's work are easier to illustrate and analyse than the complicated origins of his attempts to marry Eastern and Western thought. The whole approach to psychiatry was undergoing radical developments when he received his training. We have already seen in some detail the interpersonal and professional struggles between Bleuler and Jung, and it is clear that Jung underestimated the impetus given to his work by Bleuler's new attempt to repsychologise psychiatry. In his letters to Freud, Jung was similarly scathing about Pierre Janet, but at least four major categories were anticipated by Janet and later developed by Jung – subconscious fixed ideas, the function of synthesis, psychological automatism and dual personality can be traced in embryonic form in Janet's work. As for Binet, he anticipated Jung's introvert and extravert types in his description of two differently directed kinds of intelligence. Flournoy's research into the spiritualistic séances of Hélène Smith provided a base for some of Jung's insights into his young niece's equivalent experiences, and a phenomenon resembling cryptomnesia can also be traced in Flournoy's work.

Among Jung's contemporaries it is obvious that both Freud and Adler had considerable influence, if differences between Freud and Jung frequently crystallised contradictions in his theories. Jung subdivided the unconscious into personal and collective, and did not regard the unconscious as primarily regressive, but the whole concept had historical derivations in the work of von Hartmann, who described three levels of the unconscious – the quintessential unconscious, which constituted the substance of the universe, the psychological unconscious, which was directly related to the origin, development and evolution of all living organisms including man, and relative unconscious forming the wellspring of conscious life. The unconscious was, for Jung, a 'power-house' which could express itself creatively in a compensatory relationship with the conscious, not a repository of repressed material liable to disrupt conscious life. Jung took Freud's sexual libido and converted it into psychic energy, developed Freud's racial memory into the collective unconscious, put greater emphasis on the contemporary situation, saw dreams as experiences far richer than wish fulfilments which 'might contain ineluctable truths, philosophical

pronouncements, illusions, wild fantasies, memories, plans, anticipations, irrational experiences, even telepathic visions'.[1]

The persona and the shadow may or may not have had their origin in
Freud's ego and id, but there were some resemblances. Derivative as he
undoubtedly was in many ways from Freud, Jung eventually constructed a model which diverged at more points than it coincided and
contradicted Freud's whole approach to the life experience of the
psyche.

Jung repeatedly acknowledged Adler's influence on his work,
accepting the drive towards superiority as characteristic of some
neuroses and admitting the validity of some parts of Adler's dream
techniques. Agreeing with Adler that neurotics tend to manipulate
people in their life situations, he believed in therapeutic re-education.
Ernst Kretschmer produced his *Physique and Character* in 1921, the same
year as Jung's *Typology*.

The classics were automatically read by any intellectual young man
of Jung's generation, and there were many references in his work to
Schiller, Goethe, Homer, Plato, Socrates and Shakespeare. A number
of unexpected English writers also figured in his reading, including
Shaw, Blake, Rider Haggard, and H. G. Wells' novel *Christina Alberta's
Father* which successfully evokes an archetypal image of the animus.
Léon Daudet foreshadowed some parts of Jung's model in his novel
L'Hérèdo; Alphonse Daudet's *Tartarin sur les Alpes* anticipated the 'living
lie' of many patients' contemporary situation, and inspiration came
from Spitteler's *Imago*. 'Jung valued books like Rider Haggard's *She* and
H. G. Wells' novel *Christina Alberta's Father* just because they were naïve
and not psychologically sophisticated. Such books he thought revealed
the nature of the unconscious more clearly than did complicated works
like those of Proust.'[2] Works like *Psychological Types* had the most
complex origins, including authors as different as William Blake,
Martin Buber, Sandor Ferenczi, Jean-Jacques Rousseau, Johann
Holderlin, Theodore Lipps, Arthur Schopenhauer, Thomas Aquinas,
Arthur Waley and Wilhelm Wundt.

In maturity both Freud and Jung developed their psychotherapies
into philosophic reflections on God, man and the human condition,
Jung attempting a marriage of Eastern and Western philosophy. Jung's
sources, as we have seen, began in 1914 when he discovered Gnosticism
and claimed that the Gnostics were pioneers in the exploration of the
unconscious. Jung read Marcellin Berthelot, a historian of science who
regarded alchemy as 'a semi-rational semi-mystical science', and
Silberer, who pioneered the psychological interpretations of alchemical
operations. Paracelsus came to fascinate him, and he wrote a brilliant
essay analysing his work and personality, seeing him once more as a
pioneer of the psychologist of the unconscious. Jakob Boehme's work
inevitably played its part.

In the history of religion Jung read, of course, Origen and turned very early to the sacred books of the East, among them the Tibetan Book of the Dead where the experiences of the soul between death and reincarnation are beautifully described. The pilgrimage through the abode of the dead is divided into three parts, the first carried out in trance-like sleep, the second awakening to visions and the third a process similar to purgation by which the soul can pass into paradise. Known as the journey through the Bardo Thödel, Jung saw striking resemblances between that and a reversed process of individuation. Sir James Frazer's *Golden Bough* and *Totemism and Exogamy* were closely read. Lévy-Bruhl also figured in his bibliographies.

By 1929 Jung read the *Secret of the Golden Flower*, the Chinese book translated into German by his friend Richard Wilhelm, and discovered identities between Chinese symbols and those thrown up in his patients' dreams and fantasies, finally developing a link with Christian and alchemical symbols. Then came another Richard Wilhelm translation, the *I Ching* (*Book of Mutations*), based on the principle that each event is immortally endowed with characteristics belonging only to the moment of its occurrence. The book became an inspirational point for Jung's theory of synchronicity.

Yoga and its exponents Heinrich Zimmer and J. W. Hauer drew his close attention and, if he never practised Yoga, the Tantric symbolism enriched his understanding of the symbols of the collective unconscious. 'Viewed as training systems', Ellenberger wrote, 'certain varieties of Yoga could find parallels in the exercises of St Ignatius Loyola, with Schulz's autogenic training, and with Freud and Jung's methods of dynamic psychotherapy.' The experiments and writings of Professor J. B. Rhine in the field of extrasensory perception gave a fresh impetus to Jung's interests, but Rhine's meaningful coincidences Jung saw as the result of archetypal elements exerting their powers. Professor W. Pauli's scientific writings reaffirmed some of Jung's findings, as did the work of J. W. Dunne.

Any attempt to summarise the sources of Jung's thought and work must do serious violence to its encyclopedic complexity in many languages. Philosophers, theologians, psychologists, psychiatrists, novelists, poets, mystics, orientalists, ethnologists all figured multitudinously in his erudition. Philosophically, Nietzsche remained a writer who persistently drew him back to book after book, partly because Jung saw him as a man with a shadow personality which broke through to shower the reader with fascinating archetypal material straight out of the unconscious. In the library of the Jung Institute in Zürich, Jung deposited ten typewritten volumes containing reports of seminars he gave between 1934 and 1939 on *Zarathustra*. They make fascinating reading and constitute one of the most elaborate and penetrating analyses of Nietzsche's work. Nietzsche is sometimes seen as Jung's Old Wise Man but demoniacally possessed by the Collective Unconscious. Kant, of course, was also obligatory reading in philosophy. Inevitably, the philosophers of the unconscious also figured large in his library, from Carl Gustav Carus through Schopenhauer to von Hartmann. Whether Schleirermacher was important is in doubt, but he certainly pioneered the idea of total self-realisation as the only way to true freedom which must be achieved by calling into being man's primordial self-image. Friedrich Creuzer recurs in his reading and provided a wealth of cleverly interpreted myths and symbols where the primitive mind enshrined its experiences mythologically. Bachofen achieves little mention in Jung's work but was a pioneer in symbolic decipherment. Especially he unravelled the theme of patriarchy overwhelming matriarchy, the struggle being enshrined, once more symbolically, in mankind's memory. Ellenberger believes that this may have been one point of inspiration for Jung's formulation of the anima and animus. There is a reference as early as 1871 to the anima and animus in Professor E. B. Tylor's *Primitive Culture*, but it is uncertain whether Jung read Tylor.[3]

Justinius Verner and his celebrated medium Friedericke Hauffe certainly predisposed Jung to believe in Hélène Preiswerk's mediumistic performance. Rose Mehlich's *Fichtes Seelenlehre und ihre Beziehung zur Gegenwart* found certain correlatives between Fichte's notion of the soul and Jung's archetype of the Self and Soul. Boehme, Saint-Martin, Swedenborg and von Baader all contributed to the psychology of the unconscious. The work of the German ethnologist Adolf Bastian deeply influenced the Italian psychiatrist Tanzi, who saw a connection between the rituals of primitive tribes and the fantasies of his patients – as did Jung. It would need another book to give any satisfactory account of Jung's sources, their application to his work and his intellectual development. Each of the volumes of the *Collected Works* contains a bibliography.

Appendix III

Jung's Influence

WHEREAS no one needs to question Jung's influence on the development of psychoanalysis, analytical psychology and psychotherapy, there are those among his overzealous disciples who can easily trace his thinking in practically every sphere of human thought. Not only philosophy, politics, religion, science, art, they claim, have interacted in one way or another with the work of the Master: it is difficult to exclude him from any area of human culture.

A particularly dangerous example of extrapolation occurs in Marie Louise von Franz's attempt to correlate modern physics with the concepts of analytical psychology in *Man and His Symbols*. Taking Niels Bohr's principle of complementarity, she compares it with Jung's conscious and unconscious mind – an analogy as dangerously inexact as deriving free will from Heisenberg's *Principle of Indeterminacy*.[1] Certainly the physicist Wolfgang Pauli, an old friend of Jung, studied the role of archetypal symbolism in scientific concepts. He also pointed out that 'our idea of the evolution of life requires a revision that might take into account an area of interrelation between the unconscious psyche and biological processes', but that was a very different statement.

Jung's influence on psychoanalysis is not only much clearer but also recognised by the Freudians.[2] Jung introduced the principle of analysts being analysed, he coined the terms 'imago' and 'complex', 'introvert' and 'extravert', and inspired Freud to revise his libido theory to accommodate the term 'narcissism' – although Havelock Ellis would have claimed priority. As Ellenberger said: 'Jung's pre-occupation with myths and his Metamorphoses and Symbols of Libido stimulated Freud to write his *Totem and Taboo*.'[3]

The Neo-Freudians owe much to Jung, whose concept of individuation anticipated notions of self-actualisation, and existential analysts are similarly indebted. Three of Erikson's eight stages of development in the individual can be traced to Jung's equivalent model. Painting as a means of insight into the unconscious has developed widely, and Eysenck employed introversion–extraversion as one of the dimensions of personality.

Jung's earlier work was as influential as his later, even if it has now been superseded and no longer impresses academic psychologists. Word-association tests became part of the daily round in Swiss mental hospitals, inspired the Rorschach tests and led the way to the invention of a lie detector. His work in schizophrenia refined and developed Bleuler's, he identified the complexes and archetypes, he applied his findings to a new psychotherapy contra-distinguished at many points from Freud's, he gave another dimension to analytical theory in his concept of the collective unconscious, and discovered – in company with others – the similarity between schizophrenic dreams, fantasies and experiences and the fundamental material of universal myths. The collective and personal unconscious could henceforth be seen as creative, not repressive or distorting forces. Sexuality ceased to be the central driving force for any self-respecting Jungian, and was replaced with psychic energy. His preoccupation with myths, fairy tales, symbols and archetypes led into a new understanding of their psychological significance. Jung opened up widespread research into the relationship between mythology and psychology, and several comparative studies by mythologists and Jungians have been published such as Karl Kerenyi's joint publication with Jung.[4]

In literary criticism the cross-fertilisation has been equally rich. Throughout Northrop Frye's *The Anatomy of Criticism* Jung's influence emerges. Maud Bodkin's *Archetypal Patterns in Poetry* is directly derivative in its very title. She points out that Jung attributes the special emotional significance possessed by certain poems to a stirring in the reader's mind, 'within or beneath his conscious response, of unconscious forces which he terms "primordial images" or archetypes. These archetypes he describes as "psychic residue of numberless experiences of the same type", experiences which have happened not to the individual but to his ancestors and of which the results are inherited in the structure of the brain, a priori determinants of individual experience.'[5]

She carries her examination into prose as well as poetry, citing H. G. Wells's story of 'Preemby' as an example – ' "a small, irrelevant fledgling of a personality" to whom is presented in dream and fantasy the figure of Sargon King of Kings in such compelling fashion that he is led to identify himself with it'. This, she says, is a clear example of archetypal experience.[6] She quotes Professor Gilbert Murray in support of Jung. Describing the effect of great poetic drama, he said that such themes were strange to us, 'yet there is that within us which leaps at the sight of them, a cry of the blood which tells us we have known them always'.[7] Jung's influence can also be traced in J. B. Priestley's *Literature and Western Man*, Gottfried Diener's *Faust's Weg zu Helena* and James Kirsch's *Shakespeare's Hamlet*.

Artistically, Eric Neumann's analysis of Henry Moore, Herbert Read's studies of painting and Michael Tippett's musical criticism all fall within the shadow of the Master. In fact a whole aesthetic has been worked out based on Jungian principles.[8] The sociologist David Reisman in *The Lonely Crowd* developed Jung's concept of introversion and extraversion in sociological terms. As for religion, Ellenberger remarks, 'Jung's concepts of the natural function of religion and the existence of religious archetypes . . . provoked lively discussion in religious circles. Several theologians thought that they had found in

Jung an ally against atheism, others blamed his psychologism.' Paul
Tillich certainly found Jung's archetypal patterns a reaffirmation of
Protestant theology. No less than three Catholic theologians were suf-
ficiently influenced by Jung to write comprehensive studies – Father
Goldbrunner, Father Victor Whyte and Father Hostie.

Dietrich Schindler brought Jungian psychology into the study of
political philosophy, and Hans Fehr performed a similar feat in
jurisprudence. The Swiss economist Eugen Böhler, a friend of Jung,
attempted to show that economic life was deeply influenced by forms of
thinking structured like those in myth and fantasy. Historically, Arnold
Toynbee classified many world religions in terms of Jung's psychological types.[9]

Chomsky's innate structures and Lévi-Strauss's structuralism derive
from a methodology similar to Jung's. The theoretical programmes of
Chomsky, de Sassure and Piaget are based on the analysis of surface
phenomena derived from underlying structures through the interpo-
sition of transformational rules. It is indeed possible to see them
justifying Jung's attempt to 'structure' the collective unconscious, but it
would be a mistake to identify or even correlate the very different types of
structure. There is also a sense in which recent neurophysiological
research sets up echoes of Jung's theory of synchronicity. As Colin
Blakemore said in his 1976 Reith Lectures: 'the past two decades suggest
that there is a feed forward mechanism in neural functioning by which an
about to occur action is transmitted by an efferent copy of that action
around the nervous system'.

Observation of the response to drugs reported in such studies as *The
Varieties of Psychedelic Experience* by R. L. Masters and J. Houston also
demonstrates that subjects produce collective archetypal material of the
type brought to light by Jung.[10]

Extrapolate some of the structures underlying Jung's thinking – the
principle of opposites, of complementarity, of phylogenetic structures,
of feminine and masculine, conscious and unconscious – and it is not
difficult to find analogies in many fields.

Notes and Sources

Prologue
1. This, according to those who knew his library, was odd. They were not aware that he had ever read Popper.
2. *Journal of Analytical Psychology*, 20.2.xxx (1975).
3. Ernest Jones, author's interview, 14 July 1955.
4. M. Fordham (ed.), *Contact with Jung*, 218.
5. A. I. Allenby, author's interview, 10 July 1974.
6. Ibid.
7. Ibid.
8. Fordham, *Jung*, 191.
9. Letter to the author, 31 July 1974.
10. Fordham, *Jung*, 222.
11. Ibid.
12. Ernest Jones, author's interview, 10 July 1955.
13. Ernest Jones, author's interview, 7 May 1975. Franz Jung, letter to the author, 5 Sept 1975.
14. The Eranos meetings were held annually at the home of Frau Olga Froebe-Kapteyn in a hall specially built for that purpose near Ascona, Switzerland.
15. Dr Michael Fordham, author's interview, June 1974.
16. J. L. Henderson, letter to the author, 31 July 1974.
17. *Freud–Jung Letters*, 2 June 1910.
18. Jung, *Memories, Dreams, Reflections*, 328.
19. Ibid. 329.

Chapter 1. Forebears
1. *Eduard His Basler Gelehrte des 19 Jahunderts*, 69–76.
2. Lancelot Whyte, author's interview, 10 June 1970.
3. H. Haupt, *Ein vergessener Dichter* . . .
4. G. Steiner, *Erinnerungen au Carl Gustav Jung*, 122–3.
5. Ibid.
6. Ibid.
7. E. Jung (ed.), *Aus den Tagebuchen meines Vaters*.
8. There is no reference to the legend in the grandfather's diaries. He mentions that he once saw Goethe in Weimar.
9. Jung, *Letters*, vol. 2, 30 Dec 1959.
10. H. F. Ellenberger, *The Discovery of the Unconscious*, 661.
11. A. Jaffé, *Jung Erinnerungen, Traume, Gedanken*, 399–407.
12. Jung, *Memories*.
13. Jaffé, *Jung Erinnerungen*, 399–407.
14. Ellenberger, *Discovery*, 662.
15. Jaffé, *Jung Erinnerungen*, 399–407.
16. Jung, *Memories*, 96.
17. Ibid. 96.
18. Ibid. 58.

Chapter 2. The First Years
1. Ellenberger, *Discovery*, 660.
2. Ibid.
3. P. Berteaux, *La Vie quotidienne en Allemagne au temps de Guillaume II*, 27.

4. Jung, *Memories*, 21.
5. Ibid.
6. Ibid.
7. John Layard, author's interview, 10 June 1959.
8. Jung, *Memories*, 22.
9. Ibid. 23.
10. Ernest Jones, author's interview, June 1955.
11. Jung, *Memories*, 22.
12. John Layard, author's interview, 10 June 1959.
13. A. Oeri, *Die Kulturelle Bedeutung der Komplexen Psychologie*.
14. John Layard, author's interview, 10 June 1959.
15. Jung, *Memories*, 26.
16. Hugo Charteris, author's interview, 14 March 1963.

Chapter 3. Village School to Gymnasium
1. Jolande Jacobi, author's interview, 6 Jan 1968.
2. Oeri, *Die Kulturelle*.
3. Jung, *Memories*, 31.
4. Laryngeal spasm is common in children, and very alarming when it happens.
5. Jung, *Memories*, 30.
6. E. A. Bennet, author's interview, 6 Jan 1968.
7. Jung, *Memories*, 34.
8. Jolande Jacobi, author's interview, 6 Jan 1968.
9. Jung, *Memories*. John Layard, author's interview, 14 June 1956.
10. John Freeman, BBC interview, 22 Oct 1959.
11. *Freud–Jung Letters*, letter 49J, 28 Oct 1907.
12. John Freeman, BBC interview, 22 Oct 1959.
13. Ibid.
14. Hugo Charteris, author's interview, 14 March 1963.
15. John Layard, author's interview, 10 June 1959.
16. Ruth Bailey, author's interview, 17 Sept 1974.
17. Jung, *Memories*. John Layard, author's interview, 10 June 1959.
18. Franz Jung, author's interview, 7 May 1975.
19. Ibid.
20. Oeri, *Die Kulturelle*.
21. Jung's diary, 26 Oct 1859. Quoted in *Die Kulturelle*.
22. Ibid.
23. Confirmed by Hugo Charteris, author's interview, 14 March 1963.
24. Jung, *Memories*, 72.
25. Ibid. H. G. Wells, author's interview, 14 Jan 1941.
26. Jung, *Memories*, 55.

Chapter 4. Early Religious Struggles
1. Lancelot Whyte, author's interview, 10 July 1970.
2. Ernest Jones, author's interview, 12 June 1955.
3. He elaborated on this to E. A. Bennet, author's interview, 18 June 1974.
4. Ernest Jones, author's interview, 12 June 1955.
5. Jolande Jacobi, author's interview, 6 Jan 1968.
6. Jung, *Memories*, 50.
7. John Freeman, BBC interview, 22 Oct 1959.

Chapter 5. Intellectual Beginnings
1. Jung, *Memories*, 79.
2. John Freeman, BBC interview, 22 Oct 1959.
3. Dr James Hillman, author's interview, 7 Sept 1974.
4. Jung, *Memories*, 78.

5. Once again in his last years Jung seemed to adopt his father's attitude, as confirmed in an interview with John Layard.
6. Jung, *Memories*, 83.
7. Ibid. 84.

Chapter 6. University and a Career

1. A. Oeri, *Spring 1970*, 182.
2. Ellenberger, *Discovery*, 665.
3. Oeri, *Die Kulturelle*.
4. Ibid. 524–8.
5. Ibid.
6. Ibid.
7. Oeri, *Spring 1970*, 186.
8. Ibid. 185.
9. Jung, *Memories*, 100.
10. Ibid.
11. Verbal evidence – Ruth Bailey, who became his companion for the last six years of his life.
12. Oeri, *Die Kulturelle*, 524–8.
13. Oeri, *Spring 1970*, 185; *Die Kulturelle*.
14. Oeri, *Spring 1970*, 185; *Die Kulturelle*.
15. Oeri, *Spring 1970*, 185; *Die Kulturelle*.
16. Minutes of Student Association.
17. Steiner, *Erinnerungen*, 146–7.
18. Minutes of Student Association.
19. Steiner, *Erinnerungen*, 150.
20. Ibid. 154.
21. Ellenberger, *Discovery*, 688.
22. Steiner, *Erinnerungen*, 154.
23. Ellenberger, *Discovery*, 689.
24. A member of the Forestry Commission.
25. Lancelot Whyte, author's interview, 10 July 1970.
26. Ellenberger, *Discovery*, 689.
27. Jung, *On the Psychology and Pathology of So-Called Occult Phenomena*, 43.
28. Ellenberger, *Discovery*, 690–1.
29. Notes on the Seminar in Analytical Psychology . . . Jung, Zürich, 23 March–6 July 1925.
30. *Archives de Psychologie*, II, 85–6.
31. Basel University Archives.
32. Jung, *Memories*, 111.

Chapter 7. The Young Psychiatrist

1. Ellenberger, *Discovery*, 667.
2. Jung confirmed this description by Ernest Jones.
3. Oeri, *Spring 1970*, 185.
4. Anthony Storr, letter to the author, 21 April 1975.
5. Oeri, *Spring 1970*, 185.
6. Ellenberger quotes Dr Alphonse Maeder, then on the staff of the Burghölzli, *Discovery*, 739.
7. E. A. Bennet, author's interview, 4 Aug 1974.
8. Information supplied by Dr Peter Johnson.
9. Dr Alphonse Maeder.
10. A typescript discovered in Jung's posthumous papers, 'On Dreams', 25 June 1901.
11. Ellenberger, *Discovery*, 287.
12. Alphonse Maeder: Ellenberger interview.
13. Ibid.

14. Jung, *Diagnostische Assoziationsstudien*, 1906.
15. Jung, *The Psychogenesis of Mental Illness*, 99; *Collected Works*, vol. 3.
16. Ibid. p. 102.
17. Ellenberger, *Discovery*, 692.
18. Jung, *Memories*, 118.
19. Jung, *On the Psychology and Pathology of So-Called Occult Phenomena; Collected Works*, vol. 1, p. 48.
20. Ibid. 49.
21. Ibid. 56.

Chapter 8.   Family Life Begins
 1. Ruth Bailey, author's interview, 19 June 1975.
 2. Author's interview, letter to author, 2 July 1974.
 3. Stephen Black, BBC interview, 24 July 1955.
 4. Dr Gerhard Adler, interview. The letters are in the Jung family archive and will not be available for twenty years.
 5. Ellenberger, *Discovery*, 668. Lancelot Whyte interview.
 6. E. Jones, *Freud*, vol. 1, pp. 304-5.
 7. An English psychiatrist, interviewed June 1974, who wishes to remain anonymous.
 8. Author's interview, 7 May 1975. Franz Jung, letter to the author, 2 July 1974.
 9. *Freud–Jung Letters*, letter J256, 18 May 1911.
10. Ernest Jones, author's interview, 15 June 1957.
11. Jung, *Memories*, 120.
12. Ibid.
13. C. G. Jung, 'Zur Psychologischen Tatbestandsdiagnostik', *Zentralblatt für Nervenheilkunde und Psychiatrie*, XXVIII (1905), 813–15.
14. Aniela Jaffé defines the psychogalvanic reflex as 'a momentary decrease in the apparent electrical resistance of the skin, resulting from the activity of the sweat glands in response to mental excitement'.
15. There are many folders in the archives of the Burghölzli preserving case-histories. L. van der Post, *Jung and the Story of Our Time*, 127.
16. Jung, *Memories*, 145.
17. First published as 'Experimentelle Untersuchung uber Assoziationen Gesunder', *Journal für Psychologie und Neurologie* (Leipzig, 1904), III.
18. *Freud–Jung Letters*, letter 1F, 11 April 1906.
19. Jones, *Freud*, vol. 2, p. 124.
20. First published as *Die Hysterielehre Freuds: Eine Erwiderung auf die Aschaffenburg Kritik; Collected Works*, vol. 4, p. 3.

Chapter 9.   Friendship with Freud – First Phase
 1. Freud, *Sammlung Kleiner Schriften zür Neurosenlehre* (1906), vol. 1.
 2. *Freud–Jung Letters*, letter 2J.
 3. Ibid.
 4. *Collected Works*, vol. 3, paras 123–32.
 5. *Freud–Jung Letters*, letter 9J, 29 Dec 1906.
 6. Ibid.
 7. See subsequent correspondence of Emma Jung – quoted later.
 8. *Freud–Jung Letters*, letter 12J, 8 Jan 1907.
 9. Jung, *Dementia Praecox*, para 132.
10. Ernest Jones has the wrong date for this meeting in his Life of Freud – Sunday, 27 Feb.
11. Jung, *Memories*, 147.
12. M. Freud, *Glory Reflected*, 109.
13. Ibid.
14. Ernest Jones, author's interview, 15 June 1957.
15. Information supplied by Franz Jung to William McGuire from Frau Jung's diary.

16. *Freud–Jung Letters*, letter 18F, 7 April 1907.
17. Ibid. letter 19J, 11 April 1907.
18. Jones, *Freud*, vol. 2, p. 125.
19. Jung, *Memories*, 146.
20. Jung, *Mental Disease and the Psyche; Collected Works*, vol. 3, p. 227.
21. Jung, *Dementia Praecox*, 162.
22. *Freud–Jung Letters*, letter 33J, 28 June 1907.
23. K. Abraham, *Selected Papers*, 37.
24. *Freud–Jung Letters*, letter 39J, 19 Aug 1907.
25. Ibid. letter 42F, 2 Sept 1907.
26. Ibid. letter 49J, 28 Oct 1907.
27. *Freud Letters to Ferenczi*, 8 Dec 1912.
28. Ibid. 6 Oct 1910.
29. *Freud–Jung Letters*, letter 49J, 28 Oct 1907.
30. Ernest Jones gave the author a fairly detailed account of what took place.
31. *Letters of Sigmund Freud and Karl Abraham, 1907–26*, 13 Oct 1907.
32. Ernest Jones, author's interview, 14 June 1955.
33. Ibid.
34. *Freud–Jung Letters*, letter 54J, 30 Nov 1907.

Chapter 10.   Freud – the Second Phase

1. Meyer was a professor of psychiatry and neurology in Konigsberg University.
2. E. Jones, *Free Association*, 165.
3. Jones, *Freud*, vol. 2, p. 47.
4. Ibid. p. 52.
5. Ernest Jones, author's interview, 10 June 1955.
6. Jones, *Freud*, vol. 2, p. 49.
7. *Letters of Freud and Abraham*, 34.

Chapter 11.   The Quarrel Develops

1. Ruth Bailey, author's interview, 2 Aug 1974.
2. *Collected Works*, vol. 3, 102:114.
3. Ernest Jones, author's interview, 15 June 1955.
4. Jung, *Memories*, 128.
5. *Freud–Jung Letters*, letter 129F, 25 Jan 1909. Prof. Manfred Bleuler stated categorically to me in a letter that there had been no question of his father depriving Jung of his job.

Chapter 12.   First Visit to America

1. *Freud–Jung Letters*, letter 115J, 27 Nov 1908.
2. *Collected Works*, vol. 17, p. 11.
3. Emma repeated many of these details to Ruth Bailey, Jung's companion later in life.
4. Franz Jung, author's interview, 7 May 1975.
5. Ibid.
6. Psychiatrist at the Burghölzli 1902–4, who collaborated with Jung on word-association tests. He was married to a cousin of Jung.
7. *Freud–Jung Letters*, letter 133, 7 March 1909.
8. Jung, *Memories*, 152.
9. Ibid.
10. Brome, *Freud and His Circle*, 97–8.
11. Jung, *Memories*, 153.
12. E. A. Bennet, *C. G. Jung*, 44.
13. Brome, *Freud*, 100.
14. Jung, *Memories*, 154.
15. Ibid. 155.
16. Ernest Jones, author's interview, 15 June 1955.

17. Jung, *Memories*, 156.
18. Bennet, *Jung*, 41.
19. Jung, *Memories*, app. 2, 6 Sept 1909.
20. Ibid. app. 2, 6 Sept 1909.
21. Ibid. app. 2, 8 Sept 1909.
22. Brome, *Freud*, 106.
23. 8 Sept 1909.
24. Ernest Jones, author's interview, 10 June 1955.
25. 14 Sept 1909.

Chapter 13.   Struggles in the Zürich Circle
 1. Lancelot Whyte, author's interview, 7 Feb 1969.
 2. *Freud–Jung Letters*, 180J, 20 Feb 1910.
 3. Ibid. 181J, 2 March 1910.
 4. In the boxes of papers which contain some of Ernest Jones's material for his biography of Freud, there occur letters from Putnam to Jones, from Brill, Ferenczi and Hans Sachs to Freud. Some details of what follows are drawn from this source.
 5. Jones, *Free Association*, 215.
 6. Ibid.
 7. Ferenczi to Freud, 8 Feb 1910.
 8. Jones, *Freud*, vol. 2, p. 77.
 9. 3 April 1910.
10. *Freud–Jung Letters*, letter 189J, 30 April 1910.
11. *Letters of Freud and Abraham*, 95.
12. *Freud–Jung Letters*, letter 193J, 24 May 1910.
13. These letters were recently discovered.
14. *Freud–Jung Letters*, letter 259J, 12 June 1911.
15. Ibid. 196J, 2 June 1910.
16. This is, of course, a Latin translation from the Greek deriving from the Delphic Oracle.
17. *Freud–Jung Letters*, letter 221F, 25 Nov 1910.
18. Ibid. letter 230J, 18 Jan 1911.

Chapter 14.   A Love-Affair
 1. Following details from an unpublished document provided by Dr Gerhard Adler.
 2. Two long interviews with Dr Gerhard Adler yielded invaluable material, some of which occurs in the following pages, but Dr Adler must not be held responsible for all I say. There were several other carefully questioned witnesses. Dr Adler is, of course, a leading figure among the Jungians in London. The interviews took place on 24 Nov 1973 and 17 July 1974.
 3. *Freud–Jung Letters*, letter 175J, 30 Jan 1910.
 4. Ibid. letter 269J, 29 Aug. 1911.
 5. This information does not come from Dr Gerhard Adler.
 6. John Layard, author's interview, 15 Sept 1960.
 7. *Freud–Jung Letters*, 24 Nov 1911. Emma Jung.
 8. Ibid. 6 Nov 1911. Emma Jung.
 9. Jones, *Freud*, vol. 2, p. 102.
10. *Freud–Jung Letters*, 14 Nov 1911. Emma Jung.
11. Jung, 'Wandlungen und Symbole', *Jahrbuch der Psychoanalyse* (1911), III, 120–227; *Zweiter Teil* (1912), IV.
12. *Freud–Jung Letters*, 14 Nov 1911. Emma Jung.
13. Interview with Mrs Lucy Baynes, first wife of H. G. Baynes who became Jung's assistant in Zürich.

Chapter 15.   Freud–Jung: the Climax
 1. Jung, *Memories*, 159.

2. Brome, *Freud*, 116.
3. Jung, 'Wandlungen und Symbole'.
4. *Collected Works*, vol. 5, pp. 223–4.
5. Ibid. This anticipated the Kleinian paranoid-schizoid position of very early childhood, the good and bad breast involving the introjection of two mothers, the good and bad mother.
6. 2 Jan'1912. *Neue Züricher Zeitung*. The correspondence quoted here runs from 2 Jan–19 Feb 1912.
7. N. Malcolm, *Ludwig Wittgenstein: A Memoir*.
8. Based on many newspaper reports in the Swiss popular press.
9. *Freud–Jung Letters*, letter 297J, 15 Feb 1912.
10. Ibid. letter 285J, 24 Nov 1911.
11. Ibid. letter 286F, 30 Nov 1911.
12. John Layard, author's interview, 15 Sept 1960.

Chapter 16. Jung Attacks Freud
1. Brill, *Journal of Nervous and Mental Diseases*, vol. 95, no. 5 (May 1912), p. 547.
2. *Collected Works*, vol. 4, p. 89.
3. Ibid. p. 105.
4. Ibid. pp. 164–5.
5. Ernest Jones, author's interview, 14 June 1955.
6. *Collected Works*, vol. 4, pp. 118–22.
7. Ibid. p. 166.
8. Jones archive for Freud biography.
9. *Letters of Freud and Abraham*, 125.
10. Minutes, IV, and *Zeitschrift*, I (1912), 112; Stekel's account of the break, *Autobiography of Wilhelm Stekel* (1950), 142.
11. Jones, *Freud*, vol. 2, p. 165.
12. Holograph: *Ihrigen* ('yours') in place of *ihrigen* ('theirs'). *Freud–Jung Letters*, letter 335J.
13. Ibid. letter 338J, 18 Dec 1912.
14. Ibid. letter 340F, 22 Dec 1912.

Chapter 17. The Final Break
1. *Zeitschrift*, I. 3 (1913), 310, Bulletin section.
2. L. Andreas-Salomé, *The Freud Journal*, 168.
3. Freud, *History of the Psycho-Analytic Movement, Collected Works*, vol. 14, p. 45.
4. 13 Nov 1913.
5. *Freud–Jung Letters*, letter 357J. 27 Oct 1913.
6. Jung, *Memories*, 162.
7. Freud, *History*, pp. 42–3.
8. M. Robert, *La Révolution psychanalytique*, vol. 1, p. 226.

Chapter 18. Jung's Breakdown
1. Foreword to the 4th Swiss ed.
2. Jolande Jacobi, author's interview, 24 Nov 1963.
3. No equivalent appointment exists in England. It gives the appointee the right to lecture at the University, usually in an unpaid capacity.
4. Anthony Storr, letter to the author, 21 April 1975.
5. John Layard, author's interview, 15 Sept 1960.
6. Notes on the Seminar in Analytical Psychology (Zürich, 23 March–6 July 1925).
7. Lancelot Whyte, author's interview, 10 June 1970.
8. Jung, *Memories*, 168–9.
9. John Layard, author's interview, 15 Sept 1960.
10. Jung, *Memories*, 169.
11. A. Storr, *Jung*, 33.

12. Ibid.
13. Ibid.
14. J. W. von Goethe, *Faust*, pt 1.
15. L. Frey-Rohn, author's interview, 5 May 1975.
16. van der Post, *Jung*, 177.
17. Elliott Jaques showed in *Death and the Mid-Life Crisis* that many creative people experience a crisis around the age of thirty-eight from which they emerge to produce a different kind of work.
18. Anthony Storr disagrees with this diagnosis. 'I don't think Jung was a manic depressive. I think that his psychosis or near-psychosis was more of the nature of a schizophrenic episode' (letter, 10 Nov 1975).

    D. W. Winnicott, reviewing Jung's reminiscences (*International Journal of Psycho-Analysis*, April-July 1964) describes Jung as a 'recovered case of infantile psychosis'. Jung, he says, 'gives us a picture of childhood schizophrenia'. His defences settled down into 'a splitting of the personality'.

Chapter 19. Recovery, and Work Resumed

1. *Collected Works*, vol. 18, p. 67.
2. Franz Jung, author's interview, 7 May 1975.
3. BBC interview, 27 July 1975.
4. Author's interview with X, who wishes to remain anonymous, 7 Sept 1974.
5. Author's interviews carried out in Zürich, May 1975, and elsewhere June 1970.
6. Ibid.
7. L. Frey-Rohn, author's interview, 5 May 1975.
8. Anthony Storr, letter to the author, 10 Nov 1975.
9. Erna Naeff, Toni's sister, showed the author some beautiful mandalas painted and presented by Jung to Toni. One, at least, revealed considerable artistic talent.
10. *Collected Works*, vol. 8, pp. 350–2.
11. Jung, *Memories*, 187.
12. Ibid.
13. *Collected Works*, vol. 10, par. 803.
14. Ellenberger, *Discovery*, 672.
15. Jung, 'La Structure de l'inconscient', *Archives de Psychologie*, XVI (1910) 152–9.
16. *Collected Works*, vol. 7, p. 43.
17. A. Teilhard, *L'Ame et l'écriture*, 89–94.

Chapter 20. Some Case-Histories

1. R. Ellmann, *James Joyce*, 475.
2. Lancelot Whyte, author's interview, 10 July 1970.
3. Ibid.
4. Ellmann, *Joyce*, 435.
5. Lancelot Whyte, author's interview, 10 July 1970.
6. Oscar Schwarz, interview, 10 Oct 1956.
7. Interview, Prof. Siegfried Giedion and Dr Casola Giedion-Welcker. Ellmann, *Joyce*.
8. 16 Oct 1934.
9. P. Hutchins, *James Joyce's World* (1957), 184–5.
10. Ibid.
11. Ruth Bailey, author's interview, 12 July 1974.
12. A series of interviews established her story, June–July and Aug 1973.
13. Lancelot Whyte, author's interview, 10 July 1970.
14. Jung's literary executor Walther Niehus.
15. Lancelot Whyte, author's interview, 10 July 1970.
16. *Collected Works*, vol. 16, p. 41.
17. Montagu Norman, *Diaries*, 25 Feb 1913.
18. A. Boyle, *Montagu Norman*, 91.
19. Ibid. 92.

20. Norman, *Diaries*, 21 April 1913.
21. R. Norman, *Autobiographical Notes*.

Chapter 21.   Travels Abroad
1. Jolande Jacobi, author's interview, 4 July 1960.
2. Franz Jung, author's interview, 7 May 1975.
3. Ibid.
4. BBC interview, 27 July 1975. Jolande Jacobi, author's interview, 24 Nov 1963.
5. Dr Gerhard Adler, author's interview, 24 Nov 1973.
6. *Journal of Analytical Psychology*, 20 Feb 1975.
7. Lancelot Whyte, author's interview, 1 Jan 1971.
8. Jung, *Memories*, 225.
9. Ibid. 228.

Chapter 22.   Bollingen and New Mexico
1. Jung, *Memories*, app. 4, p. 342.
2. Ibid. 343.
3. Aniela Jaffé, author's interview, 8 May 1975.
4. Lancelot Whyte, author's interview, 1 Jan 1971.
5. Jung, *Memories*, 213.
6. Ruth Bailey, author's interview, 19 June 1974.
7. Lancelot Whyte, author's interview, 1 Jan 1971.
8. Barbara Hannah, author's interview, 7 May 1975.

Chapter 23.   Middle Age and Africa
1. Jolande Jacobi, author's interview, 24 Nov 1963.
2. Storr, *Jung*.
3. Franz Jung, author's interview, 7 May 1975.
4. *Neue Züricher Zeitung*, 2116, Blatt 9, 8 Nov 1928.
5. H. G. Wells, author's interview, 10 July 1942.
6. BBC interview, 27 July 1975.
7. Jung, *Letters*, vol. 1, 1 Jan 1926.
8. Ruth Bailey, author's interview, 19 June 1974.
9. Jung, *Memories*, 239.
10. Ruth Bailey, author's interview, 19 June 1974.
11. Ibid.
12. Jung, *Memories*, 240.
13. Ibid.
14. Anthony Storr, author's interview, 6 Aug 1974.
15. Edward Glover, author's interview, 5 Jan 1952.
16. Jung, *Letters*, vol. 1, 1 Jan 1926.
17. Ruth Bailey, author's interview, 19 June 1974.
18. Ibid.
19. *Asia*, Jan 1939.
20. Ibid.
21. Jung, *Memories*, 251.
22. Ruth Bailey, author's interview, 18 June 1974.
23. Lancelot Whyte, author's interview, 1 Jan 1971.
24. Ruth Bailey, author's interview, 19 June 1974.
25. Ruth Bailey, letter to the author, 1 Dec 1974.

Chapter 24.   Eranos
1. Lancelot Whyte, author's interview, 1 Jan 1974.
2. Jung, *Letters*, vol. 1, 24 Sept 1926.
3. *Seminar Notes*, ed. Mary Foote.
4. Author's interview, 20 May 1974.

5. A. I. Allenby, author's interview, 10 July 1974.
6. *Spirit and Nature*, ed. Joseph Campbell, p. xi.
7. Ibid. p. xiii.
8. Ibid.
9. Lancelot Whyte, author's interview, 1 Jan 1971.
10. Eranos, like the Jung Institute in Zürich, was criticised by several English students. They complained that there was little free-ranging criticism and everything was very commercial.
11. A. Jaffé, *Life and Work of Jung*, 105.
12. Author's interview, 4 May 1975.
13. Jaffé, *Jung*, 119.
14. Ibid. 119.
15. Ibid. 120.

Chapter 25.   The Anti-Semitic Legend
1. A relative of Herman Göring.
2. January 1934.
3. Jung, *Letters*, vol. 1, 2 March 1934.
4. Ibid. vol. 1, 13 April 1934.
5. Dr Michael Fordham points out that he was President of the General Medical Society for Psychotherapy not the International Society.
6. Jung, *Letters*, vol. 1, 26 March 1938.
7. 'The Concept of the Collective Unconscious', originally given as a lecture to the Abernethian Society at St Bartholomew's Hospital, London, on 19 Oct 1936, and published in the hospital's journal, XLIV (1936–7), 46–9, 64–6.
8. Dieterich, *Eine Mithras liturgie*, 7, 62.
9. Dr Michael Fordham states that a second edition was available.
10. *Collected Works*, vol. 9, pt 1, p. 291.
11. Author's interview, 10 July 1955.
12. *Collected Works*, vol. 9, pt 1, p. 292.

Chapter 26.   A Visit to India
1. Barbara Hannah, author's interview, 7 May 1975.
2. Ibid.
3. BBC interview, 27 July 1975. Author's interview, 7 May 1975.
4. BBC interview, 27 July 1975.
5. Ibid. Author's interview, 7 May 1975.
6. This does not come from Barbara Hannah. Anonymous interview.
7. L. Frey-Rohn, author's interview, 9 May 1975.
8. Ibid.
9. Jolande Jacobi, author's interview, 6 Jan 1968.
10. Barbara Hannah, author's interview, 7 May 1975.
11. Jung, *Letters*, vol. 1, 11 July 1944.
12. Bennet, *Jung*, 6.
13. E. A. Bennet, author's interview, 4 Aug 1974.
14. Jung, *Letters*, vol. 1, 27 Oct 1936.
15. E. A. Bennet, author's interview, 4 Aug 1974.
16. Ibid.
17. *Collected Works*, vol. 11, p. 7.
18. Jung, *Letters*, 4 April 1938, vol. 1.
19. *Asia*, Jan 1939.
20. Ibid. p. 4.
21. Ibid. p. 5.
22. Jung, *Memories*, 258.
23. *Asia*, Jan 1939, p. 6.

24. *Collected Works*, vol. 12, p. 231.
25. Jung, *Memories*, p. 196.

Chapter 27. The Second World War
1. Jung, *Letters*, vol. 1, 5 Oct 1939.
2. Anonymous, 5 Oct 1939.
3. Jung, *Letters*, vol. 1, 5 Oct 1939.
4. Ibid. 4 Dec 1939.
5. Ibid. 20 May 1940.
6. Ibid.
7. Communication from Aniela Jaffé.
8. 3 January 1939.
9. Jung, *Letters*, vol. 1, 12 Aug 1940.
10. Ibid. 7 Jan 1941.
11. Ibid. 18 April 1941.
12. Ibid. note, p. 319.
13. Ibid. 28 July 1942.
14. *Collected Works*, vol. 14, p. xiii.
15. Ibid. p. 14.
16. XIII: 12 March 1944.
17. Jung, *Letters*, vol. 1, 12 Jan 1944.
18. Ibid. 22 Dec 1942.
19. This should have read Royal Society of Medicine. He was never a member of the British Royal Society.
20. Brinkman, a psychiatrist, read a paper on 9 Feb at the Schweizerische Gesellschaft für praktische Psychologie, Zürich.

Chapter 28. A Serious Illness
1. Franz Jung, author's interview, 5 May 1975. Franz Jung, letter to the author, 21 Oct 1975.
2. Jung, *Memories*, 270.
3. Ibid. 270.
4. Ibid. 272.
5. L. Frey-Rohn, interview, 9 May 1975.
6. Ibid.
7. M. Fordham, author's interview, 13 Jan 1976.
8. Jung, *Letters*, vol. 1, 22 Sept 1944.
9. Ibid. 22 Sept 1944.
10. Ibid. 7 April 1945.
11. *Collected Works*, vol. 10, p. 197.
12. Ibid. 195.
13. First published as *Neue Schweizer Rundschau, Zürich*, n.s., XIII (1945).
14. Originally published as *Über das Unbewusste Schweizerland Montashefte für Schweizer Art und Arbeit (Zürich)*, IV (1918).
15. *Collected Works*, vol. 10, p. 220.
16. The doyen of London Jungians, 18 April 1946. Dr Fordham states that Jung was reluctant to defend himself. He only did so in reply to a request from Fordham. Author's interview, 13 Jan 1976.
17. Letter to Aniela Jaffé, 7 May 1963.

Chapter 29. Growing Old
1. Mrs Edith Forster, author's interview, 7 July 1974.
2. Jung, *Letters*, vol. 1, 18 Sept 1945.
3. Ibid. 31 Aug 1945.
4. BBC interview, 27 July 1975. Jolande Jacobi, author's interview, 6 Jan 1970.
5. Ibid.

6. BBC interview, 27 July 1975. Jolande Jacobi, author's interview, 6 Jan 1970.
7. Ibid.
8. *Journal of Analytical Psychology*, 20 Feb 1975.
9. Dr Michael Fordham, author's interview, 15 May 1974.
10. Author's interview, 30 June 1974.
11. Dr Gerhard Adler, author's interview, 24 Nov 1973.
12. A. I. Allenby, author's interview, 16 July 1974.
13. Marie Louise von Franz, lecture.
14. Anthony Storr, author's interview, 4 Sept 1974.
15. *Collected Works*, vol. 9, pt 2, foreword, p. ix.
16. Ibid. vol. 11, p. 366.
17. Jung, *Letters*, vol. 2, 4 May 1953.
18. Ibid. 5 Jan 1952.
19. Interview by Frederick Sands, *Daily Mail*, 29 April 1955.
20. Jung, *Letters*, vol. 2, 5 Dec 1959.
21. Ibid. 28 Feb 1952.
22. White wrote a highly critical review of *Answer to Job* in *Blackfriars*, March 1955.

Chapter 30. Death of Toni and Emma
1. Ruth Bailey, author's interview, 14 June 1975.
2. Jung, *Letters*, vol. 1, 31 Dec 1949.
3. Barbara Hannah, author's interview, 7 May 1975.
4. Dr Gerhard Adler, author's interview, 24 Nov 1973.
5. Barbara Hannah, author's interview, 7 May 1975.
6. Dr Fordham states that it was definitely a heart attack. Author's interview, 13 Jan 1976.
7. Frau Erna Naeff, author's interview, 8 May 1975.
8. Barbara Hannah, author's interview, 7 May 1975.
9. Unpublished document supplied by Dr Gerhard Adler.
10. Jung, *Letters*, vol. 2, 10 April 1954.
11. Ibid. 13 March 1953.
12. Ibid. 6 May 1955.
13. Ibid. 16 Sept 1953.
14. Ibid. 8 Nov 1954.
15. Jaffé, *Jung*, 123.
16. Jung, *Letters*, vol. 2, 15 Dec 1955.
17. Ruth Bailey, author's interview, 19 June 1974.
18. Dr Michael Fordham, author's interview, 13 Jan 1976.
19. L. Frey-Rohn, 9 May 1975.
20. Jung, *Letters*, vol. 2, 17 July 1956.
21. Jung, *Memories*, 276.

Chapter 31. Old Age
1. Ruth Bailey, letter to the author, 14 June 1975.
2. Stephen Black, BBC interview, 24 July 1955.
3. E. A. Bennet, author's interview, 4 Aug 1974.
4. *Studien zür Analytischen Psychologie*, 1955.
5. Ludwig Marcuse, 'Der Fall C. G. Jung', *Der Zeitgeist*, no. 36, pp. 13–15. (Monthly supplement of *Der Aufbau*.)
6. *Israelitisches Wochenblatt*, 2 March 1956, 39–40.
7. Jung, *Letters*, vol. 2, 30 May 1957.
8. Ibid. 14 June 1957.
9. Ibid. 24 May 1958.
10. From a partly unpublished manuscript. Hugo Charteris.
11. Aniela Jaffé, author's interview, 8 May 1975.
12. Ibid.

13. Ibid.
14. Jung, *Letters*, vol. 2, 29 April 1960.
15. Aniela Jaffé, author's interview, 8 May 1975.
16. Interview, Georges Duplain, *Gazette de Lausanne*, nos. 208–11, 4–8 Sept 1959.
17. Jaffé, *Jung*, 115.
18. Ibid. 117.

Chapter 32.   The Last Year
 1. Jung, *Letters*, vol. 2, 9 Jan 1960.
 2. Hugo Charteris, author's interview, 10 July 1963.
 3. M. Serrano, *Jung and Herman Hesse*, 97–8.
 4. *Journal of Analytical Psychology*, 20 Feb 1975.
 5. Letter, 16 June 1961.
 6. Ibid.
 7. Ruth Bailey, author's interview, 19 June 1975.
 8. Franz Jung, author's interview, 5 May 1975. Franz Jung, letter to the author, 2 July
    1974.

Appendix I.   Jung's Model of the Psyche
 1. *Collected Works*, vol. 6, p. 425.
 2. Ibid. vol. 9, pt 2, foreword, iii.
 3. J. Jacobi, *The Psychology of Jung*, 10.
 4. Ibid. 12.
 5. *Collected Works*, vol. 17, p. 198.
 6. Ibid. vol. 9, pt 2, p. 14.
 7. Storr, *Jung*, 52.
 8. *Collected Works*, vol. 7, p. 208.
 9. Storr, *Jung*, 52.
10. Jung, *Modern Man in Search of a Soul*, 90.
11. Jacobi, *Psychology of Jung*, 21.
12. Ibid. 46.
13. Ellenberger, *Discovery*, 712.
14. *Collected Works*, vol. 11, p. 167.
15. Jacobi, *Psychology of Jung*, 122.
16. *Collected Works*, vol. 10, p. 170.
17. Jung, *The Practice of Psychotherapy*, 20.
18. Ibid. 27.
19. E. Glover, *Freud or Jung*, 51.
20. Storr, *Jung*, 112.
21. 1956, ed. Alan Pryce-Jones.
22. M. Fordham, *The Objective Psyche*, 1.

Appendix II.   Jung's Sources
 1. Jung, *Practice of Psychotherapy*, 147.
 2. Anthony Storr, letter to the author, 10 Nov 1975.
 3. E. B. Tylor, *Primitive Culture*, vol. 1, p. 435.

Appendix III.   Jung's Influence
 1. *Man and His Symbols*, ed. Jung. M. L. von Franz, 306.
 2. Sheldon T. Selesnick, 'C. G. Jung's Contributions to Psycho-Analysis', *American Journal of Psychiatry*, cxx (1963), 350–6.
 3. Ellenberger, *Discovery*, 732.
 4. C. G. Jung and Karl Kerenyi, *Eine Einfuhrung in das Wesen der Mythologie* (1941).
 5. M. Bodkin, *Archetypal Patterns in Poetry*, 1.

6. Ibid. 18.
7. Gilbert Murray, *The Classical Tradition in Poetry*, 239.
8. M. Philipson, *Outline of a Jungian Aesthetic*.
9. Arnold Toynbee, *A Study of History*, vol. VII, pp. 722–36.
10. Masters and Houston, 213–46.

The Collected Works of
C. G. Jung

Editors: Sir Herbert Read, Dr Michael Fordham and Dr Gerhard Adler. William McGuire Executive Editor Volumes 2 and 6.

1. PSYCHIATRIC STUDIES

On the Psychology and Pathology of So-Called Occult Phenomena (1902)
On Hysterical Misreading (1904)
Cryptomnesia (1905)
On Manic Mood Disorder (1903)
A Case of Hysterical Stupor in a Prisoner in Detention (1902)
On Simulated Insanity (1903)
A Medical Opinion on a Case of Simulated Insanity (1904)
A Third and Final Opinion on Two Contradictory Psychiatric Diagnoses (1906)
On the Psychological Diagnosis of Facts (1905)

2. EXPERIMENTAL RESEARCHES

Studies in Word Association
The Associations of Normal Subjects (by Jung and Riklin) (1906)
Experimental Observations on Memory (1905)
On the Determination of Facts by Psychological Means (1906)
An Analysis of the Associations of an Epileptic (1906)
The Association Method (1910)
Reaction-Time in Association Experiments (1906)
On Disturbances in Reproduction in Association Experiments (1909)
Psychoanalysis and Association Experiments (1906)
Association, Dream, and Hysterical Symptoms (1909)

Psychophysical Researches
On Psychophysical Relations of the Association Experiment (1907)
Psychophysical Investigations with the Galvanometer and Pneumograph in Normal and Insane Individuals (by Petersen and Jung) (1907)
Further Investigations on the Galvanic Phenomenon and Respirations in Normal and Insane Individuals (by Ricksher and Jung) (1907–8)

3. THE PSYCHOGENESIS OF MENTAL DISEASE

The Psychology of Dementia Praecox (1907)
The Content of the Psychoses (1908/1914)
On Psychological Understanding (1914)
A Criticism of Bleuler's Theory of Schizophrenic Negativism (1911)
On the Importance of the Unconscious in Psychopathology (1914)
On the Problem of Psychogenesis in Mental Disease (1919)
Mental Disease and the Psyche (1928)
On the Psychogenesis of Schizophrenia (1939)
Recent Thoughts on Schizophrenia (1957)
Schizophrenia (1958)

4. FREUD AND PSYCHOANALYSIS

Freud's Theory of Hysteria: A Reply to Aschaffenburg (1906)
The Freudian Theory of Hysteria (1908)
The Analysis of Dreams (1909)
A Contribution to the Psychology of Rumour (1910/1911)
On the Significance of Number Dreams (1910/1911)
Morton Prince, 'Mechanism and Interpretation of Dreams': A Critical Review (1911)
On the Criticism of Psychoanalysis (1910)
Concerning Psychoanalysis (1912)
The Theory of Psychoanalysis (1913)
General Aspects of Psychoanalysis (1913)
Psychoanalysis and Neurosis (1916)
Some Crucial Points in Psychoanalysis: The Jung–Loy Correspondence (1914)
Prefaces to 'Collected Papers on Analytical Psychology' (1916, 1917)
The Significance of the Father in the Destiny of the Individual (1909/1949)
Introduction to Kranefeldt's 'Secret Ways of the Mind' (1930)
Freud and Jung: Contrasts (1929)

5. SYMBOLS OF TRANSFORMATION (1912/1952)

Original German version, *Wandlungen und Symbole der Libido*, 1912 (= *Psychology of the Unconscious*); present extensively revised edition, 1952.

6. PSYCHOLOGICAL TYPES (1921)

The Problem of Types in the History of Classical and Medieval Thought
Schiller's Ideas on the Type Problem
The Apollinian and the Dionysian
The Type Problem in Human Character
The Type Problem in Poetry
The Type Problem in Psychopathology
The Type Problem in Aesthetics
The Type Problem in Modern Philosophy
The Type Problem in Biography
General Description of the Types
Definitions

7. TWO ESSAYS ON ANALYTICAL PSYCHOLOGY

The Psychology of the Unconscious (1917/1926/1943)
The Relations Between the Ego and the Unconscious (1929)
Appendixes:
New Paths in Psychology (1912)
The Structure of the Unconscious (1916)

8. THE STRUCTURE AND DYNAMICS OF THE PSYCHE

On Psychic Energy (1928)
The Transcendent Function ([1916]/1957)
A Review of the Complex Theory (1934)
The Significance of Constitution and Heredity in Psychology (1929)
Psychological Factors Determining Human Behaviour (1937)
Instinct and the Unconscious (1919)
The Structure of the Psyche (1927/1931)
On the Nature of the Psyche (1947/1954)
General Aspects of Dream Psychology (1916/1948)
On the Nature of Dreams (1945/1948)

The Psychological Foundations of Belief in Spirits (1920/1948)
Spirit and Life (1926)
Basic Postulates of Analytical Psychology (1931)
Analytical Psychology and *Weltanschauung* (1928/1931)
The Real and the Surreal (1933)
The Stages of Life (1930/1931)
The Soul and Death (1934)
Synchronicity: An Acausal Connecting Principle (1952)
Appendix: On Synchronicity (1951)

9. PART I
THE ARCHETYPES AND THE COLLECTIVE UNCONSCIOUS

Archetypes of the Collective Unconscious (1934/1954)
The Concept of the Collective Unconscious (1936)
Concerning the Archetypes, with Special Reference to the Anima Concept (1936/1954)
Psychological Aspects of the Mother Archetype (1938/1954)
Concerning Rebirth (1940/1950)
The Psychology of the Child Archetype (1940)
The Psychological Aspects of the Kore (1941)
The Phenomenology of the Spirit in Fairytales (1945/1948)
On the Psychology of the Trickster-Figure (1954)
Conscious, Unconscious, and Individuation (1939)
A Study in the Process of Individuation (1934/1950)
Concerning Mandala Symbolism (1950)
Appendix: Mandalas (1955)

9. PART II
AION (1951)
Researches into the Phenomenology of the Self

The Ego
The Shadow
The Syzygy: Anima and Animus
The Self.
Christ, a Symbol of the Self
The Sign of the Fishes
The Prophecies of Nostradamus
The Historical Significance of the Fish
The Ambivalence of the Fish Symbol
The Fish in Alchemy
The Alchemical Interpretation of the Fish
Background to the Psychology of Christian Alchemical Symbolism
Gnostic Symbols of the Self
The Structure and Dynamics of the Self
Conclusion

10. CIVILISATION IN TRANSITION

The Role of the Unconscious (1918)
Mind and Earth (1927/1931)
Archaic Man (1931)
The Spiritual Problem of Modern Man (1928/1931)
The Love Problem of a Student (1928)
Woman in Europe (1927)
The Meaning of Psychology for Modern Man (1933/1934)
The State of Psychotherapy Today (1934)

Rex and Regina
Adam and Eve
The Conjunction

15. THE SPIRIT IN MAN, ART, AND LITERATURE

Paracelsus (1929)
Paracelsus the Physician (1941)
Sigmund Freud: A Cultural Phenomenon (1932)
Sigmund Freud: An Obituary (1939)
Richard Wilhelm: An Obituary (1930)
Psychology and Literature (1930/1950)
On the Relation of Analytical Psychology to the Poetic Art (1922)
Picasso (1932)
'Ulysses' (1932)

16. THE PRACTICE OF PSYCHOTHERAPY

General Problems of Psychotherapy
Principles of Practical Psychotherapy (1935)
What Is Psychotherapy? (1935)
Some Aspects of Modern Psychotherapy (1930)
The Aims of Psychotherapy (1931)
Problems of Modern Psychotherapy (1929)
Psychotherapy and a Philosophy of Life (1943)
Medicine and Psychotherapy (1945)
Psychotherapy Today (1945)
Fundamental Questions of Psychotherapy (1951)

Specific Problems of Psychotherapy
The Therapeutic Value of Abreaction (1921/1928)
The Practical Use of Dream-Analysis (1934)
Psychology of the Transference (1946)

17. THE DEVELOPMENT OF PERSONALITY

Psychic Conflicts in a Child (1910/1946)
Introduction to Wickes's 'Analyse der Kinderseele' (1927/1931)
Child Development and Education (1928)
Analytical Psychology and Education: Three Lectures (1926/1946)
The Gifted Child (1943)
The Significance of the Unconscious in Individual Education (1928)
The Development of Personality (1934)
Marriage as a Psychological Relationship (1925)

18. MISCELLANEOUS

AURORA CONSURGENS (1957/1966)
A Companion to Jung's 'Mysterium Coniunctionis'
Man and His Symbols (1964)

A DRAFT BIOGRAPHY

Select Bibliography

Books

Abraham, K., *Selected Papers* (1927).
Andreas-Salomé, L., *The Freud Journal* (1965).
Bach, I., *C. G. Jung's Aion, etc.* (1952).
Barthes, R., *Mythologies* (1972).
Bennet, E. A., *C. G. Jung* (1961).
—, *What Jung Really Said* (1966).
Berteaux, P., *La Vie quotidienne en Allemagne au temps de Guillaume II* (1926).
Bertine, E., *Jung's Contribution to Our Time* (1967).
Boyle, A., *Montagu Norman* (1967).
Brown, J. A. C., *Freud and the Post-Freudians* (1961).
Campbell, J., *Papers from Eranos: Pagan and Christian Mysteries* (1963).
—, *Eranos Yearbooks* (1963).
'C. G. Jung' (articles by various authors), *Les Cahiers pensée et action*, no. 23/24.
Cox, D., *Jung and St Paul* (1958).
Crookall, R., *The Jung–Jaffé View of Out of the Body Experiences* (1970).
Daking, D. C., *Jungian Psychology and Modern Spiritual Thought* (1933).
Dry, A. M., *The Psychology of Jung* (1961).
Ellenberger, H. F., *The Discovery of the Unconscious* (1970).
Ellmann, R., *James Joyce* (1959).
Eranos, *Eranos Jahrbuch* (1965).
—, *Papers from Eranos*, 2 vols (1955).
Evans, I., *Conversations with C. G. Jung and Reactions from Ernest Jones* (1964).
Festschrift zum 80 Geburtstag von C. G. Jung, edited by F. Riklin, E. Jung and K. W. Beck, 2 vols (1955).
Fordham, F., *An Introduction to Jung's Psychology* (1953).
Fordham, M. (ed.), *Contact with Jung* (1963).
—, *New Developments in Analytical Psychology* (1957).
—, *The Objective Psyche* (1958).
Freud, M., *Glory Reflected* (1957).
Freud, Sigmund, *On the History of the Psycho-Analytic Movement*, in *Collected Works*, vol. 14.
—, *Sammlung kleiner Schriften zur Neurosenlehre* (1906).
—, *The Standard Edition of the Complete Psychological Works of Sigmund Freud*, general editor J. Strachey in collaboration with Anna Freud assisted by Alix Strachey and Alan Tyson, 21 vols (1955–61).
Freud, Sigmund and Abraham, Karl, *Letters of Sigmund Freud and Karl Abraham, 1907–26*.
Freud, Sigmund and Jung, C. G., *Freud–Jung Letters*, ed. W. McGuire (1974).
Glover, E. G., *Freud or Jung* (1950).
Hannah, B., *Jung, His Life and Work* (1976).
Haupt, H., *Ein vergessener Dichter aus der Fruhzeit der Burschenschaft Carl Gustav Jung.*
Howard, P., *Jung and the Problem of Evil* (1958).
The I Ching or Book of Changes, with a foreword by C. G. Jung (1951).
Jacobi, J., *Die Psychologie C. G. Jung* (1940).
—, *Komplex Archetypes* (1957).
—, *The Psychology of Jung* (1962).
Jaffé, A., *Der Mythus Vom Sinn in dem Werk von C. G. Jung* (1947).
—, *Life and Work of Jung* (1971).
Jones, E., *Free Association* (1959).
—, *The Life and Work of Sigmund Freud*, 3 vols (1953–7).

Jung, C. G., *Briefe 1906–1961*, edited and selected by Gerhard Adler and Aniela Jaffé, 3 vols (1972–3).

—, *Letters*, edited and selected by Gerhard Adler and Aniela Jaffé, 2 vols (1973–5).

—, *Memories, Dreams, Reflections*, recorded and edited by Aniela Jaffé (1963).

Jung, Emma and Franz, Marie Louise von, *Die Graalslegende in psychologischer Sicht. Mit siebzehn Tafeln* (1900).

—, *Psychologie Herausgegeben von Psychologischen Club – Zürich* (1935).

Jung, Ernest (ed.), *Aus den Tagebuchen meines Vaters*.

Kerenyi, C. and Jung, C. G., Introduction to *A Science of Mythology* (1970).

Malcolm, Norman, *Ludwig Wittgenstein: A Memoir* (1958).

Metman, Eva, *C. G. Jung's Essay on the Psychology of the Spirit*, Pastoral Guild Lecture no. 80 (1954).

Metman, Philip, *C. G. Jung's Psychology and the Problem of Values* (1949).

Oeri, A., *Die Kulturelle Bedeutung der Komplexen Psychologie* (1935).

—, *Spring 1970*.

Philipson, M., *Outline of a Jungian Aesthetic* (1963).

Rautenfeld, M. E. B. von, *Der Persona: Begriff von C. G. Jung, etc.* (1950).

Roazen, P., *Freud and His Followers* (1974).

Robert, M., *La Révolution psychanalytique*, 2 vols (1963).

Roth, Paul, *Anima und Animus in der Psychologie C. G. Jung's* (1954).

Sborowitz, A., *Beziehung und Bestimmung. Die Lehren von M. Buber und C. G. Jung* (1956).

Schaer, H., *Religion und Seele der Psychologie C. G. Jung's* (1946).

The Secret of the Golden Flower, with a European Commentary by C. G. Jung (1931).

Serrano, M., *C. G. Jung and Herman Hesse* (1966).

Steiner, Gustav, *Erinnerungen au Carl Gustav Jung* (1965).

Stern, P. J., *C. G. Jung: The Haunted Prophet* (1976).

Suzuki, D. T., *The Complete Works of D. T. Suzuki: An Introduction to Zen Buddhism*, with a foreword by C. G. Jung (1949).

van der Post, L., *Jung and the Story of Our Time* (1976).

Wells, H. G., *Experiment in Autobiography* (1934).

—, *A Thesis on the Quality of Illusion in the Continuity of the Individual Life in the Higher Metazoa* (1934).

White, Victor, *God and the Unconscious*, with a foreword by C. G. Jung (1952).

Whyte, L. L., *Focus and Diversions* (1963).

Newspapers and Periodicals

American Imago
American Journal of Psychiatry
Archives de Psychologie
Jahrbuch der Psychoanalyse
Journal of Nervous and Mental Diseases
Neue Züricher Zeitung
New York Times
The Times
Zentralblatt für Psychotherapie

Other Sources

Basel University Archives

'A Draft Bibliography of the Works of C. G. Jung', for eventual publication in the *Collected Works of C. G. Jung* (private circulation, 1962)

Guild of Pastoral Psychology, Lecture no. 69, 5 April 1939

Honneger, John: recently discovered letters of the period

Jung, C. G., 'On Dreams' (1901) (typescript discovered in Jung's posthumous papers).

Jung, Emma: diaries – consulted by Franz Jung to confirm facts for W. McGuire

Notes on Jung's Seminar in Analytical Psychology, 1925 (typewritten).

Vienna Psycho-Analytical Society Minutes, vol. 1
Zürich Student Association Minutes

Seminar Reports
Multigraphed for Private Circulation
Notes on the Seminar on Analytical Psychology, March 23–July 6, 1925.
Notes on Lectures given at a Seminar, November 1928. Arranged by Anne Chapin.
Notes of Seminars–Dream Analysis, 1928–1930. Compiled and edited by Charlotte H. Deady.
   Five volumes. New edition edited by Carol Baumann, 1938–9.
Zür Psychologie der Individuation.
Berichte über die Deutschen Seminare, Küsnacht 6–11 October 1930, 5–10 October 1931. 1931–2.
   Two Volumes.
Behricht über das Deutsche Seminar in Psychologischen Club, Zürich, 3–8 October 1932. Foreword
   by Lind Fierz and Toni Wolff, 1933.
Über Traume. Bericht über des Deutsche Seminar 1933 (26 June–1 July 1934). Edited by Mary
   Foote. Eleven Volumes. New edition 1939–1941.
Psychologischer Kommentar zu Hauers Seminars über den Tantra Yoga, 1935.
Psychological Aspects of Nietzsche's Zarathustra. Seminar Notes 1934–1939. Compiled by Mary
   Briner. Edited by Mary Foote. Ten Volumes.
*Fundamental Psychological Conceptions. A Report of Five Lectures given under the Auspices of the
   Institute of Medical Psychology, September 30–October 4, 1935.* Edited by Mary Baker and
   Margaret Game for the Analytical Psychology Club, 1936.
Lectures at the ETH. Zürich October 1935–July 1936. Compiled by Barbara Hannah, Una
   Gauntlett Thomas and Elizabeth Baumann.
*Seminar über Kindertraume und altere Literatur über Trauminterpretation, ETH Zürich, Winter
   1936–1937.* Edited by Hans H. Baumann.
*Dream Symbols of the Individuation Process. Volume II. Notes of a Seminar in New York City,
   October 1937.*
Ueber die Archetypen Seminar Report, Berlin 1937.
The Process of Individuation. Notes on lectures given at the ETH Zürich, October 1938–1941.
   Preface by Barbara Hannah. Five Volumes.
*Human Relationships in Relation to the Process of Individuation. Notes of a Seminar at Polzeath,
   Cornwall, Summer 1923.*
*Dreams and Symbolism. Notes of a Seminar at Swanage, 1928. Psychologische Interpretation von
   Kindertraumen. Seminar ETH Zürich, Winter 1939–1940.* Edited by Liliane Frey and
   Aniela Jaffé.

Interviews with Jung
'America Facing its Most Tragic Moment'. *New York Times.* 29 September 1912.
'Does the World Stand on the Verge of Spiritual Re-Birth?' *Hearst's International
   Cosmopolitan,* April 1934, pp. 24–5, 179–82.
'The Psychology of Dictatorship'. *Observer,* 18 October 1936.
'Diagnosing the Dictators'. *Hearst's International Cosmopolitan,* 1939, pp. 22, 116–19.
'Professor Jung Diagnoses the Dictators'. Howard L. Philip. *Psychologist,* 7 : 77, May 1939,
   pp. 2–5.
'Selbsterkenntnis und Tiefenpsychologie'. Jolande Jacobi, *Du,* 111 : 9, September 1943,
   pp. 15–18.
'Werden die Seelen Frieden Finden'. Peter Schmidt, *Weltwoche,* 13 : 600, 11 May 1945,
   p. 3.
'The Occult'. Norman Colgan. *Prediction,* 15 : 2, September 1949, pp. 7–10.
'C. G. Jung zu den Fliegenden Unterlassen'. George Gerster, *Weltwoche,* 22 : 1078, 9 July
   1954, p. 7.
'Carl Gustav (sic) Jung'. Stephen Black. *News Chronicle* 34026, 26 July, 1955, p. 4.
'Men, Women and God'. Frederick Sands. *Daily Mail,* 25–9 April 1955, p. 6 of each issue.
'C. G. Jung und die Weihnatchshaum', George Gerster. *Weltwoche,* 25 : 1259, 25
   December 1957, p. 7.

'Aux Frontieres de la Connaissance'. Georges Duplain, *Gazette de Lausanne*, 1959.
'Dr Jung Looks Back and On'. Hugo Charteris, *Daily Telegraph*, 21 January, 1960.

BBC Interviews
'Dr Jung on Life and Death'. BBC Interview, 22 October 1959.
BBC composite programme. Interviews with friends and relatives, 1975.

Index

VINCENT BROME has been working on aspects of the history of psychoanalysis and analytical psychology for many years. The author of *Freud and His Early Circle,* he has written in all some twenty books, and has contributed the main Freud entry to the new *Encyclopaedia Britannica,* together with many other articles. He lives in Bloomsbury, London.